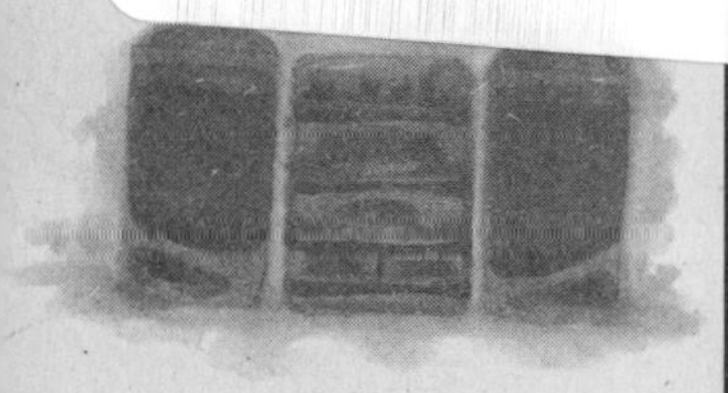

久保帯人

...e a stereo at home. I ...ht it in junior high with ...ey I earned delivering ...spapers—I know it's ...h a cliché. I've used it for over 10 years. Recently, it hasn't been working so well. I thought about replacing it, but even if I bought the latest, coolest unit, I'd probably still miss this one. So I can't bring myself to buy a new one. In other words, I'm a wimp.

Tite Kubo

BLEACH is author Tite Kubo's second title. Kubo made his debut with *ZOMBIE POWDER*, a four-volume series for *WEEKLY SHONEN JUMP*. To date, *BLEACH* has been translated into numerous languages and has also inspired an animated TV series that began airing in Japan in 2004. Beginning its serialization in 2001, *BLEACH* is still a mainstay in the pages of *WEEKLY SHONEN JUMP*. In 2005, *BLEACH* was awarded the prestigious Shogakukan Manga Award in the *shonen* (boys') category.

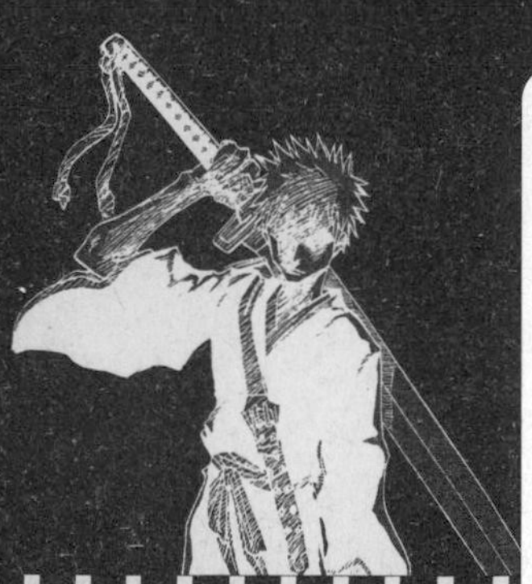

BLEACH
Vol. 9: FOURTEEN DAYS FOR CONSPIRACY
The SHONEN JUMP Graphic Novel Edition

STORY AND ART BY
TITE KUBO

English Adaptation/Lance Caselman
Translation/Joe Yamazaki
Touch-Up Art & Lettering/Andy Ristaino
Design/Sean Lee
Editor/Kit Fox

Managing Editor/Elizabeth Kawasaki
Director of Production/Noboru Watanabe
Vice President of Publishing/Alvin Lu
Vice President & Editor in Chief/Yumi Hoashi
Sr. Director of Acquisitions/Rika Inouye
Vice President of Sales & Marketing/Liza Coppola
Publisher/Hyoe Narita

Printed in the U.S.A.

Published by VIZ Media, LLC
P.O. Box 77010
San Francisco, CA 94107

SHONEN JUMP Graphic Novel Edition
10 9 8 7 6 5 4 3 2 1
First printing, September 2005

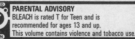

PARENTAL ADVISORY
BLEACH is rated T for Teen and is
recommended for ages 13 and up.
This volume contains violence and tobacco use.

THE WORLD'S
MOST POPULAR MANGA

SHONEN JUMP
GRAPHIC NOVEL
www.shonenjump.com

www.viz.com

Oh, all of us dream
That we are flying the skies
With our eyes open

BLEACH9

FOURTEEN DAYS FOR CONSPIRACY

Shonen Jump Graphic Novel

STARS AND

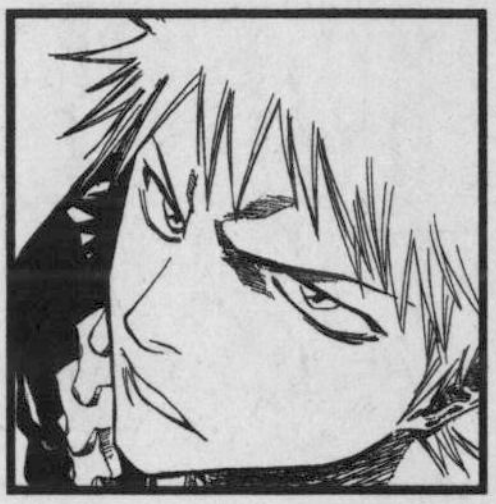

夜一

Yoruichi

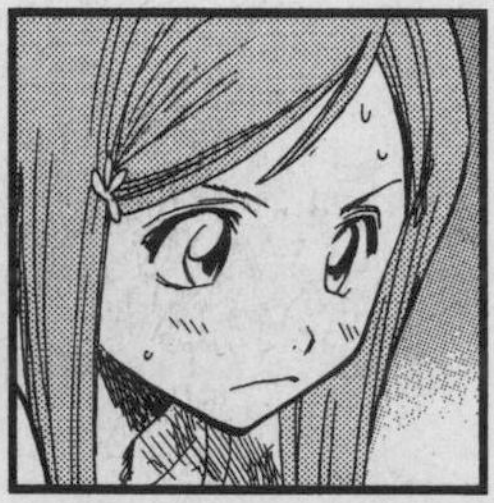

Ichigo Kurosaki

黒崎一護

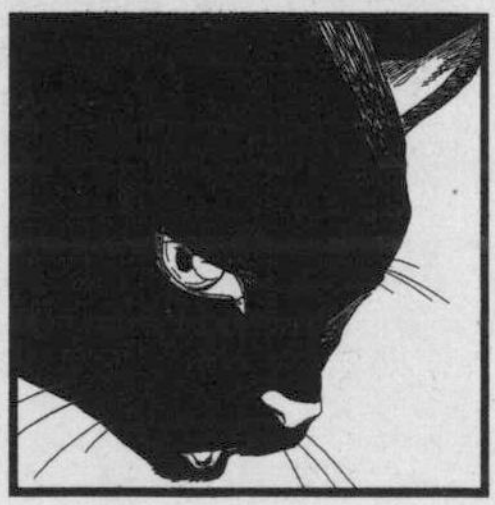

Orihime Inoue

井上織姫

plot

One fateful night, Ichigo Kurosaki encounters Soul Reaper Rukia Kuchiki and ends up helping her do her job—which is cleansing lost souls called Hollows and guiding them to the Soul Society. Eventually, Ichigo grows powerful and defeats the behemoth Menos Grande. Now Rukia has been condemned to death in the Soul Society. To save her, Ichigo, Orihime, Chad, and Uryû have endured rigorous training. With their feline guide, Yoruichi, they finally enter the Soul Society. But do they have what it takes to save Rukia—or themselves?!!

BLEACH ALL

茶渡泰虎

Yasutora "Chad" Sado

兕丹坊

Jidanbô

Uryû Ishida

石田雨竜

STORIES

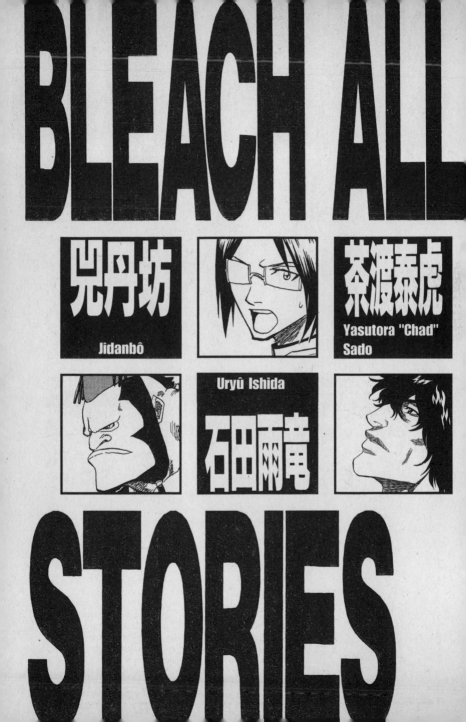

BLEACH 9

FOURTEEN DAYS FOR CONSPIRACY

Contents

71. INTRUDERZ		7
72. The Superchunk		29
73. Ax Storm		49
74. Amputation		69
75. Crimson Rain		89
76. Boarrider Comin'		109
77. My Name is Ganju		129
78. meeT 'Em iN tHE basemenT		149
79. FOURTEEN DAYS FOR CONSPIRACY		169

71. INTRUDERZ

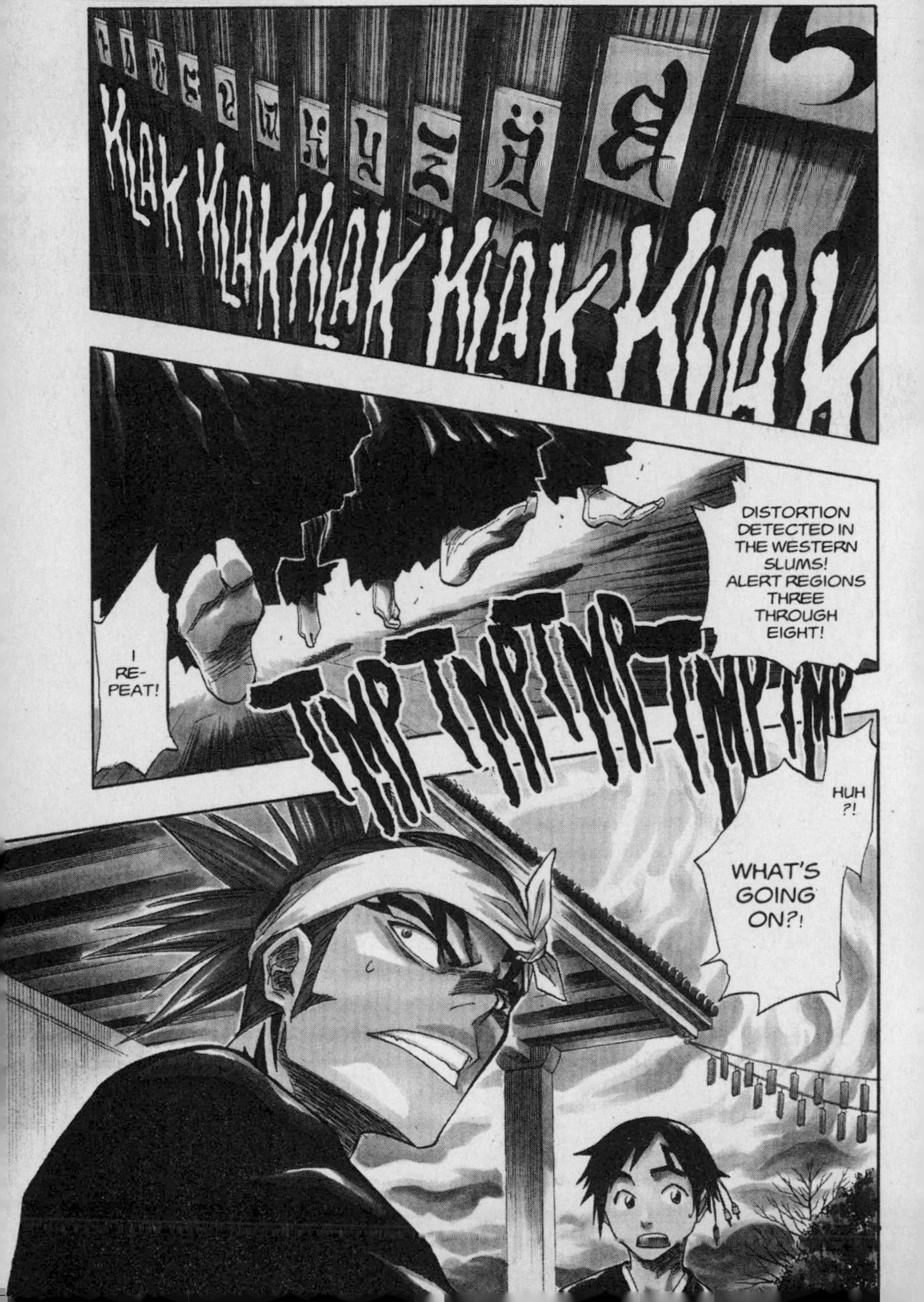
KLAK KLAK KLAK KLAK KLAK
DISTORTION DETECTED IN THE WESTERN SLUMS! ALERT REGIONS THREE THROUGH EIGHT!
TMP TMP TMP TMP TMP TMP
I REPEAT!
HUH?!
WHAT'S GOING ON?!

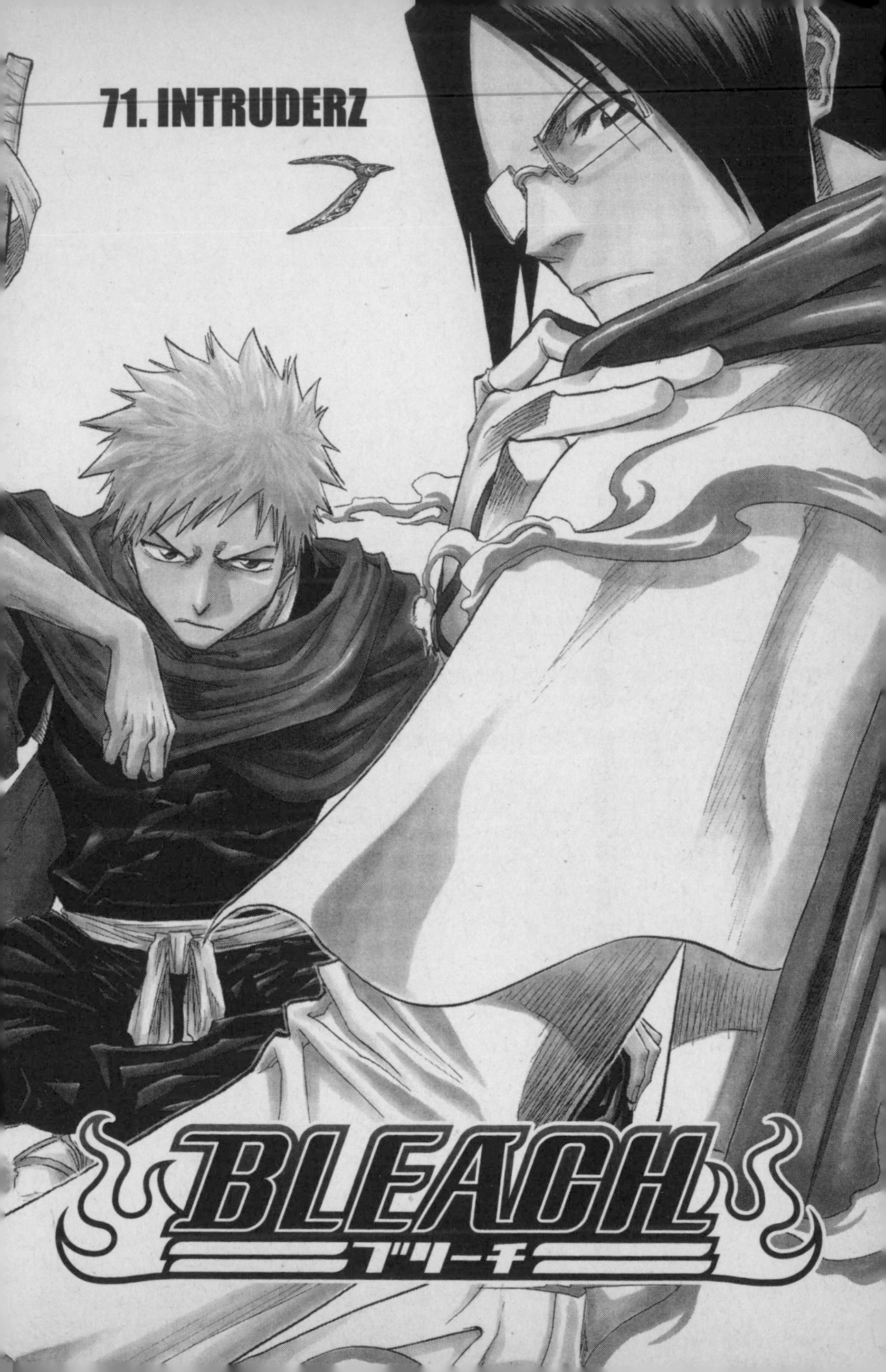
71. INTRUDERZ
BLEACH
ブリーチ

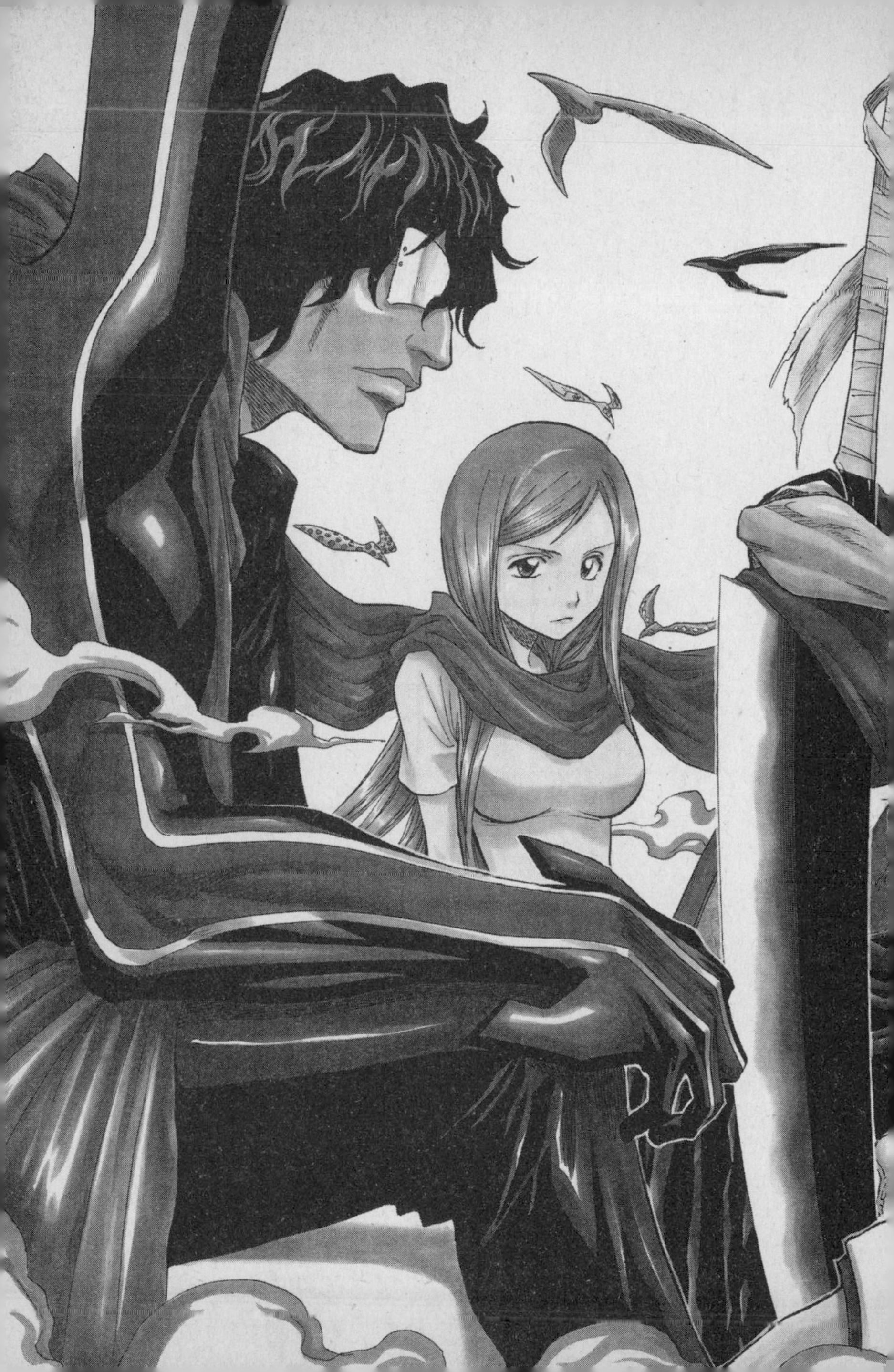

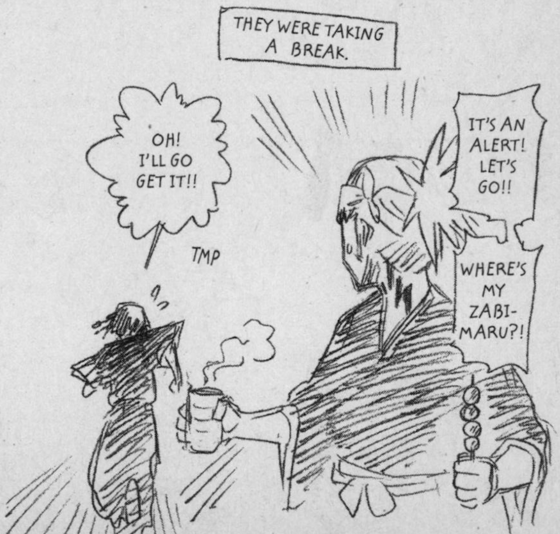
THEY WERE TAKING A BREAK.
IT'S AN ALERT! LET'S GO!!
WHERE'S MY ZABI-MARU?!
OH! I'LL GO GET IT!!
TMP

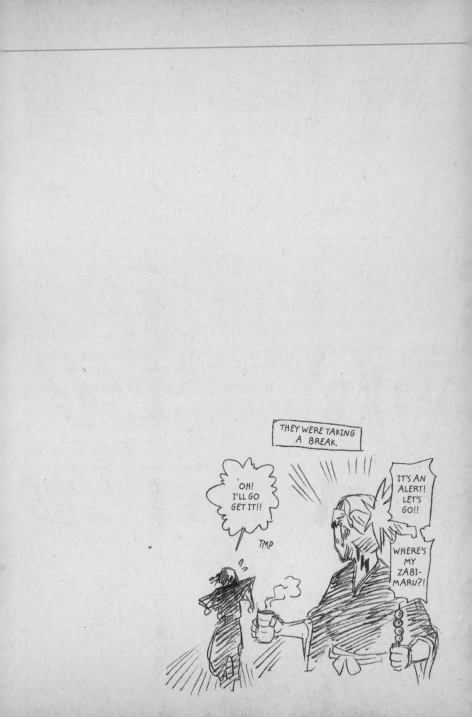

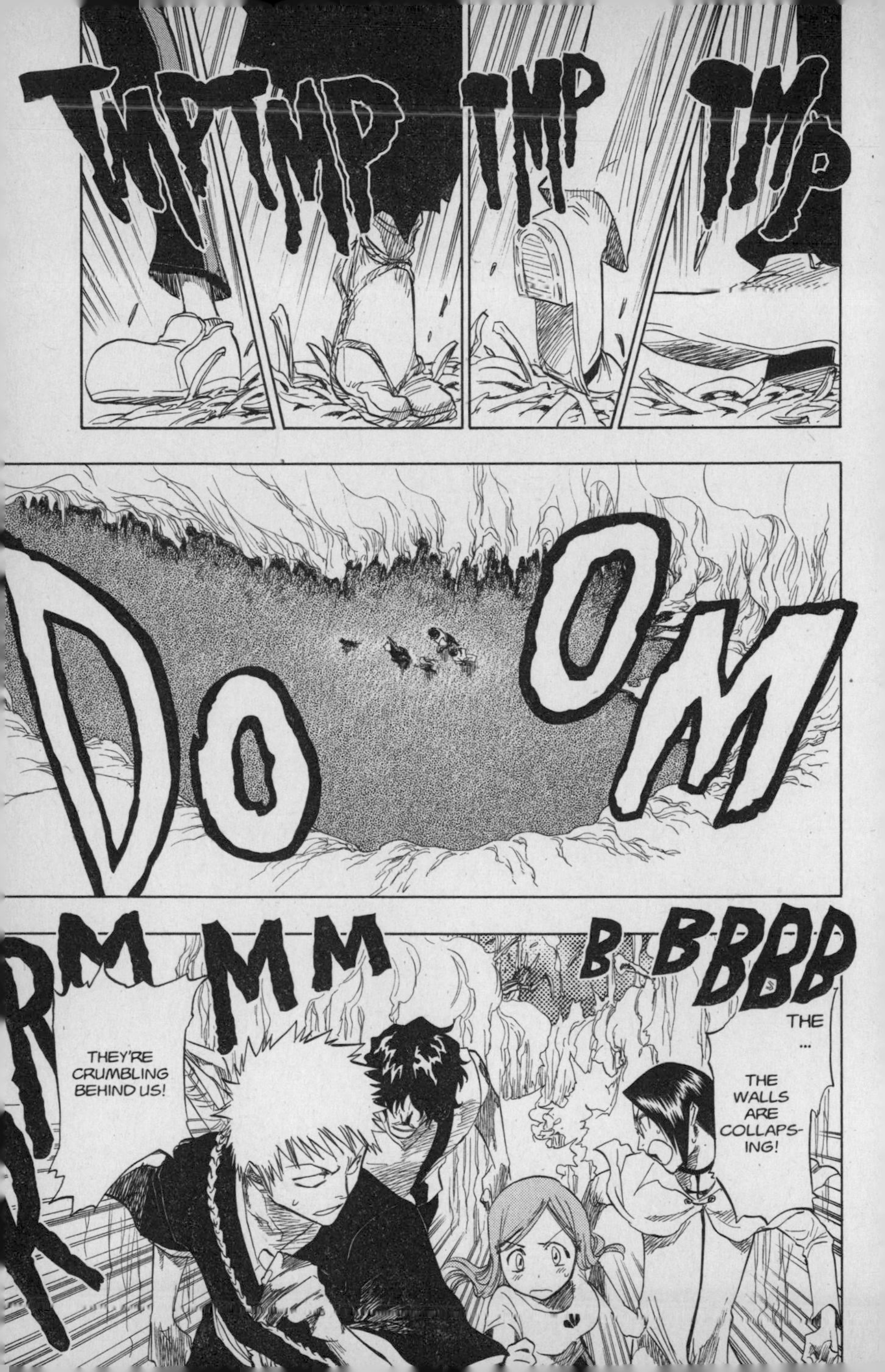
TMP
TMP
TMPTMP
DOOM
THE...
THE WALLS ARE COLLAPS-ING!
THEY'RE CRUMBLING BEHIND US!

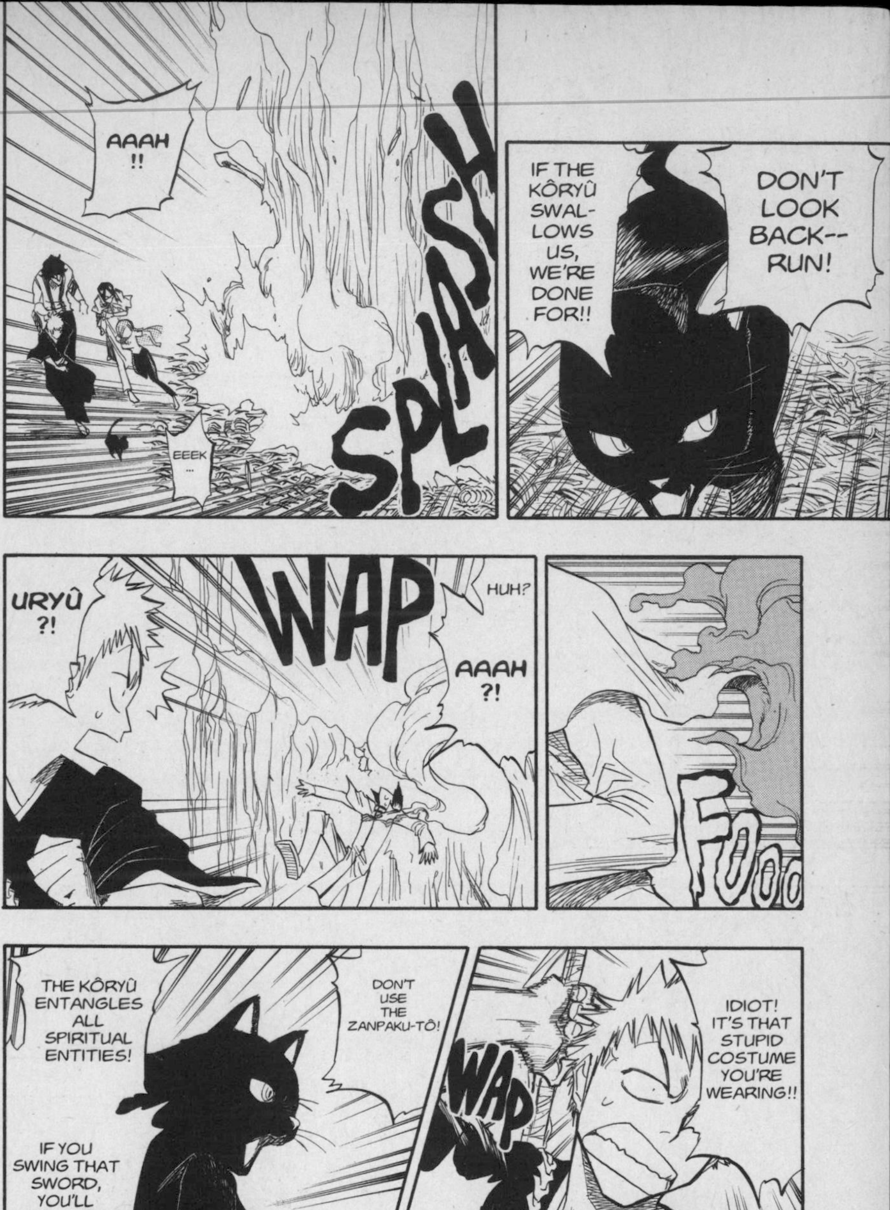
DON'T LOOK BACK-- RUN!
IF THE KÔRYÛ SWAL-LOWS US, WE'RE DONE FOR!!
SPLASH
AAAH !!
EEEK ...
FOOO
HUH?
AAAH ?!
WAP
URYÛ ?!
IDIOT! IT'S THAT STUPID COSTUME YOU'RE WEARING!!
WAP
WAIT!
DON'T USE THE ZANPAKU-TÔ!
THE KÔRYÛ ENTANGLES ALL SPIRITUAL ENTITIES!
IF YOU SWING THAT SWORD, YOU'LL BOTH BE SWALLOWED UP!!

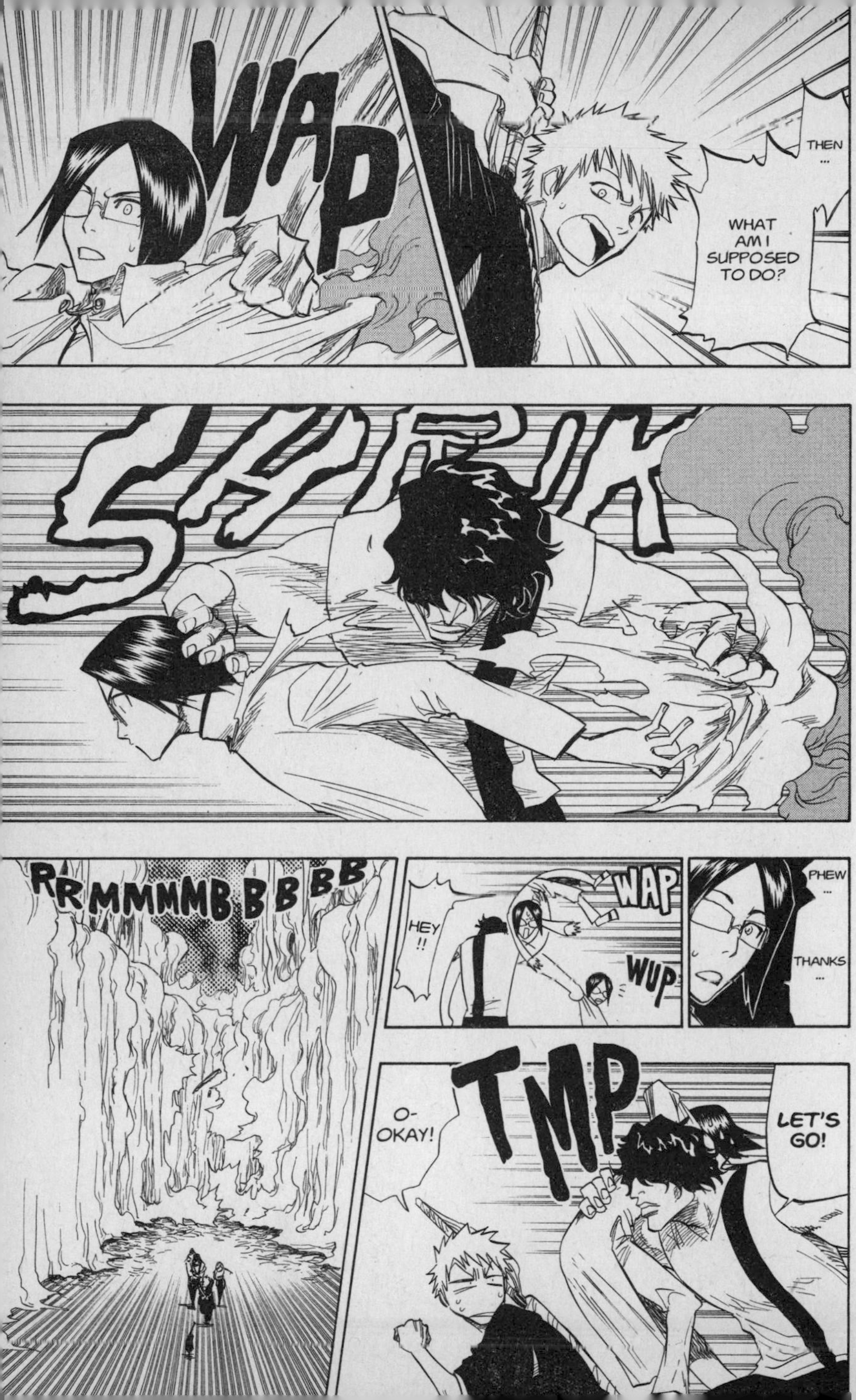
THEN ...
WHAT AM I SUPPOSED TO DO?
WAP
PHEW ...
THANKS ...
WAP
HEY !!
WUP
LET'S GO!
TMP
O-OKAY!
RRMMMMB B B B B

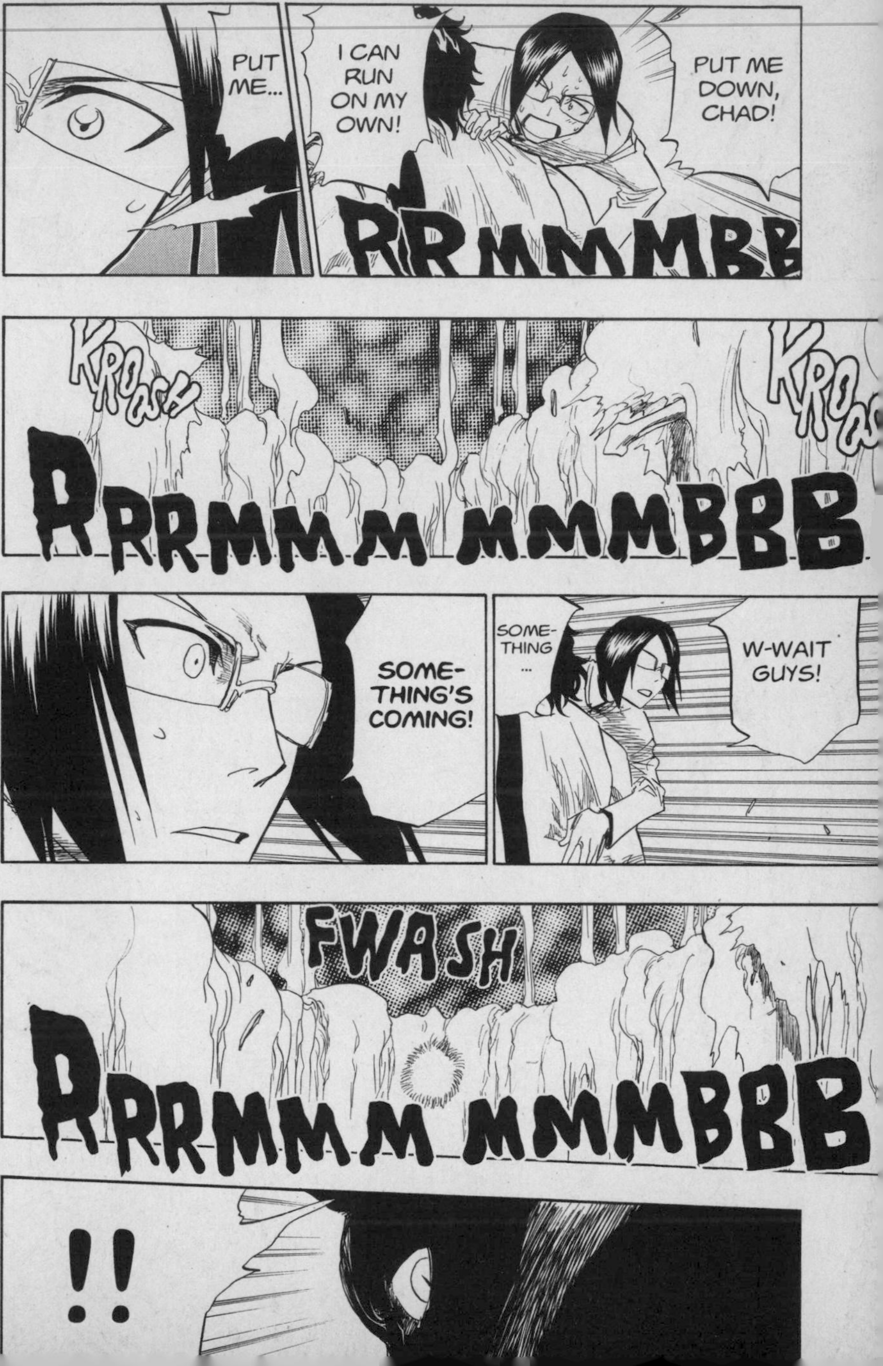
PUT ME DOWN, CHAD!
I CAN RUN ON MY OWN!
RRMMMBB
PUT ME...
KROOSH
RRRMMM MMMMBBB
W-WAIT GUYS!
SOME-THING ...
SOME-THING'S COMING!
FWASH
RRRMMM MMMMBBB
!!

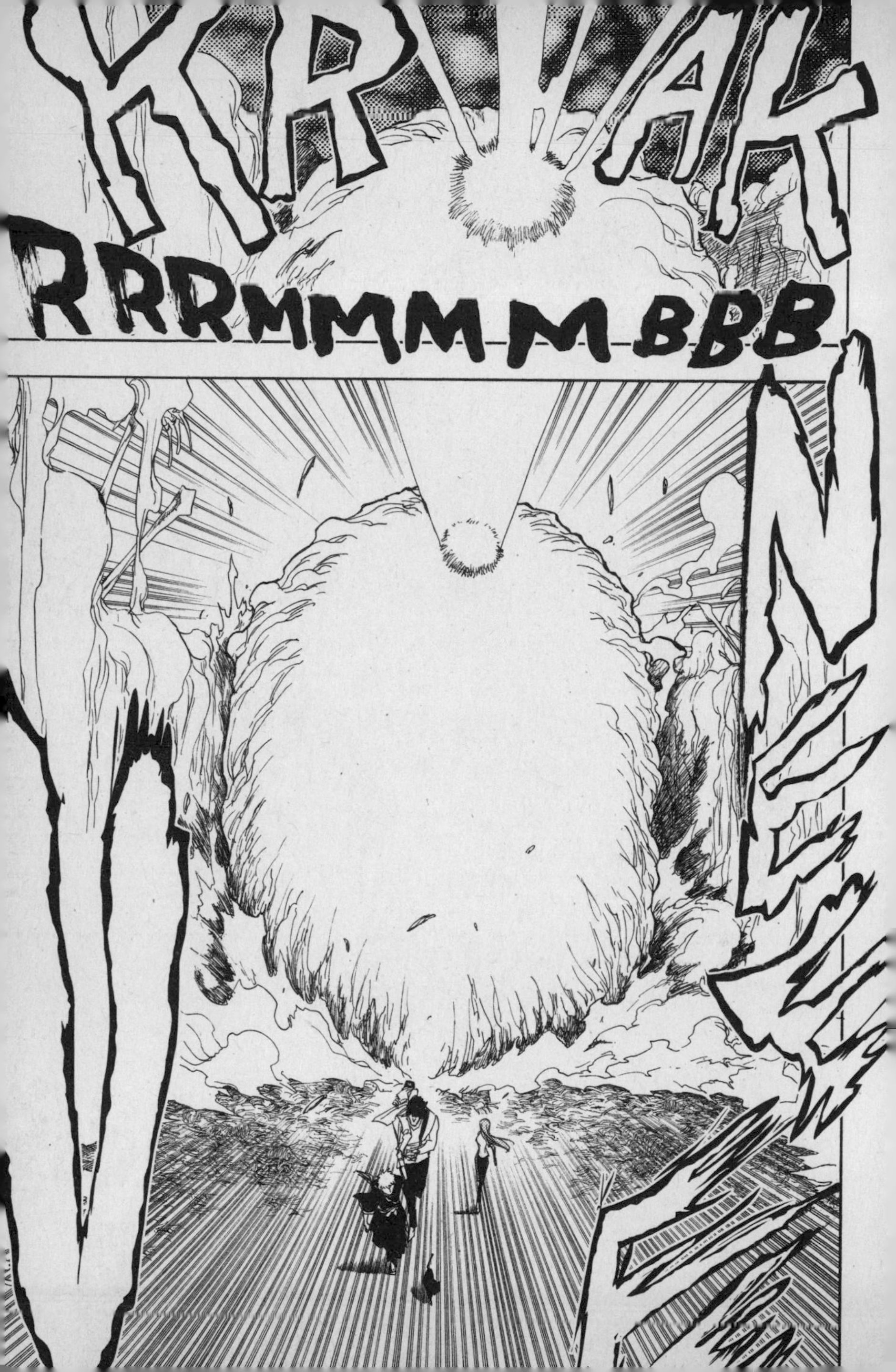
KRAAK
RRRMMMMMBBB

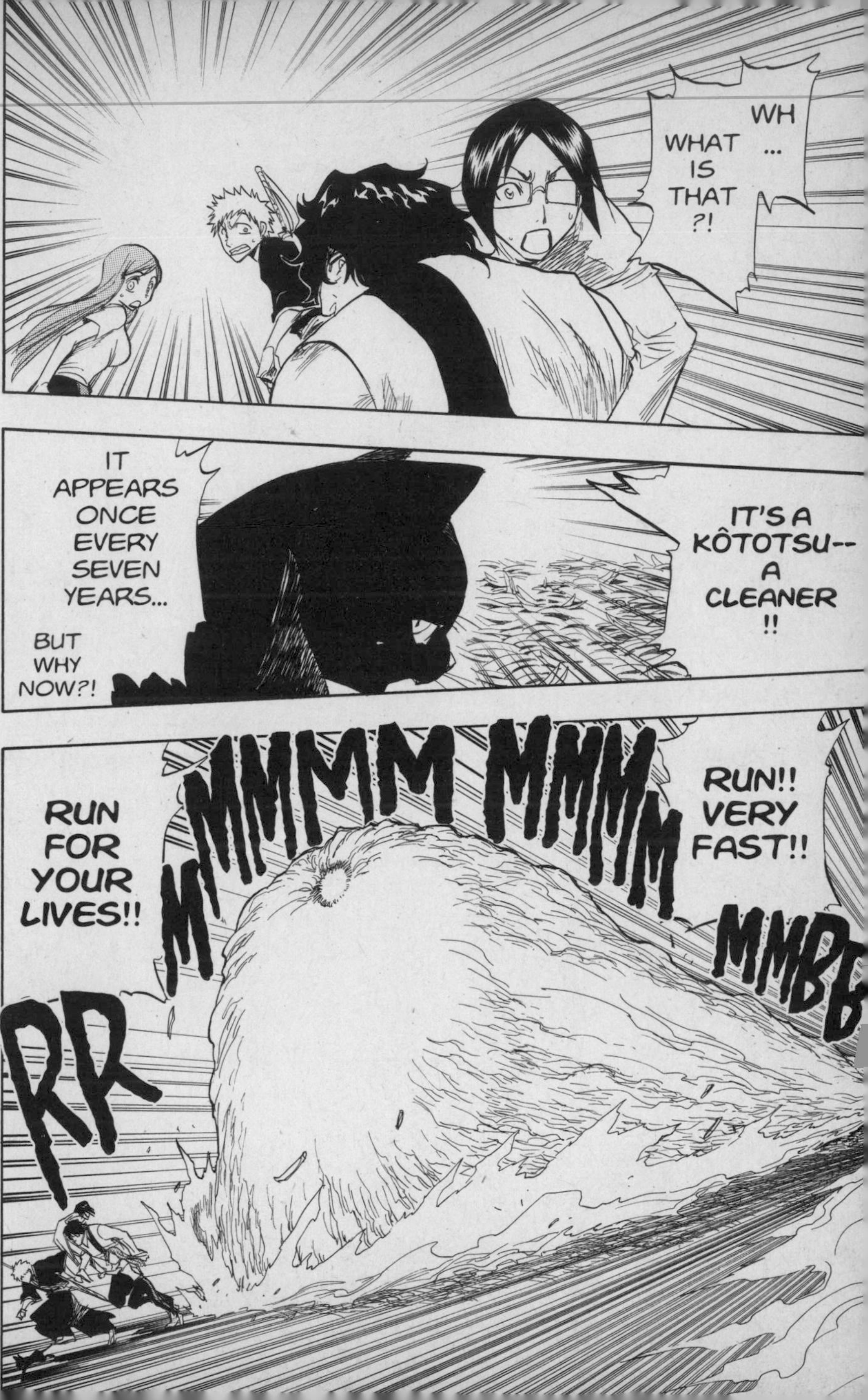

WH ... WHAT IS THAT ?!
IT'S A KÔTOTSU-- A CLEANER !!
IT APPEARS ONCE EVERY SEVEN YEARS...
BUT WHY NOW?!
RUN!! VERY FAST!!
RUN FOR YOUR LIVES!!
MMMMMM MMMMM MMBB
RR

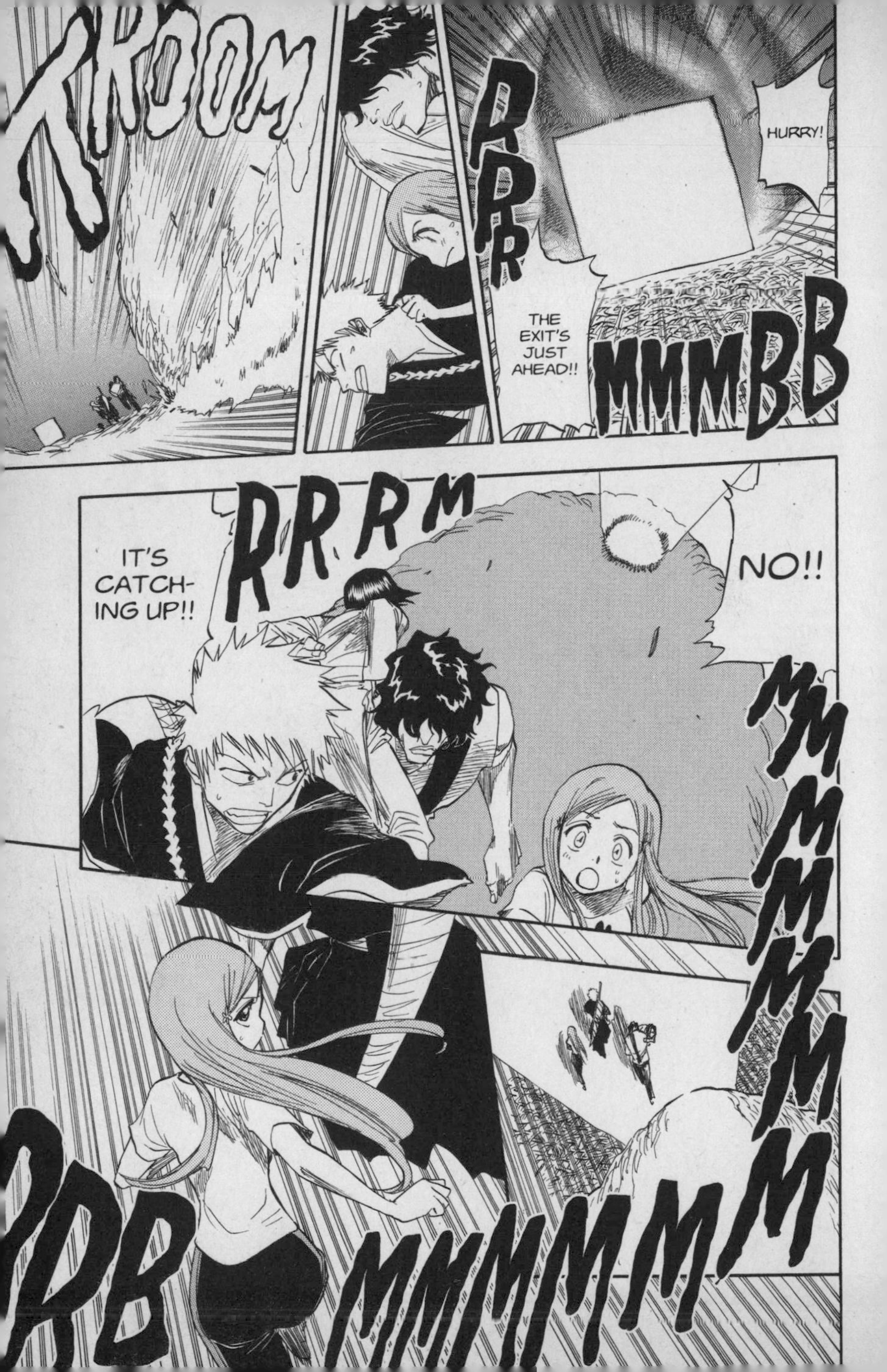
HURRY!
THE EXIT'S JUST AHEAD!!
RRRR
MMMBB
TROOM
NO!!
RRRM
IT'S CATCHING UP!!
MMMMMMMMM
RRB MMMMMMM

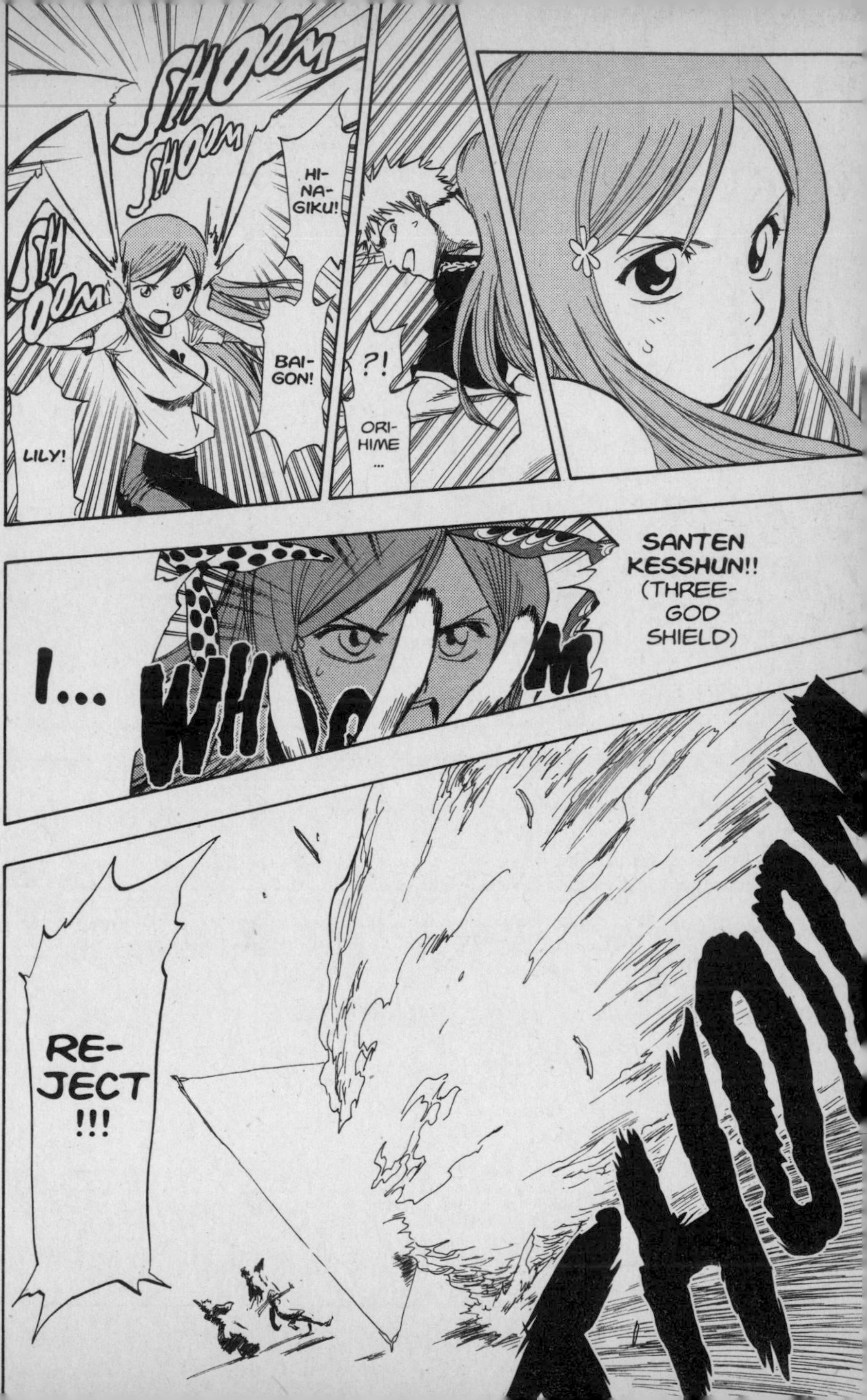
?!
ORI-HIME...
SHOOM
SHOOM
HI-NA-GIKU!
BAI-GON!
SHOOM
LILY!
SANTEN KESSHUN!! (THREE-GOD SHIELD)
I...
RE-JECT!!!

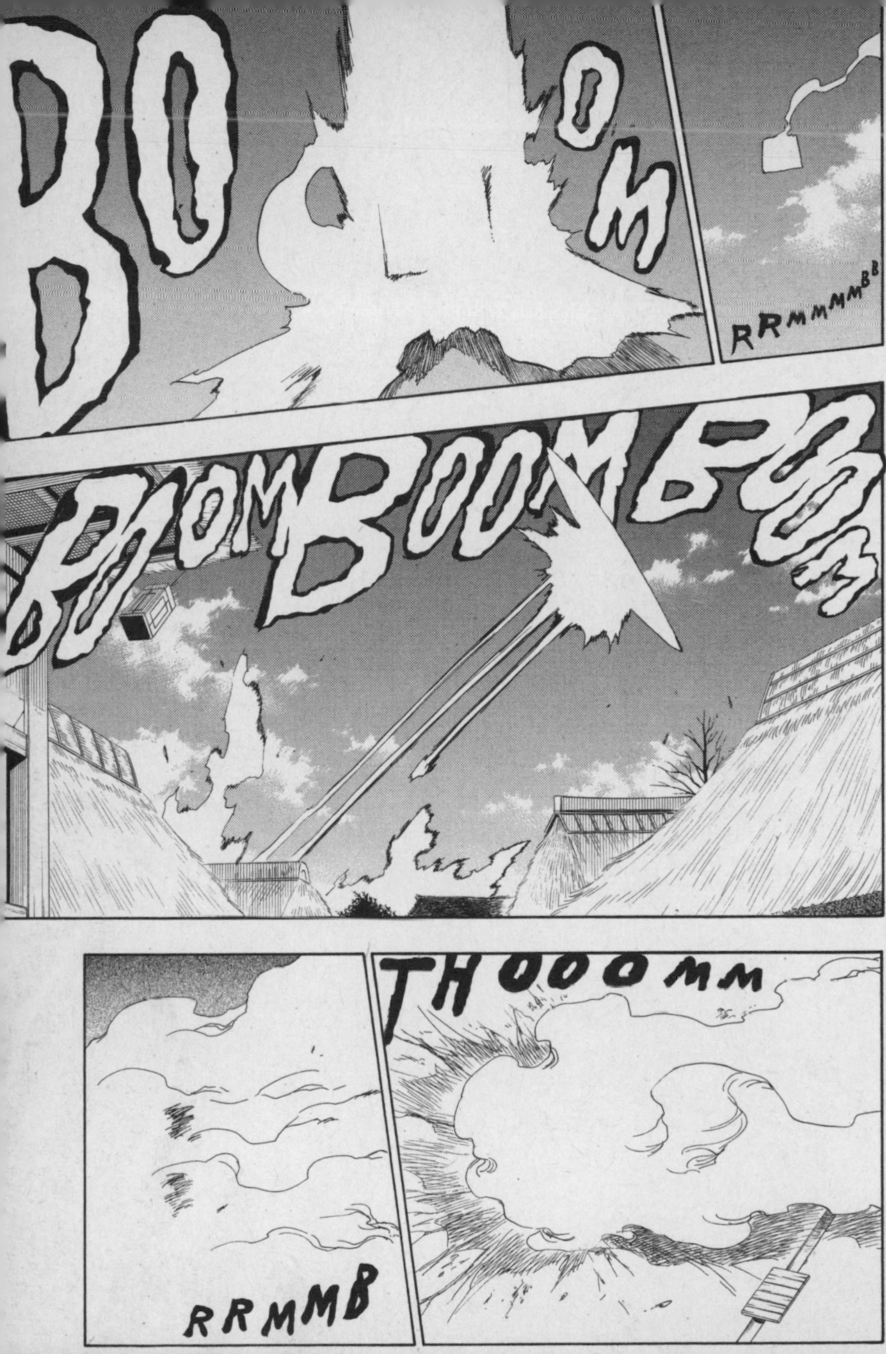
RRMMMMBB
BOOM
BOOM BOOM BOOM
THOOOMM
RRMMB

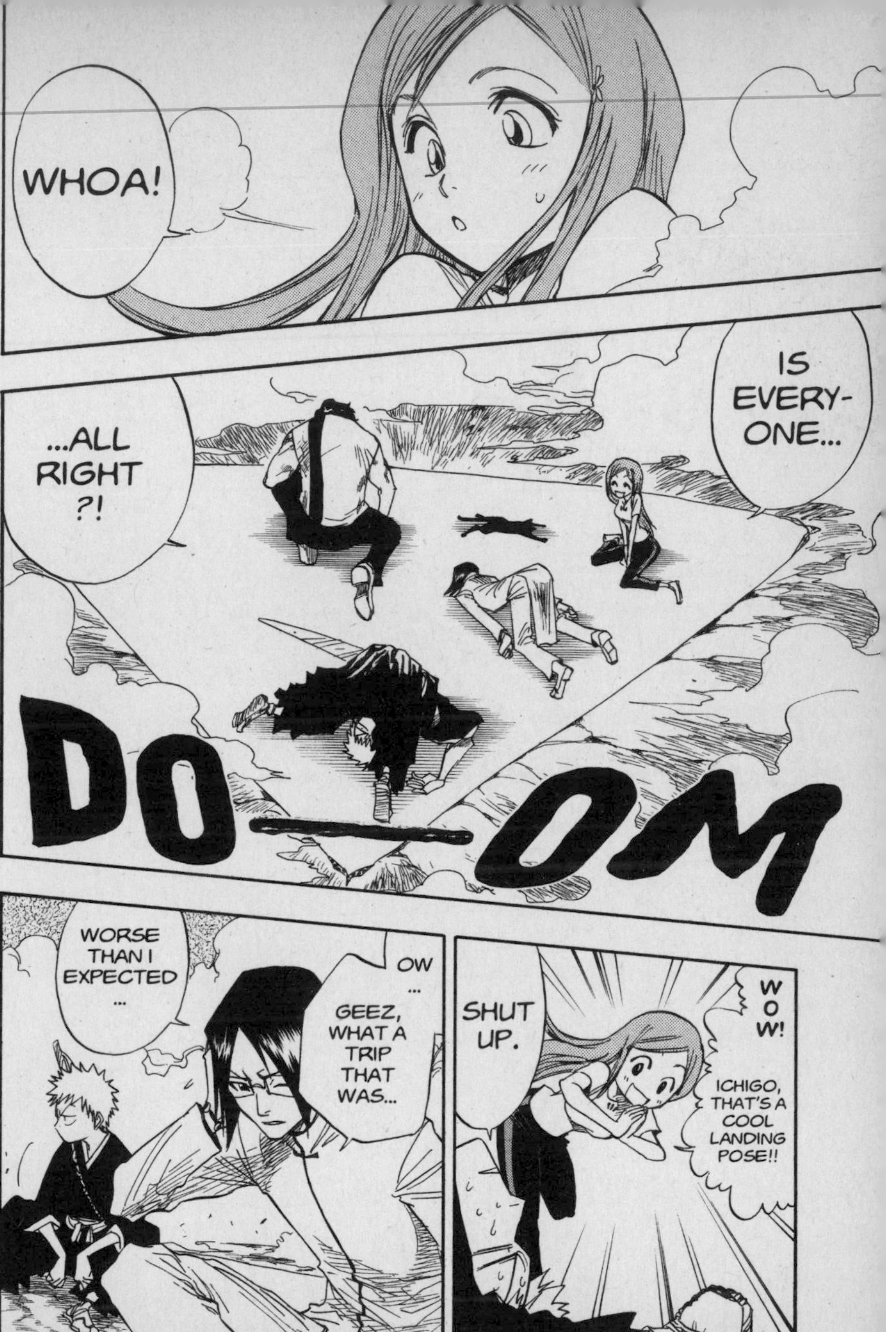
WHOA!
IS EVERYONE...
...ALL RIGHT ?!
DO—OM
WOW!
ICHIGO, THAT'S A COOL LANDING POSE!!
SHUT UP.
OW ...
GEEZ, WHAT A TRIP THAT WAS...
WORSE THAN I EXPECTED ...

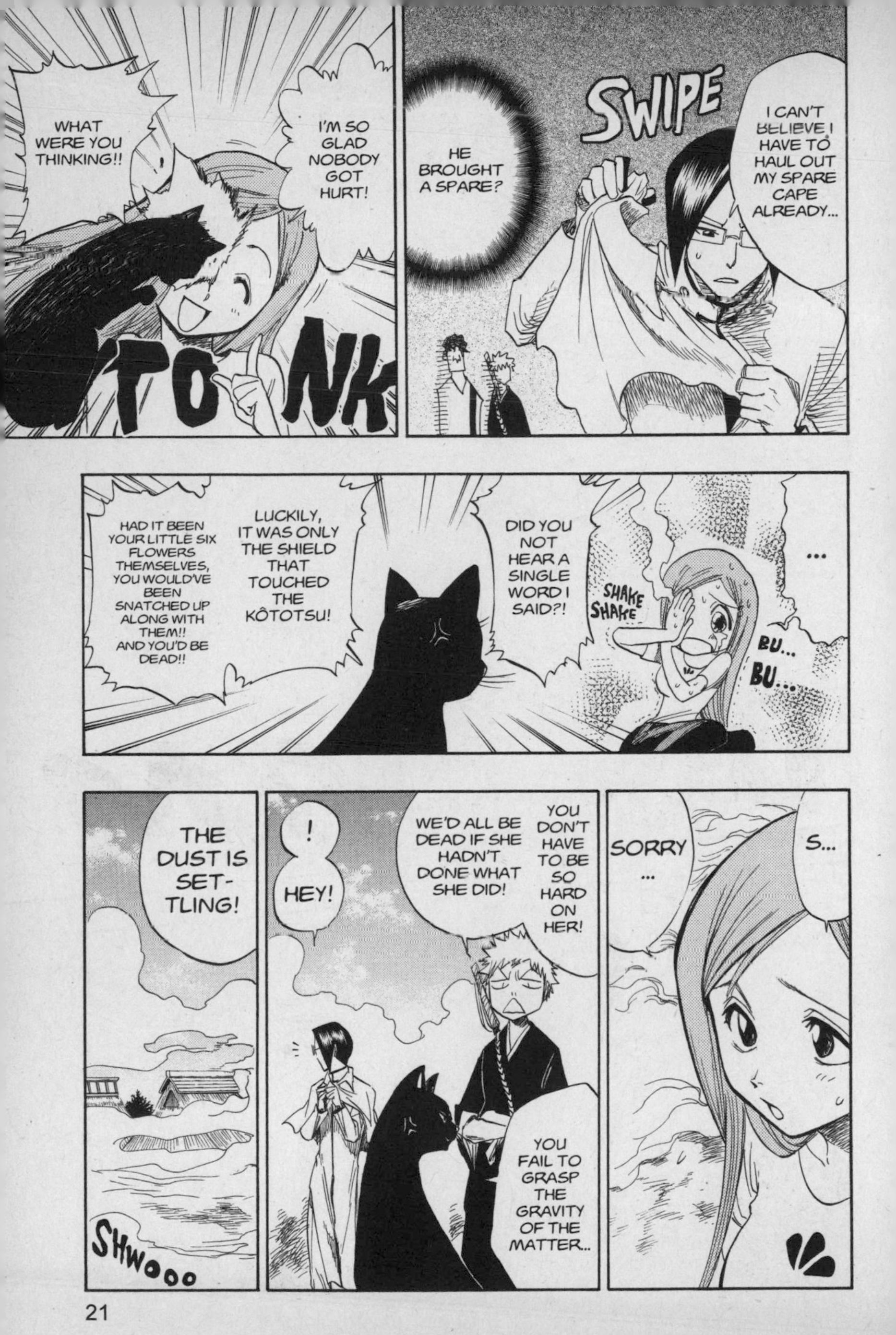
SWIPE
I CAN'T BELIEVE I HAVE TO HAUL OUT MY SPARE CAPE ALREADY...
HE BROUGHT A SPARE?
I'M SO GLAD NOBODY GOT HURT!
WHAT WERE YOU THINKING!!
TONK
...
BU... BU...
SHAKE SHAKE
DID YOU NOT HEAR A SINGLE WORD I SAID?!
LUCKILY, IT WAS ONLY THE SHIELD THAT TOUCHED THE KÔTOTSU!
HAD IT BEEN YOUR LITTLE SIX FLOWERS THEMSELVES, YOU WOULD'VE BEEN SNATCHED UP ALONG WITH THEM!! AND YOU'D BE DEAD!!
S...
SORRY ...
YOU DON'T HAVE TO BE SO HARD ON HER!
WE'D ALL BE DEAD IF SHE HADN'T DONE WHAT SHE DID!
!
HEY!
YOU FAIL TO GRASP THE GRAVITY OF THE MATTER..
THE DUST IS SET-TLING!
SHWOOO

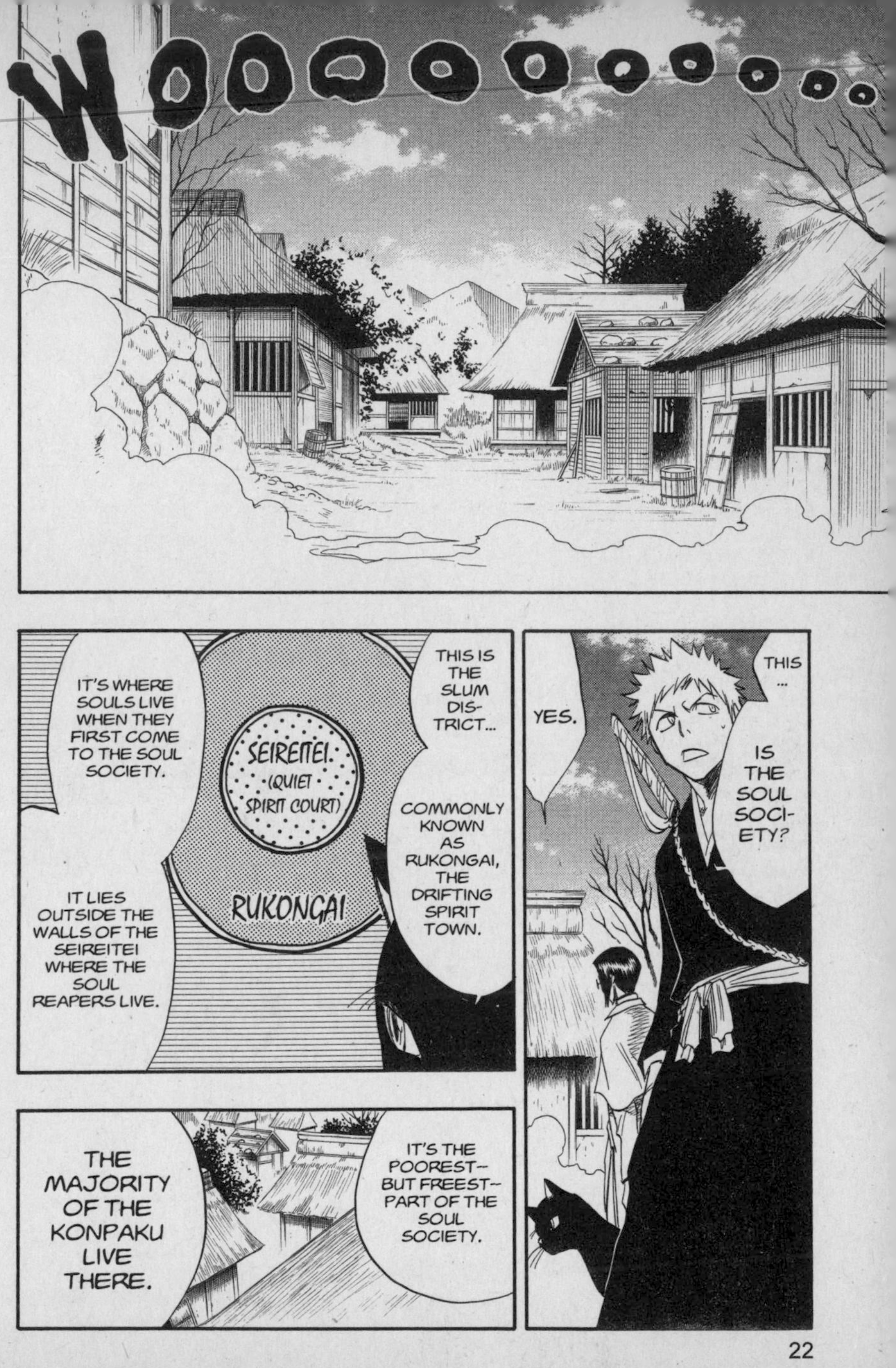

WOOOOOOOOO...
THIS ... IS THE SOUL SOCIETY?
YES.
THIS IS THE SLUM DISTRICT...
COMMONLY KNOWN AS RUKONGAI, THE DRIFTING SPIRIT TOWN.
SEIREITEI. (QUIET SPIRIT COURT)
RUKONGAI
IT'S WHERE SOULS LIVE WHEN THEY FIRST COME TO THE SOUL SOCIETY.
IT LIES OUTSIDE THE WALLS OF THE SEIREITEI WHERE THE SOUL REAPERS LIVE.
IT'S THE POOREST-- BUT FREEST-- PART OF THE SOUL SOCIETY.
THE MAJORITY OF THE KONPAKU LIVE THERE.

READ THIS WAY

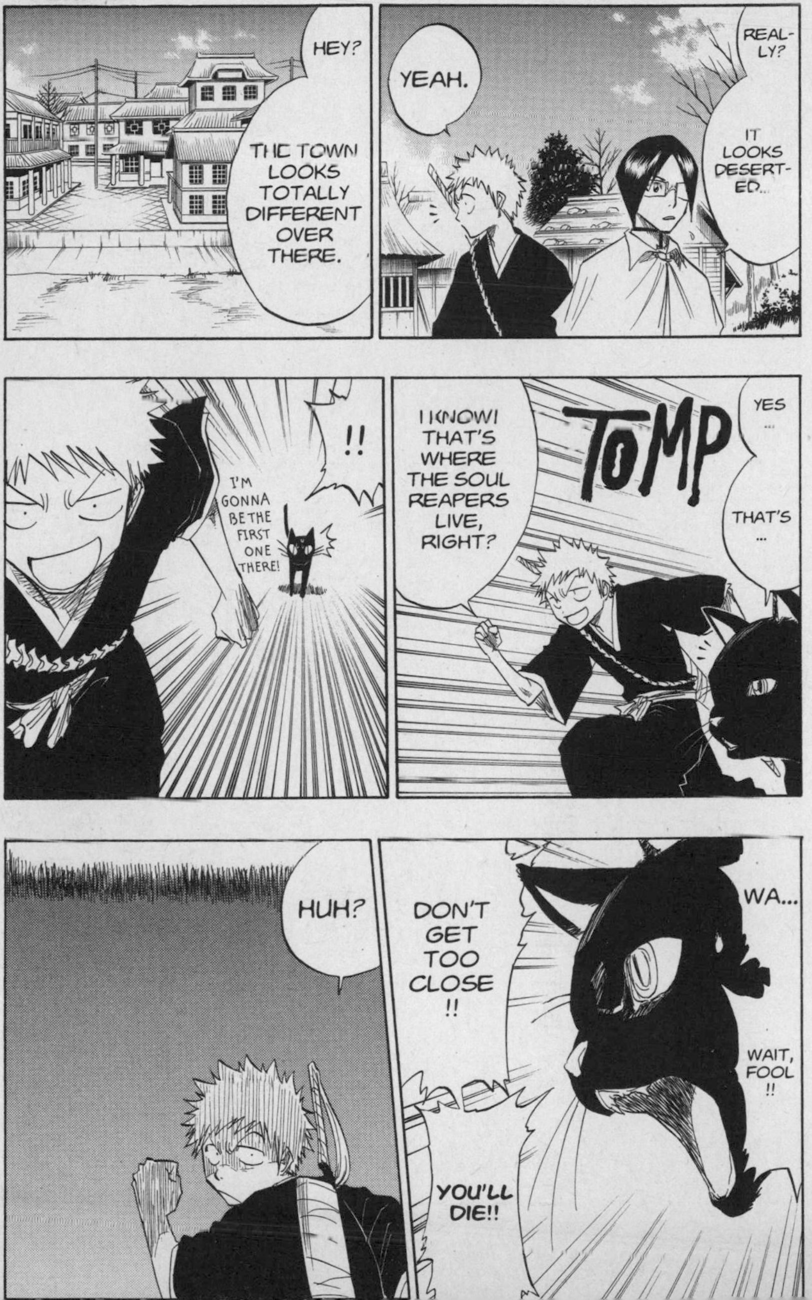
REAL-LY?
IT LOOKS DESERT-ED...
YEAH.
HEY?
THE TOWN LOOKS TOTALLY DIFFERENT OVER THERE.
YES... THAT'S...
TOMP
I KNOW! THAT'S WHERE THE SOUL REAPERS LIVE, RIGHT?
!!
I'M GONNA BE THE FIRST ONE THERE!
WA...
DON'T GET TOO CLOSE!!
WAIT, FOOL!!
YOU'LL DIE!!
HUH?

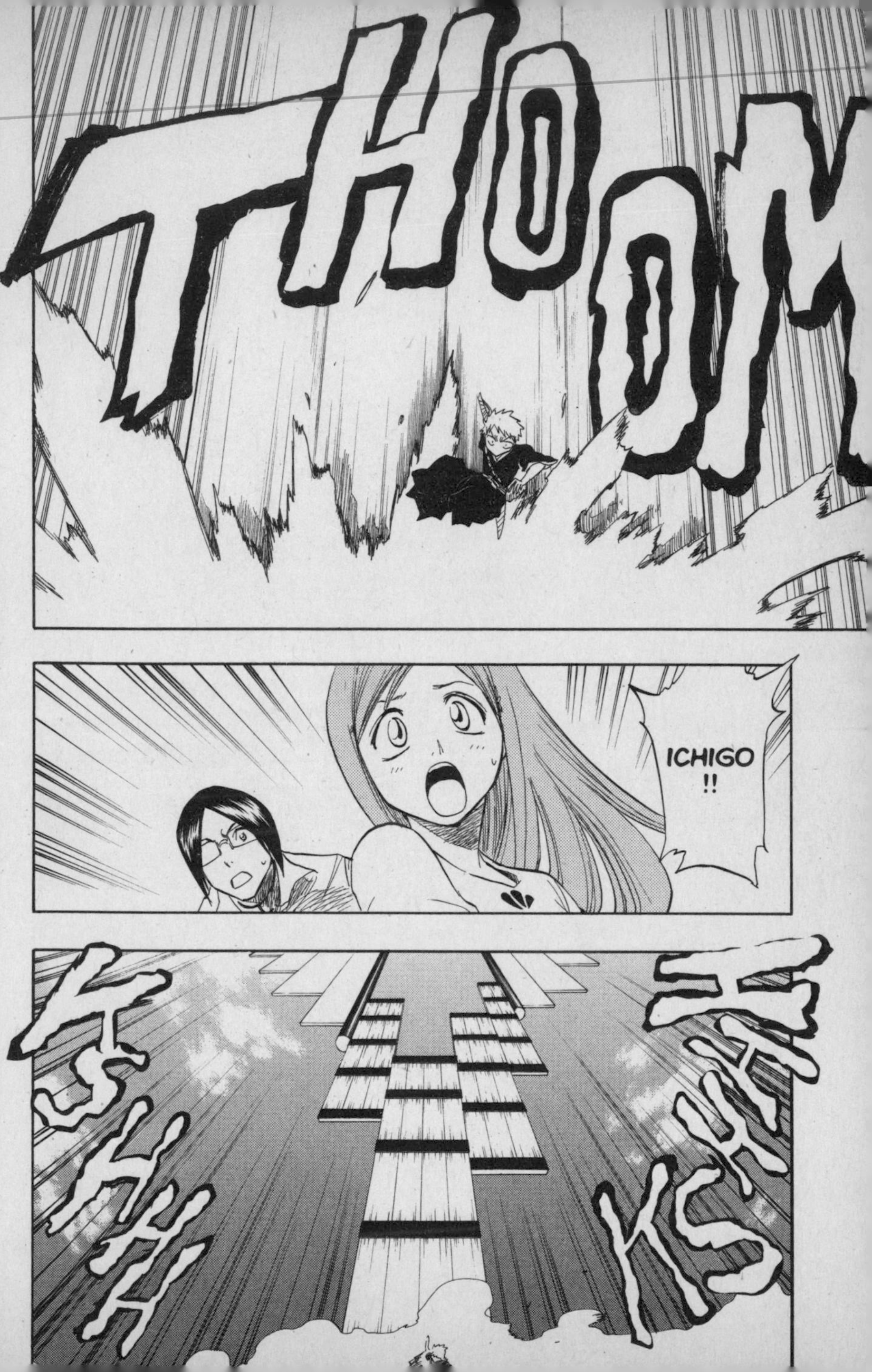
THOOM
ICHIGO
!!

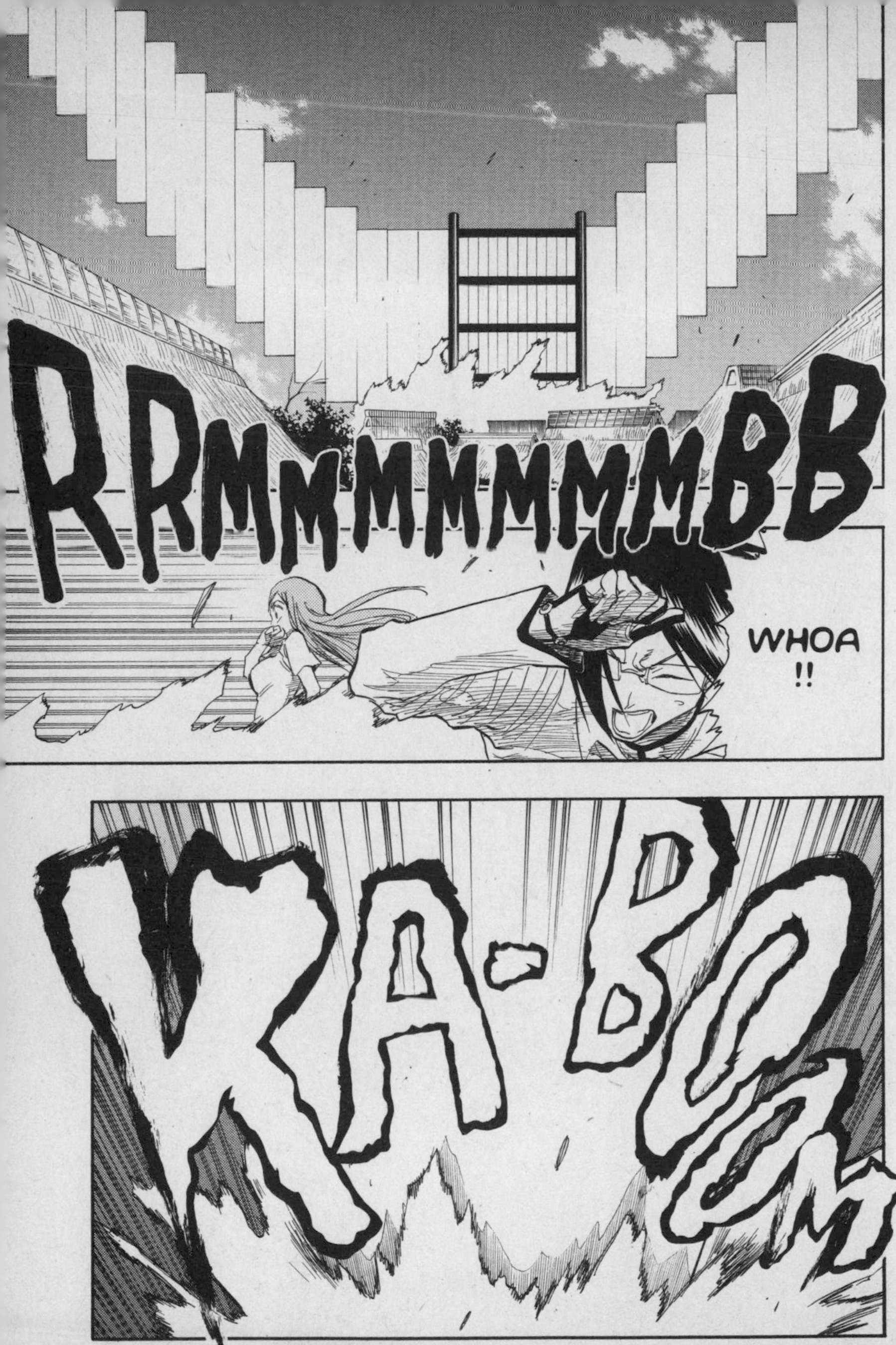
RRMMMMMMMBB
WHOA !!
KA-BOOM

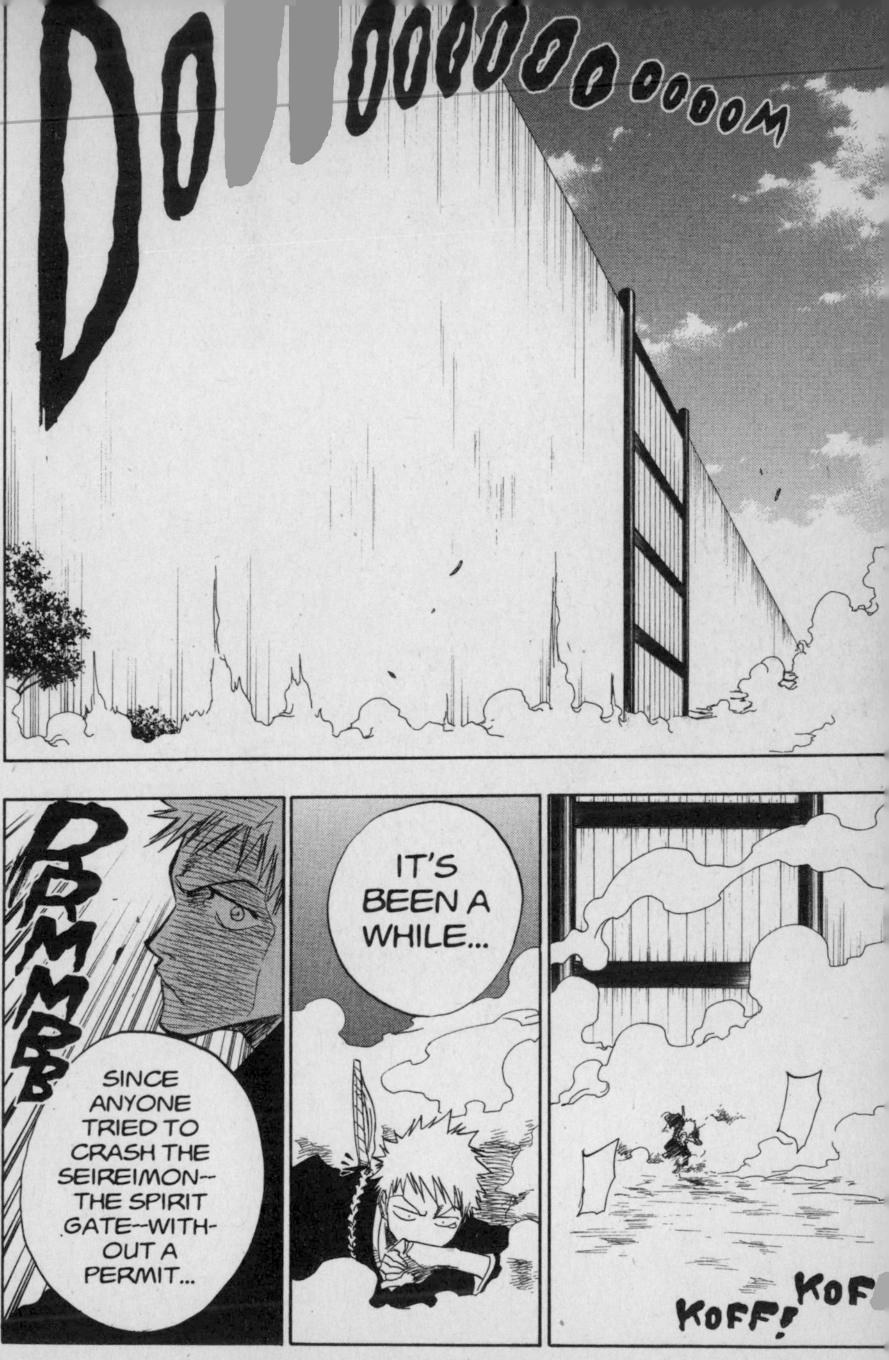
DOOOOOOOOOOOOOM
KOFF! KOF
IT'S BEEN A WHILE...
BRRMMBB
SINCE ANYONE TRIED TO CRASH THE SEIREIMON--THE SPIRIT GATE--WITHOUT A PERMIT...

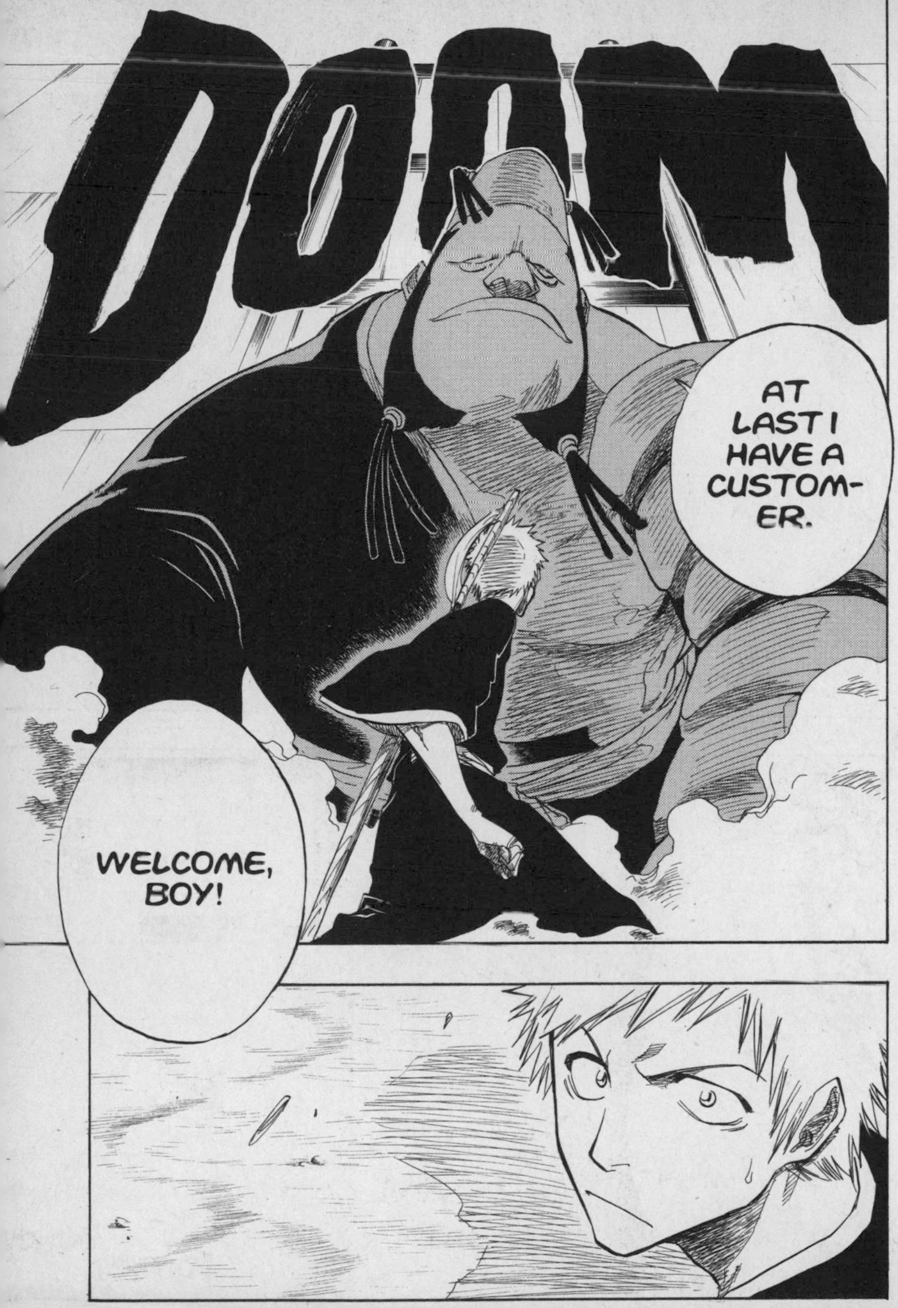
DOOM
AT LAST I HAVE A CUSTOMER.
WELCOME, BOY!

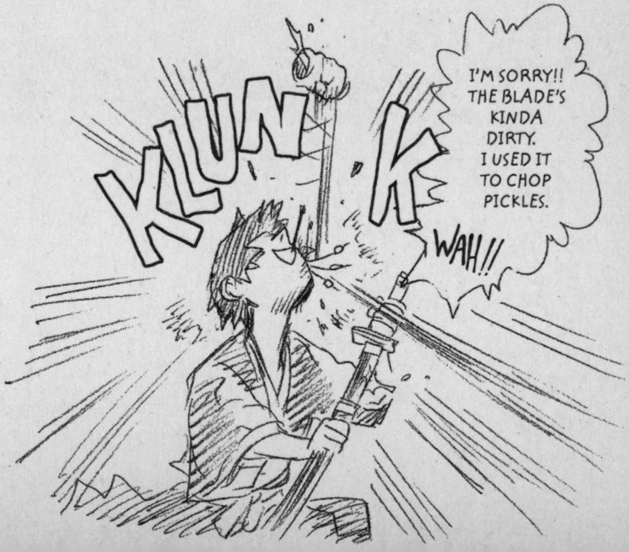
I'M SORRY!! THE BLADE'S KINDA DIRTY. I USED IT TO CHOP PICKLES.
KLUNK
WAH!!

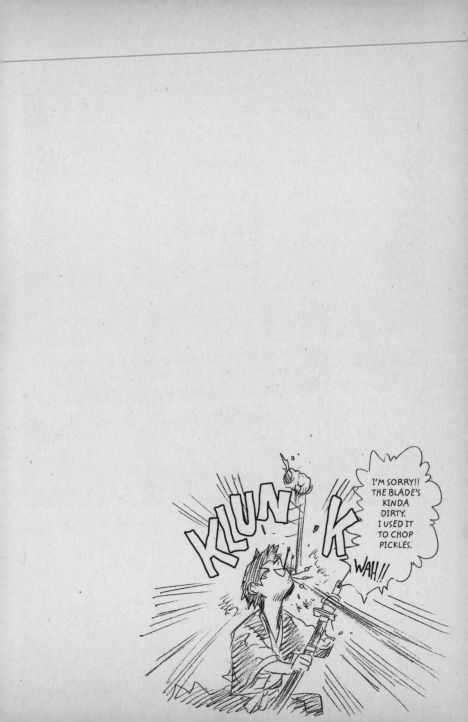

72. The Superchunk

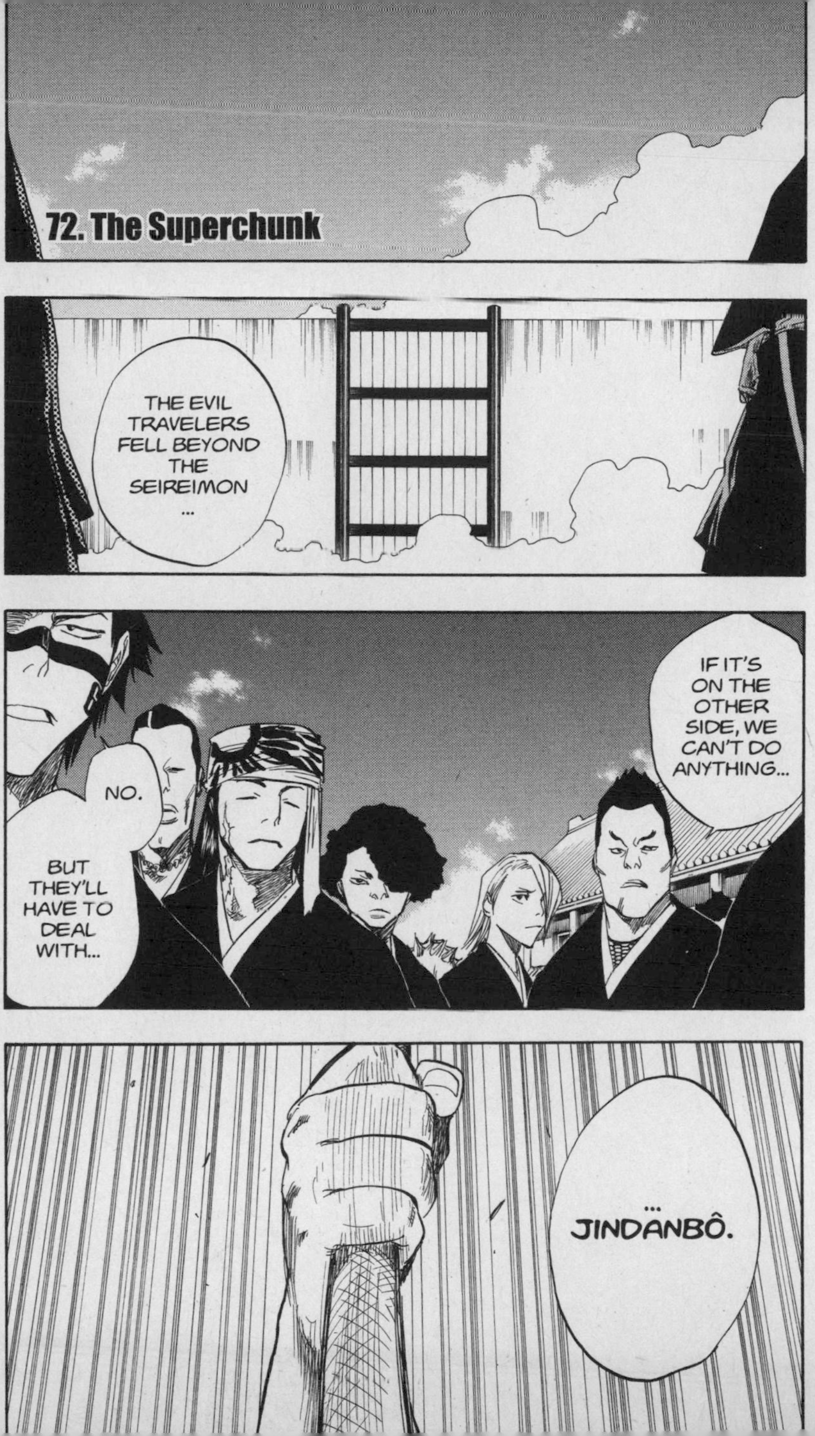
THE EVIL TRAVELERS FELL BEYOND THE SEIREIMON ...
IF IT'S ON THE OTHER SIDE, WE CAN'T DO ANYTHING...
NO.
BUT THEY'LL HAVE TO DEAL WITH...
... JINDANBÔ.

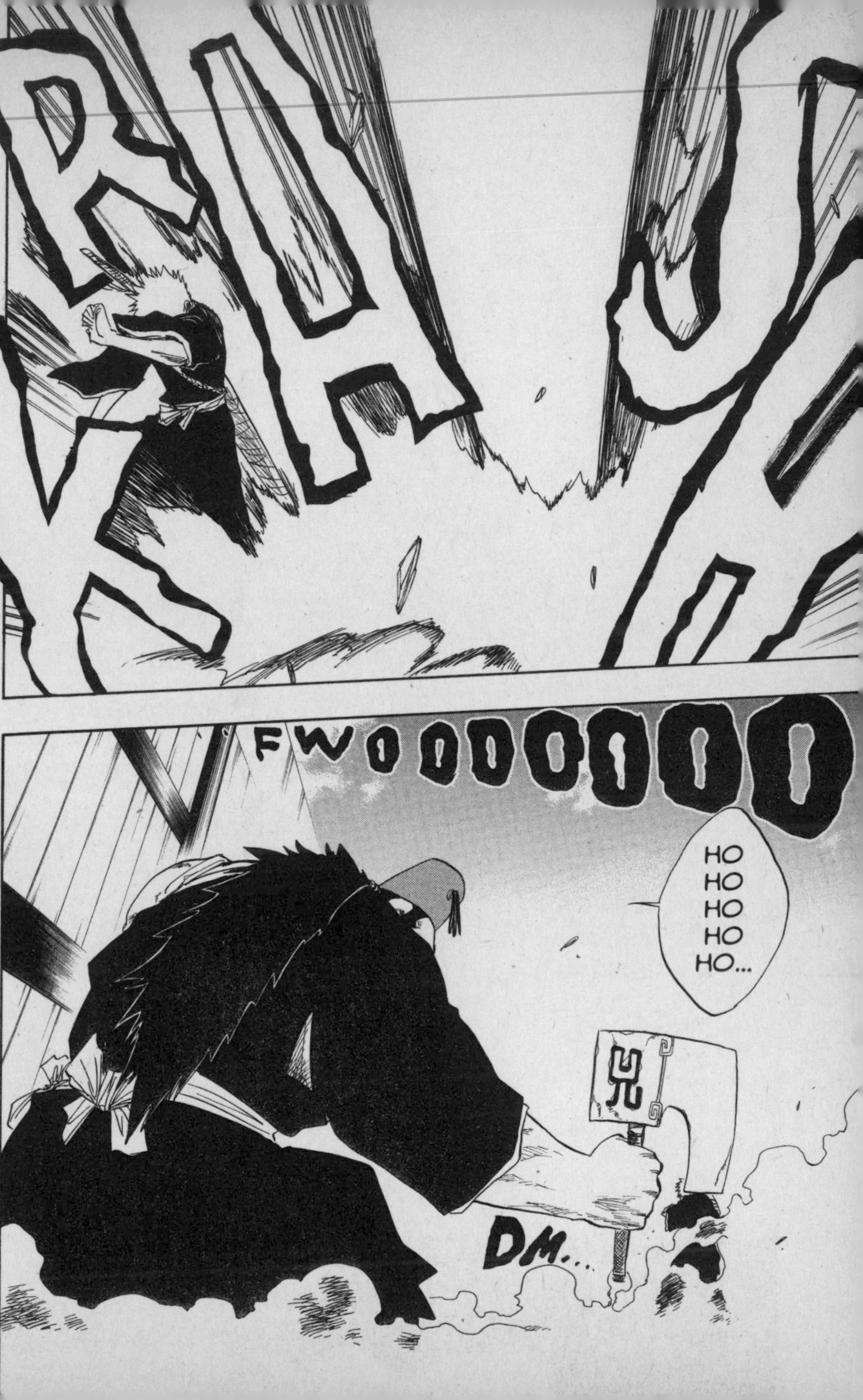
FWOOOOOOOO
HO HO HO HO HO...
DM...

AX: JI--FIRST CHARACTER OF JINDANBÔ'S NAME

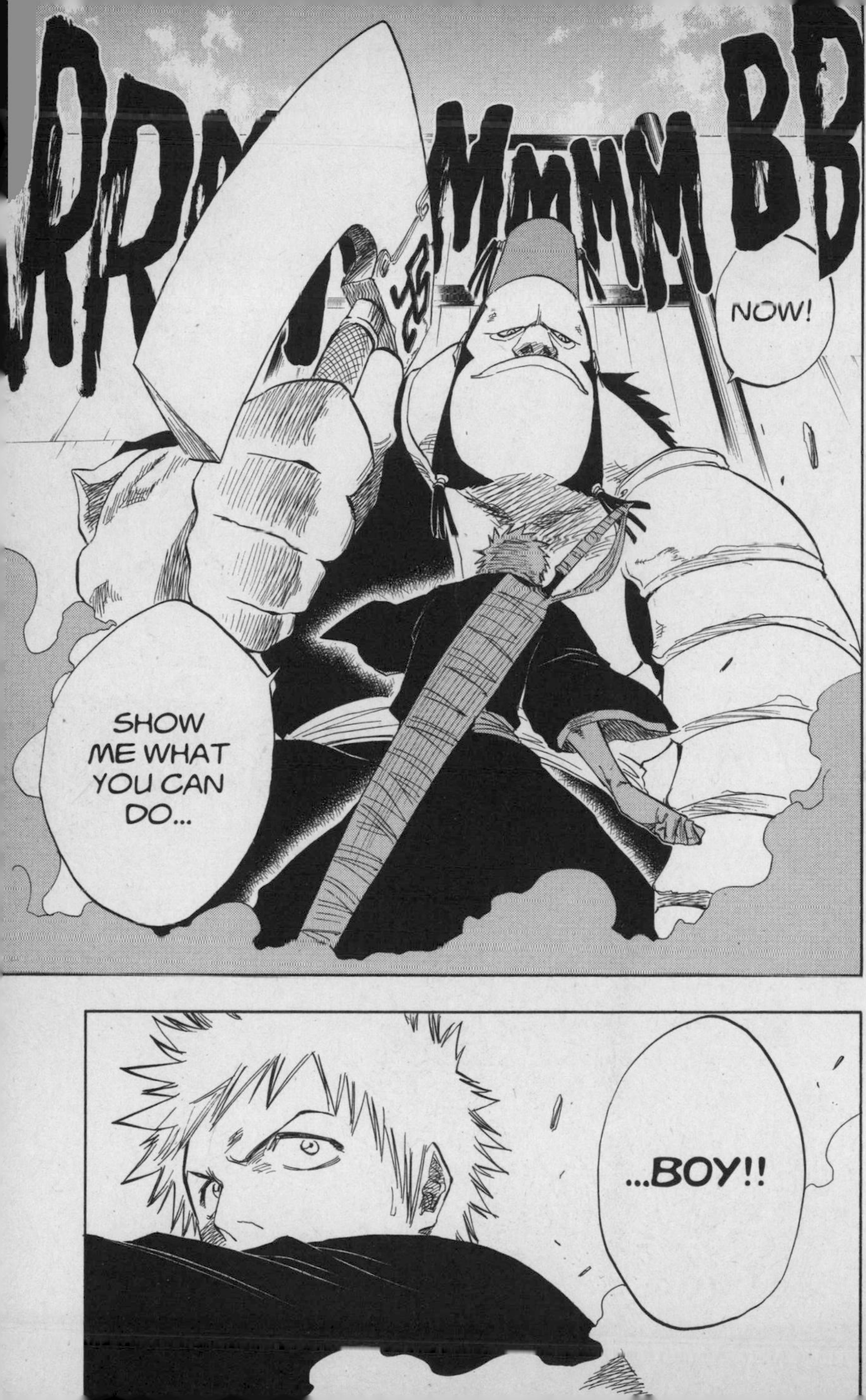
NOW!
SHOW ME WHAT YOU CAN DO...
...BOY!!

72. The Superchunk

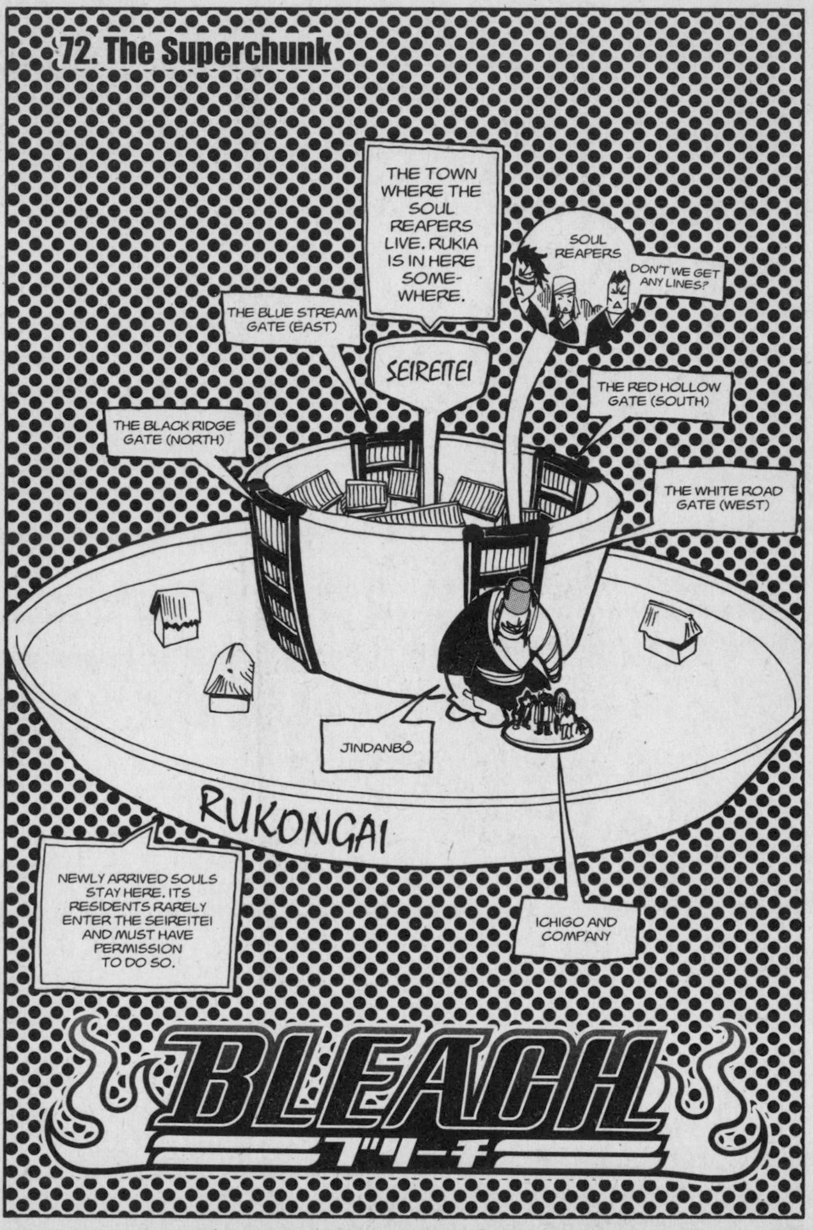

SOUL REAPERS
DON'T WE GET ANY LINES?
THE TOWN WHERE THE SOUL REAPERS LIVE. RUKIA IS IN HERE SOME-WHERE.
THE BLUE STREAM GATE (EAST)
SEIREITEI
THE RED HOLLOW GATE (SOUTH)
THE BLACK RIDGE GATE (NORTH)
THE WHITE ROAD GATE (WEST)
JINDANBÔ
RUKONGAI
ICHIGO AND COMPANY
NEWLY ARRIVED SOULS STAY HERE. ITS RESIDENTS RARELY ENTER THE SEIREITEI AND MUST HAVE PERMISSION TO DO SO.
BLEACH
ブリーチ

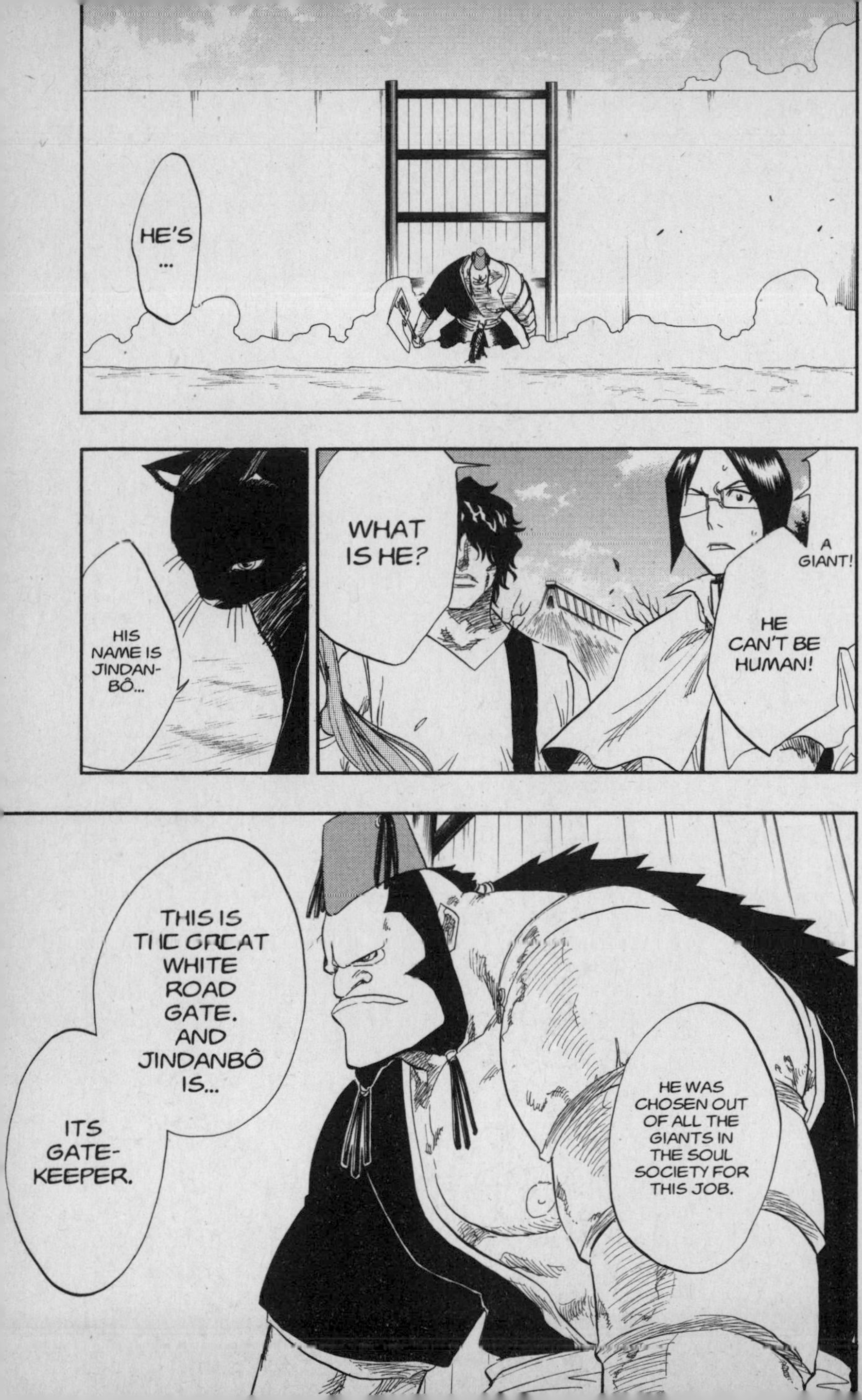
HE'S ...
A GIANT!
HE CAN'T BE HUMAN!
WHAT IS HE?
HIS NAME IS JINDANBÔ...
THIS IS THE GREAT WHITE ROAD GATE. AND JINDANBÔ IS...
ITS GATE-KEEPER.
HE WAS CHOSEN OUT OF ALL THE GIANTS IN THE SOUL SOCIETY FOR THIS JOB.

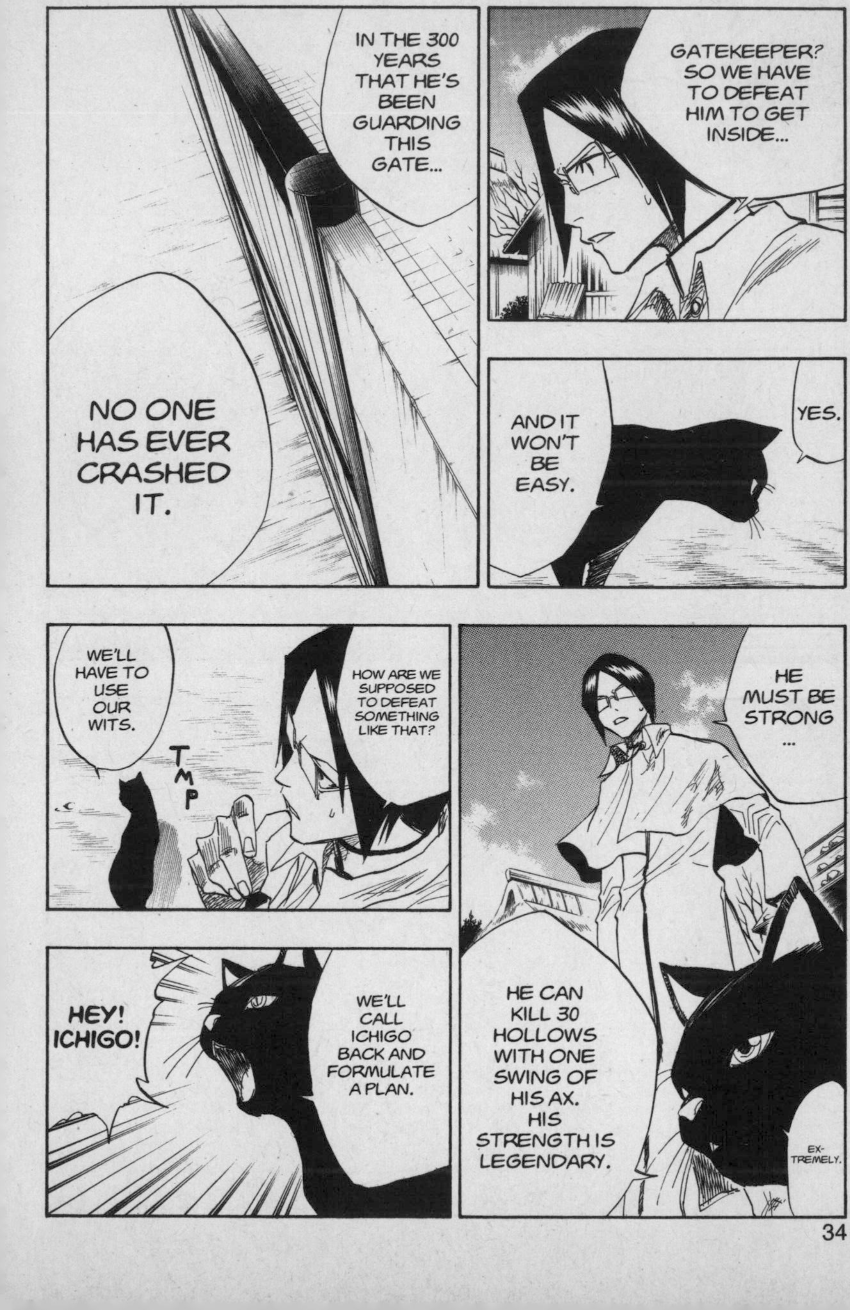
GATEKEEPER? SO WE HAVE TO DEFEAT HIM TO GET INSIDE...
YES.
AND IT WON'T BE EASY.
IN THE 300 YEARS THAT HE'S BEEN GUARDING THIS GATE...
NO ONE HAS EVER CRASHED IT.
HE MUST BE STRONG ...
EX-TREMELY.
HE CAN KILL 30 HOLLOWS WITH ONE SWING OF HIS AX. HIS STRENGTH IS LEGENDARY.
HOW ARE WE SUPPOSED TO DEFEAT SOMETHING LIKE THAT?
TMP
WE'LL HAVE TO USE OUR WITS.
WE'LL CALL ICHIGO BACK AND FORMULATE A PLAN.
HEY! ICHIGO!

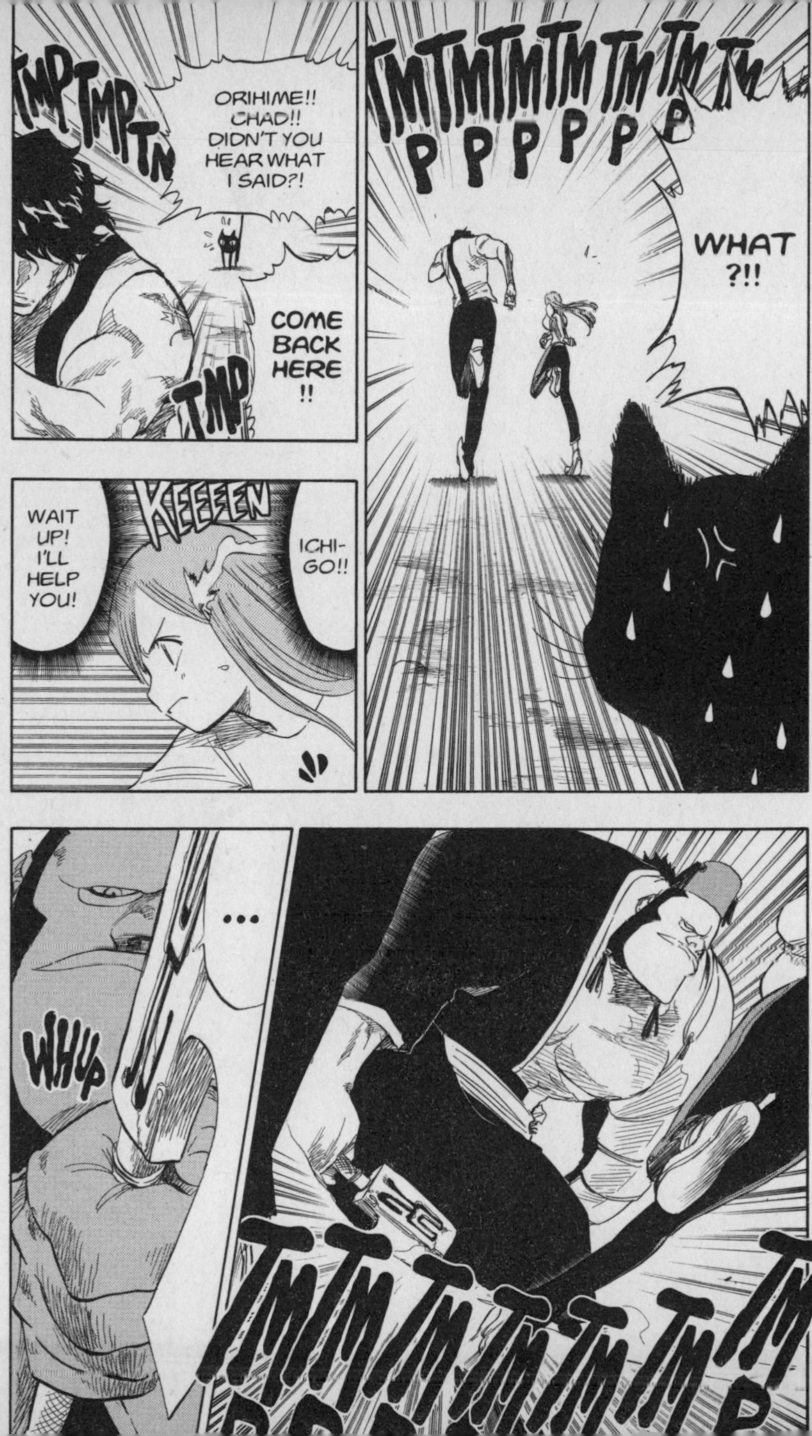
WHAT ?!!
TMPTMPTM
ORIHIME!! CHAD!! DIDN'T YOU HEAR WHAT I SAID?!
COME BACK HERE !!
TMP
KEEEEN
ICHI-GO!!
WAIT UP! I'LL HELP YOU!
...
WHUP

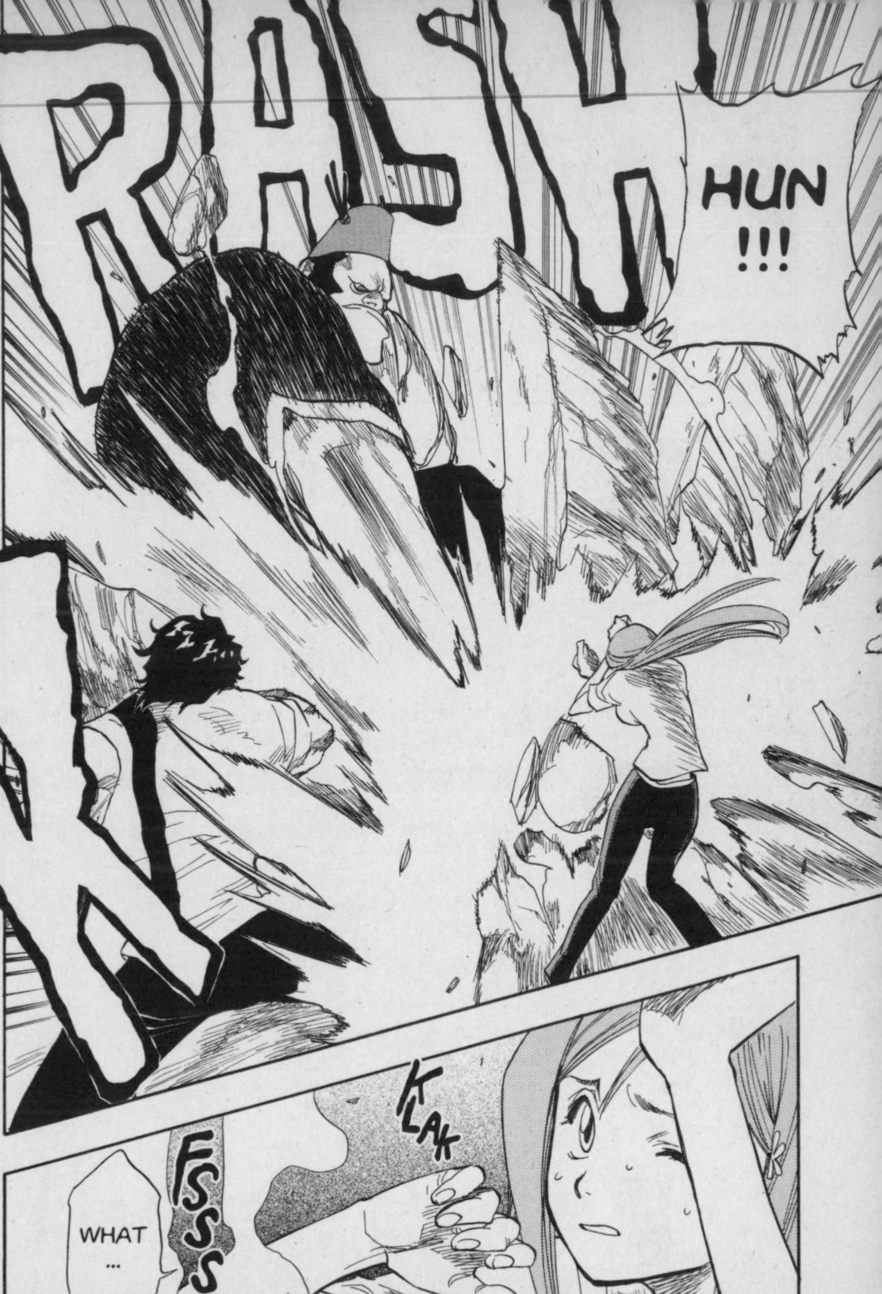
HUN !!!
KLAK
FSSS
WHAT ...

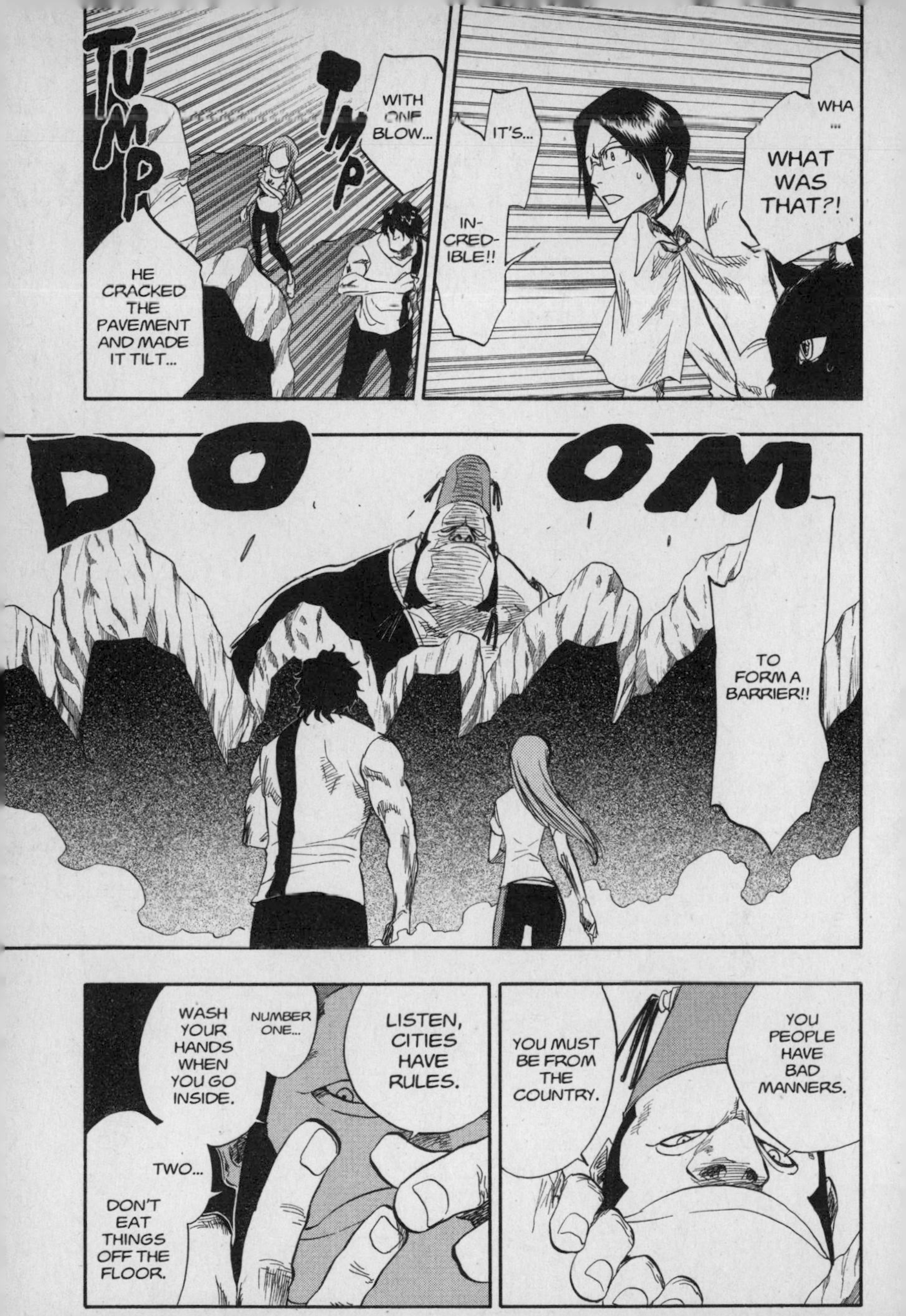
WHA... WHAT WAS THAT?!
IT'S...
IN-CRED-IBLE!!
WITH ONE BLOW...
TMP
TUMP
HE CRACKED THE PAVEMENT AND MADE IT TILT...
DOOM
TO FORM A BARRIER!!
YOU PEOPLE HAVE BAD MANNERS.
YOU MUST BE FROM THE COUNTRY.
LISTEN, CITIES HAVE RULES.
NUMBER ONE...
WASH YOUR HANDS WHEN YOU GO INSIDE.
TWO...
DON'T EAT THINGS OFF THE FLOOR.

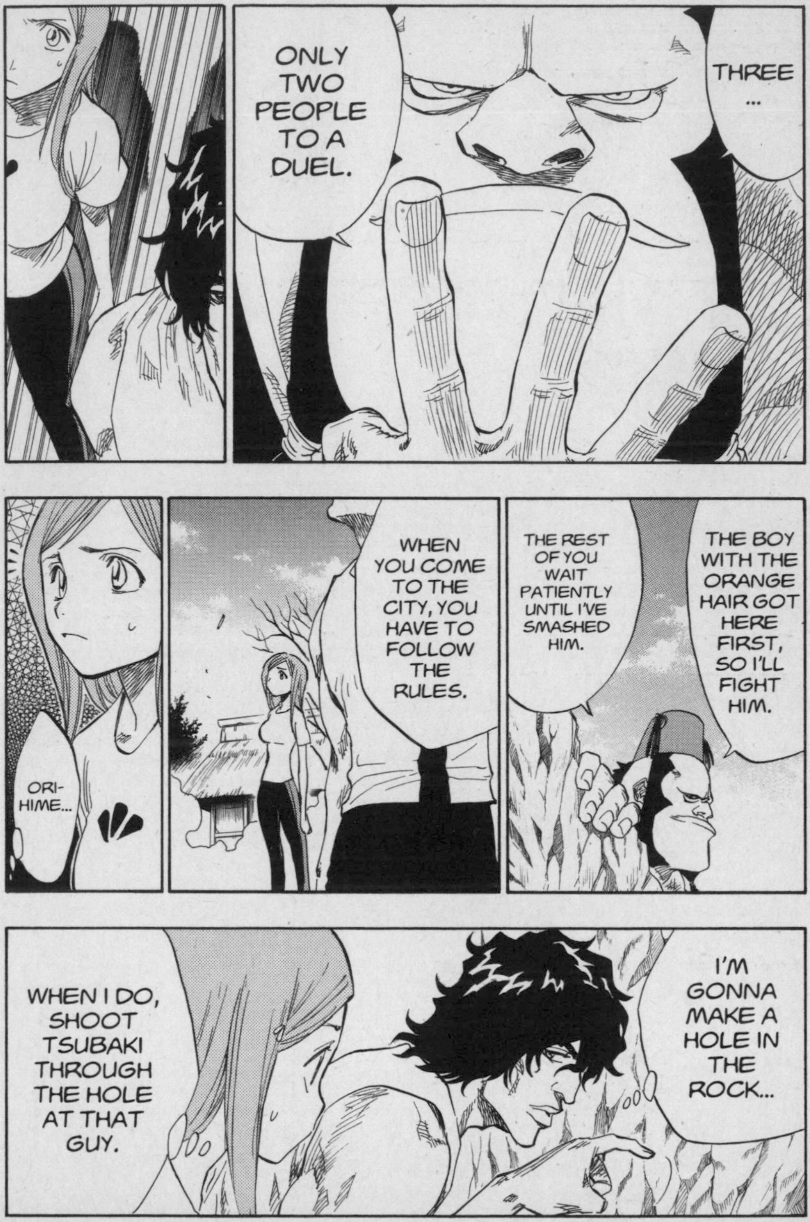
THREE ...
ONLY TWO PEOPLE TO A DUEL.
THE BOY WITH THE ORANGE HAIR GOT HERE FIRST, SO I'LL FIGHT HIM.
THE REST OF YOU WAIT PATIENTLY UNTIL I'VE SMASHED HIM.
WHEN YOU COME TO THE CITY, YOU HAVE TO FOLLOW THE RULES.
ORI-HIME...
I'M GONNA MAKE A HOLE IN THE ROCK...
WHEN I DO, SHOOT TSUBAKI THROUGH THE HOLE AT THAT GUY.

READ THIS WAY

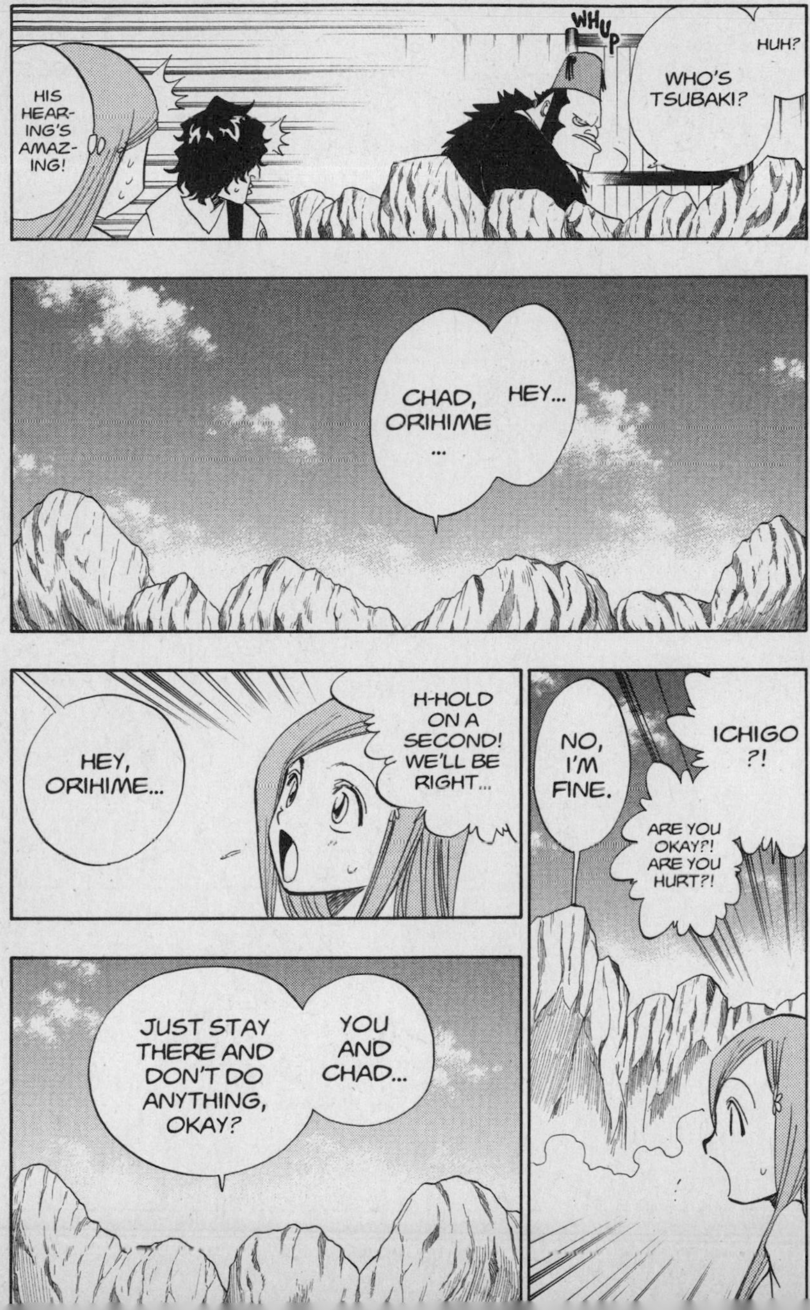
HUH? WHO'S TSUBAKI?
WHUP
HIS HEARING'S AMAZING!
HEY... CHAD, ORIHIME...
ICHIGO?!
ARE YOU OKAY?! ARE YOU HURT?!
NO, I'M FINE.
H-HOLD ON A SECOND! WE'LL BE RIGHT...
HEY, ORIHIME...
YOU AND CHAD...
JUST STAY THERE AND DON'T DO ANYTHING, OKAY?

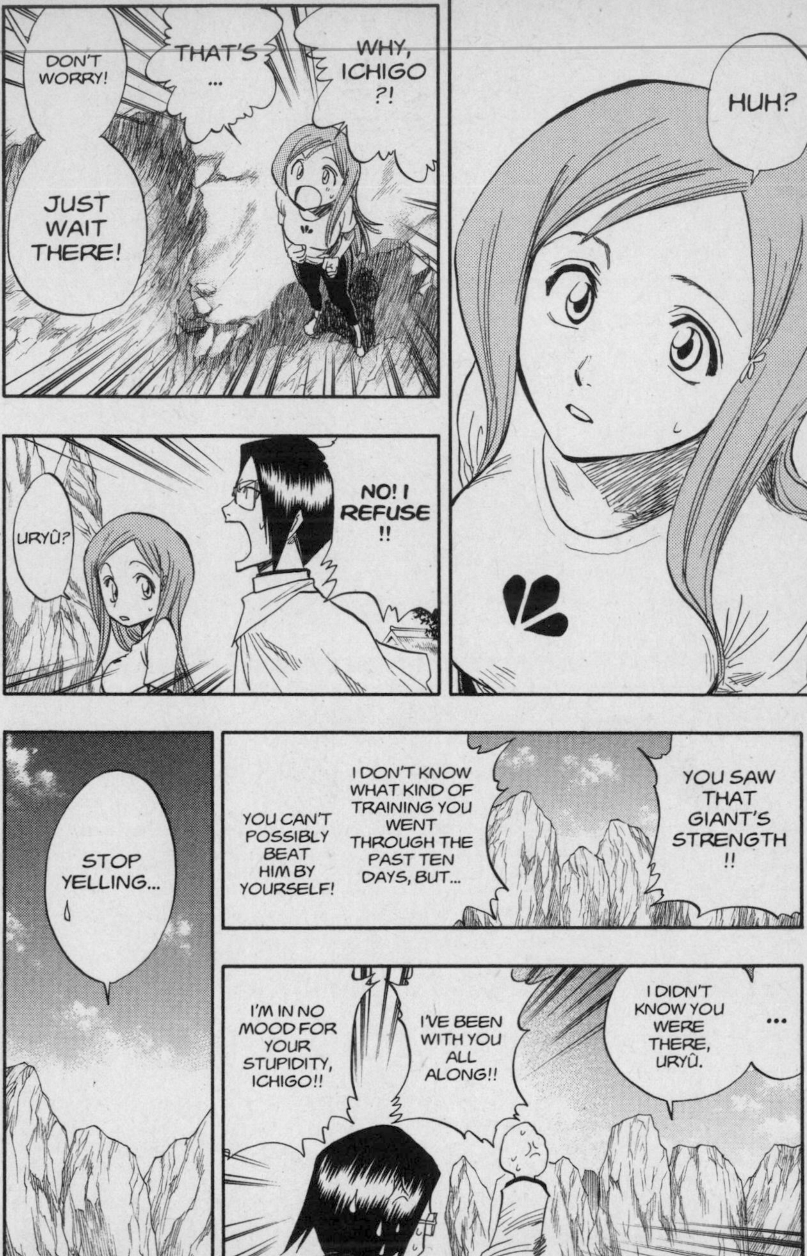
HUH?
WHY, ICHIGO ?!
THAT'S ...
DON'T WORRY! JUST WAIT THERE!
NO! I REFUSE !!
URYÛ?
YOU SAW THAT GIANT'S STRENGTH !!
I DON'T KNOW WHAT KIND OF TRAINING YOU WENT THROUGH THE PAST TEN DAYS, BUT...
YOU CAN'T POSSIBLY BEAT HIM BY YOURSELF!
...
I DIDN'T KNOW YOU WERE THERE, URYÛ.
I'VE BEEN WITH YOU ALL ALONG!!
I'M IN NO MOOD FOR YOUR STUPIDITY, ICHIGO!!
STOP YELLING...

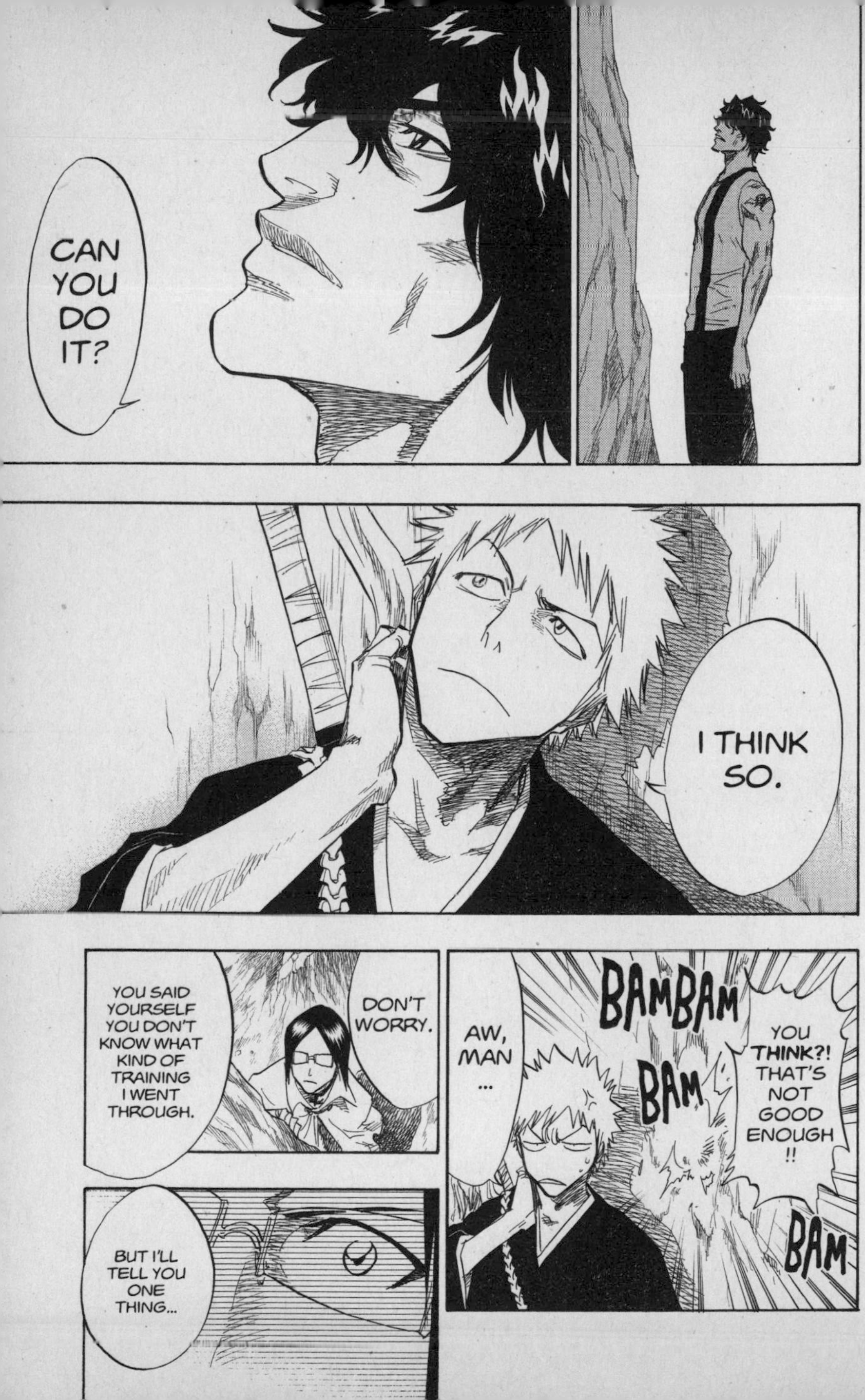

CAN YOU DO IT?
I THINK SO.
YOU THINK?! THAT'S NOT GOOD ENOUGH !!
BAMBAM
BAM
AW, MAN ...
BAM
DON'T WORRY.
YOU SAID YOURSELF YOU DON'T KNOW WHAT KIND OF TRAINING I WENT THROUGH.
BUT I'LL TELL YOU ONE THING...

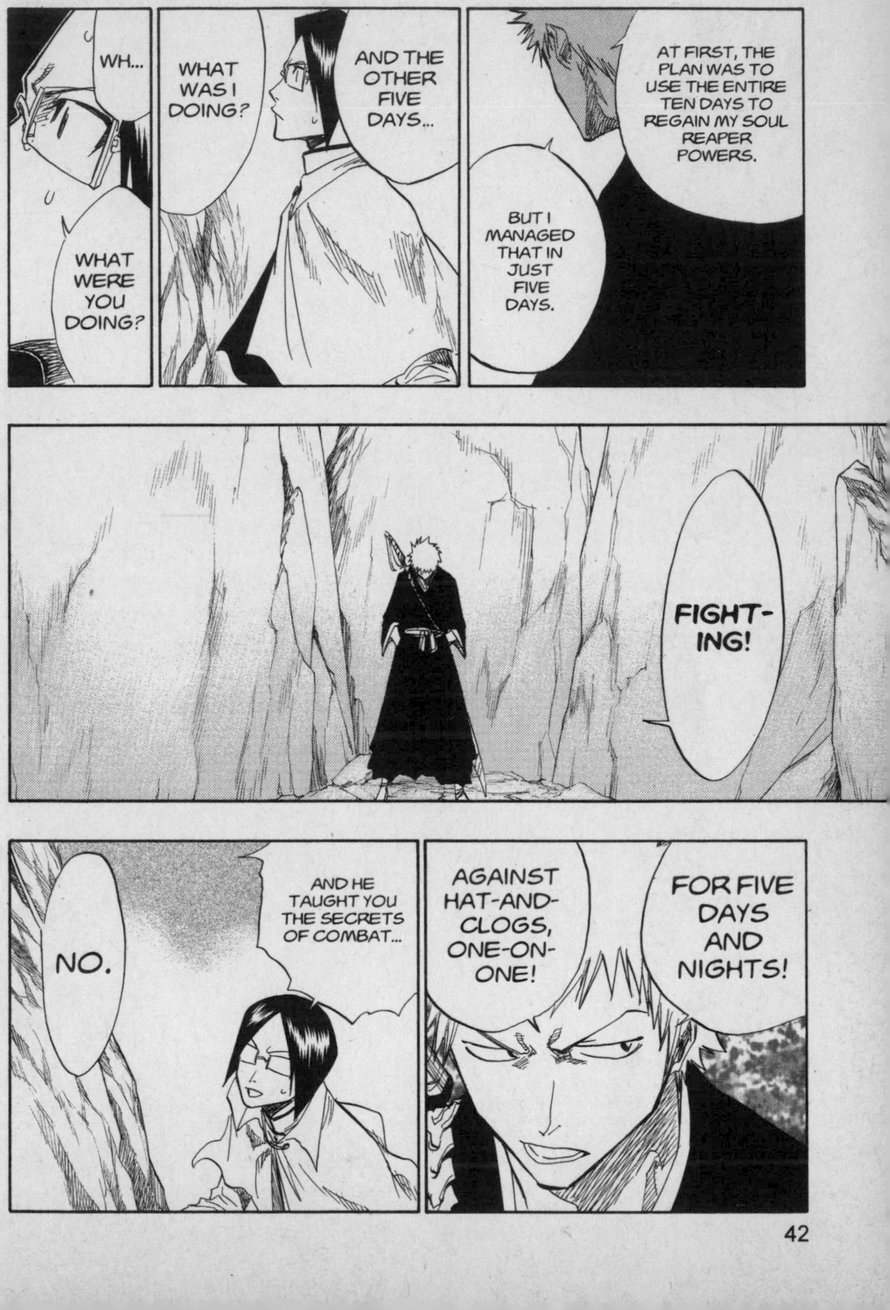
AT FIRST, THE PLAN WAS TO USE THE ENTIRE TEN DAYS TO REGAIN MY SOUL REAPER POWERS.
BUT I MANAGED THAT IN JUST FIVE DAYS.
AND THE OTHER FIVE DAYS...
WHAT WAS I DOING?
WH...
WHAT WERE YOU DOING?
FIGHT-ING!
FOR FIVE DAYS AND NIGHTS!
AGAINST HAT-AND-CLOGS, ONE-ON-ONE!
AND HE TAUGHT YOU THE SECRETS OF COMBAT...
NO.

READ THIS WAY

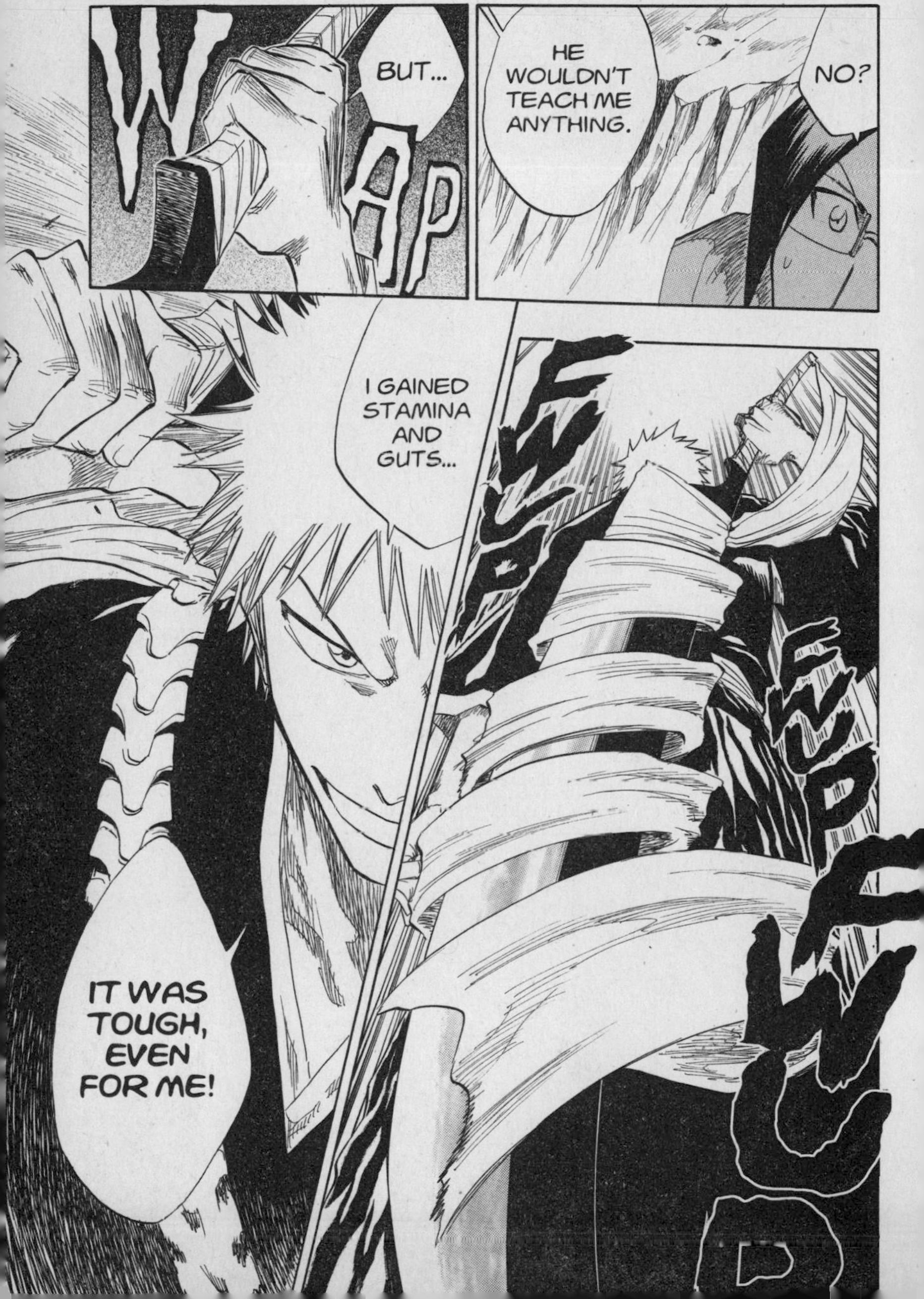
NO?
HE WOULDN'T TEACH ME ANYTHING.
BUT...
WAP
I GAINED STAMINA AND GUTS...
IT WAS TOUGH, EVEN FOR ME!

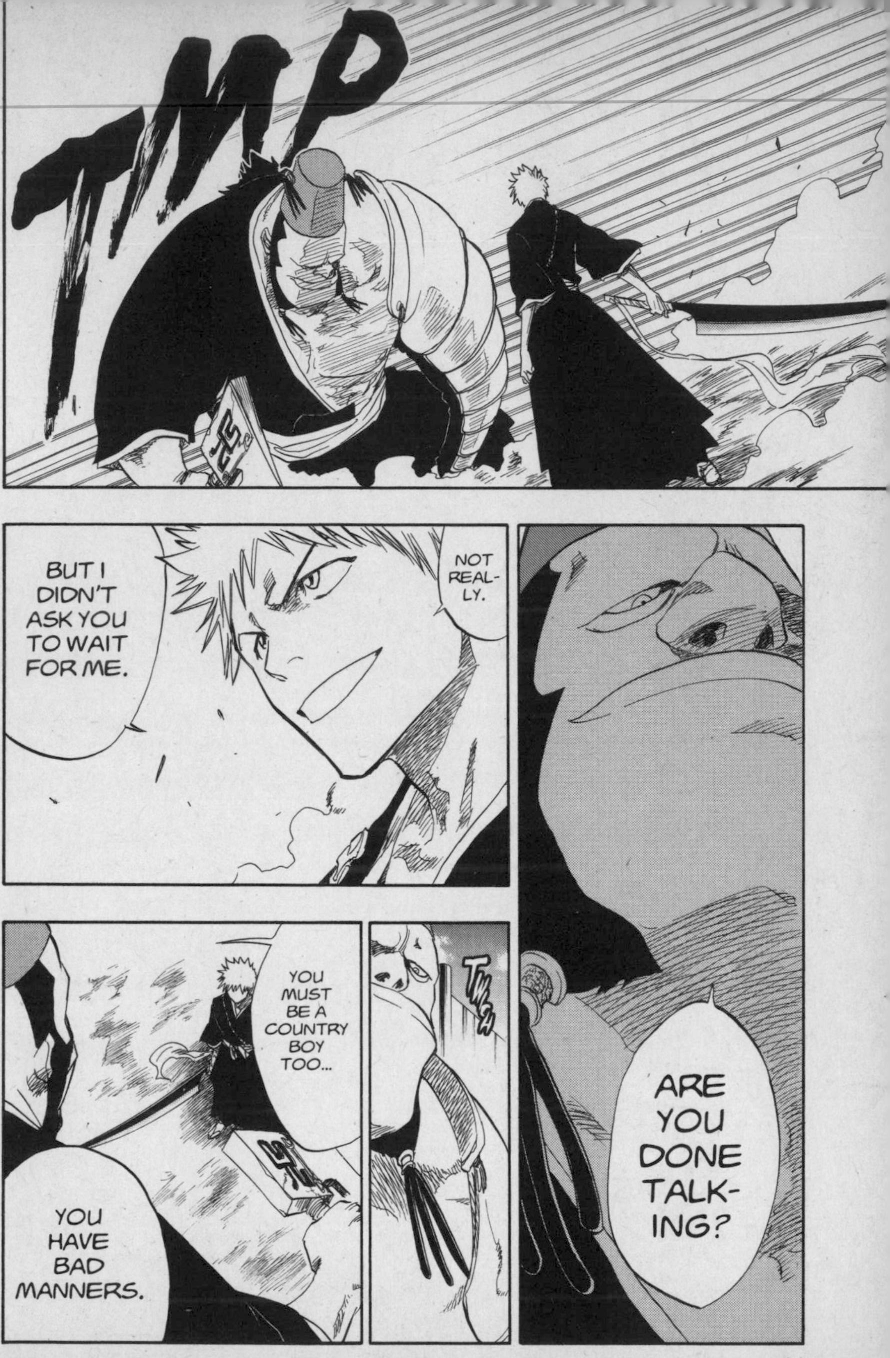
TMP
ARE YOU DONE TALKING?
NOT REALLY.
BUT I DIDN'T ASK YOU TO WAIT FOR ME.
TWICH
YOU MUST BE A COUNTRY BOY TOO...
YOU HAVE BAD MANNERS.

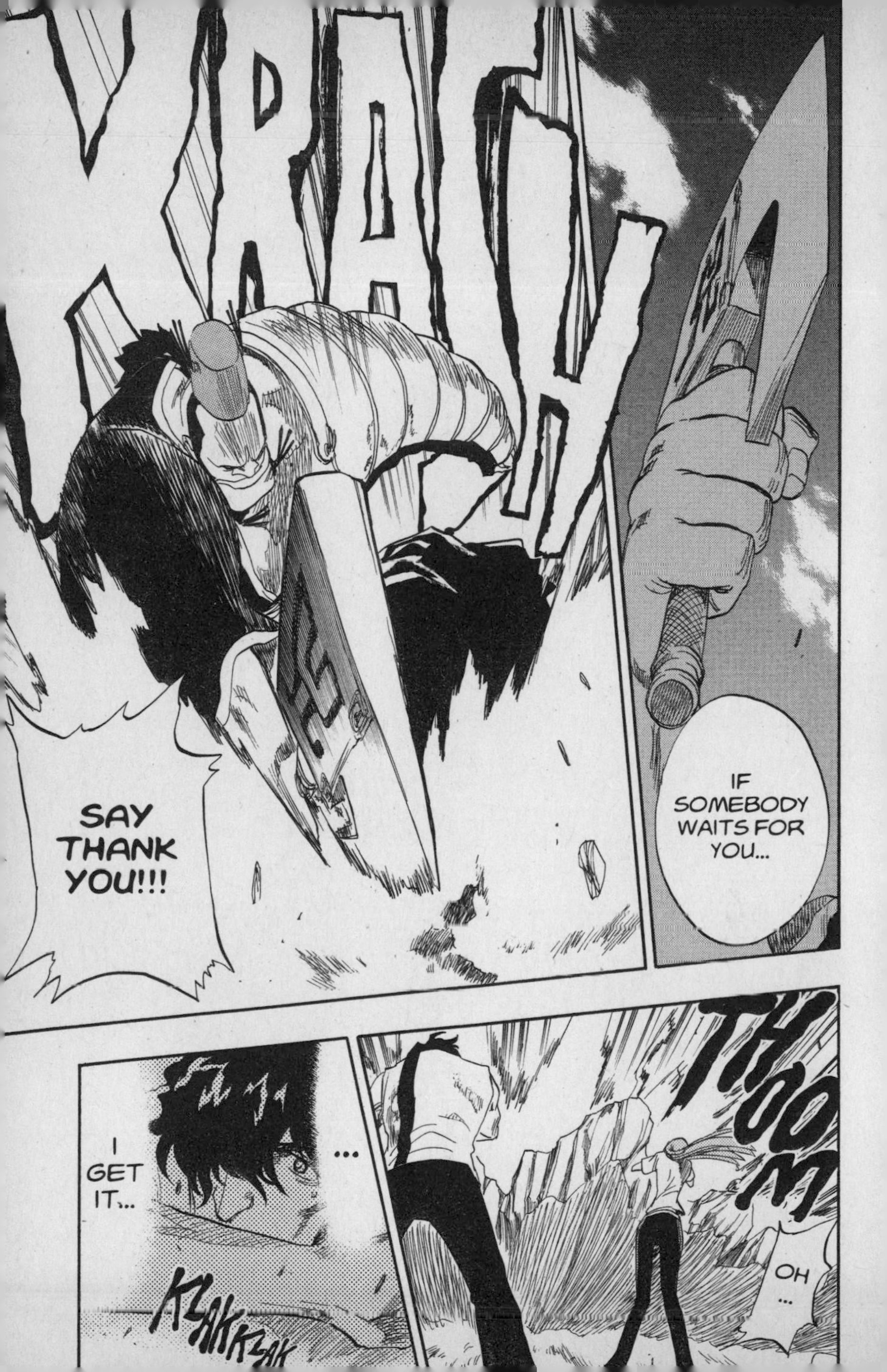
IF SOMEBODY WAITS FOR YOU...
SAY THANK YOU!!!
THOOM
OH ...
...
I GET IT...
KLAK KLAK

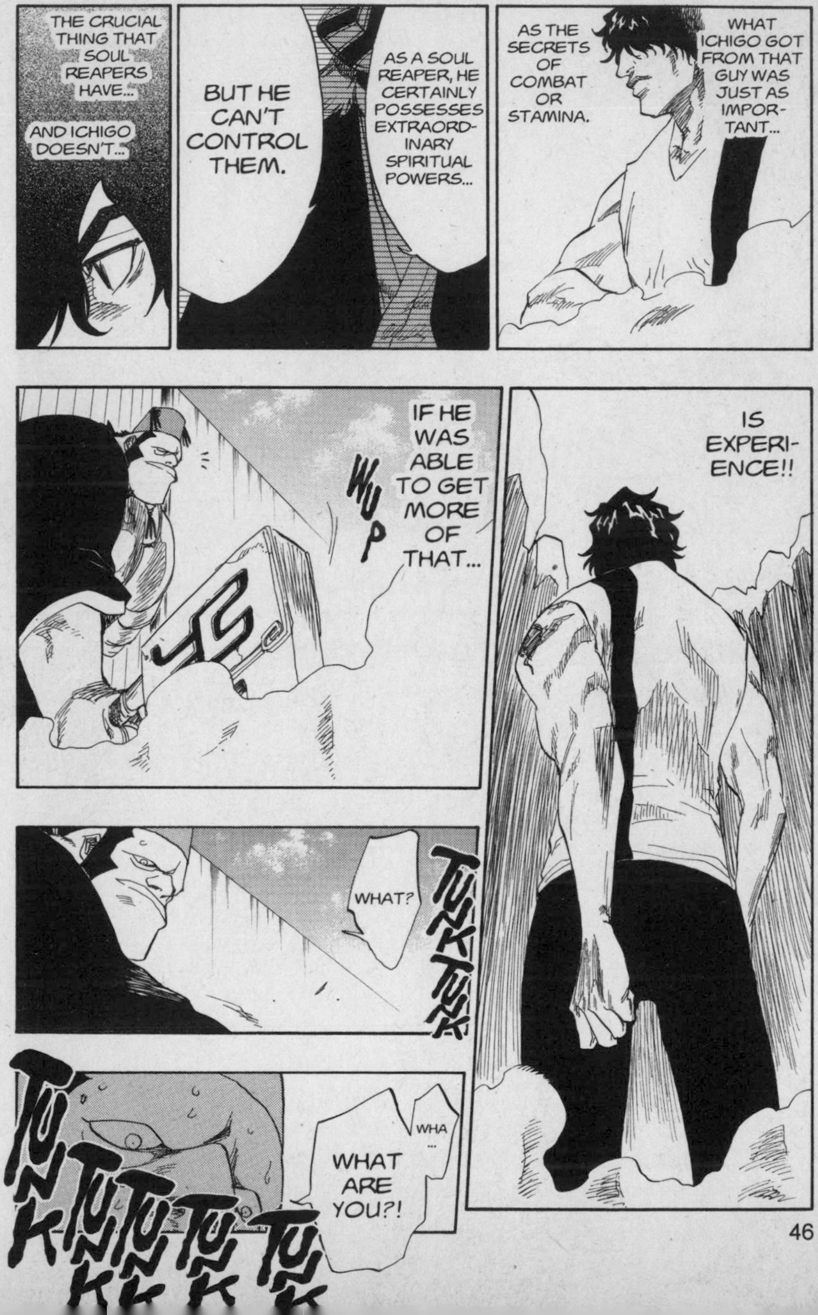
WHAT ICHIGO GOT FROM THAT GUY WAS JUST AS IMPORTANT...
AS THE SECRETS OF COMBAT OR STAMINA.
AS A SOUL REAPER, HE CERTAINLY POSSESSES EXTRAORDINARY SPIRITUAL POWERS...
BUT HE CAN'T CONTROL THEM.
THE CRUCIAL THING THAT SOUL REAPERS HAVE...
AND ICHIGO DOESN'T...
IS EXPERIENCE!!
IF HE WAS ABLE TO GET MORE OF THAT...
WUP
TUNK TUNK
WHAT?
WHA...
WHAT ARE YOU?!
TUNK TUNK TUNK TUNK TUNK

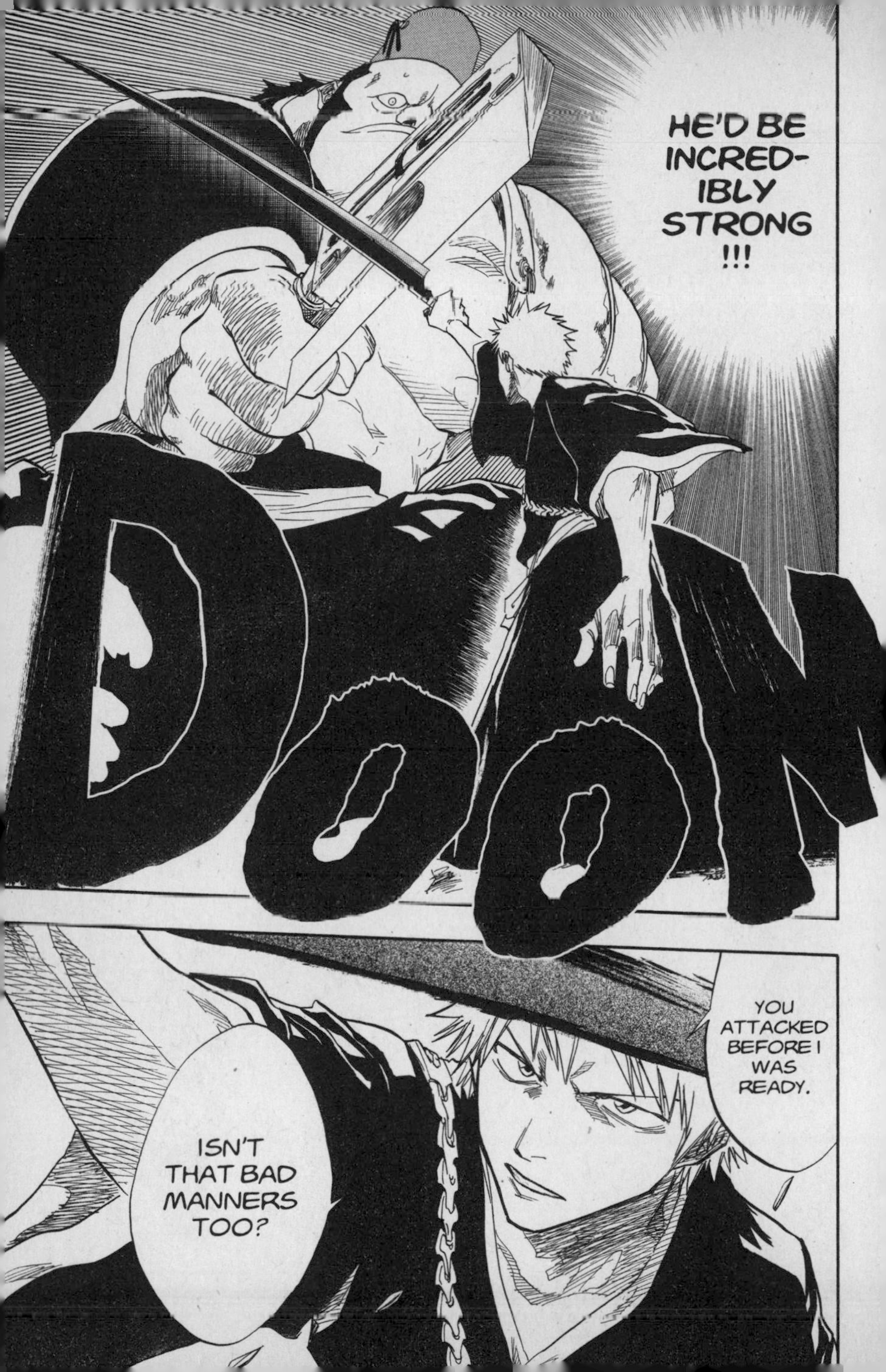
HE'D BE INCREDIBLY STRONG!!!
DOOOM
YOU ATTACKED BEFORE I WAS READY.
ISN'T THAT BAD MANNERS TOO?

G-GOOD LUCK, RENJI...

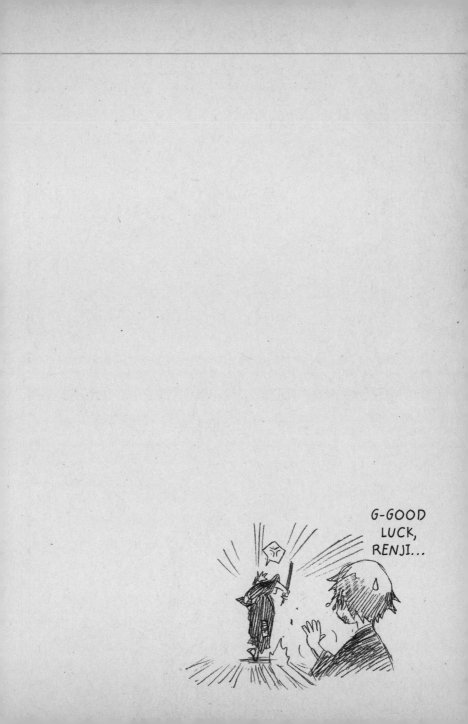

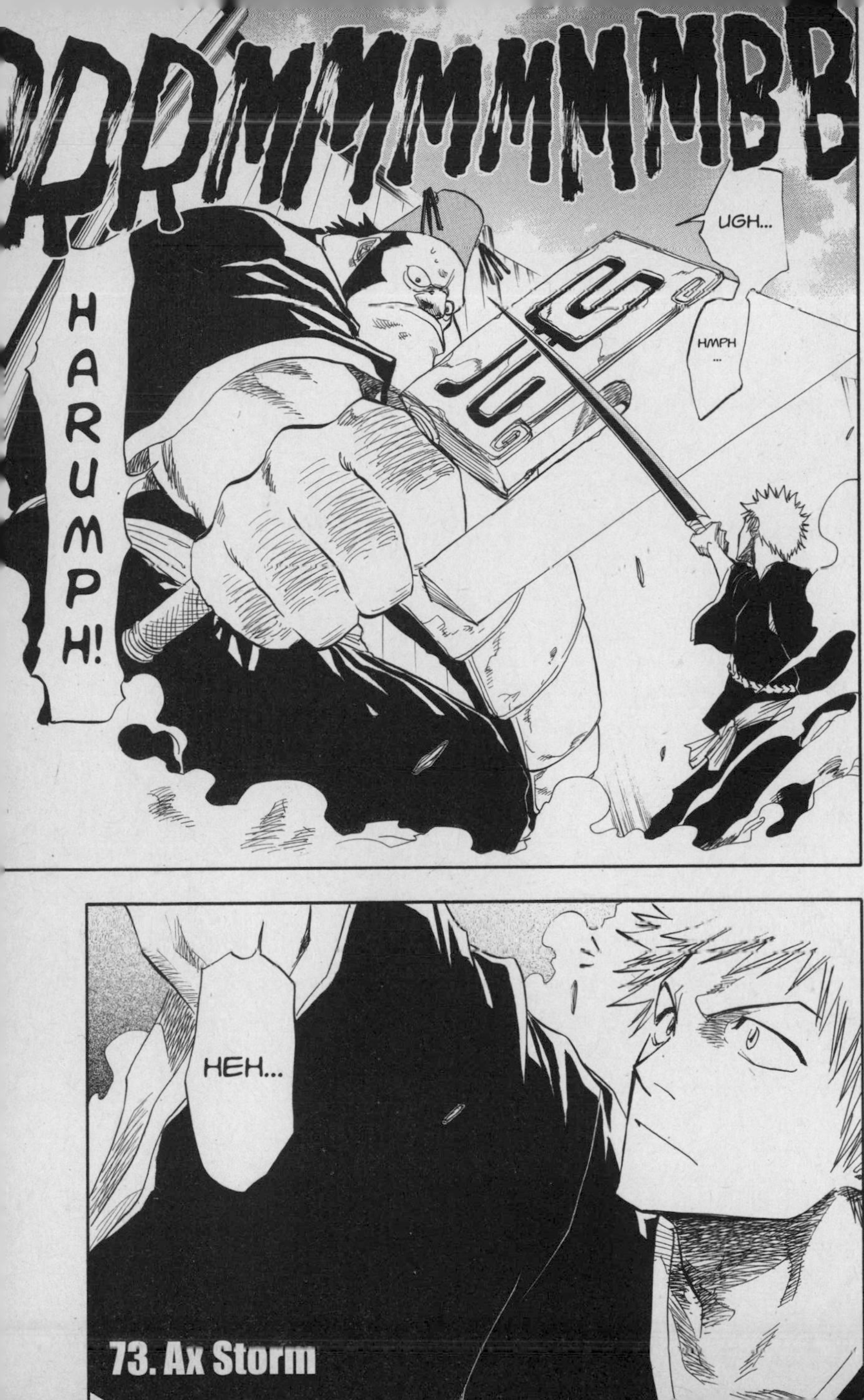
DRMMMMMMBB
UGH...
HMPH...
HARUMPH!
HEH...

73. Ax Storm

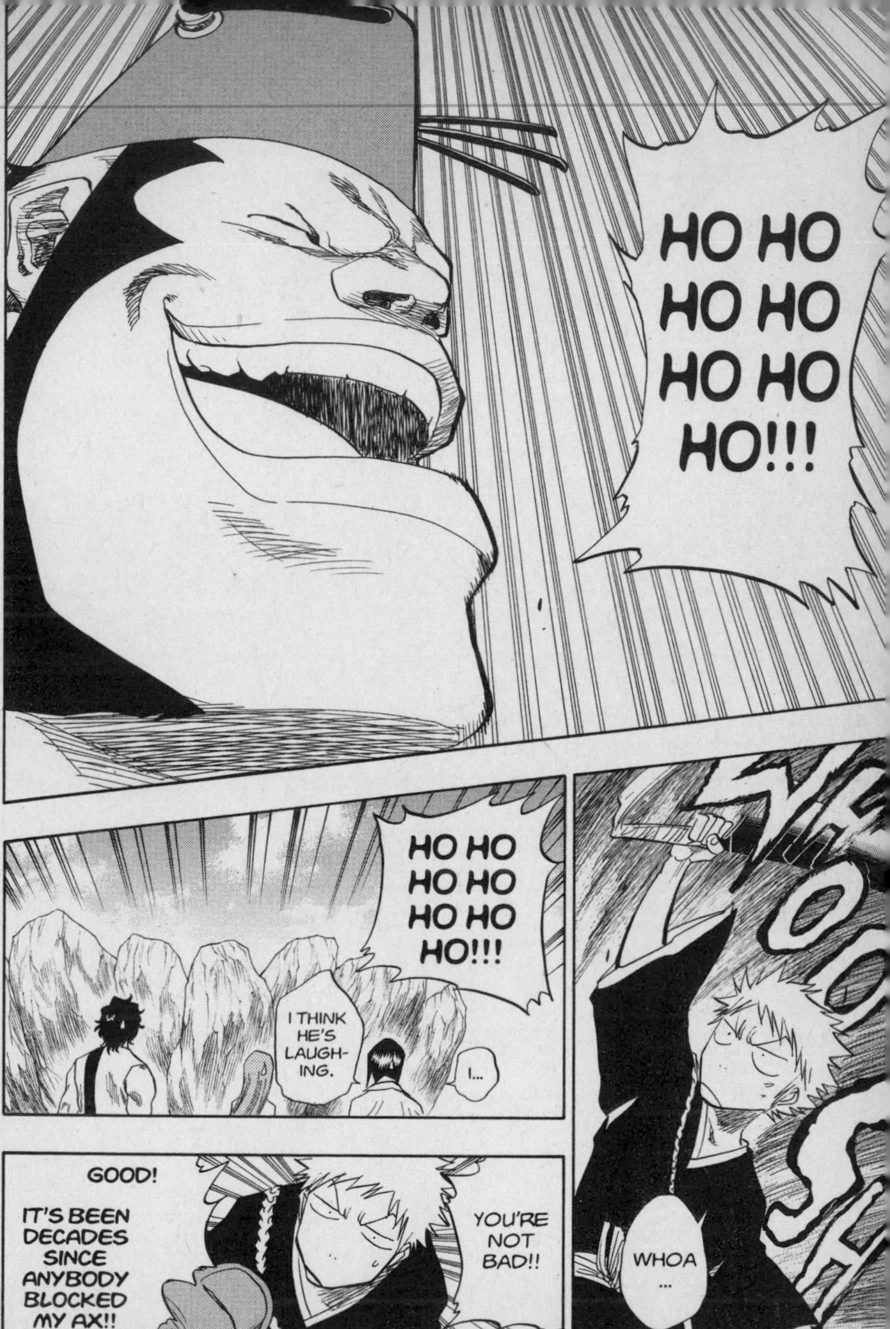
HO HO HO HO HO HO HO!!!
WHOA ...
HO HO HO HO HO HO HO!!!
I THINK HE'S LAUGH-ING.
I...
YOU'RE NOT BAD!!
GOOD!
IT'S BEEN DECADES SINCE ANYBODY BLOCKED MY AX!!

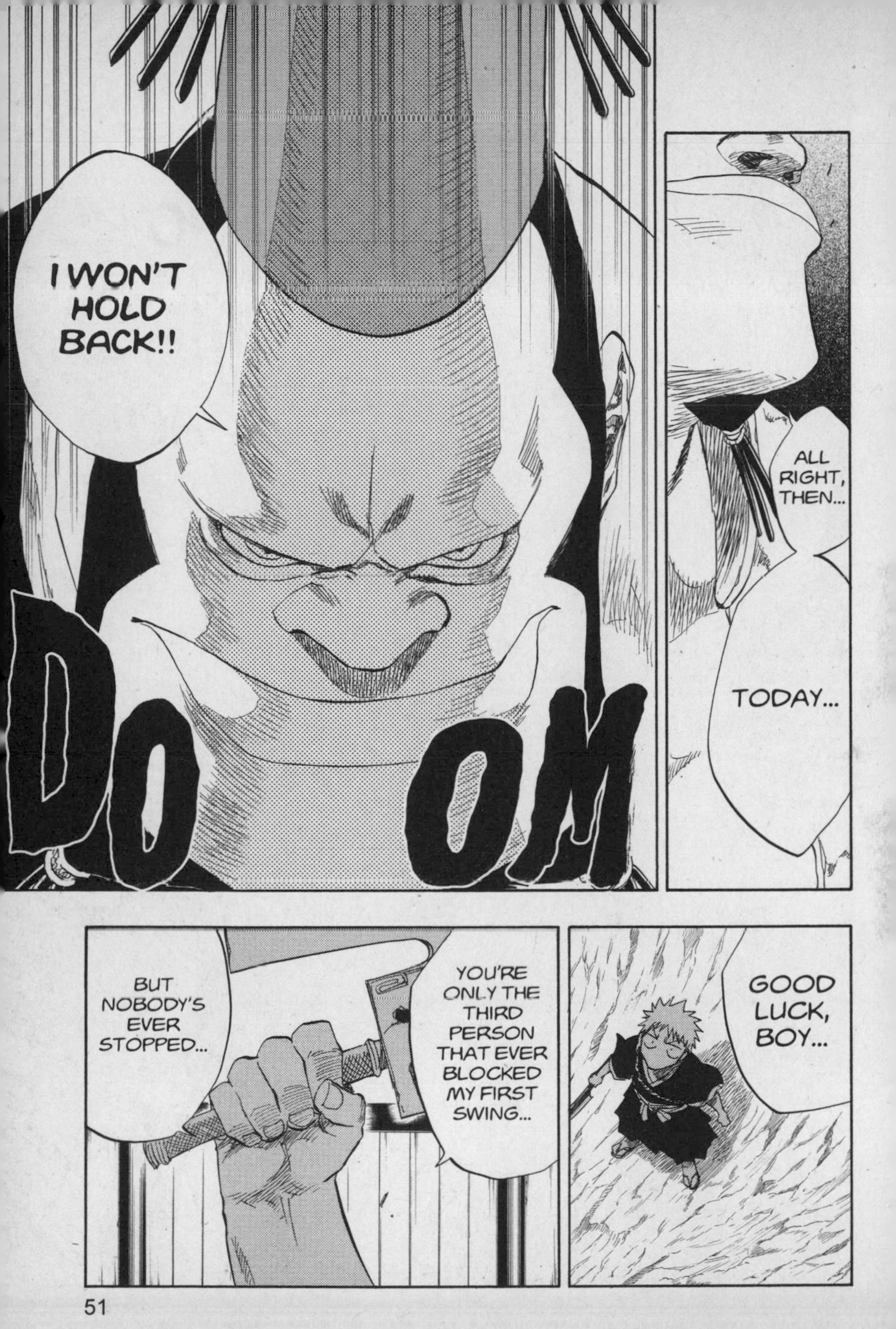
ALL RIGHT, THEN...
TODAY...
I WON'T HOLD BACK!!
DO OM
GOOD LUCK, BOY...
YOU'RE ONLY THE THIRD PERSON THAT EVER BLOCKED MY FIRST SWING...
BUT NOBODY'S EVER STOPPED...

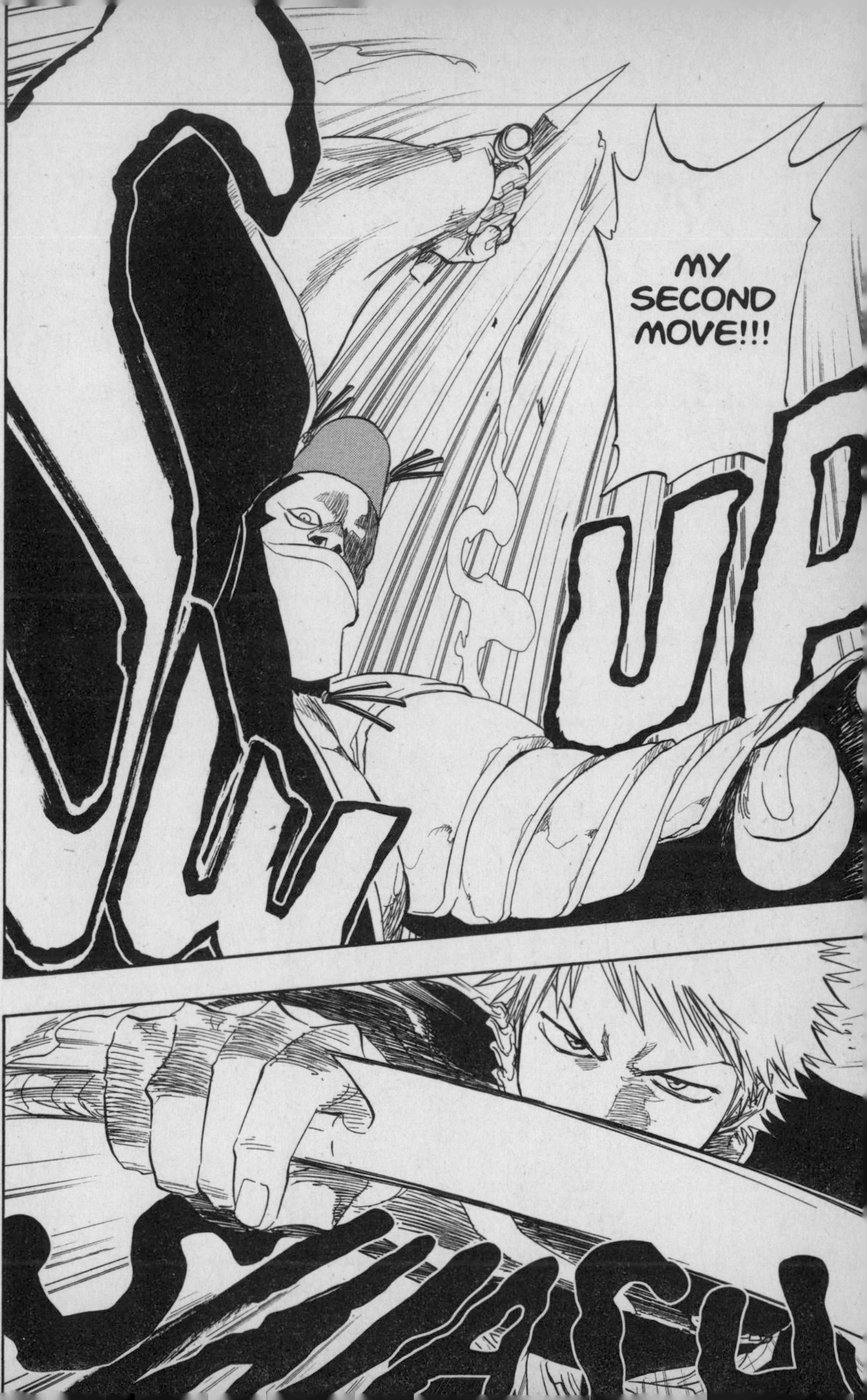
MY SECOND MOVE!!!

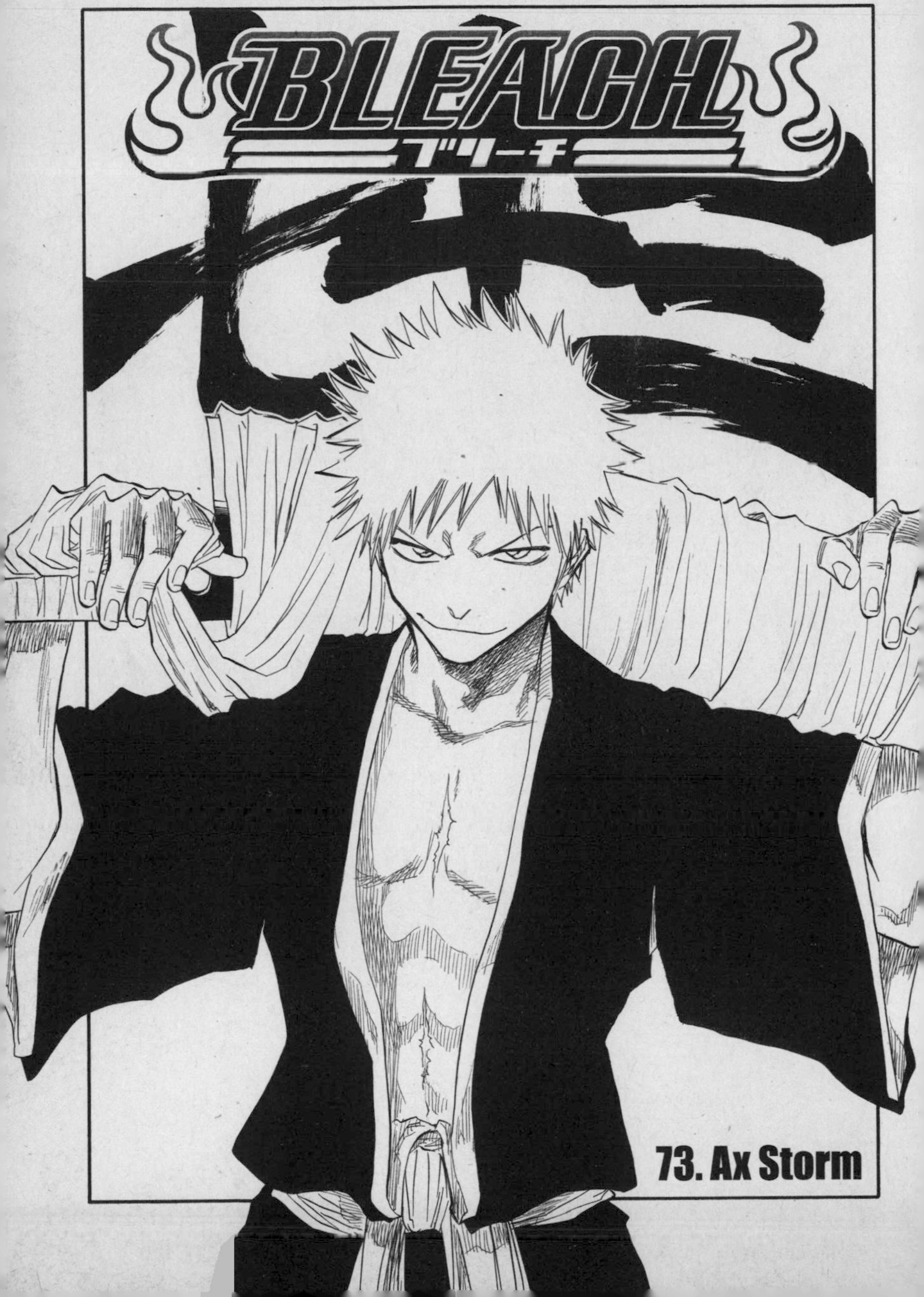
BLEACH
ブリーチ
73. Ax Storm

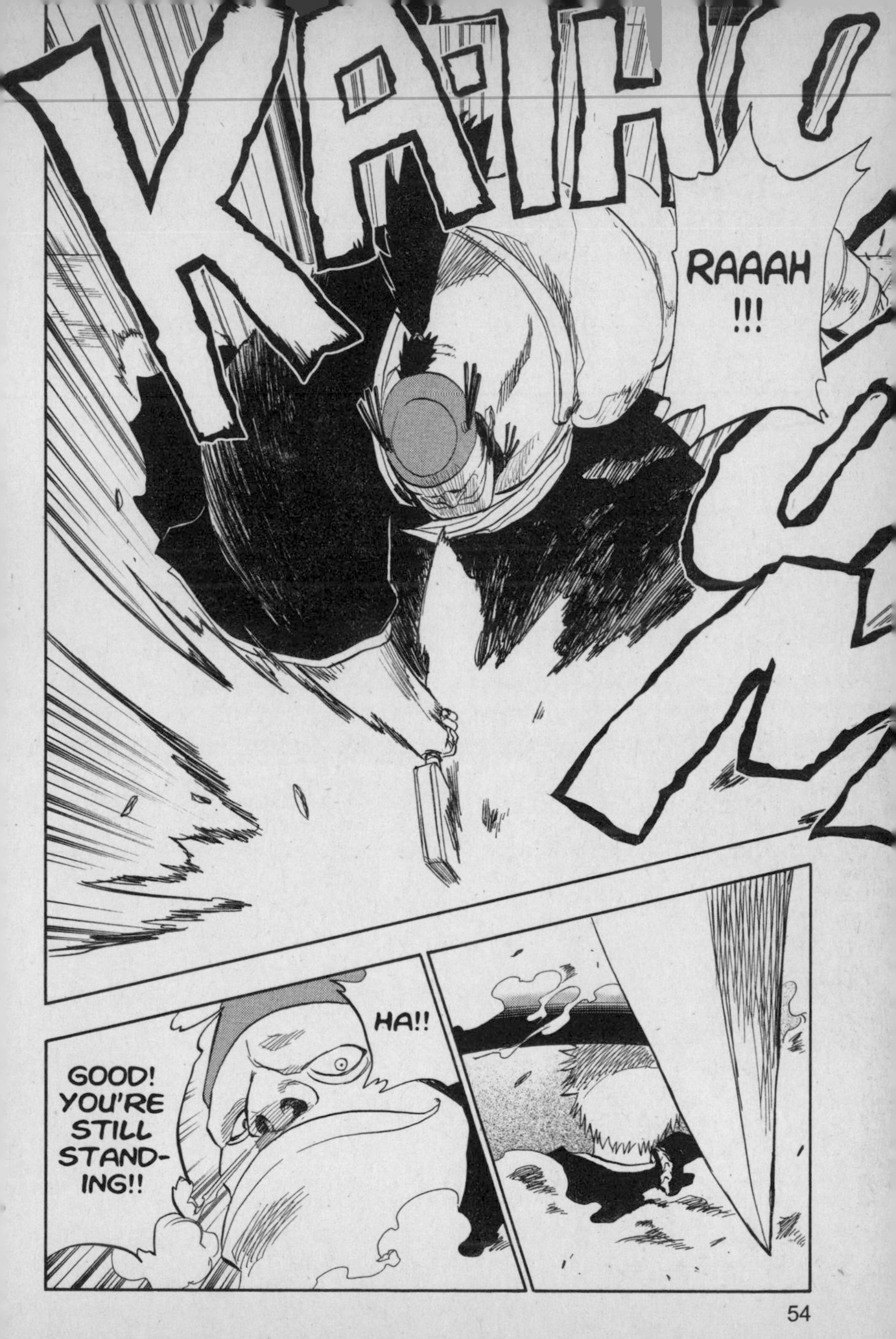
RAAAH !!!
HA!!
GOOD! YOU'RE STILL STAND-ING!!

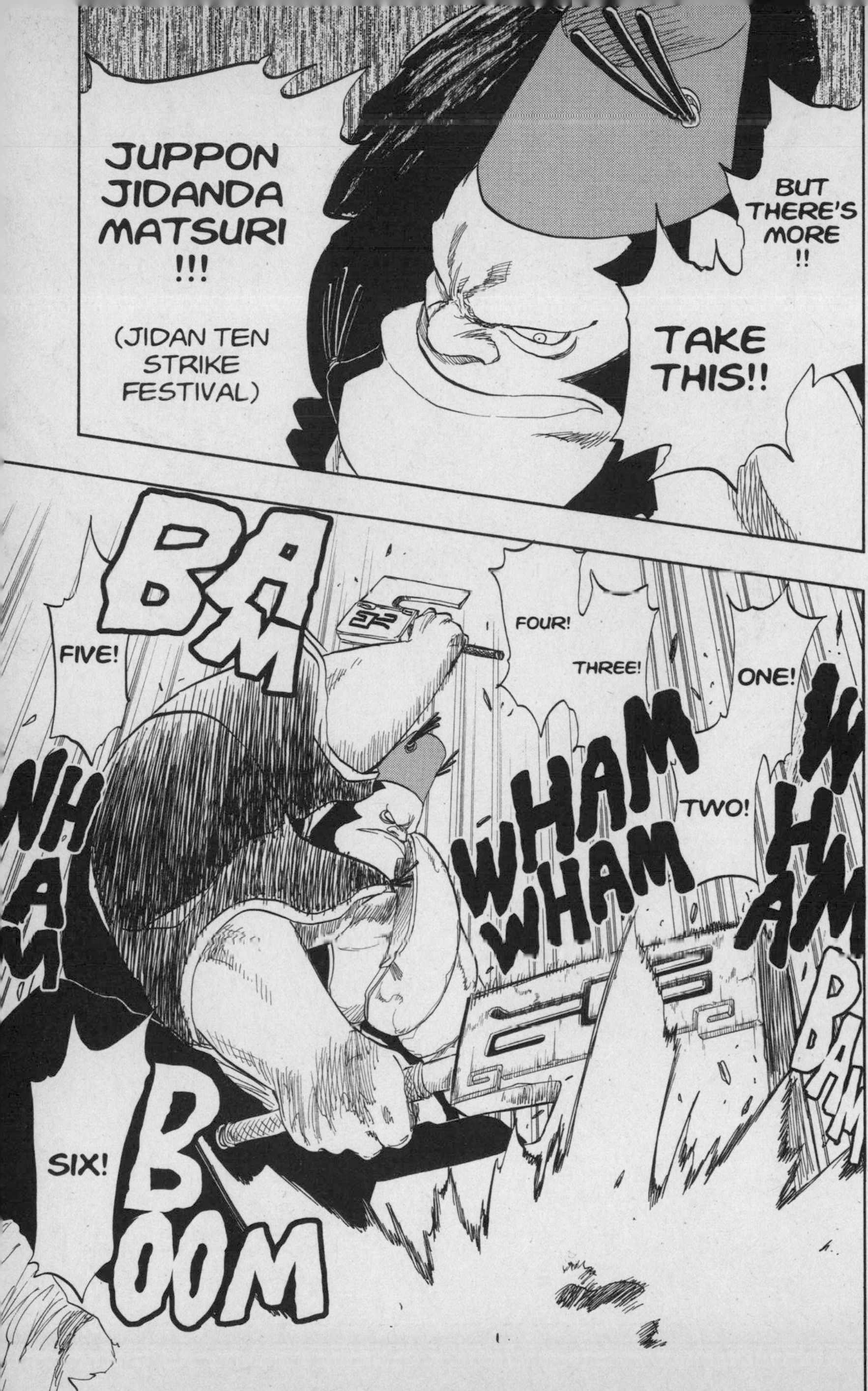
BUT THERE'S MORE !!
TAKE THIS!!
JUPPON JIDANDA MATSURI !!!
(JIDAN TEN STRIKE FESTIVAL)
ONE!
THREE!
FOUR!
WHAM
WHAM
TWO!
BAM
FIVE!
SIX!
BOOM

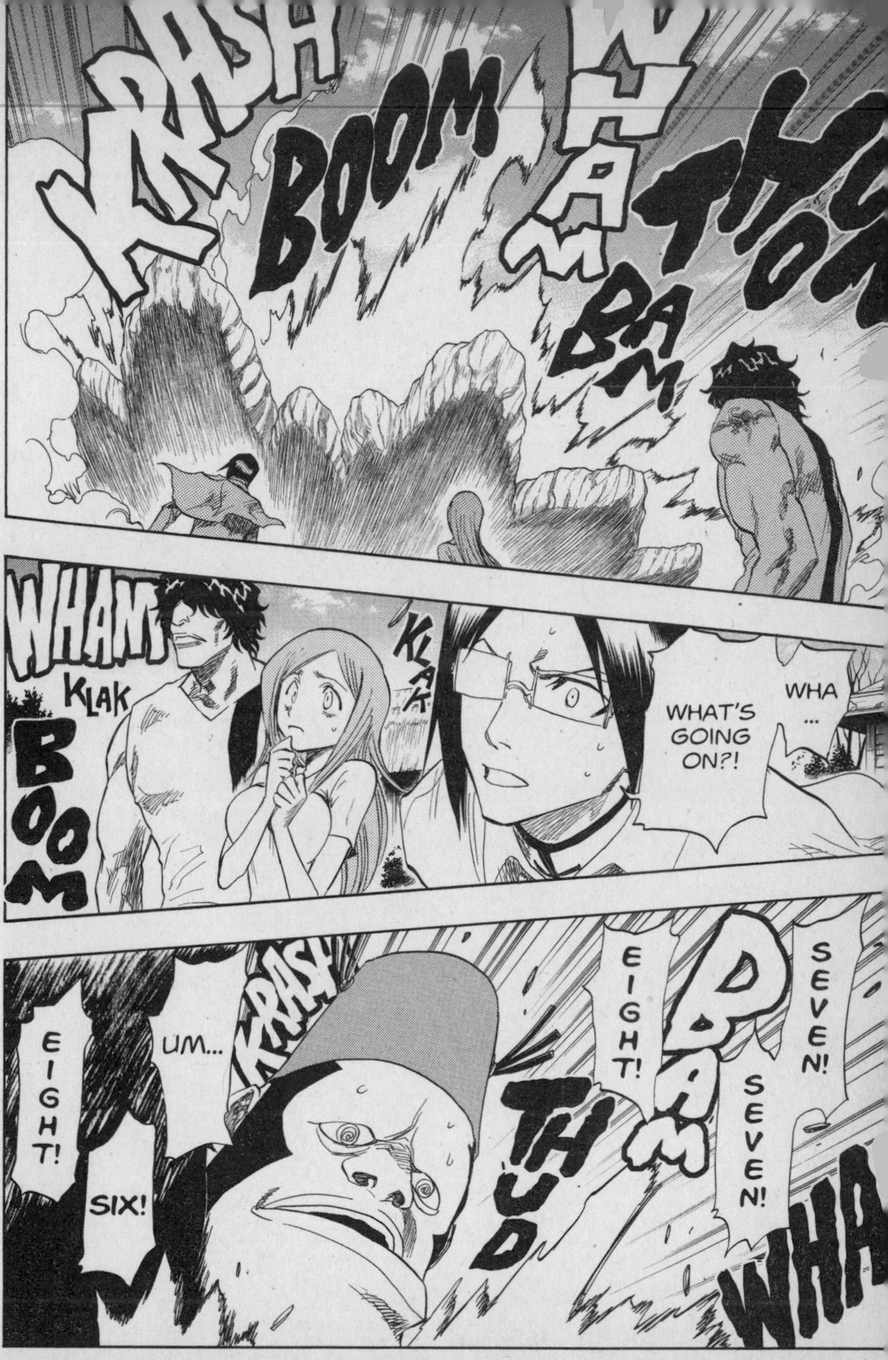

BAM
WHAM
BOOM
KRASH
WHA
...
WHAT'S GOING ON?!
KLAK
KLAK
BOOM
WHAM
SEVEN!
SEVEN!
BAM
EIGHT!
THUD
UM...
SIX!
EIGHT!

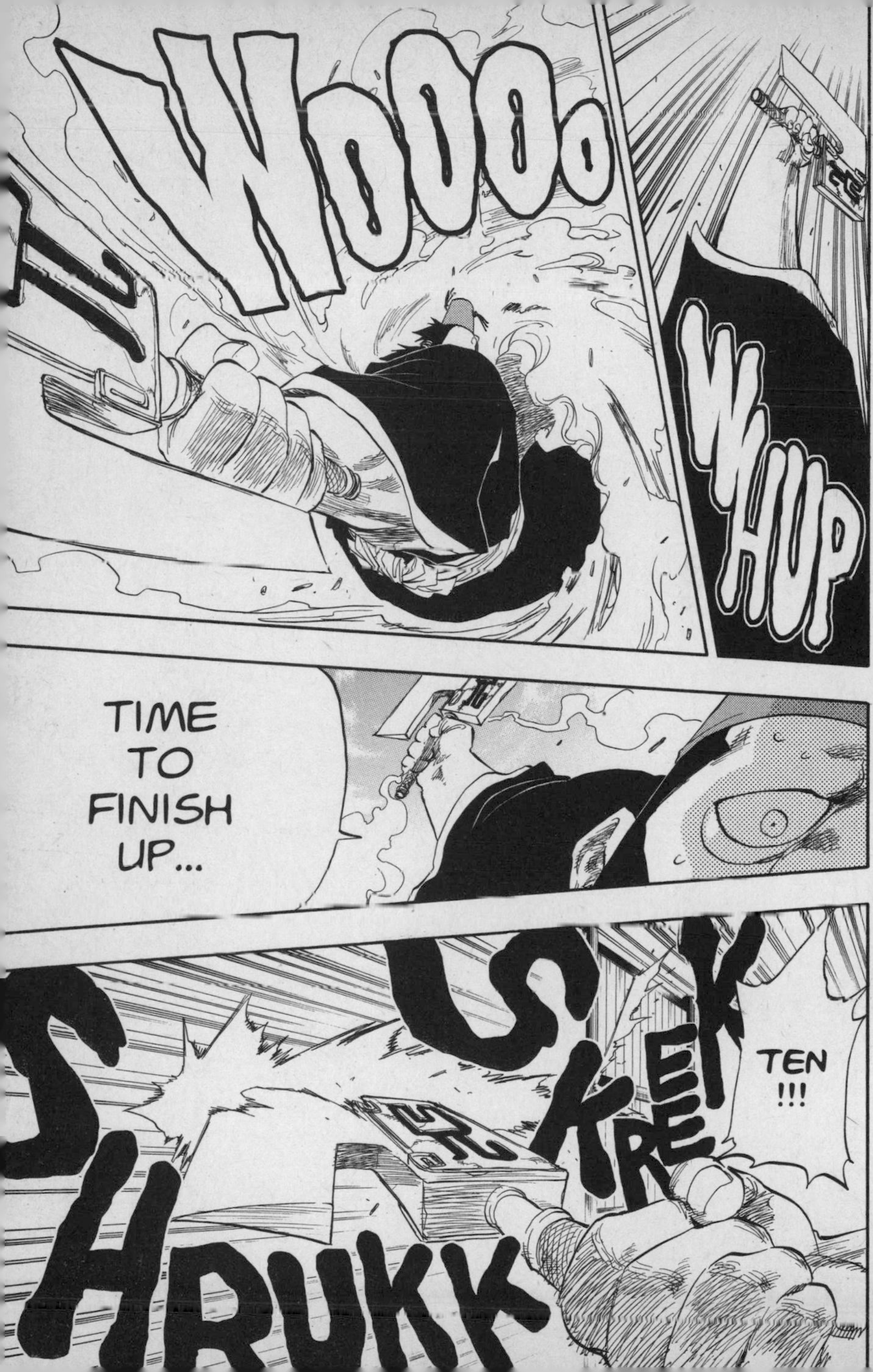
WHUP
WOOOOO
TIME TO FINISH UP...
TEN!!!
KREEK
SHRUKK

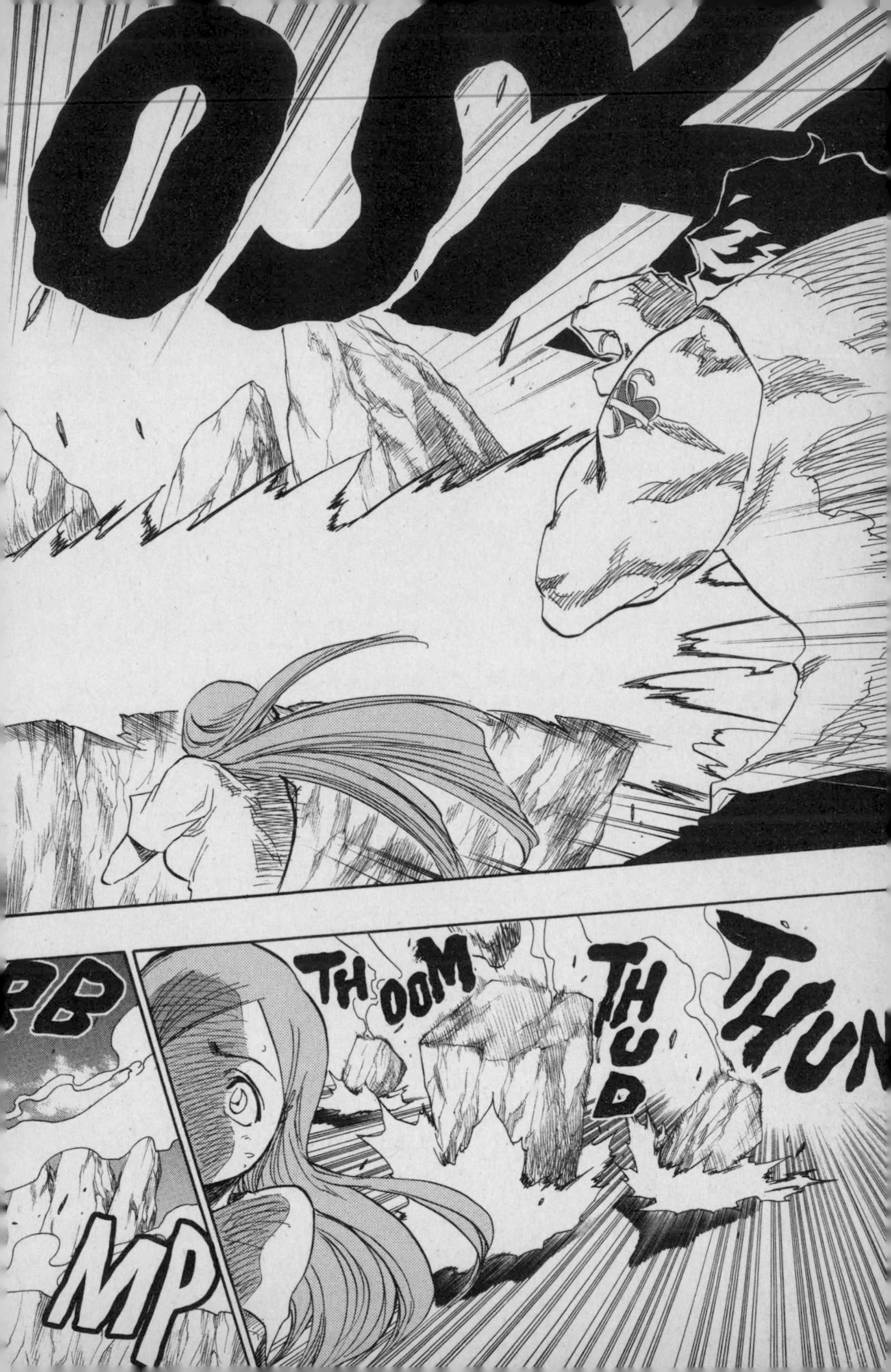

OOSH
THUN
THUD
THOOM
RB
MP

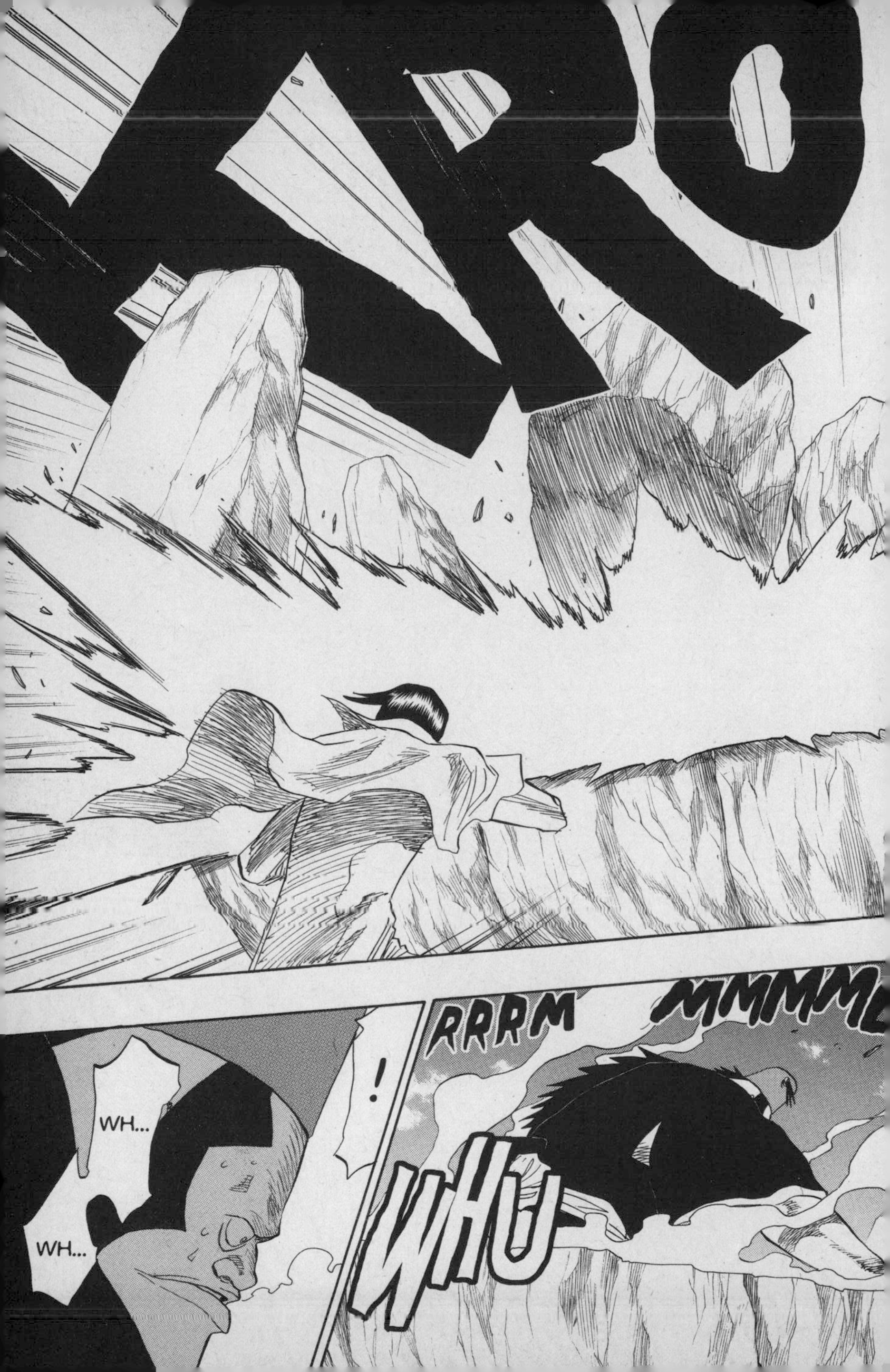
RRRM
MMMMM
WHU
!
WH...
WH...

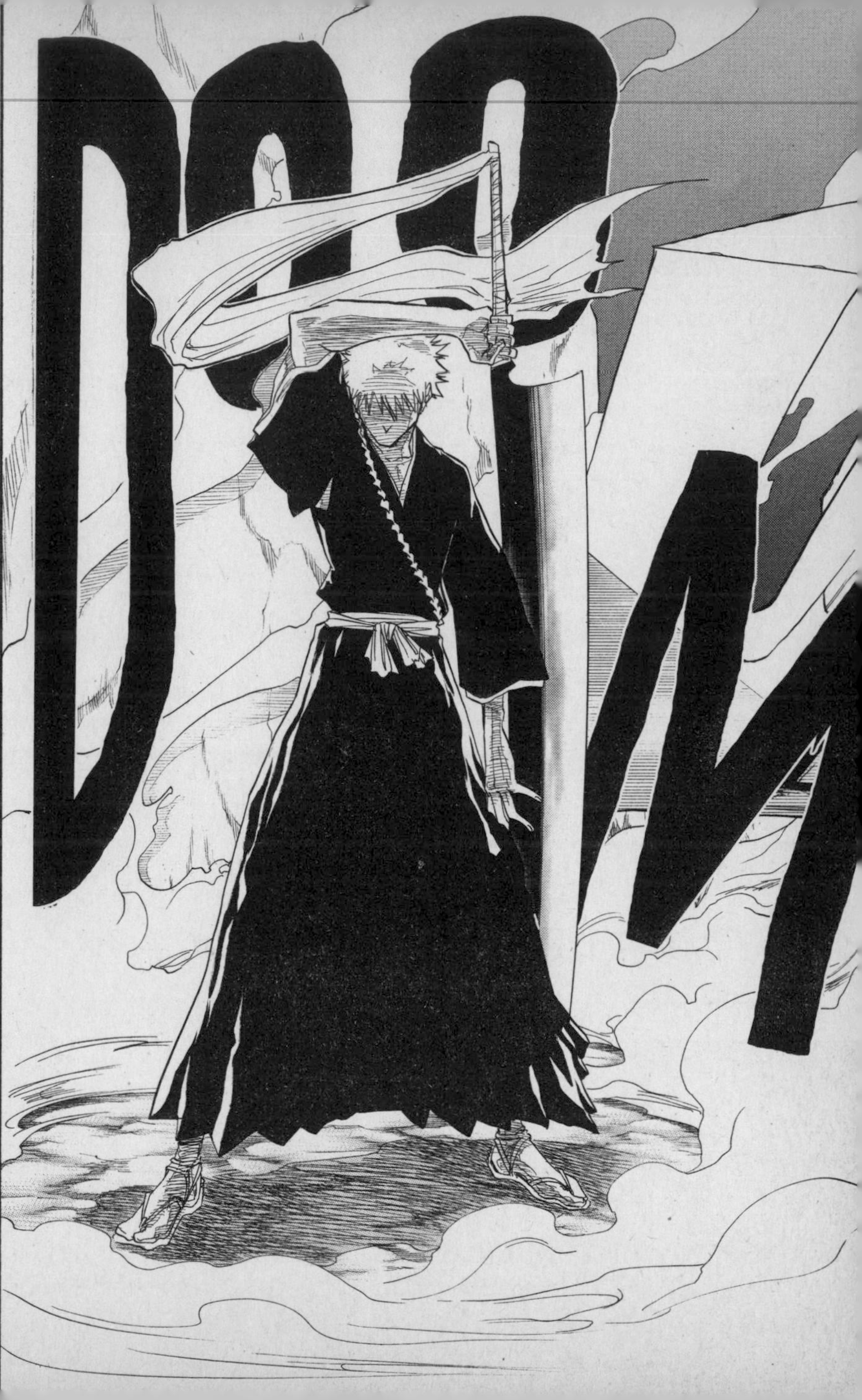
DOOM

READ THIS WAY

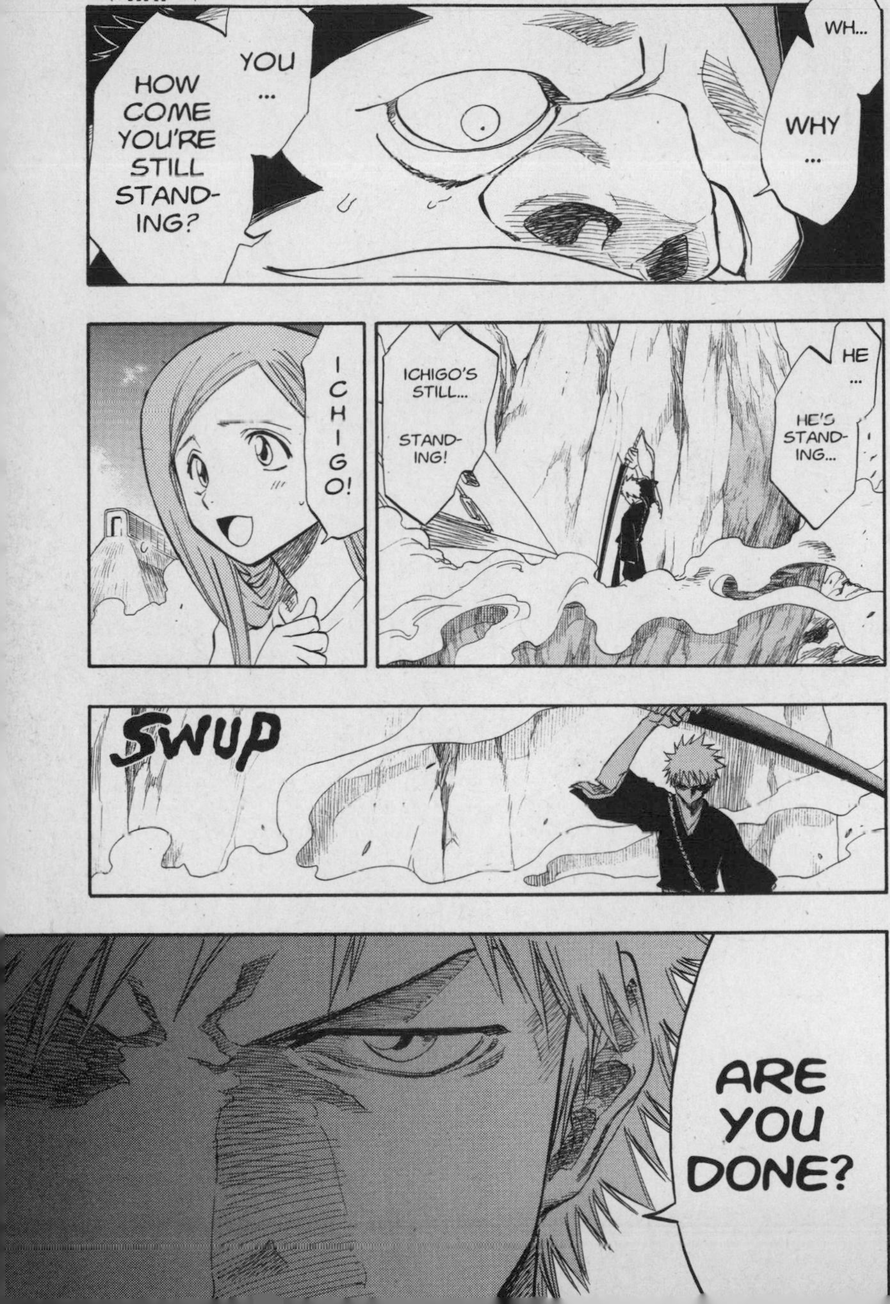
WH... WHY...
YOU... HOW COME YOU'RE STILL STANDING?
HE... HE'S STANDING...
ICHIGO'S STILL... STANDING!
ICHIGO!
SWUP
ARE YOU DONE?

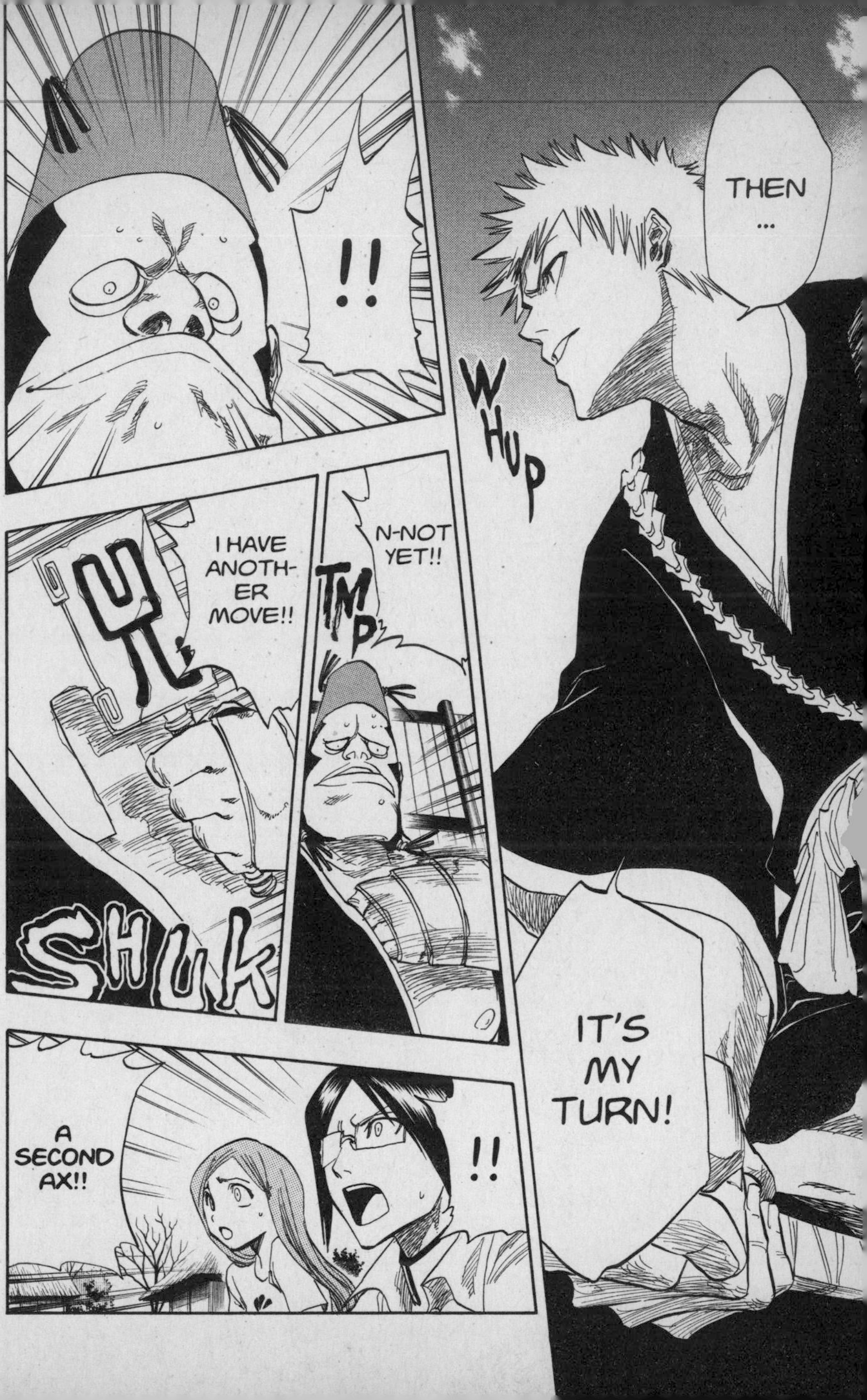
THEN ...
WHUP
IT'S MY TURN!
!!
N-NOT YET!!
TMP
I HAVE ANOTH-ER MOVE!!
SHUK
!!
A SECOND AX!!

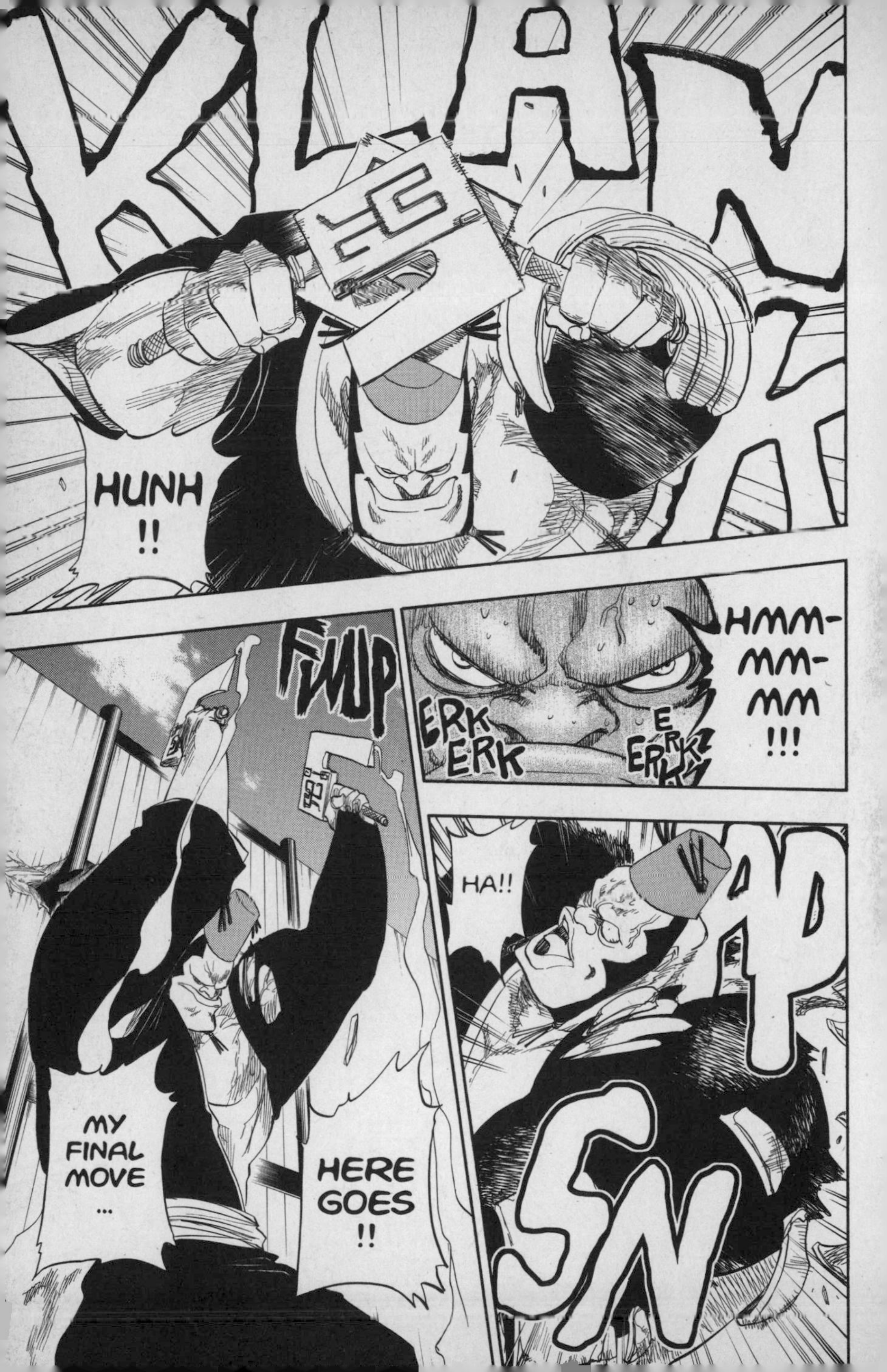
HUNH !!
HMM-MM-MM !!!
ERK ERK
ERK ERK
FWUP
HA!!
HERE GOES !!
MY FINAL MOVE ...

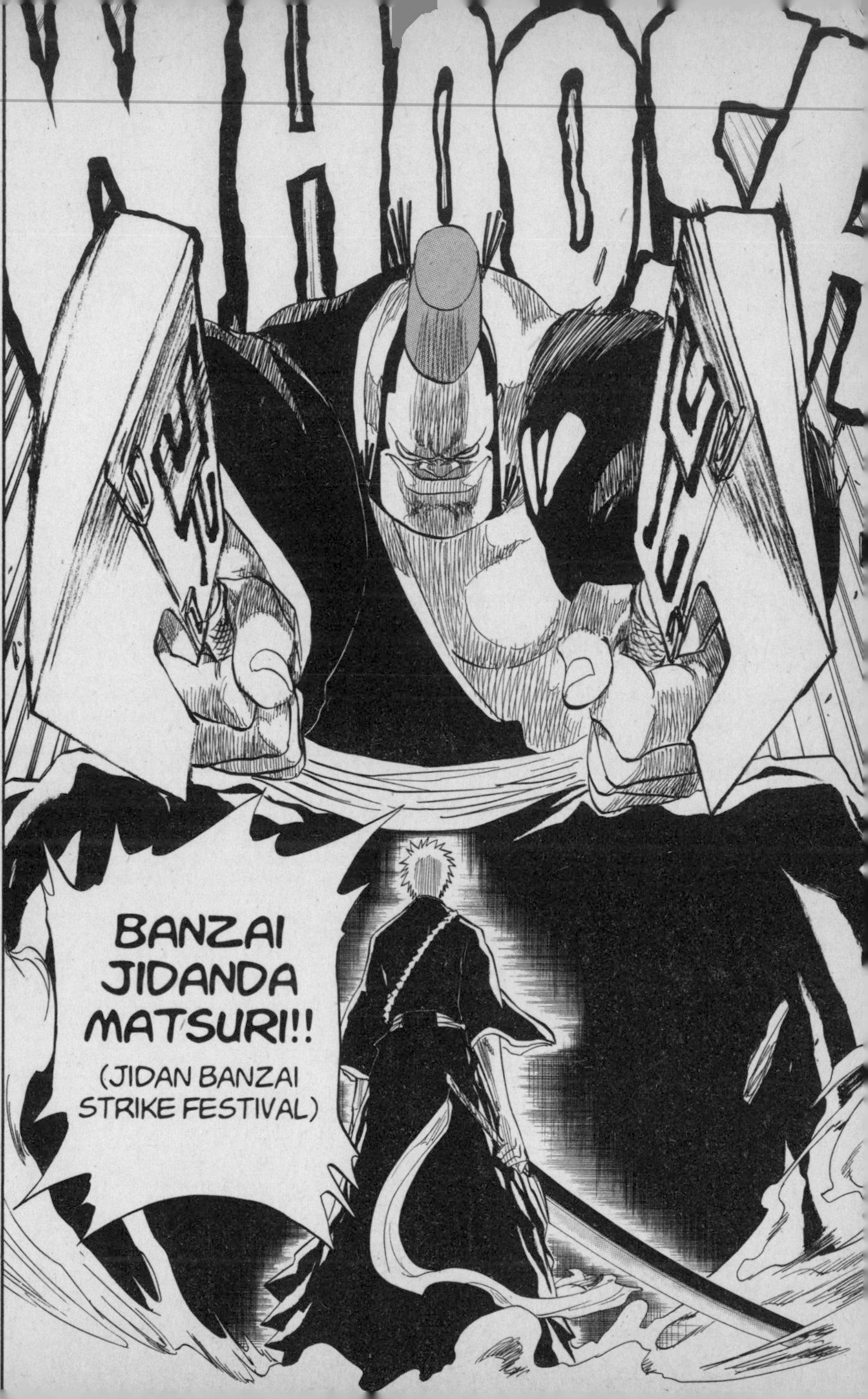
BANZAI JIDANDA MATSURI!!
(JIDAN BANZAI STRIKE FESTIVAL)

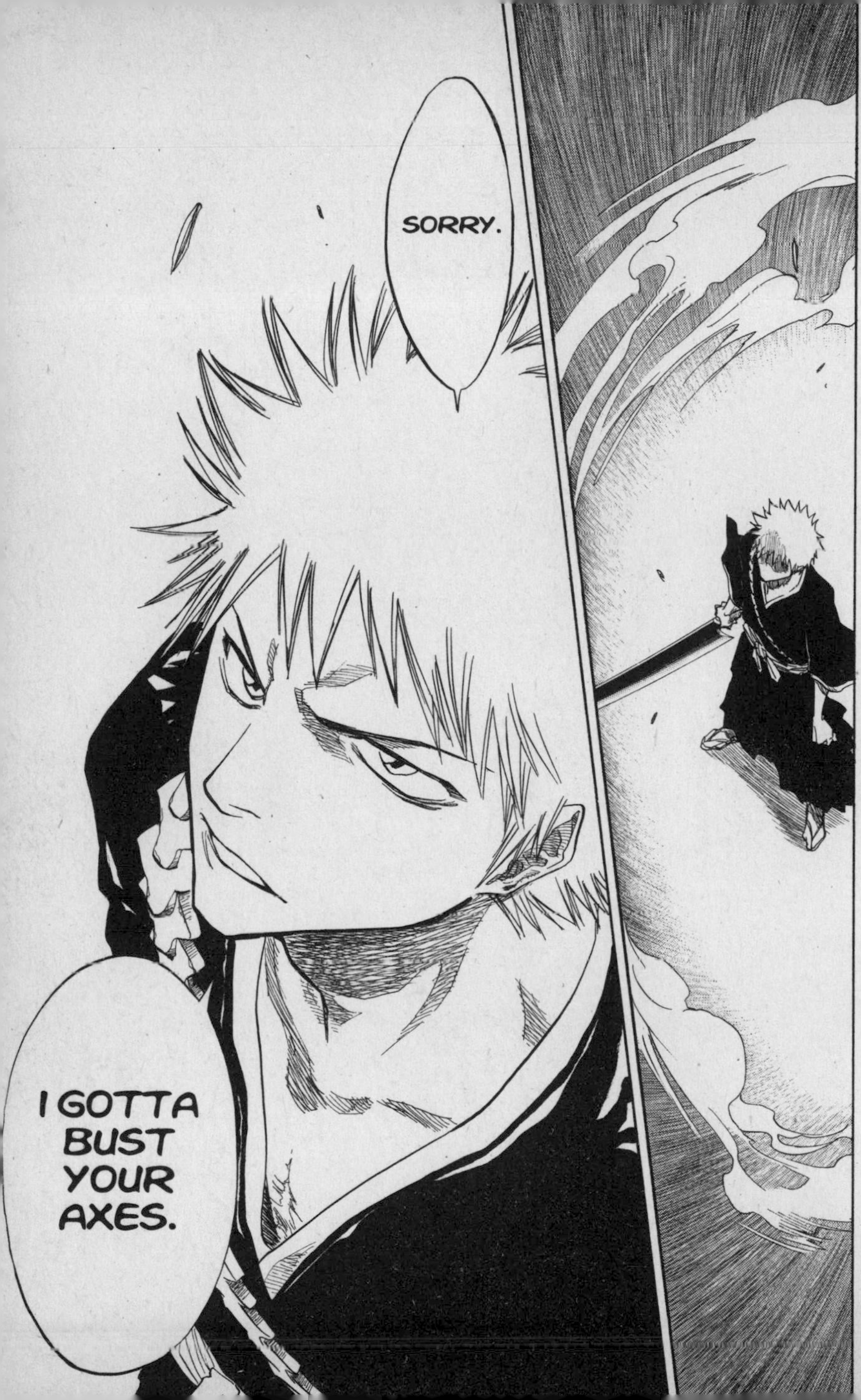
SORRY.
I GOTTA BUST YOUR AXES.

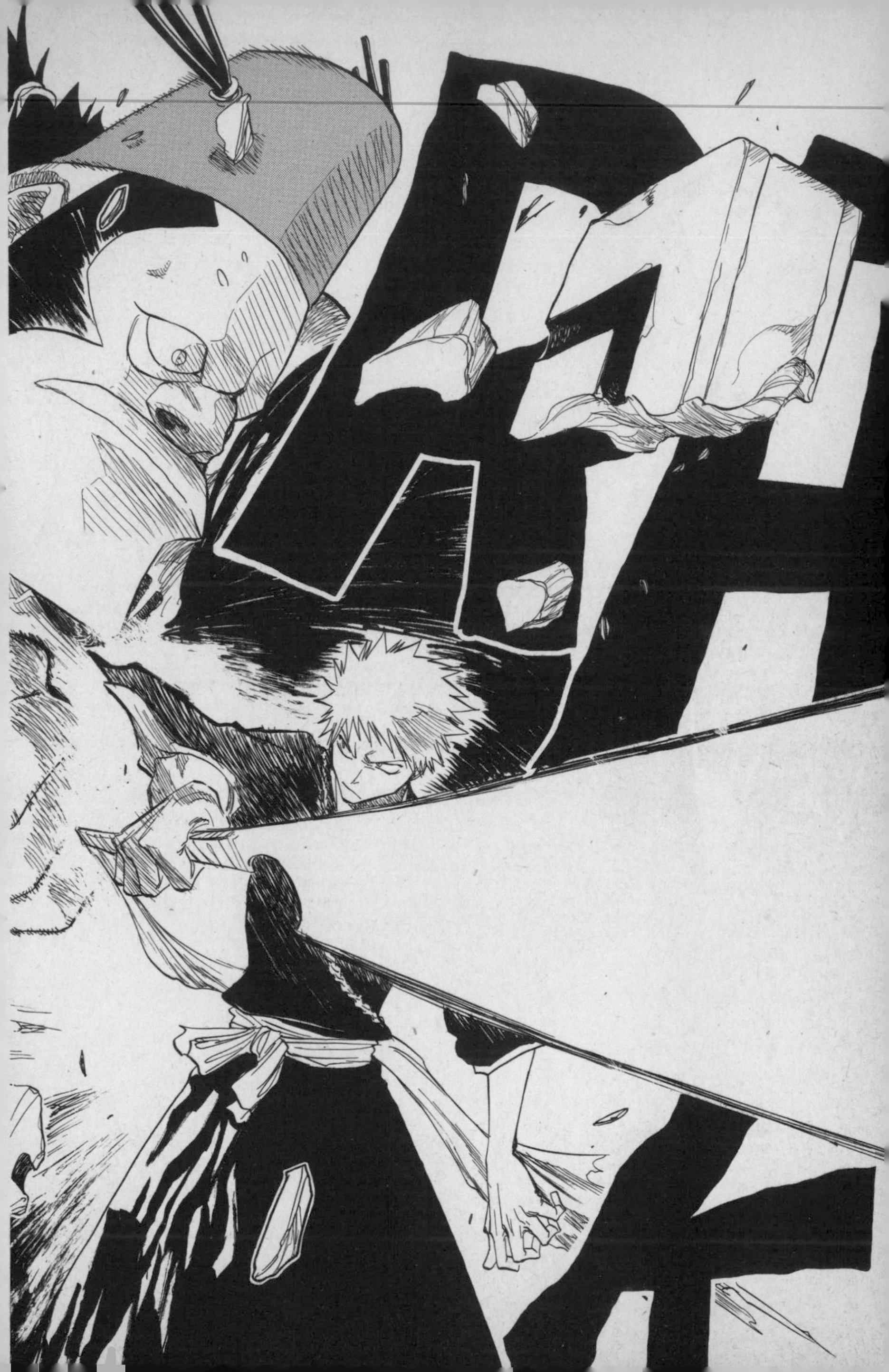

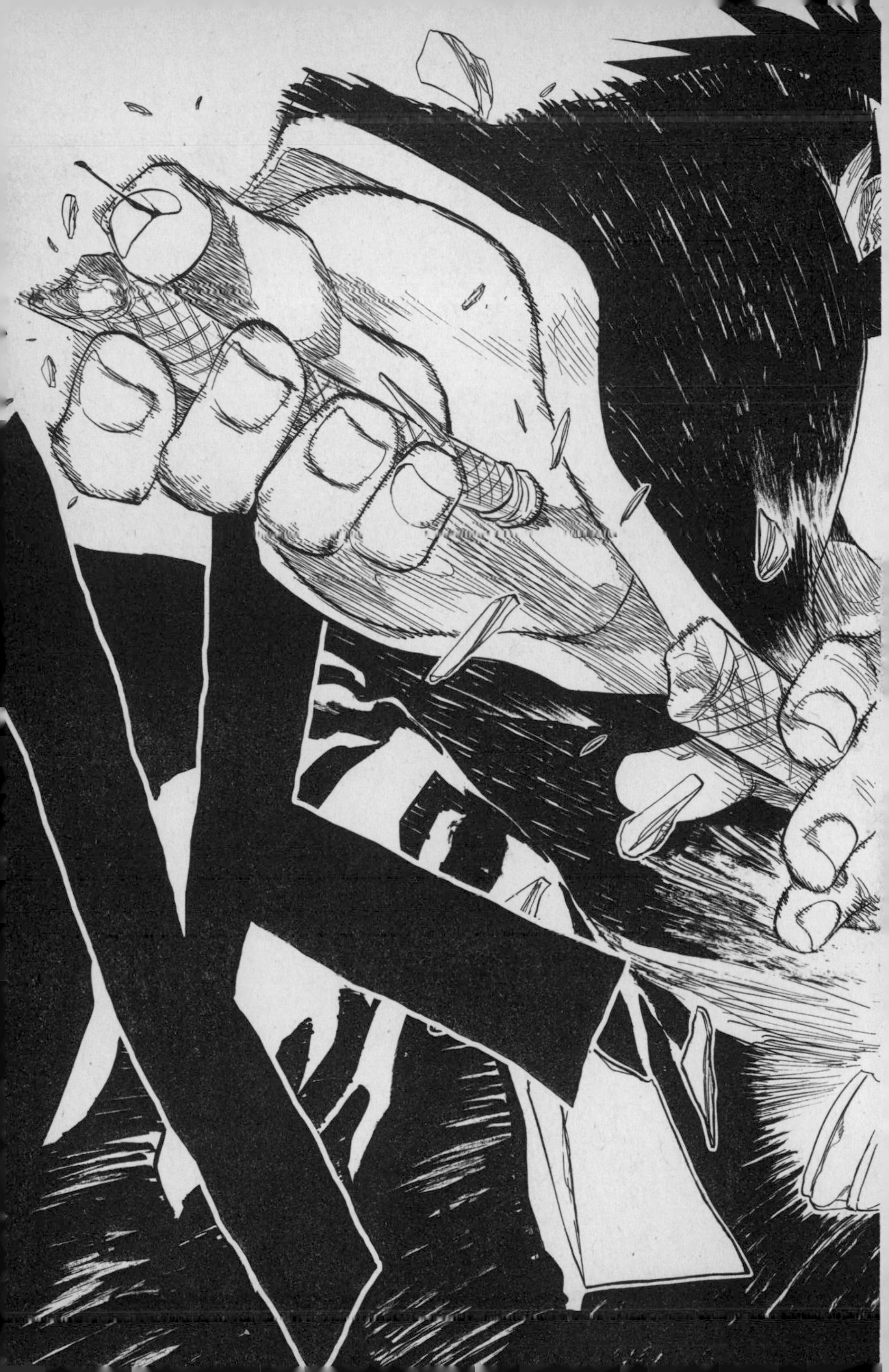

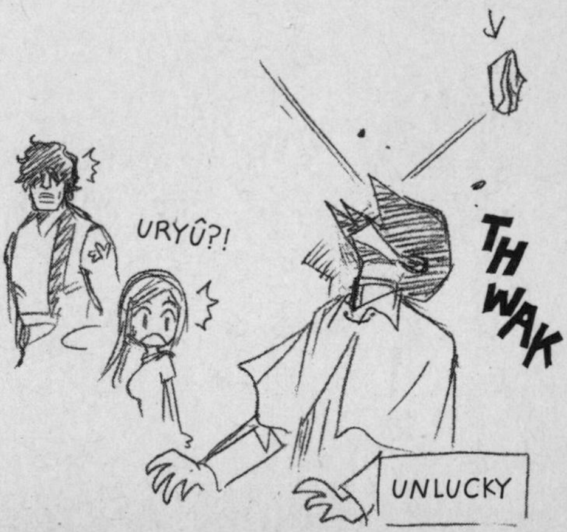
FRAGMENT
URYÛ?!
THWAK
UNLUCKY

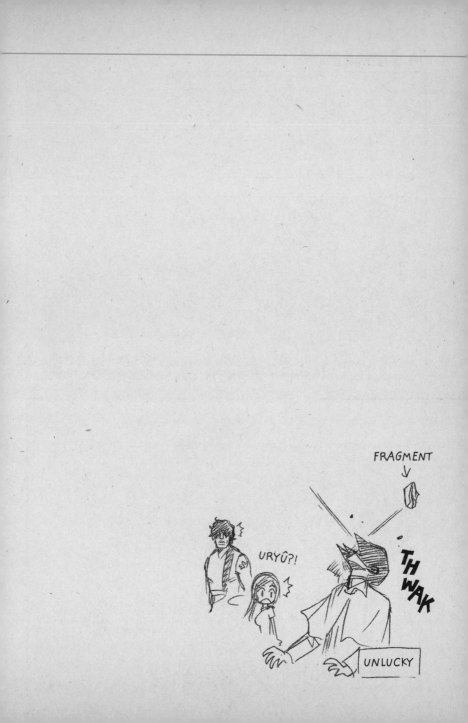

74. Amputation

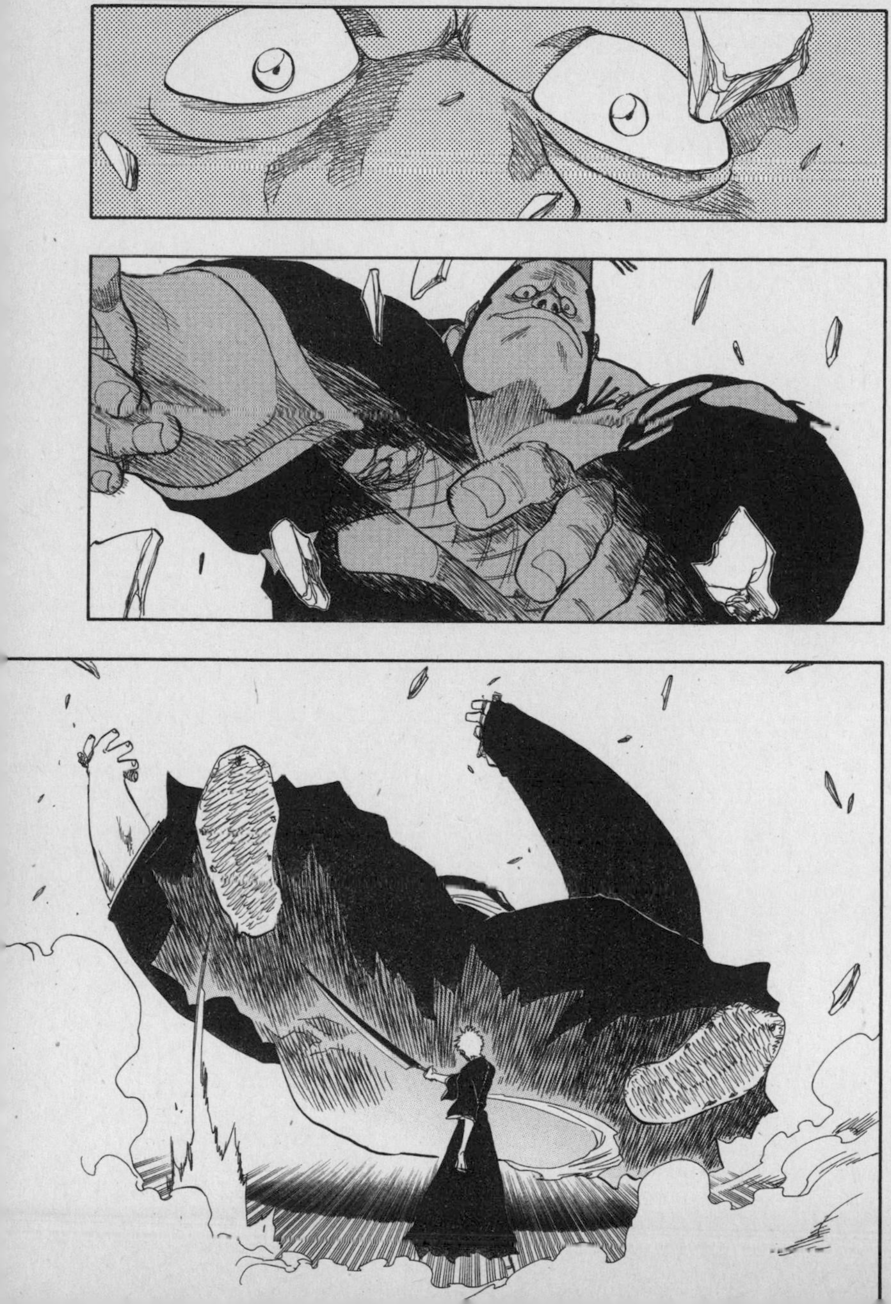

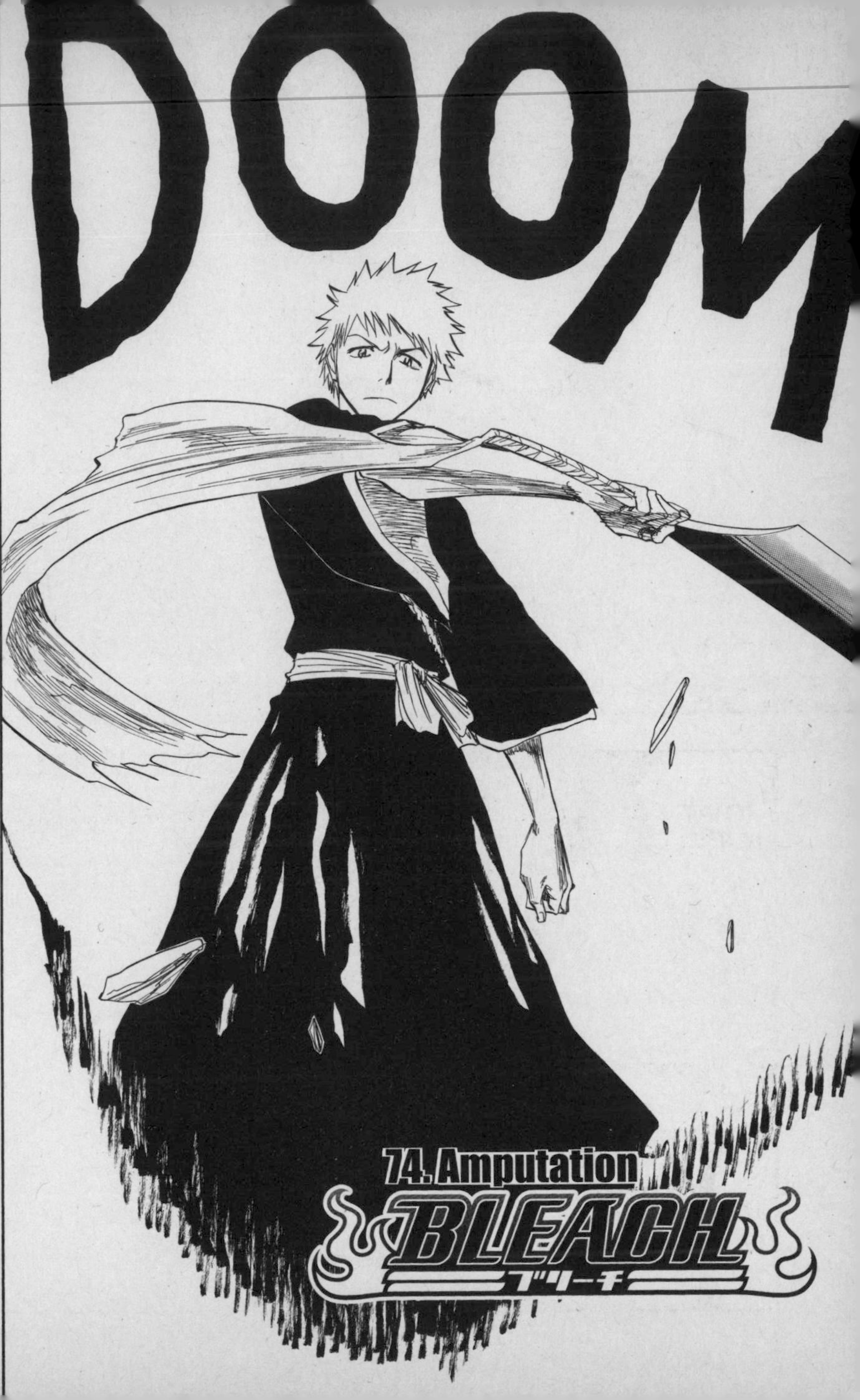
DOOM
74. Amputation
BLEACH
ブリーチ

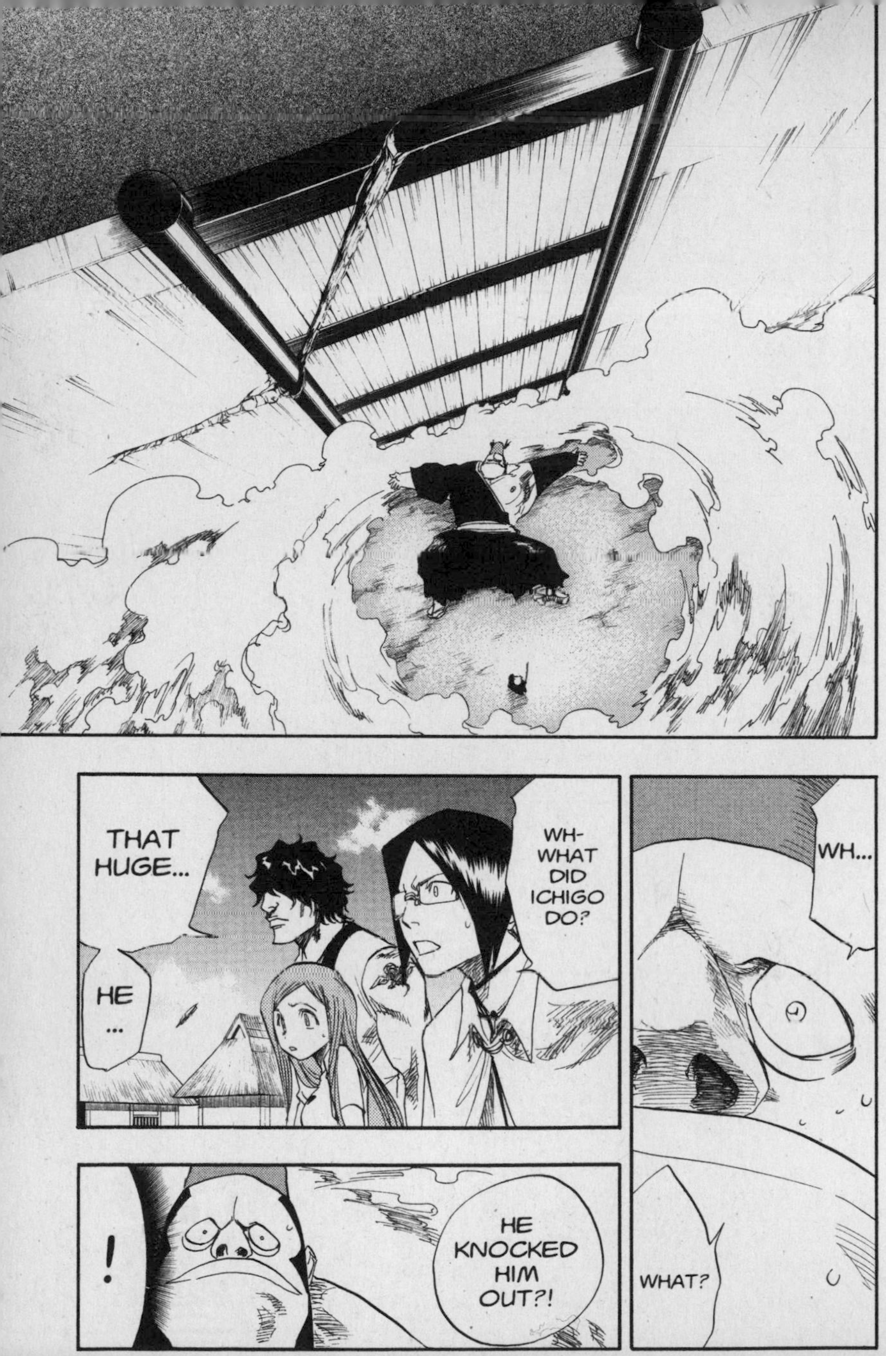
WH...
WHAT?
WH-WHAT DID ICHIGO DO?
THAT HUGE...
HE ...
HE KNOCKED HIM OUT?!
!

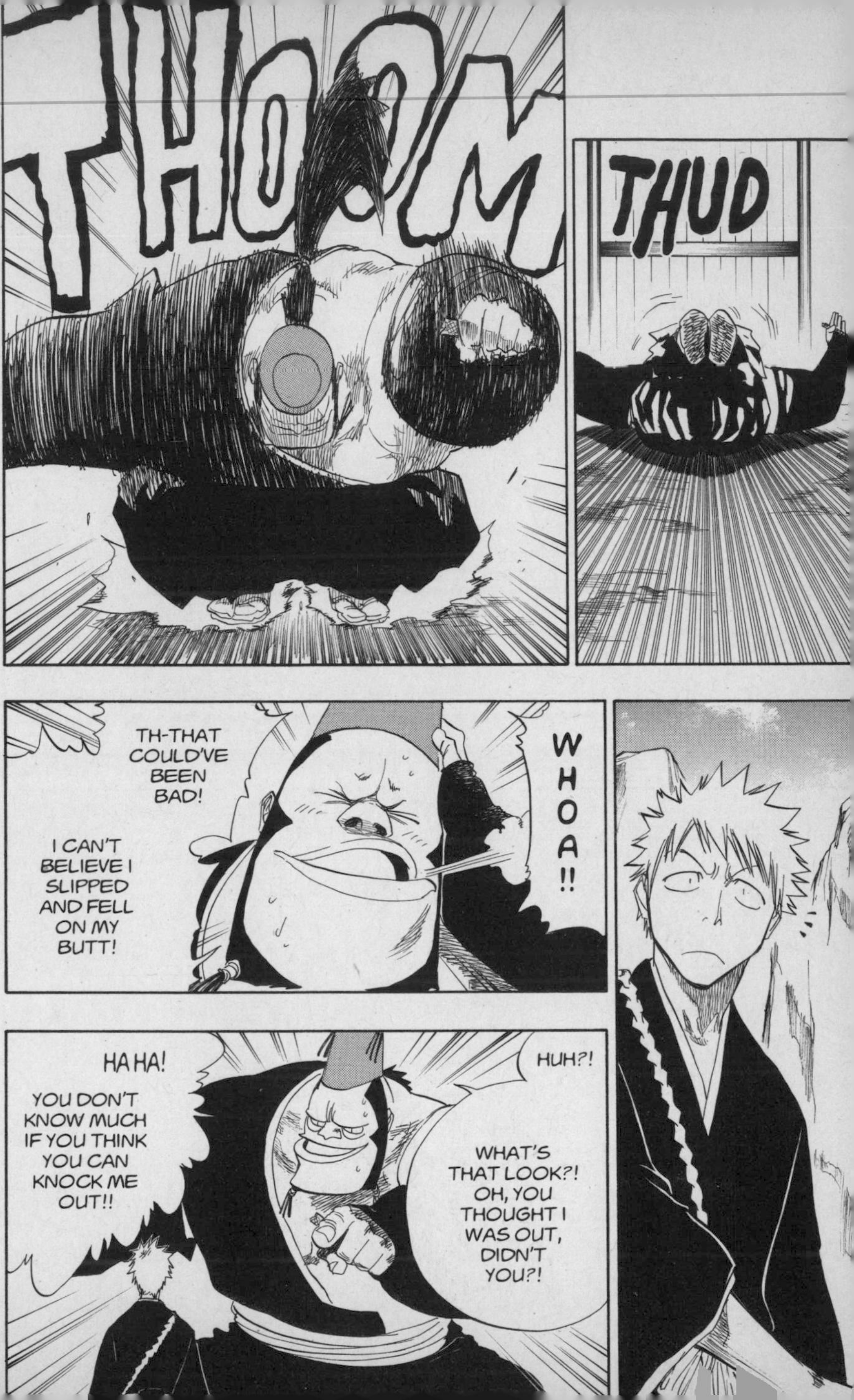
THUD
THOOM
WHOA!!
TH-THAT COULD'VE BEEN BAD!
I CAN'T BELIEVE I SLIPPED AND FELL ON MY BUTT!
HUH?!
WHAT'S THAT LOOK?! OH, YOU THOUGHT I WAS OUT, DIDN'T YOU?!
HA HA!
YOU DON'T KNOW MUCH IF YOU THINK YOU CAN KNOCK ME OUT!!

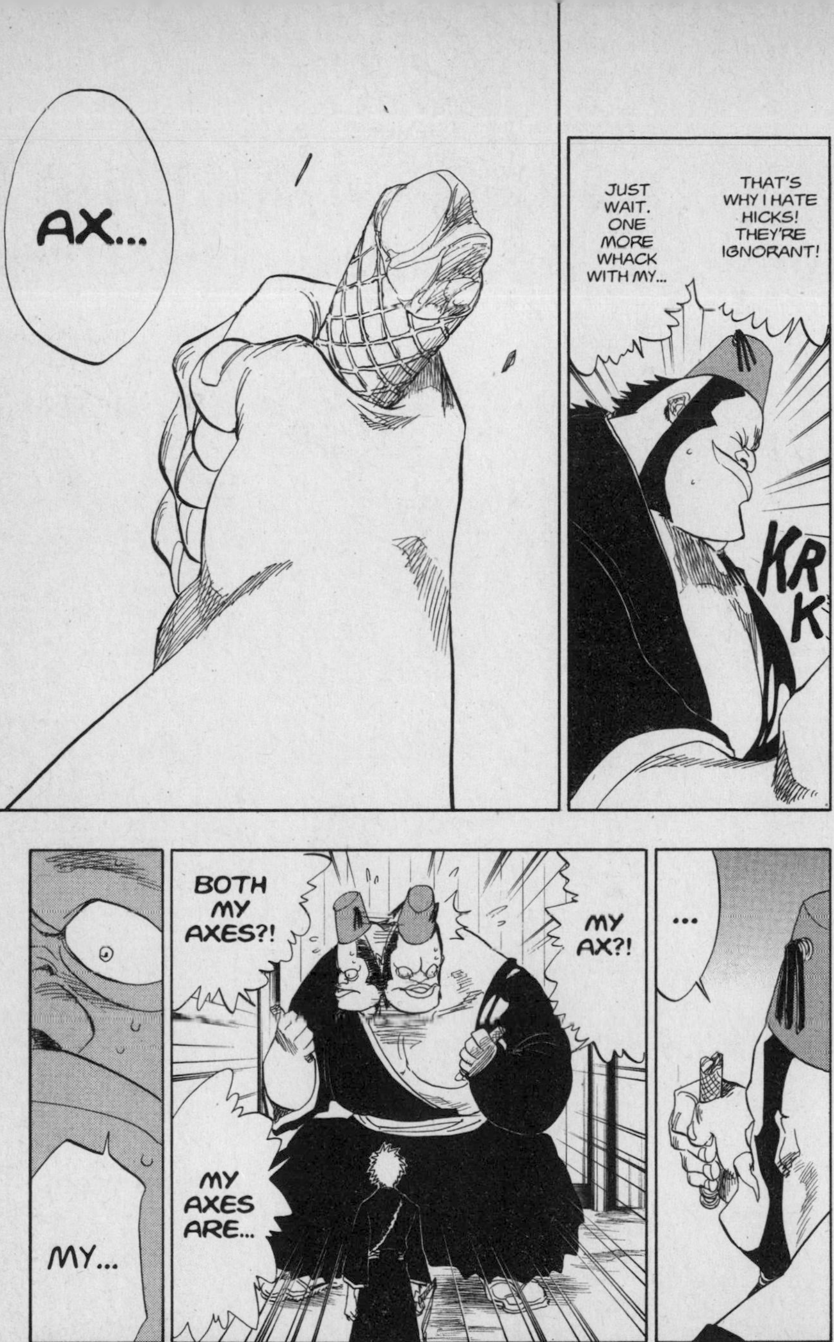
THAT'S WHY I HATE HICKS! THEY'RE IGNORANT!
JUST WAIT. ONE MORE WHACK WITH MY...
KRK
AX...
...
MY AX?!
BOTH MY AXES?!
MY AXES ARE...
MY...

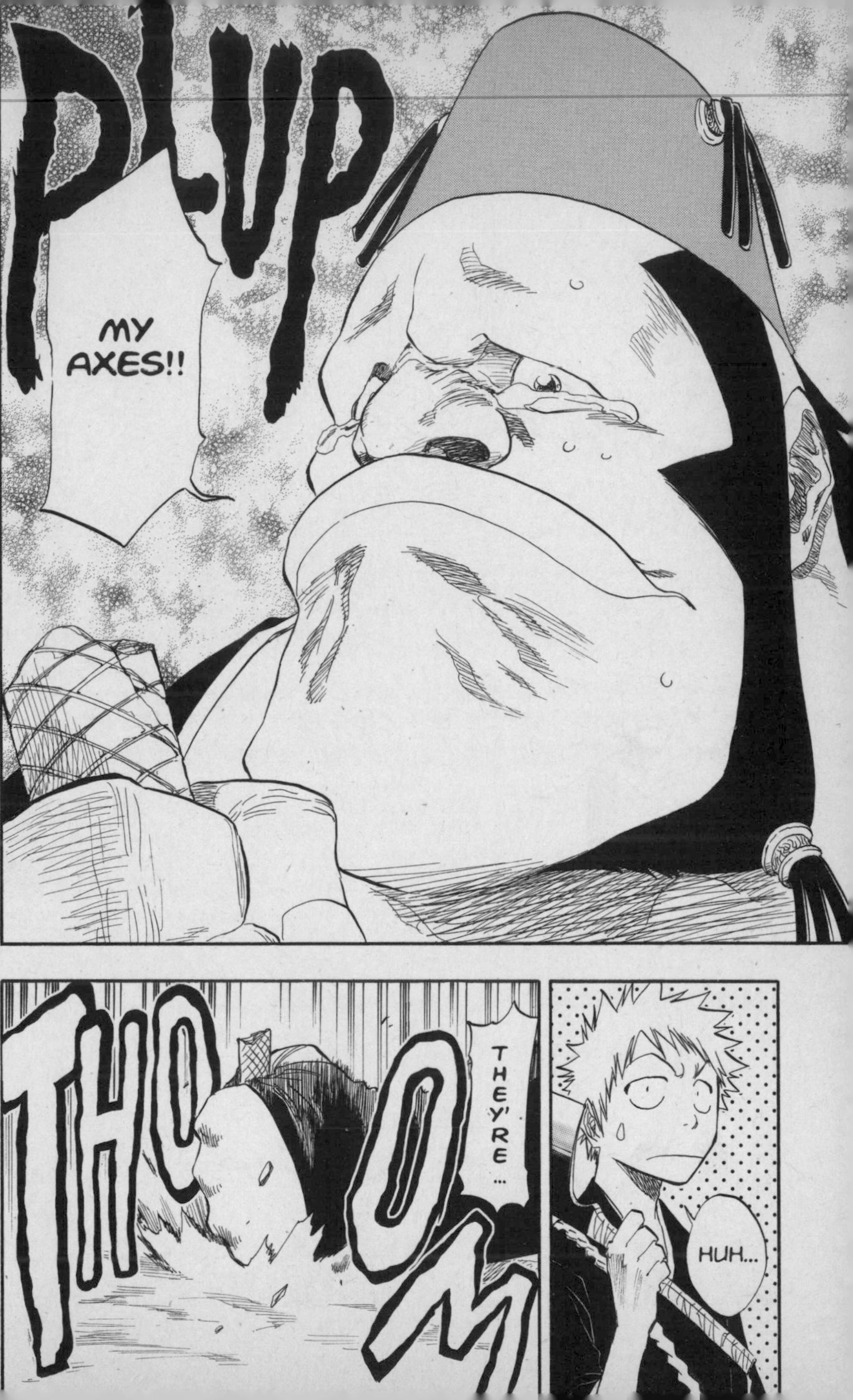
PLUP
MY AXES!!
HUH...
THEY'RE...
THOOM

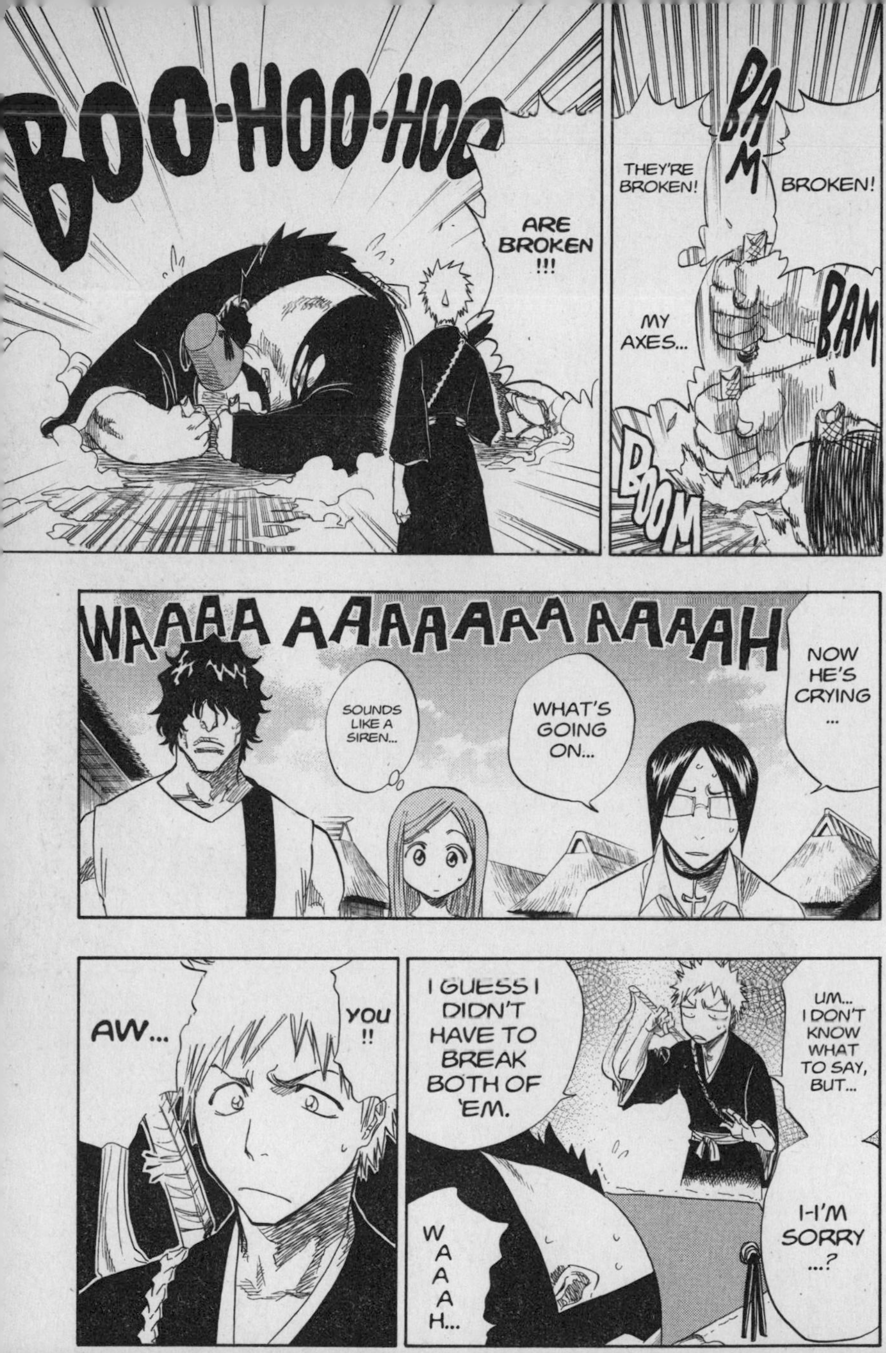
BAM
BROKEN!
THEY'RE BROKEN!
BAM
MY AXES...
BOOM
ARE BROKEN !!!
BOO-HOO-HOO
WAAAA AAAAAAA AAAAH
NOW HE'S CRYING ...
WHAT'S GOING ON...
SOUNDS LIKE A SIREN...
UM... I DON'T KNOW WHAT TO SAY, BUT...
I GUESS I DIDN'T HAVE TO BREAK BOTH OF 'EM.
I-I'M SORRY ...?
WAAAH...
YOU !!
AW...

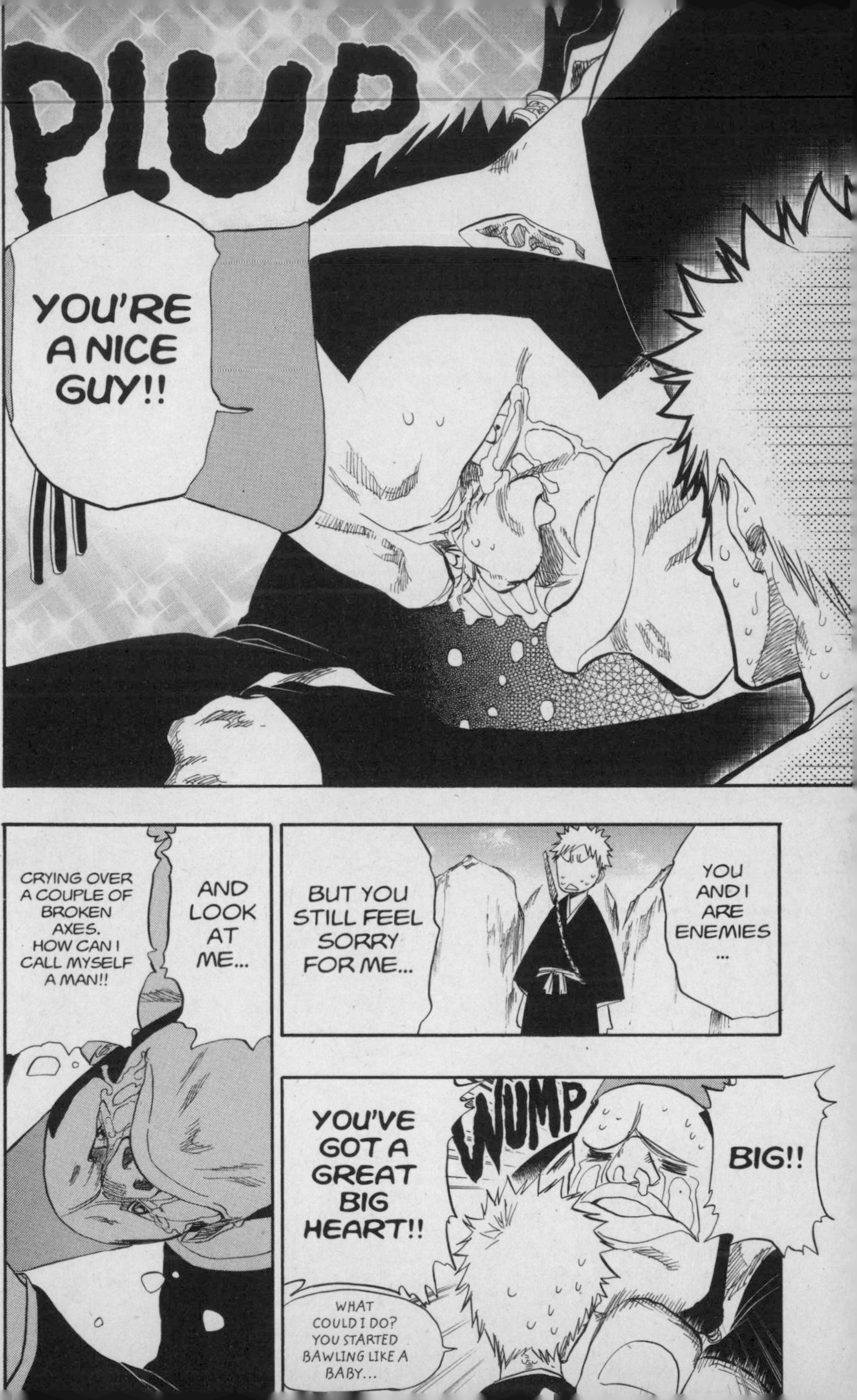
PLUP
YOU'RE A NICE GUY!!
YOU AND I ARE ENEMIES ...
BUT YOU STILL FEEL SORRY FOR ME...
BIG!!
WUMP
YOU'VE GOT A GREAT BIG HEART!!
WHAT COULD I DO? YOU STARTED BAWLING LIKE A BABY...
AND LOOK AT ME...
CRYING OVER A COUPLE OF BROKEN AXES. HOW CAN I CALL MYSELF A MAN!!

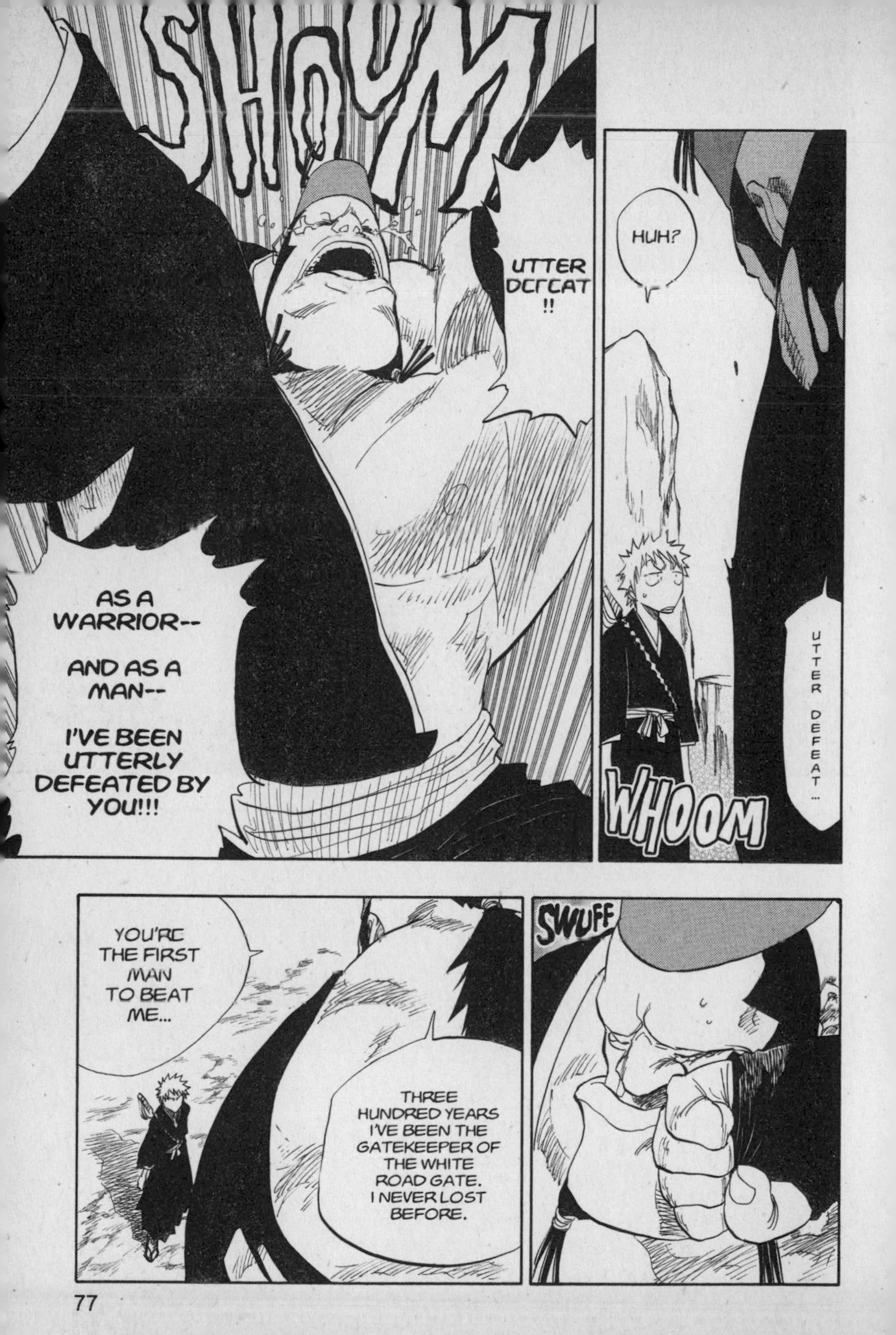
SHOOM
UTTER DEFEAT!!
AS A WARRIOR--
AND AS A MAN--
I'VE BEEN UTTERLY DEFEATED BY YOU!!!
HUH?
UTTER DEFEAT...
WHOOM
SWUFF
YOU'RE THE FIRST MAN TO BEAT ME...
THREE HUNDRED YEARS I'VE BEEN THE GATEKEEPER OF THE WHITE ROAD GATE. I NEVER LOST BEFORE.

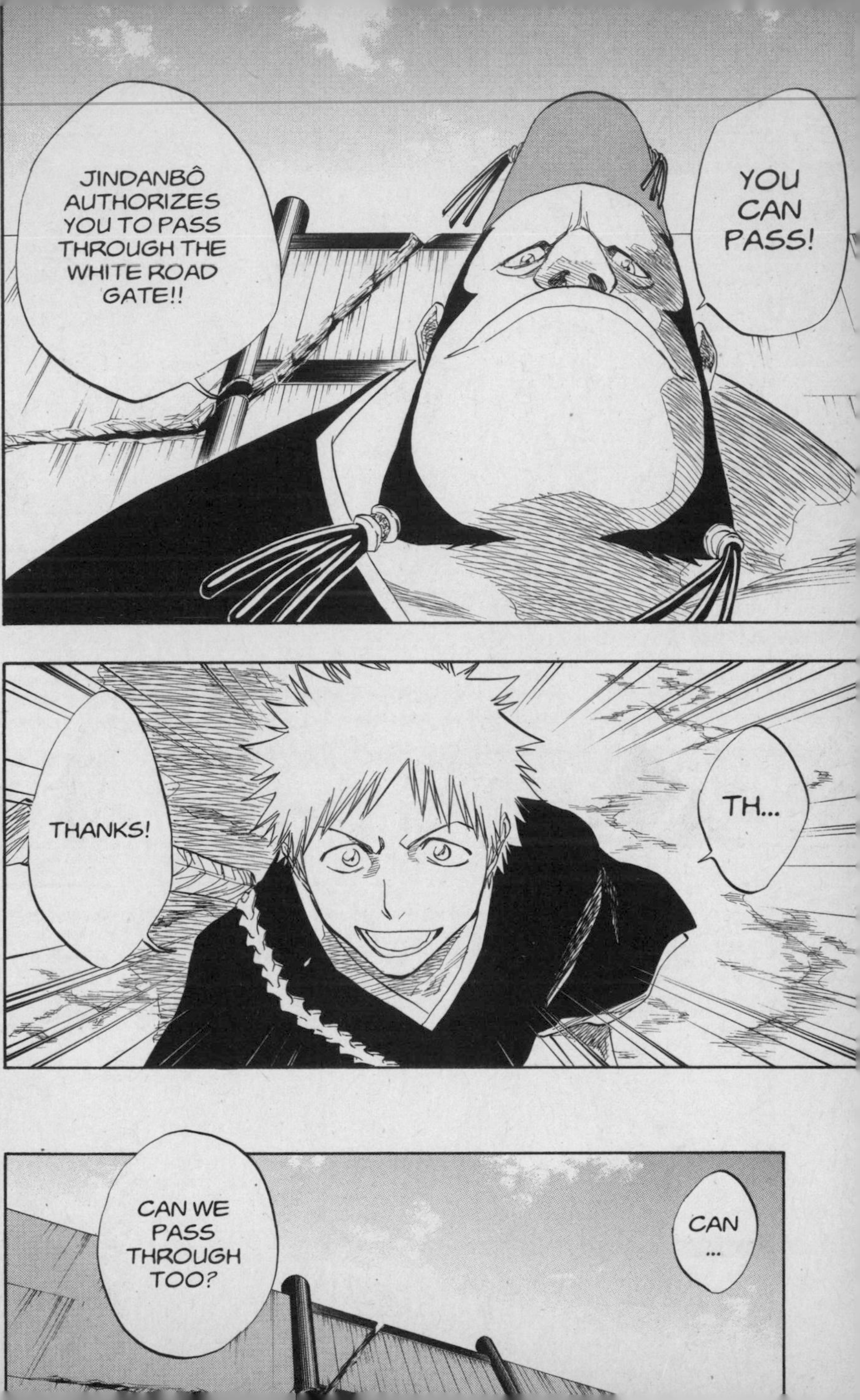
YOU CAN PASS!
JINDANBÔ AUTHORIZES YOU TO PASS THROUGH THE WHITE ROAD GATE!!
TH...
THANKS!
CAN ...
CAN WE PASS THROUGH TOO?

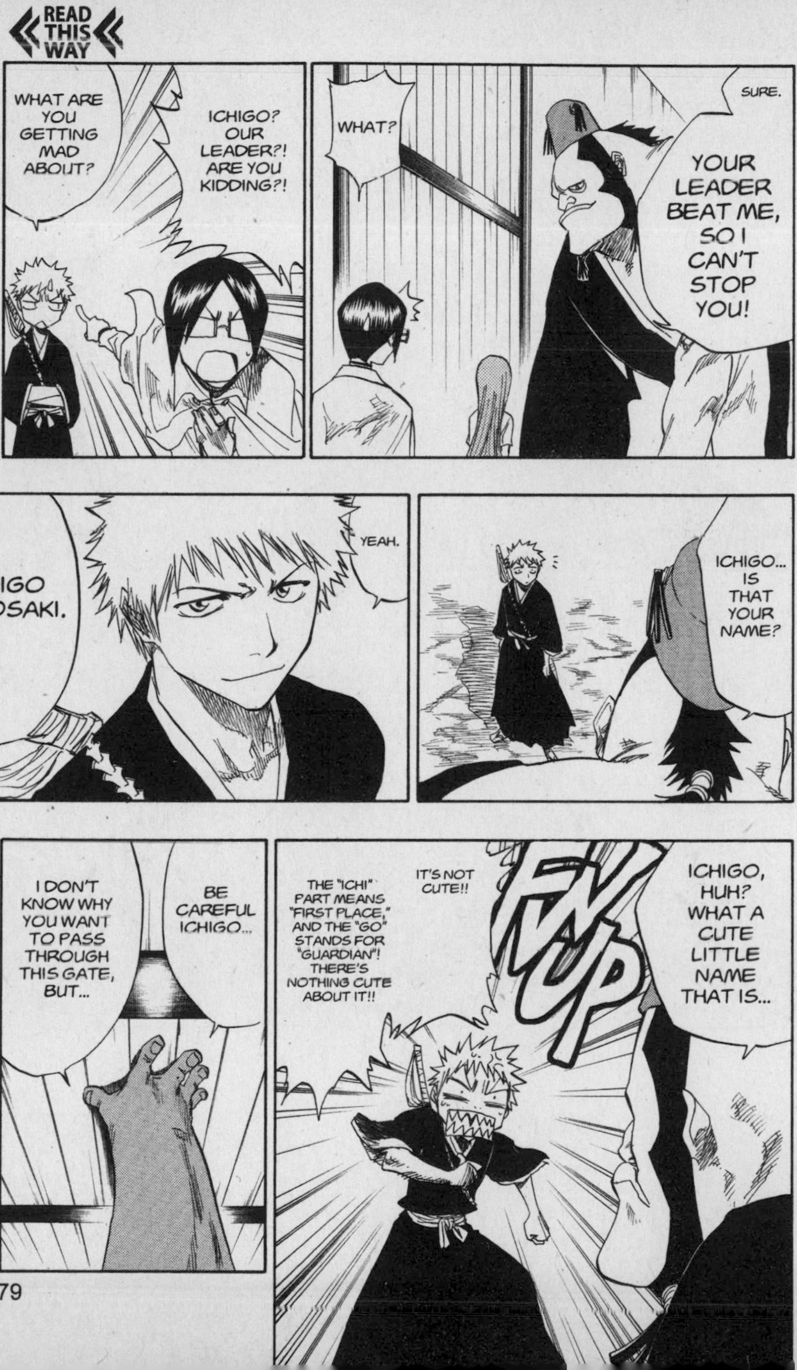
READ THIS WAY
SURE.
YOUR LEADER BEAT ME, SO I CAN'T STOP YOU!
WHAT?
ICHIGO? OUR LEADER?! ARE YOU KIDDING?!
WHAT ARE YOU GETTING MAD ABOUT?
ICHIGO... IS THAT YOUR NAME?
YEAH.
ICHIGO KUROSAKI.
ICHIGO, HUH? WHAT A CUTE LITTLE NAME THAT IS...
FWUP
IT'S NOT CUTE!!
THE "ICHI" PART MEANS "FIRST PLACE," AND THE "GO" STANDS FOR "GUARDIAN"! THERE'S NOTHING CUTE ABOUT IT!!
BE CAREFUL ICHIGO...
I DON'T KNOW WHY YOU WANT TO PASS THROUGH THIS GATE, BUT...

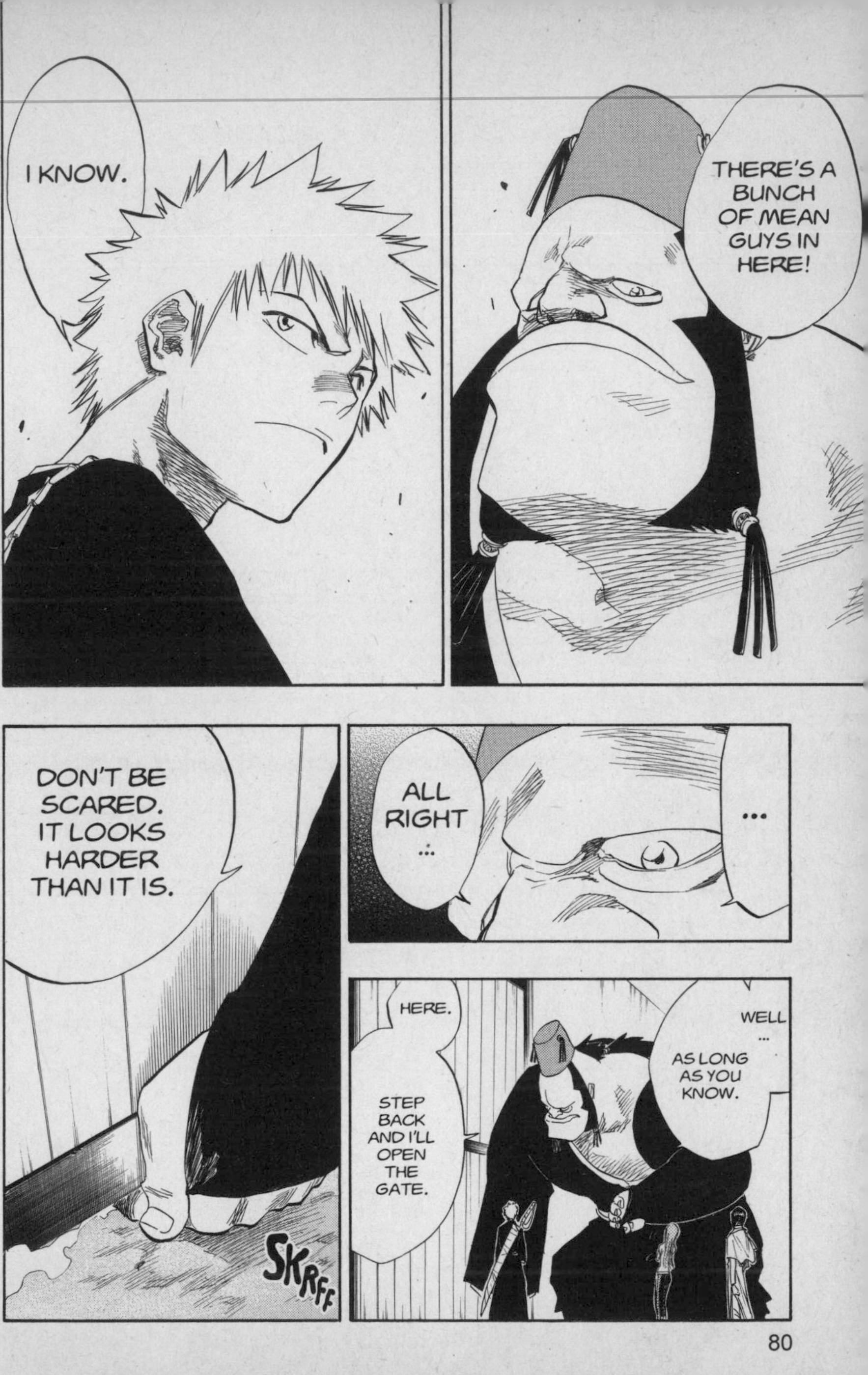
THERE'S A BUNCH OF MEAN GUYS IN HERE!
I KNOW.
...
ALL RIGHT ...
WELL ...
AS LONG AS YOU KNOW.
HERE.
STEP BACK AND I'LL OPEN THE GATE.
DON'T BE SCARED. IT LOOKS HARDER THAN IT IS.
SKRFF

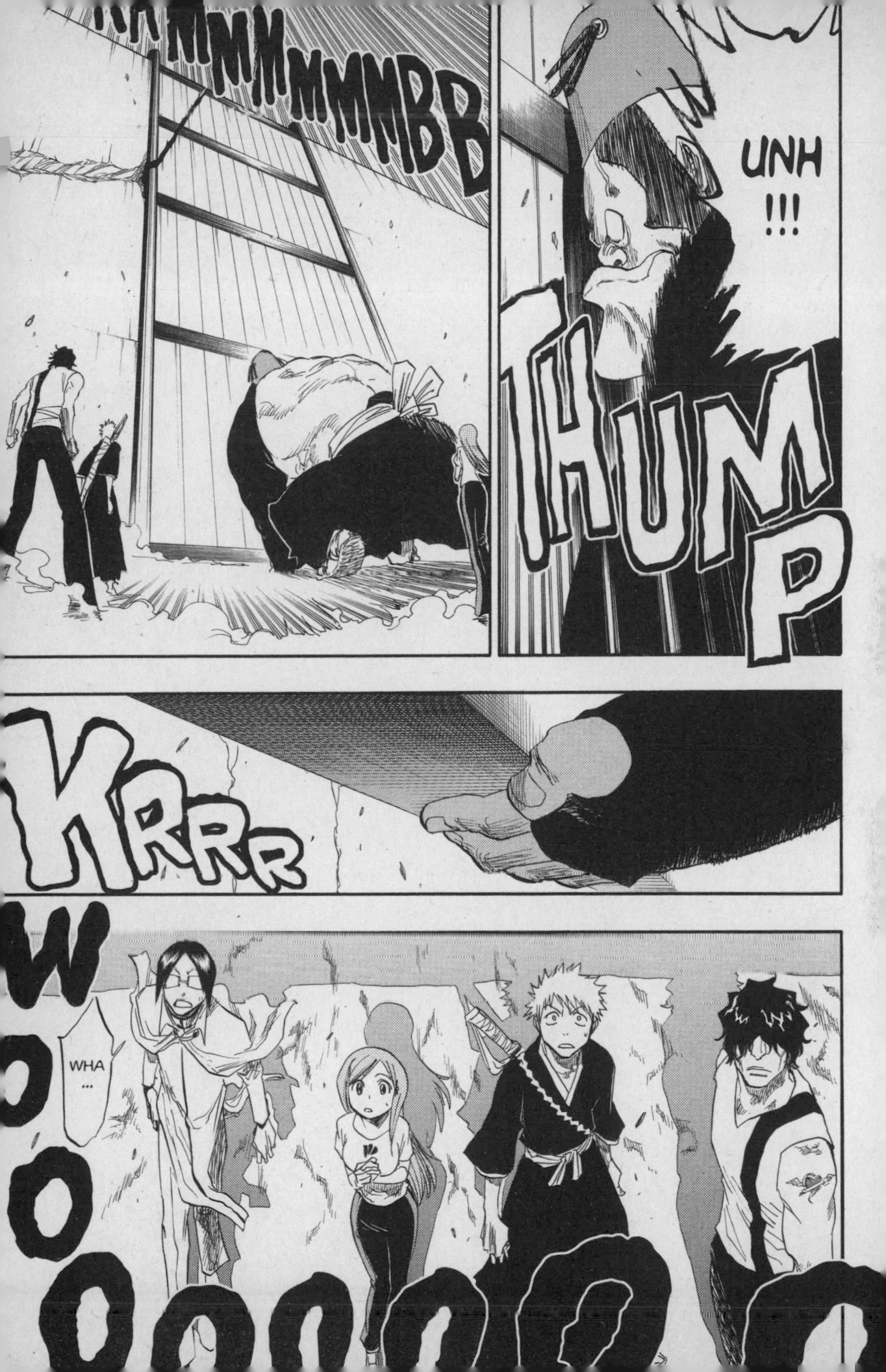
UNH !!!
THUMP
MMMMMNBB
KRRR
WOOOOOOOOO
WHA ...

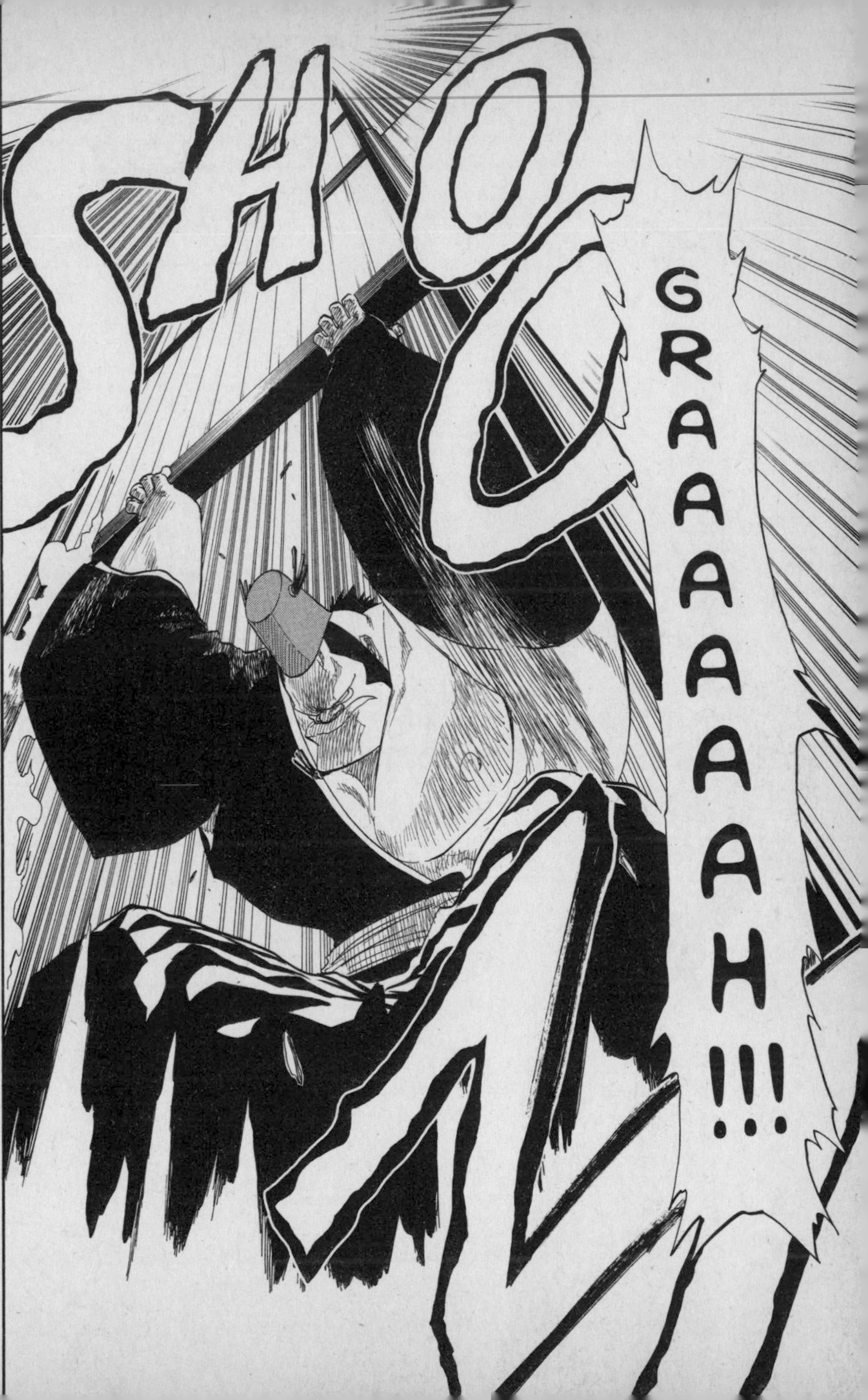
GRAAAAAAH!!!

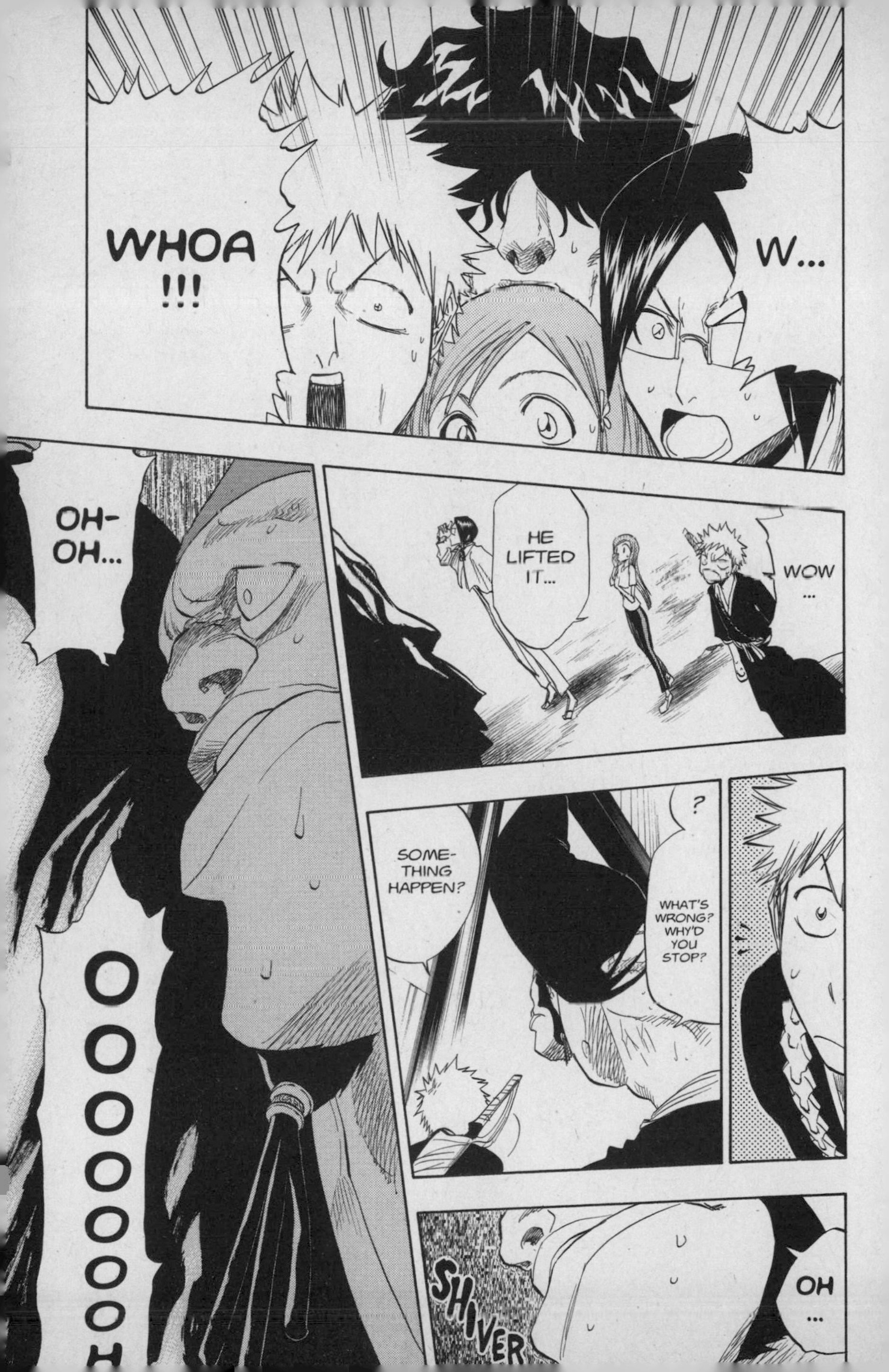
W...
WHOA !!!
WOW ...
HE LIFTED IT...
?
WHAT'S WRONG? WHY'D YOU STOP?
SOME-THING HAPPEN?
OH ...
SHIVER
OH-OH...
OOOOOOOH

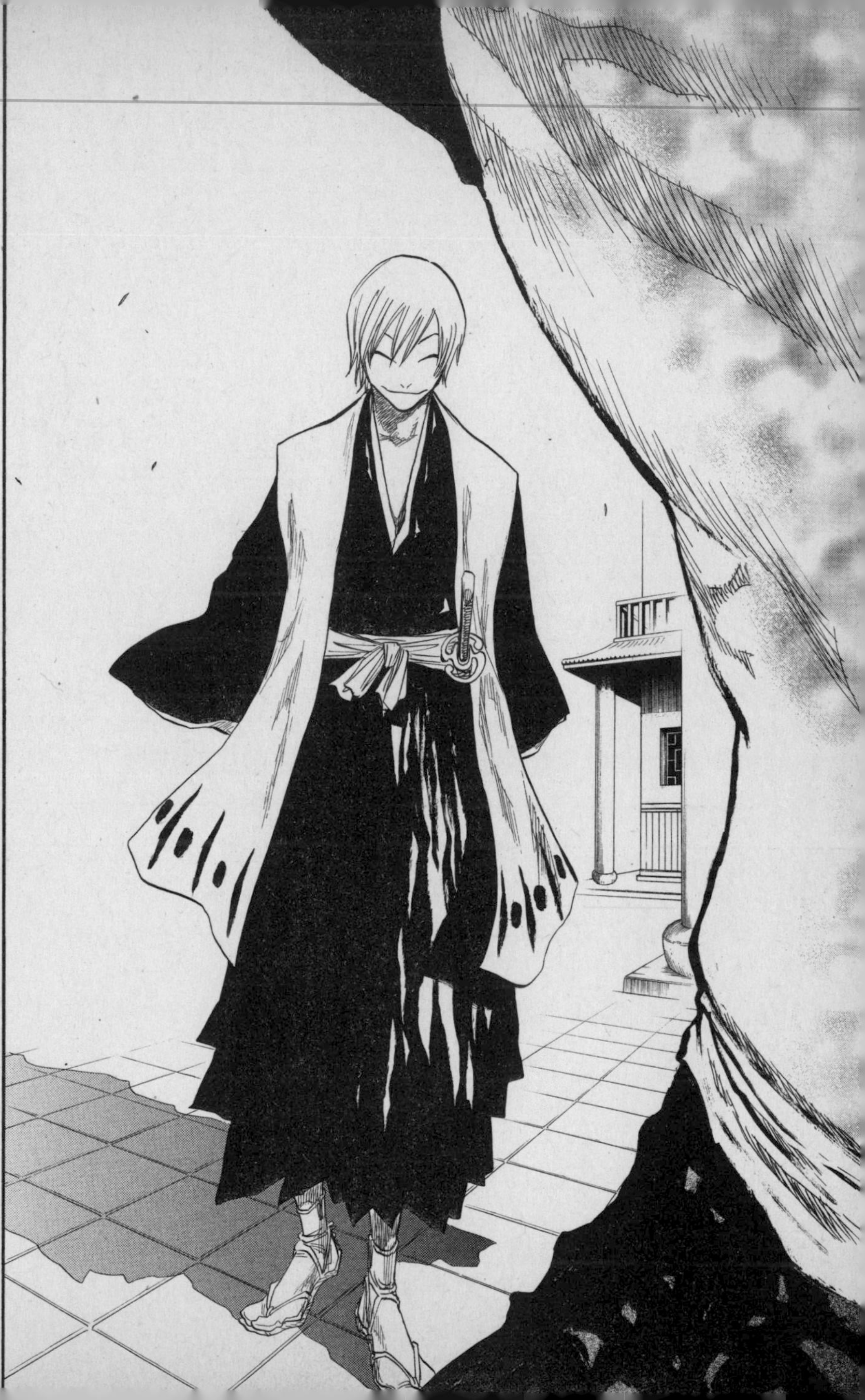

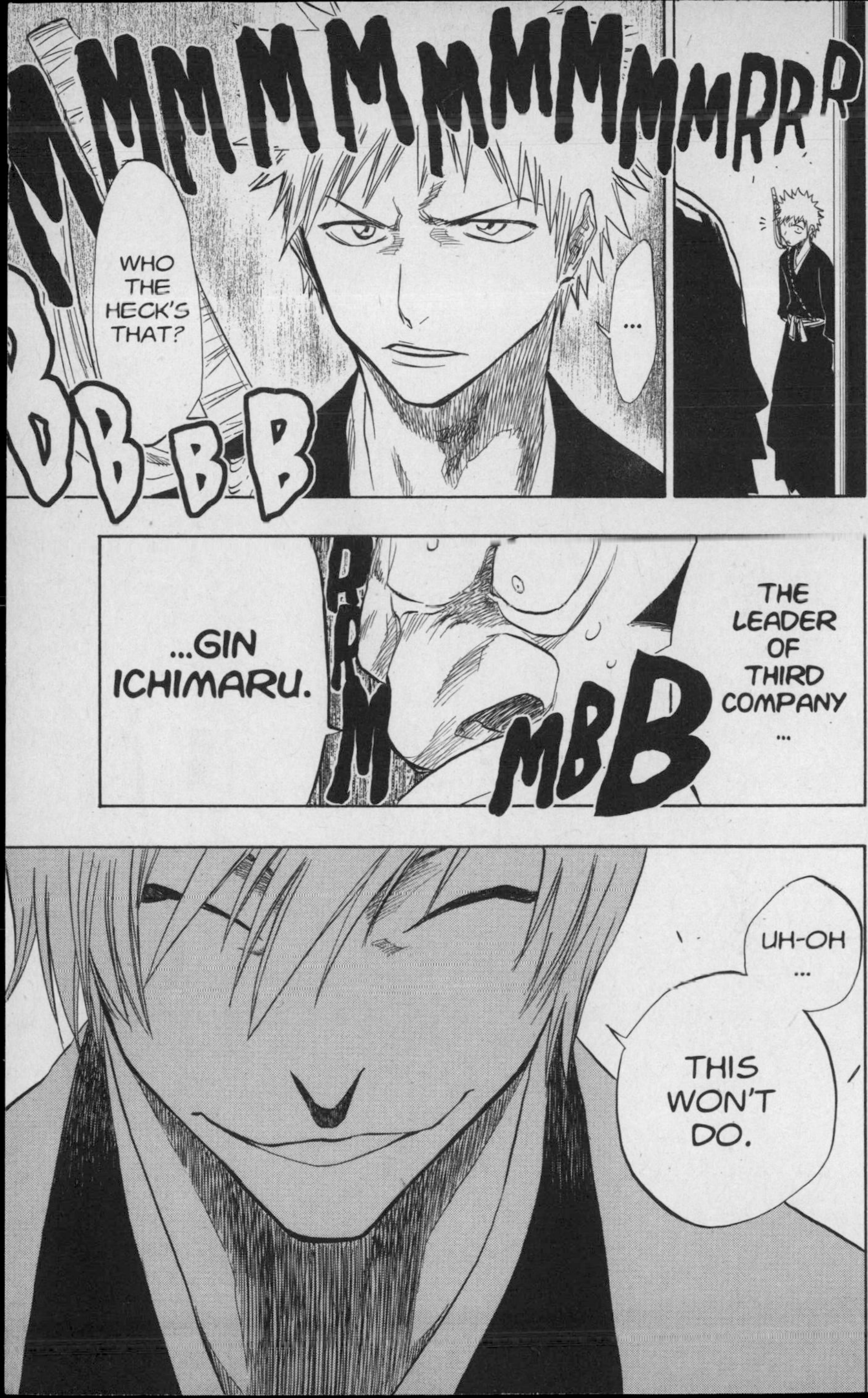
MMMMMMMMMMMMMRRR
...
WHO THE HECK'S THAT?
BBBB
THE LEADER OF THIRD COMPANY ...
...GIN ICHIMARU.
RRM
MBB
UH-OH ...
THIS WON'T DO.

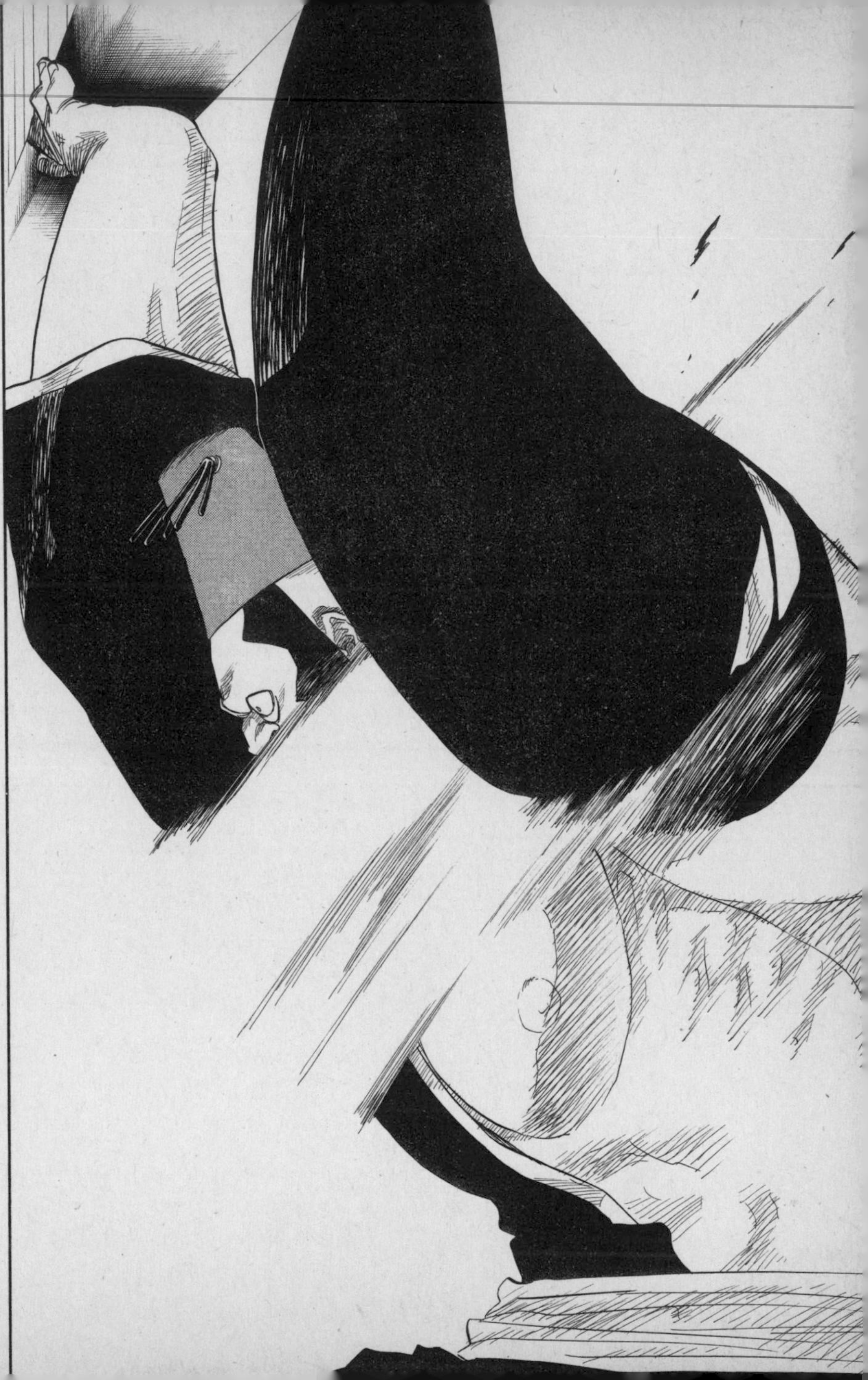

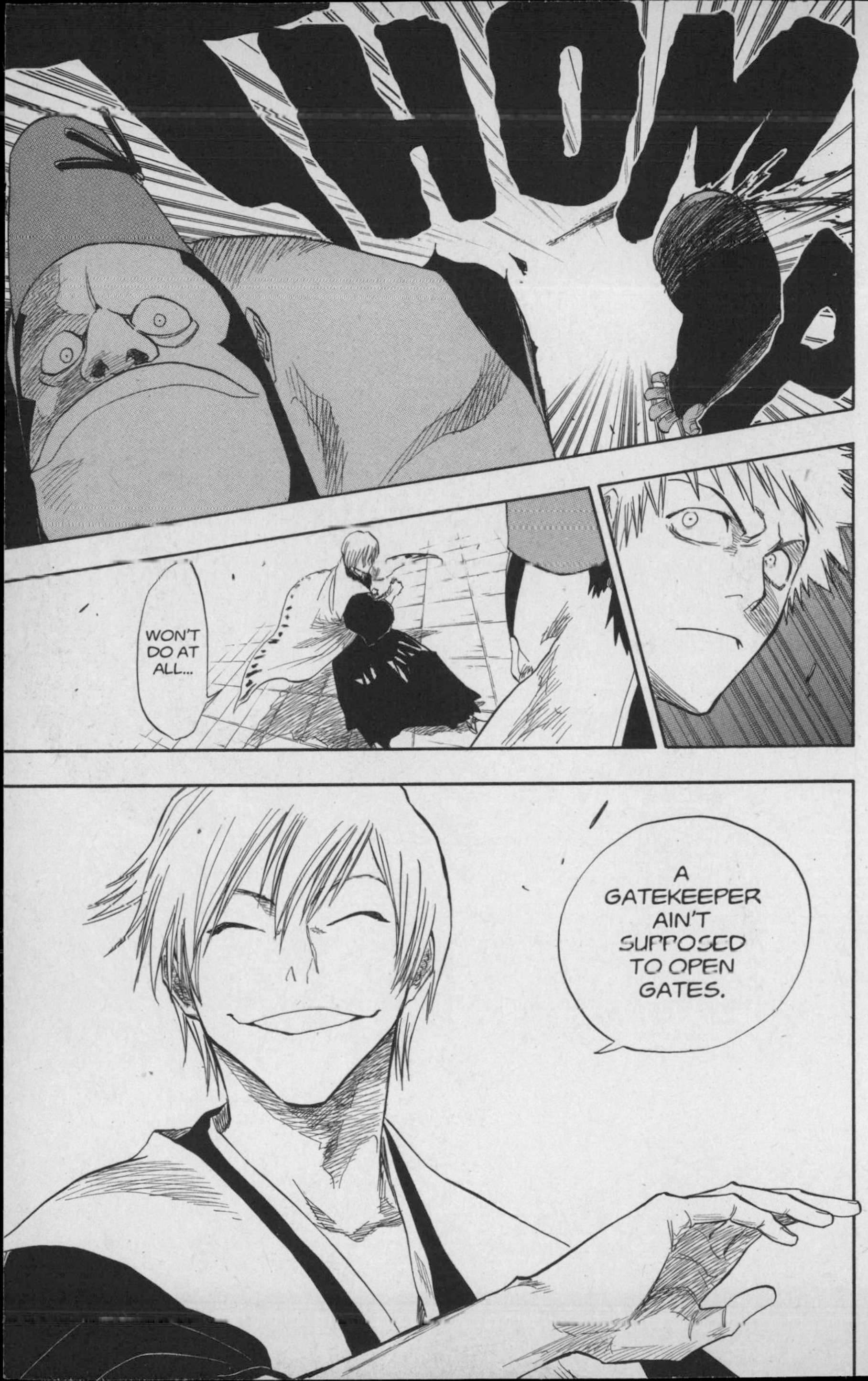
THOM
WON'T DO AT ALL...
A GATEKEEPER AIN'T SUPPOSED TO OPEN GATES.

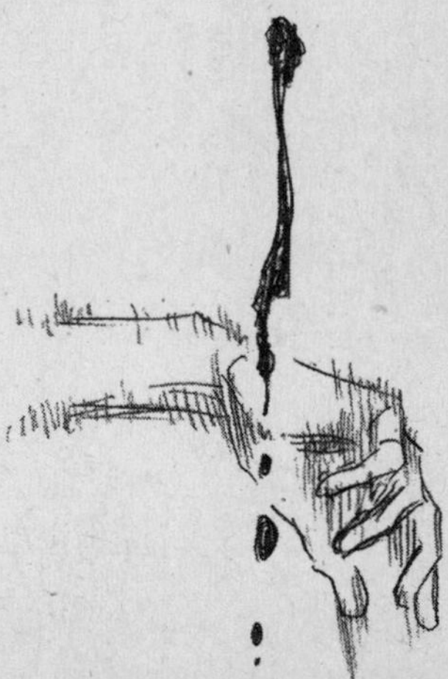

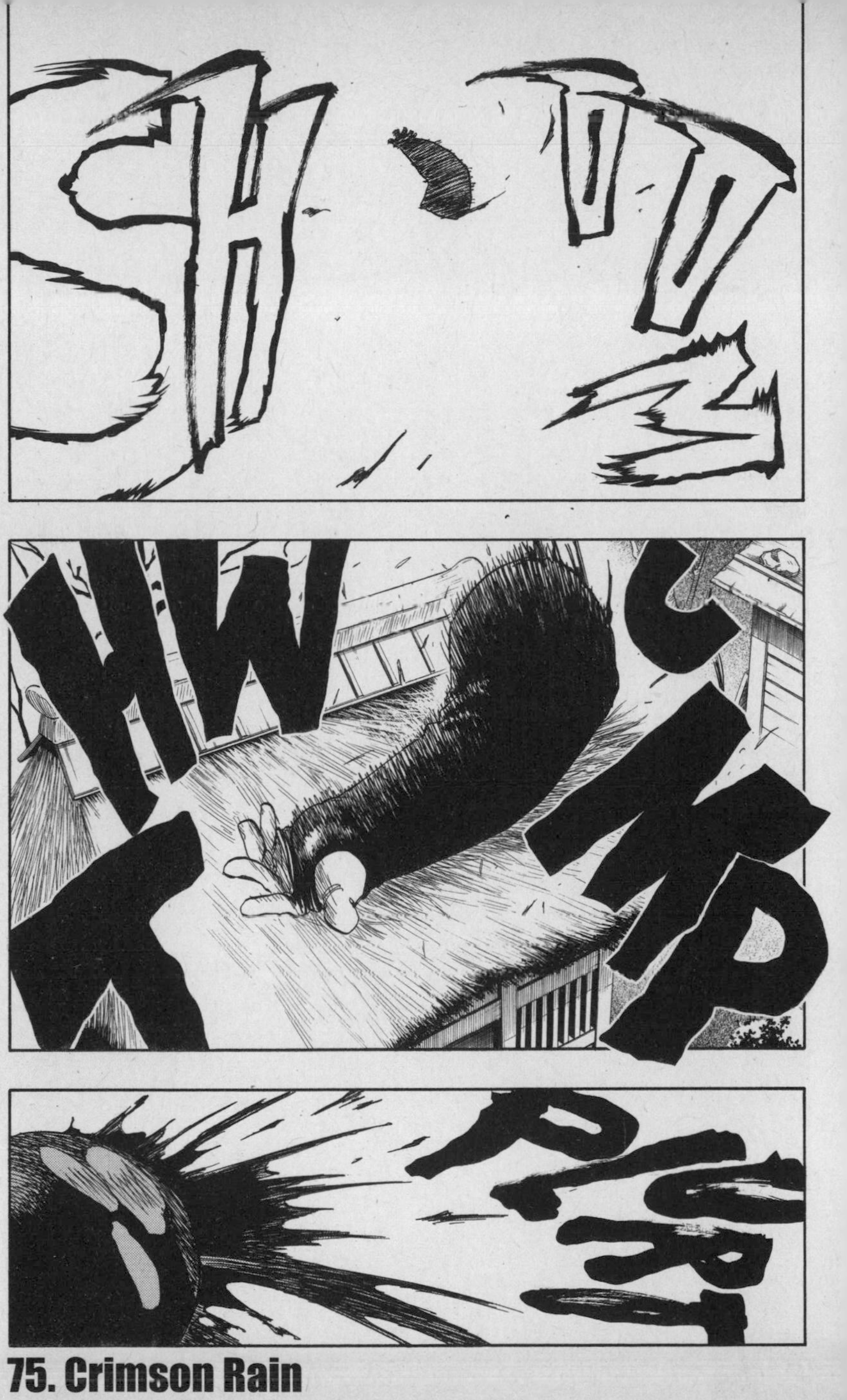
WHUMP

75. Crimson Rain

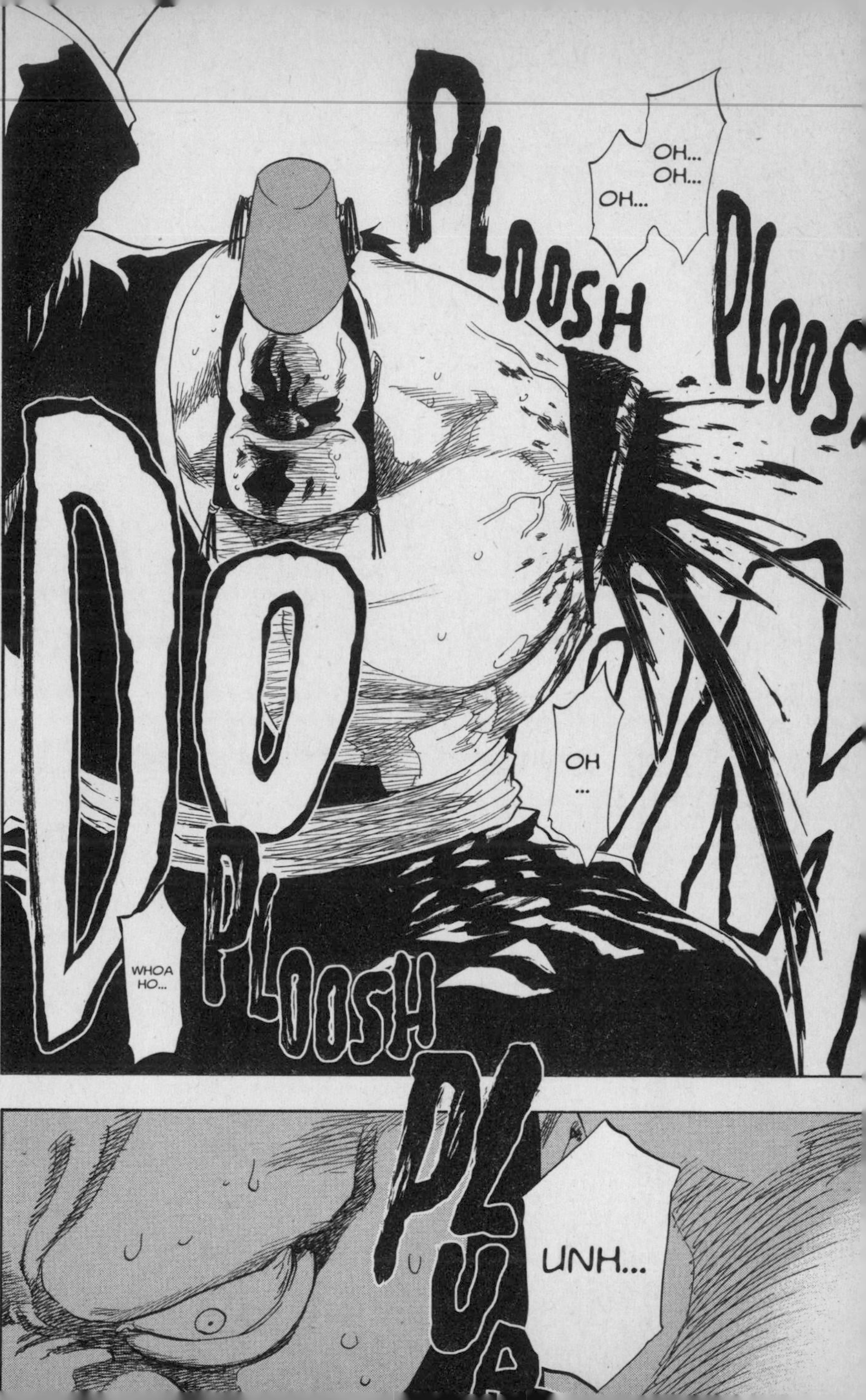
OH...
OH...
OH...
PLOOSH
PLOOSH
OH
...
DO
WHOA
HO...
PLOOSH
UNH...

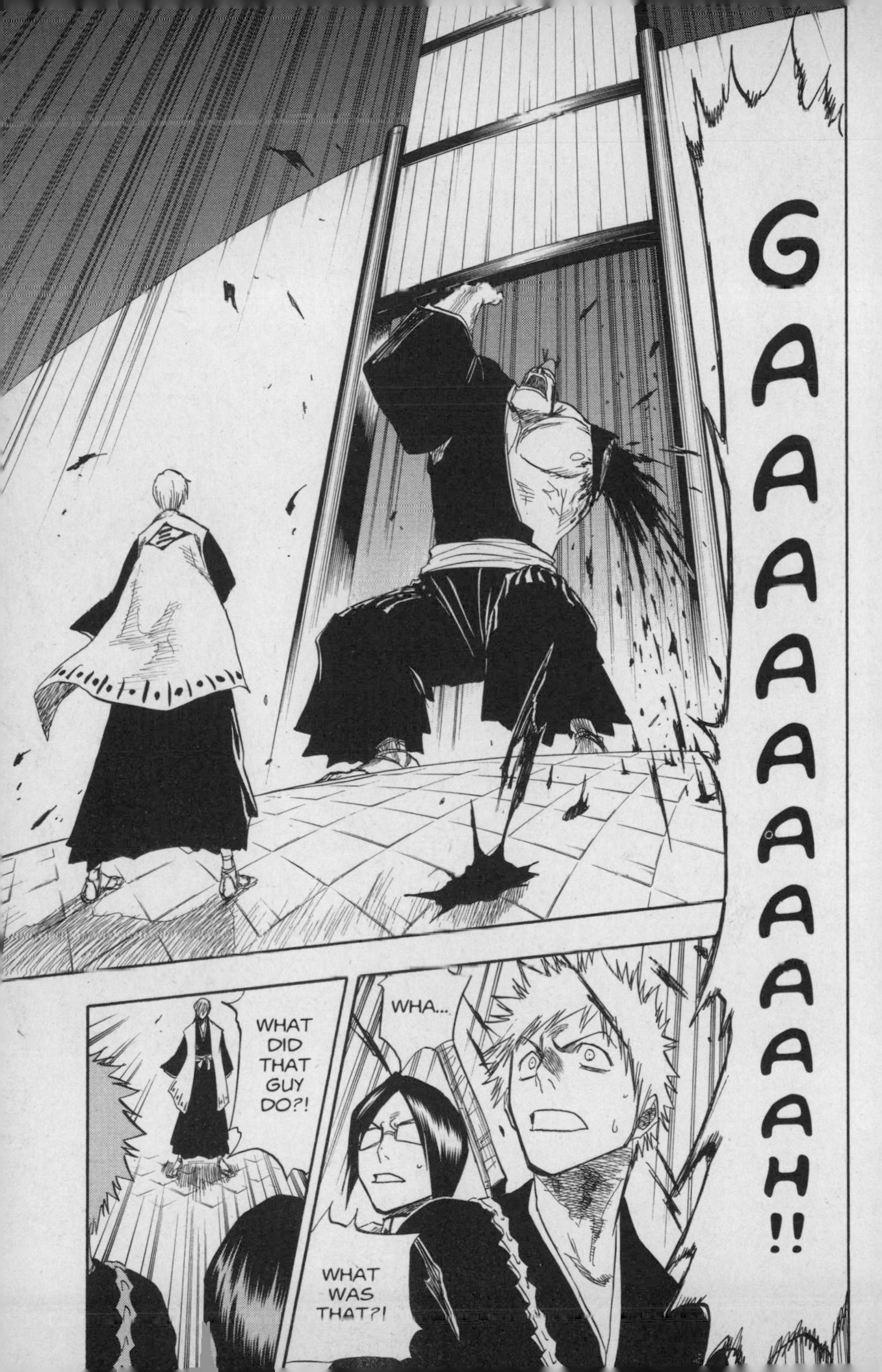
GAAAAAAAAH!!
WHA...
WHAT WAS THAT?!
WHAT DID THAT GUY DO?!

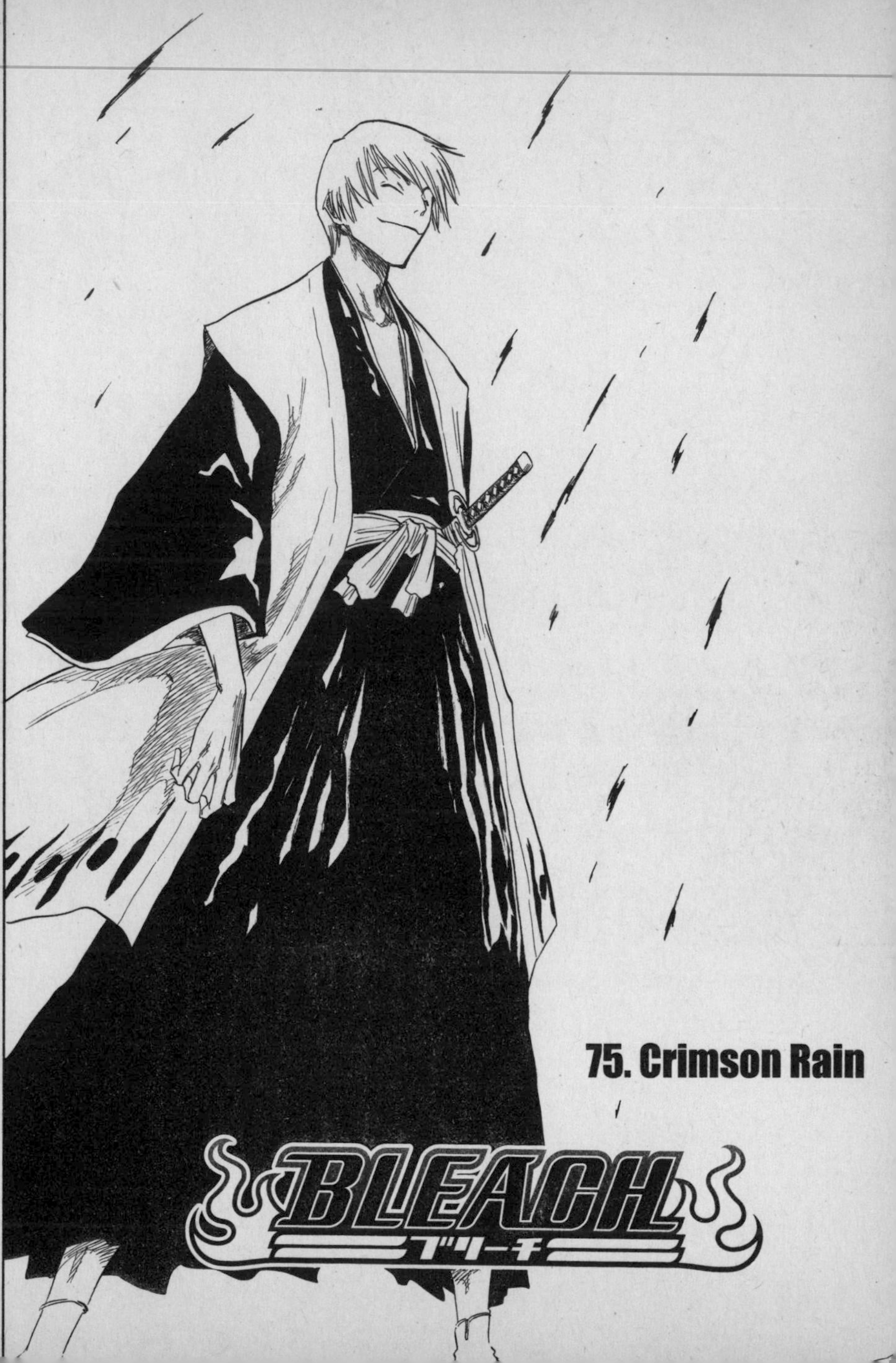
75. Crimson Rain
BLEACH
ブリーチ

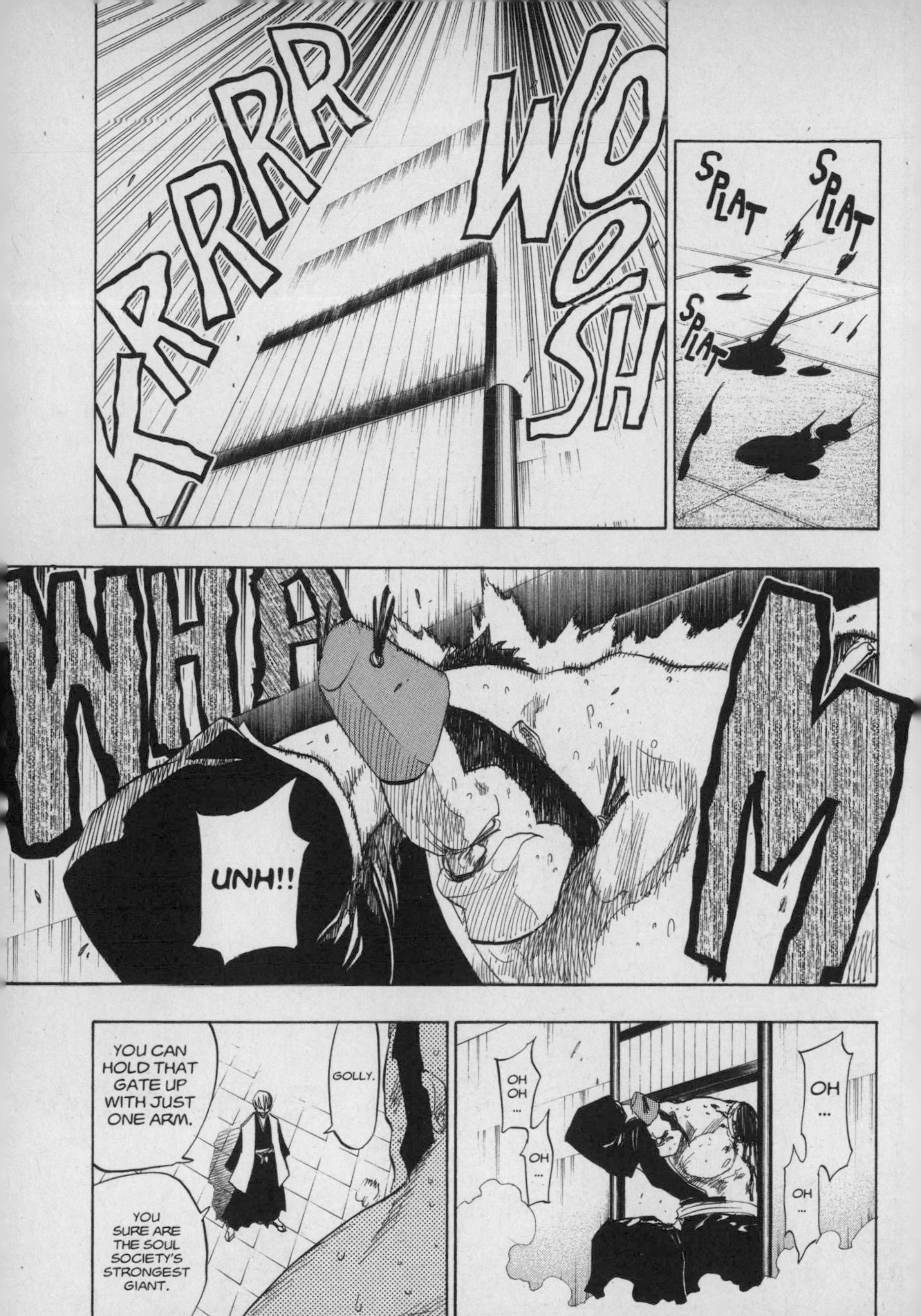
SPLAT
SPLAT
SPLAT
KRRRR
WOOSH
WHAM
UNH!!
OH ...
OH ...
OH OH ...
OH ...
GOLLY.
YOU CAN HOLD THAT GATE UP WITH JUST ONE ARM.
YOU SURE ARE THE SOUL SOCIETY'S STRONGEST GIANT.

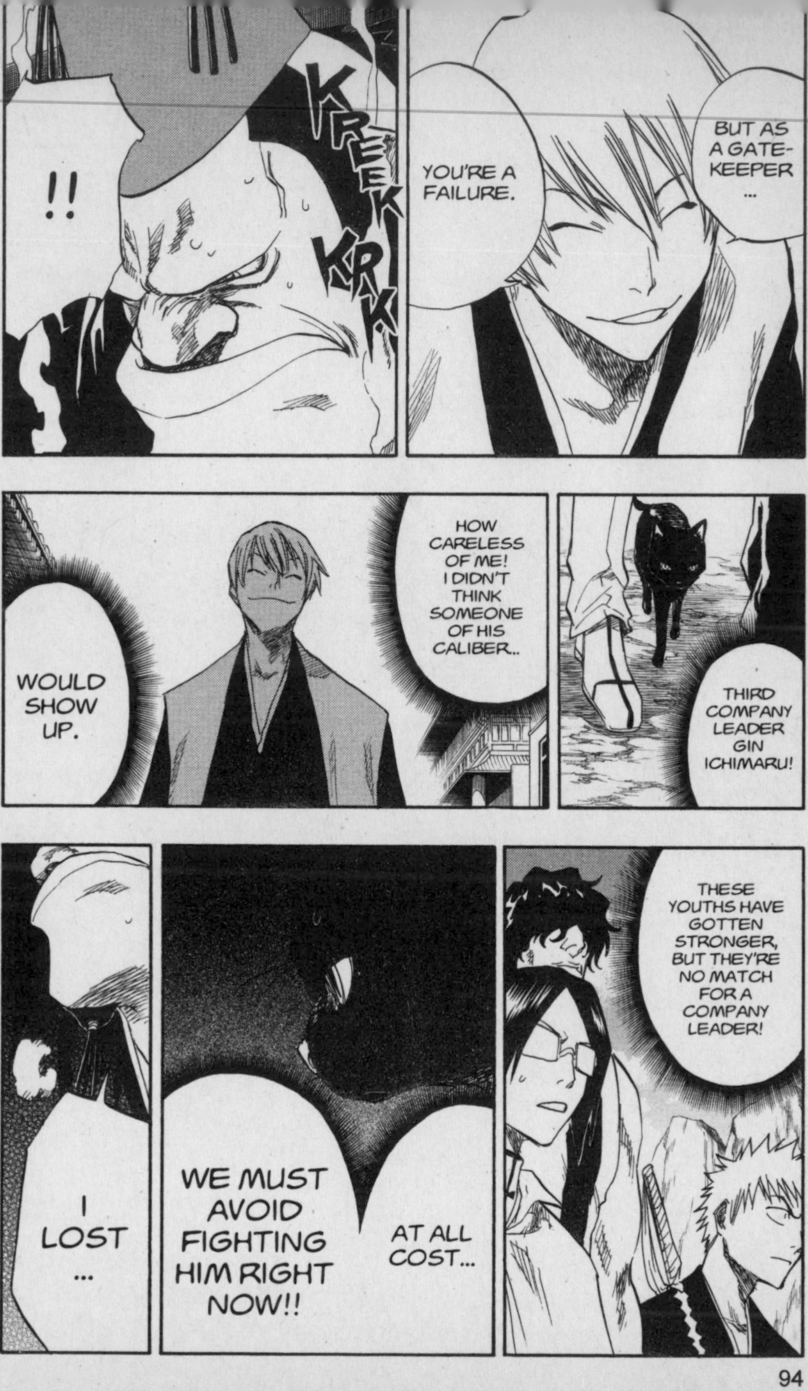
BUT AS A GATE-KEEPER ...
YOU'RE A FAILURE.
KREEK
KRK
!!
THIRD COMPANY LEADER GIN ICHIMARU!
HOW CARELESS OF ME! I DIDN'T THINK SOMEONE OF HIS CALIBER...
WOULD SHOW UP.
THESE YOUTHS HAVE GOTTEN STRONGER, BUT THEY'RE NO MATCH FOR A COMPANY LEADER!
AT ALL COST...
WE MUST AVOID FIGHTING HIM RIGHT NOW!!
I LOST ...

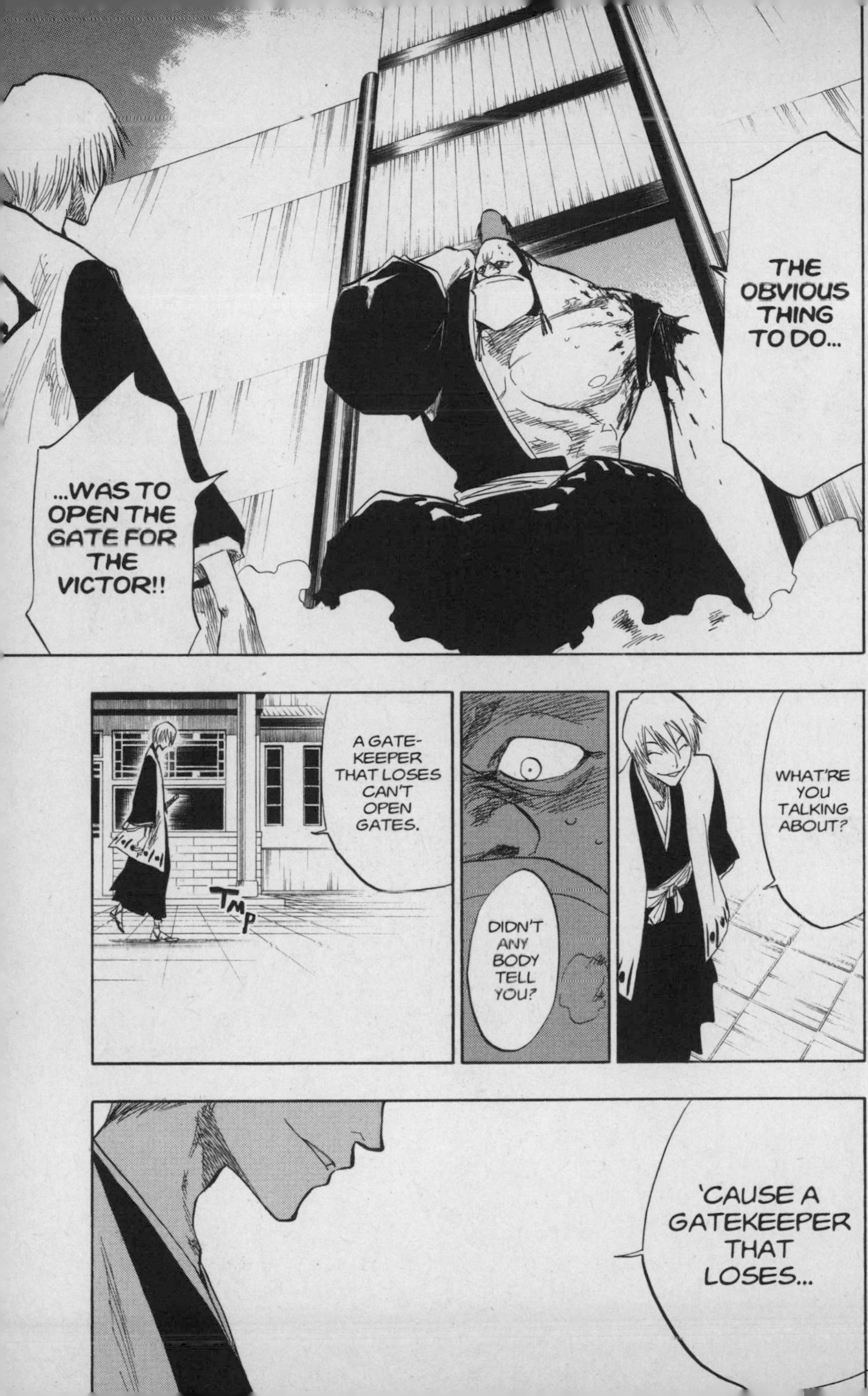
THE OBVIOUS THING TO DO...
...WAS TO OPEN THE GATE FOR THE VICTOR!!
WHAT'RE YOU TALKING ABOUT?
DIDN'T ANY BODY TELL YOU?
A GATE-KEEPER THAT LOSES CAN'T OPEN GATES.
TMP
'CAUSE A GATEKEEPER THAT LOSES...

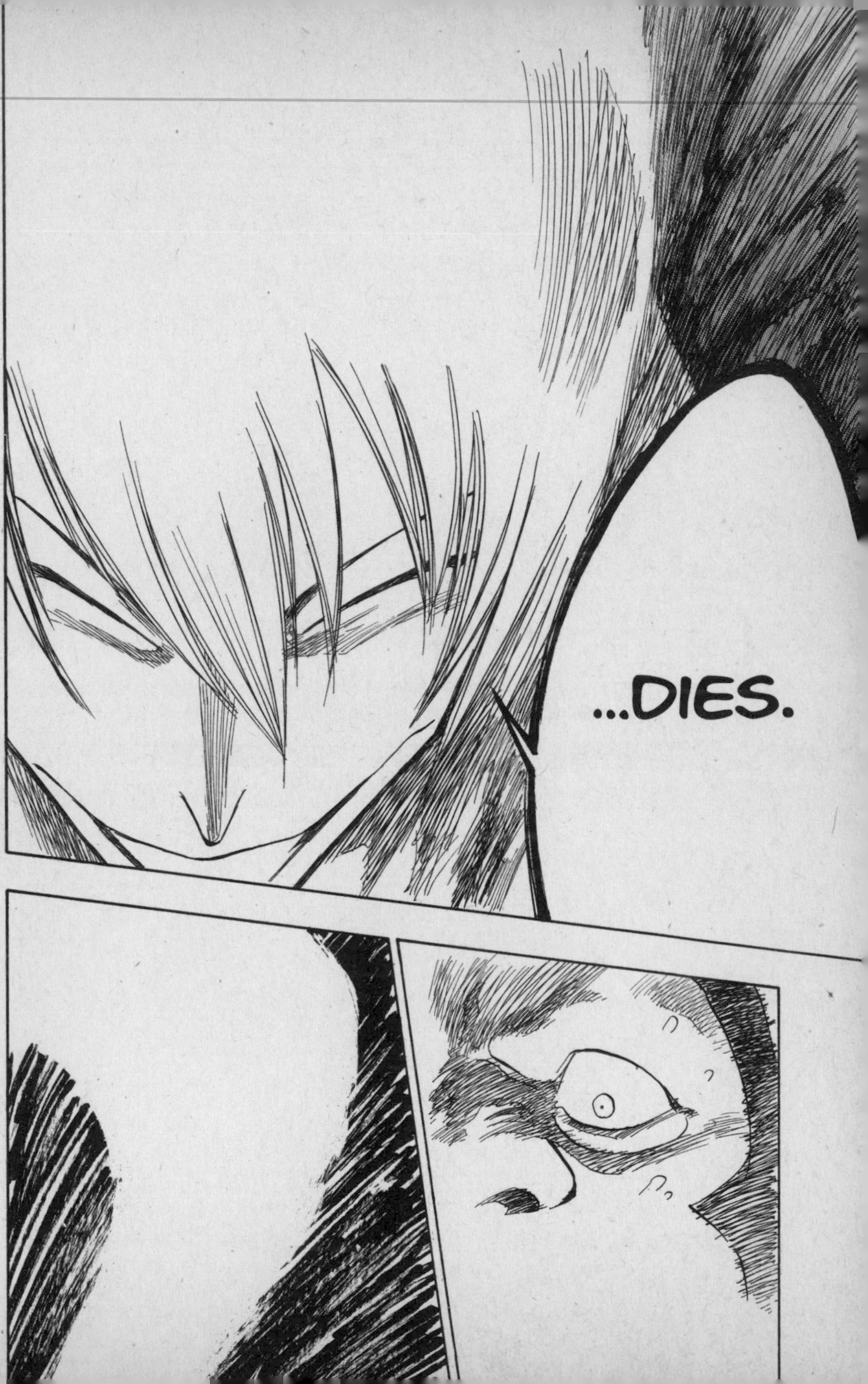
...DIES.

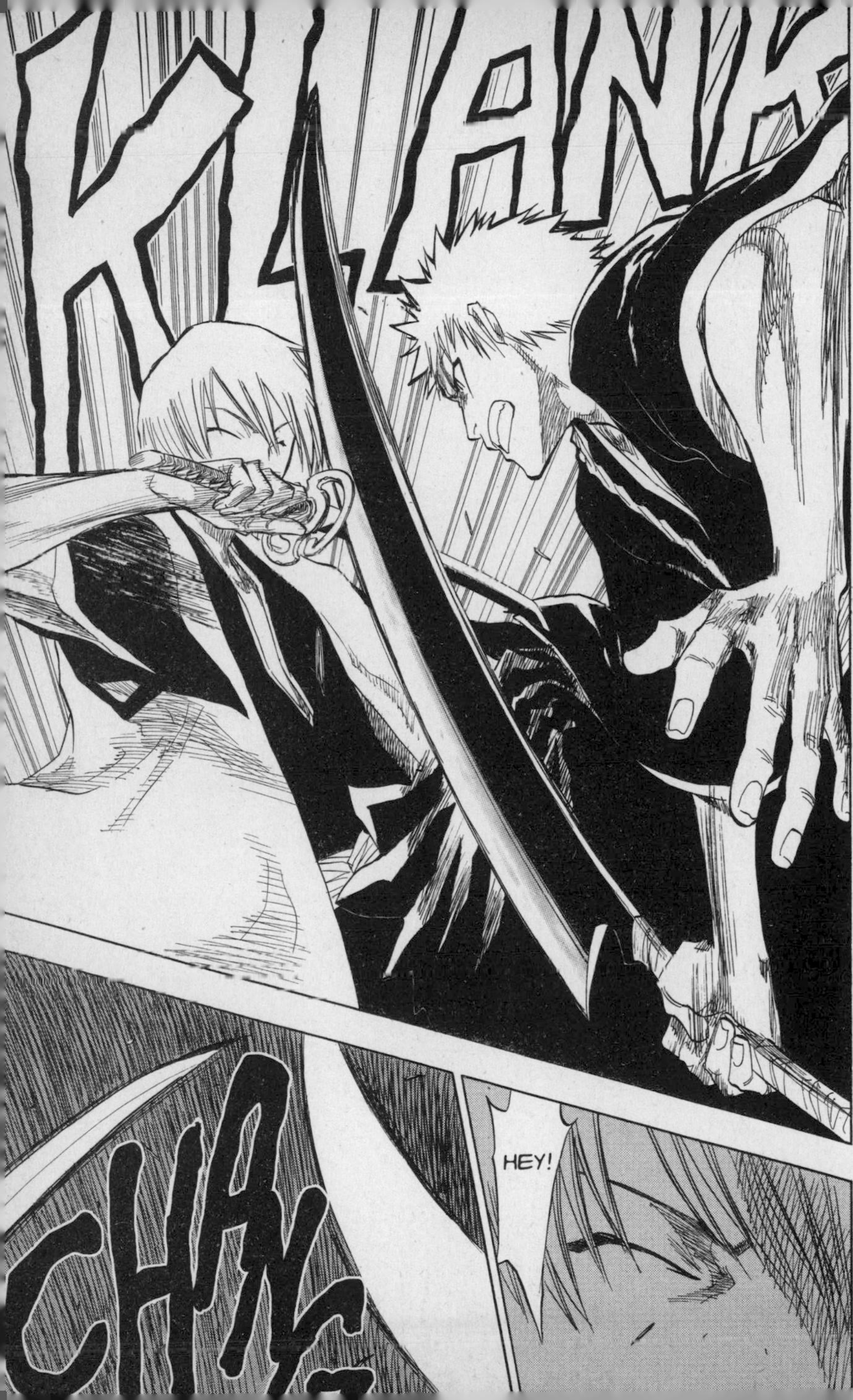
HEY!

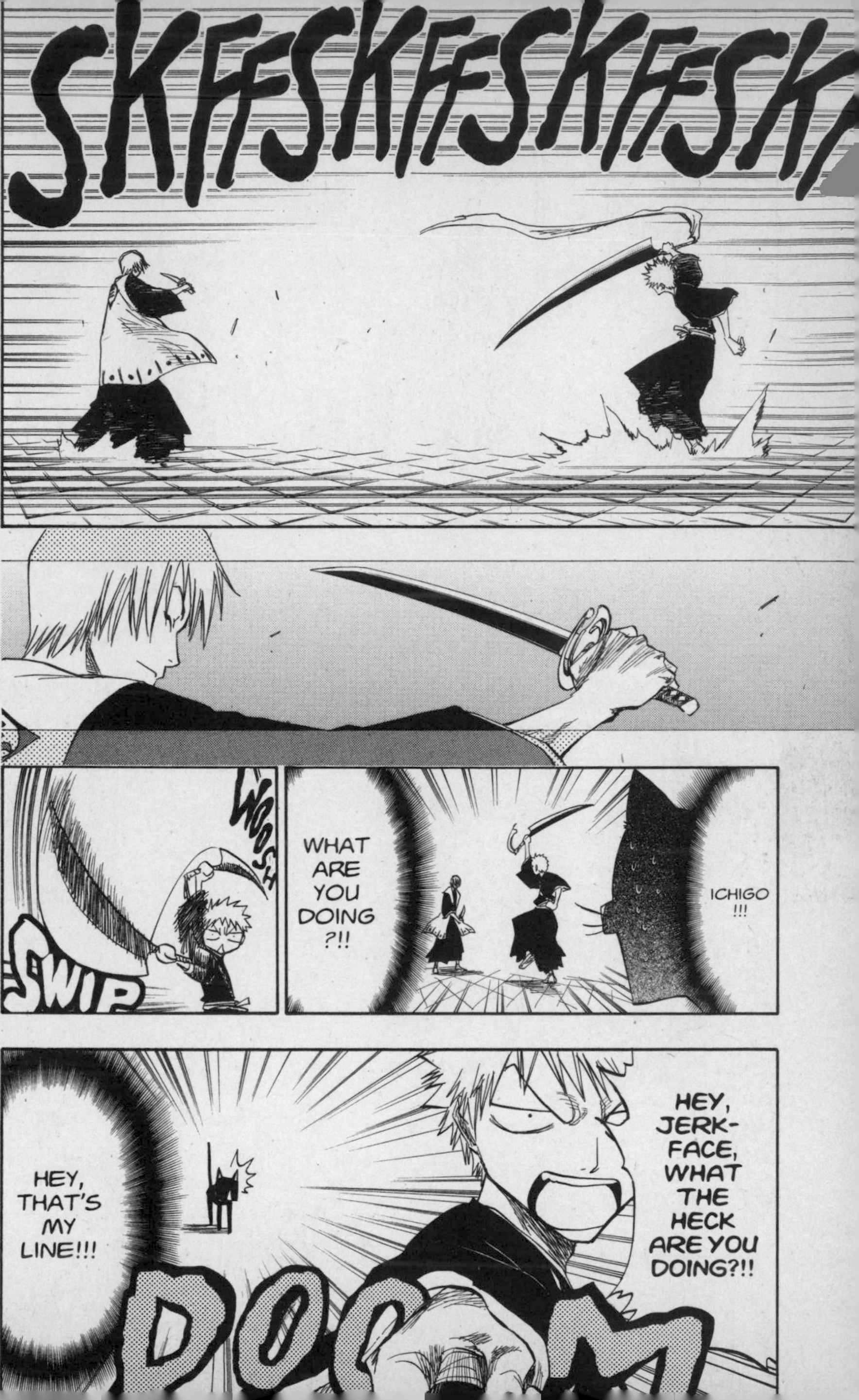
SKFFSKFFSKFFSKF
ICHIGO!!!
WHAT ARE YOU DOING?!!
WOOSH
SWIP
HEY, JERK-FACE, WHAT THE HECK ARE YOU DOING?!!
HEY, THAT'S MY LINE!!!
DOOM

READ THIS WAY

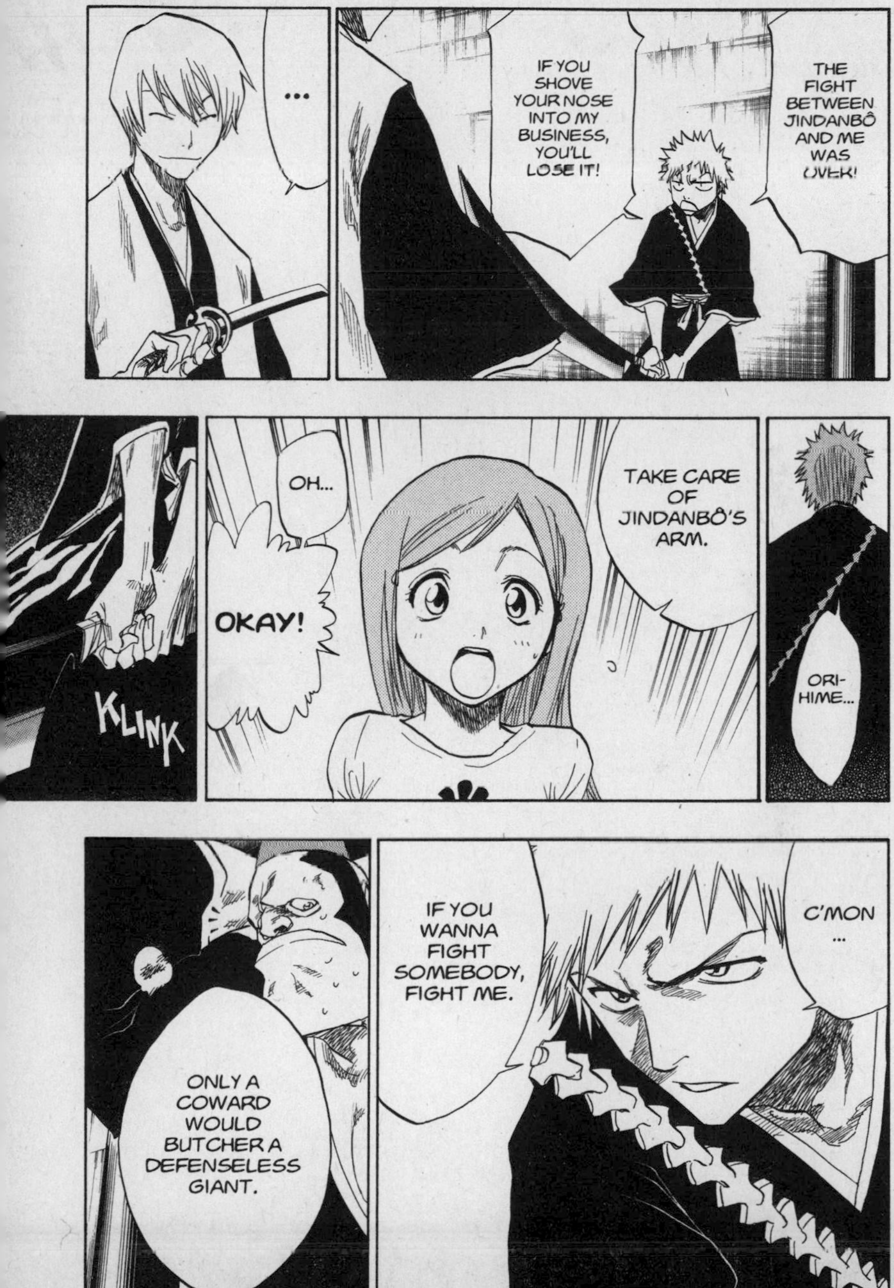
THE FIGHT BETWEEN JINDANBÔ AND ME WAS OVER!
IF YOU SHOVE YOUR NOSE INTO MY BUSINESS, YOU'LL LOSE IT!
...
ORI-HIME...
TAKE CARE OF JINDANBÔ'S ARM.
OH...
OKAY!
KLINK
C'MON ...
IF YOU WANNA FIGHT SOMEBODY, FIGHT ME.
ONLY A COWARD WOULD BUTCHER A DEFENSELESS GIANT.

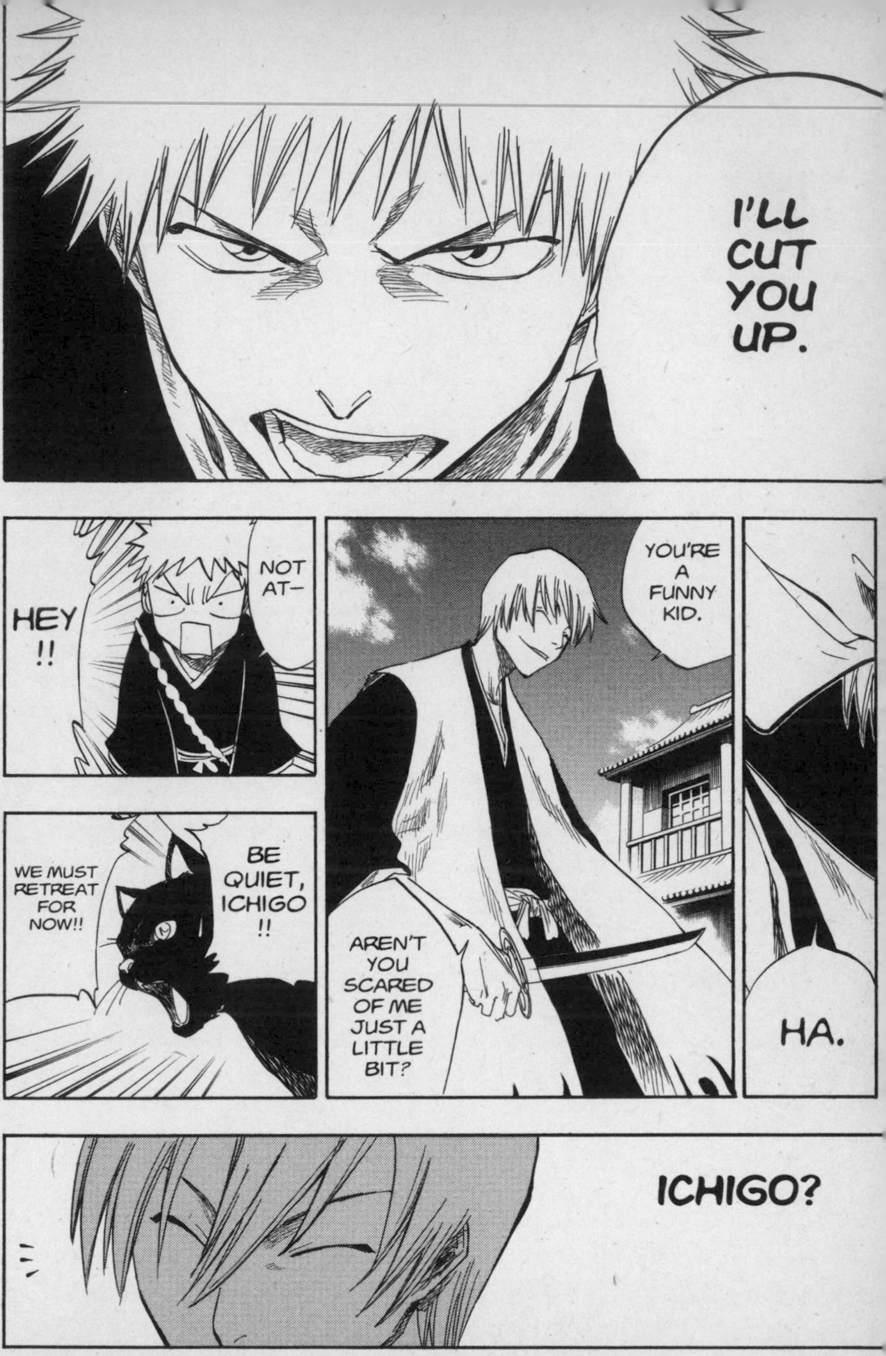
I'LL CUT YOU UP.
HA.
YOU'RE A FUNNY KID.
AREN'T YOU SCARED OF ME JUST A LITTLE BIT?
NOT AT—
HEY!!
BE QUIET, ICHIGO!!
WE MUST RETREAT FOR NOW!!
ICHIGO?

READ THIS WAY

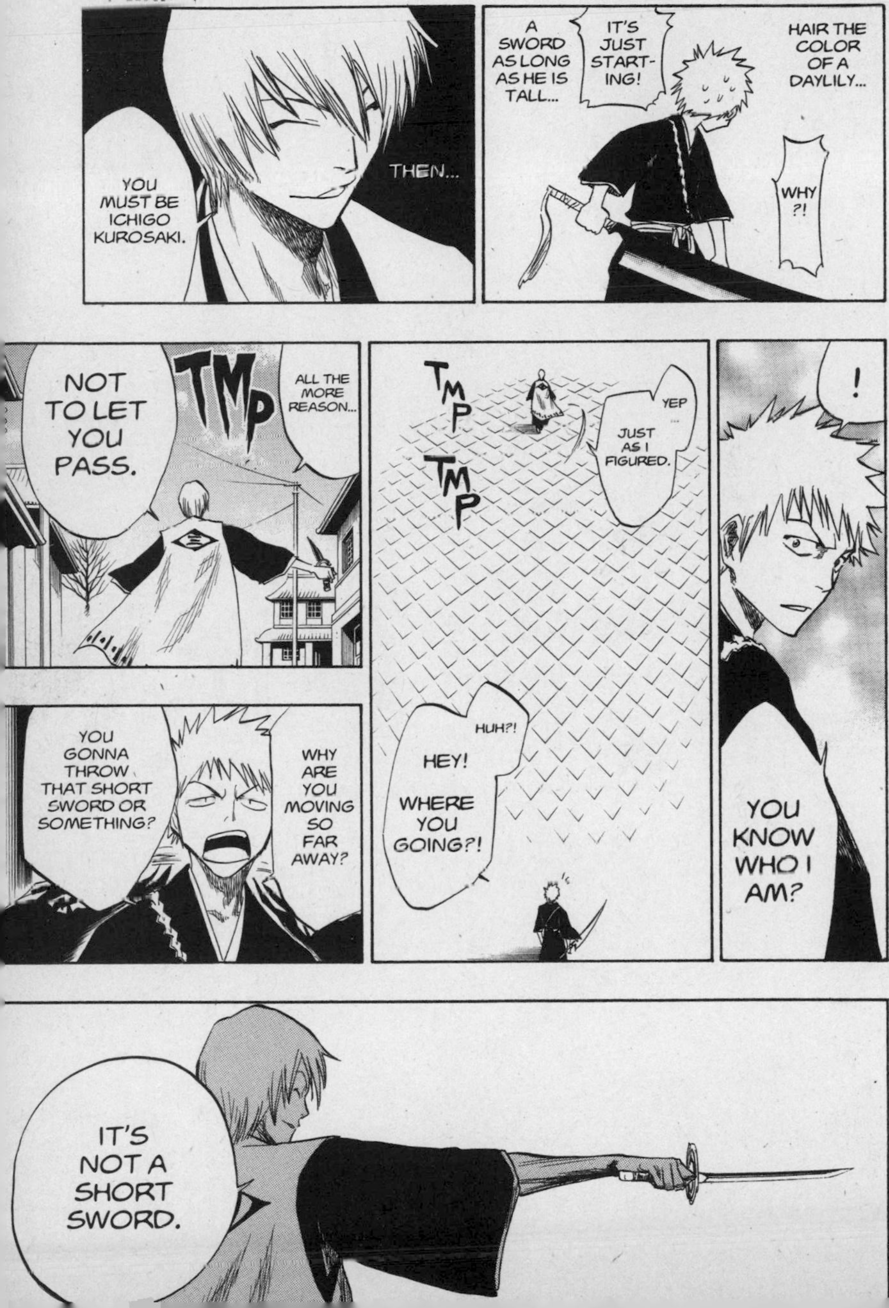
HAIR THE COLOR OF A DAYLILY...
IT'S JUST STARTING!
A SWORD AS LONG AS HE IS TALL...
WHY?!
THEN...
YOU MUST BE ICHIGO KUROSAKI.
!
YOU KNOW WHO I AM?
TMP
TMP
YEP... JUST AS I FIGURED.
HUH?!
HEY! WHERE YOU GOING?!
ALL THE MORE REASON...
TMP
NOT TO LET YOU PASS.
WHY ARE YOU MOVING SO FAR AWAY?
YOU GONNA THROW THAT SHORT SWORD OR SOMETHING?
IT'S NOT A SHORT SWORD.

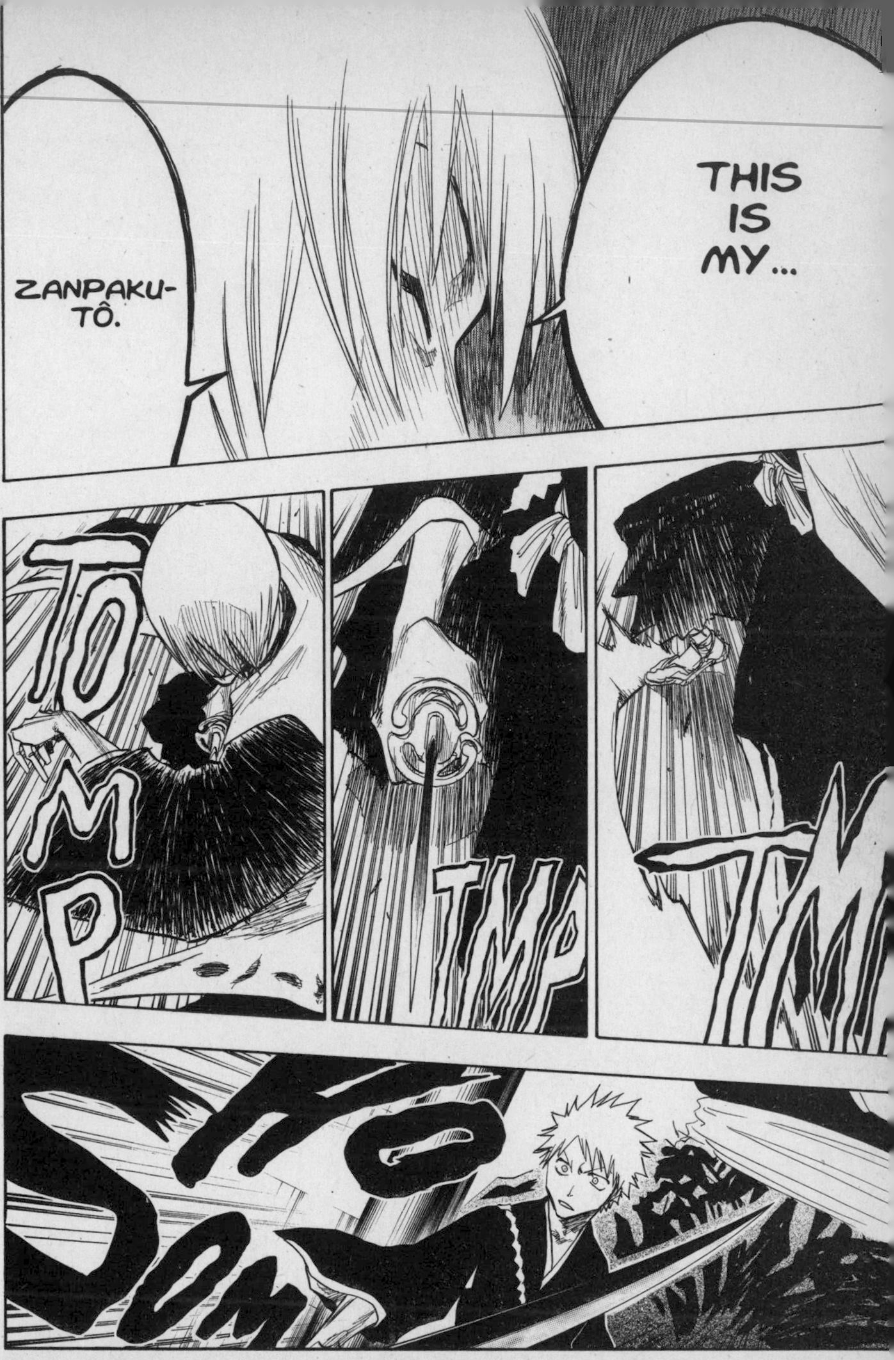
THIS IS MY...
ZANPAKU-TÔ.
TMP
TOMP

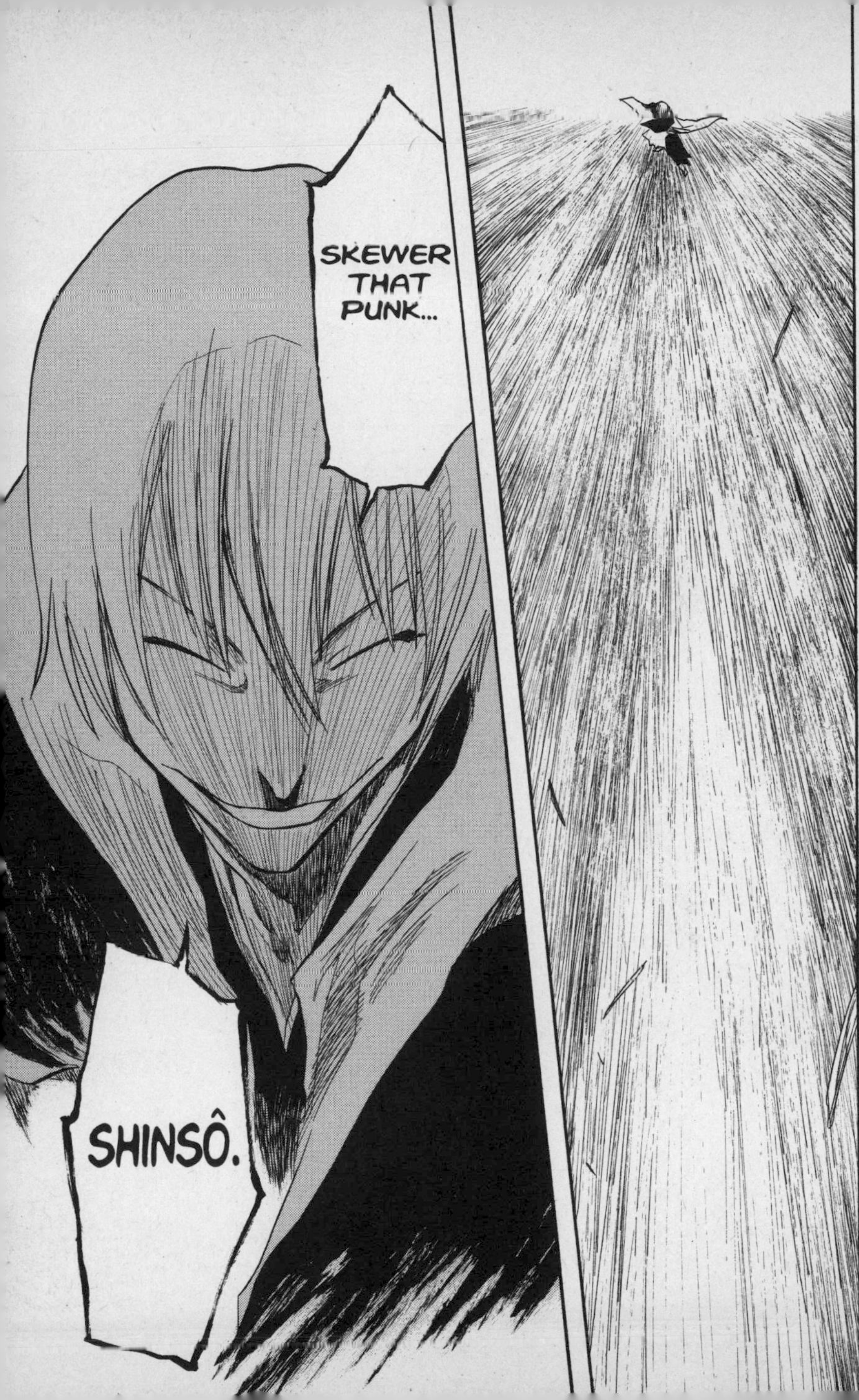
SKEWER THAT PUNK...
SHINSÔ.

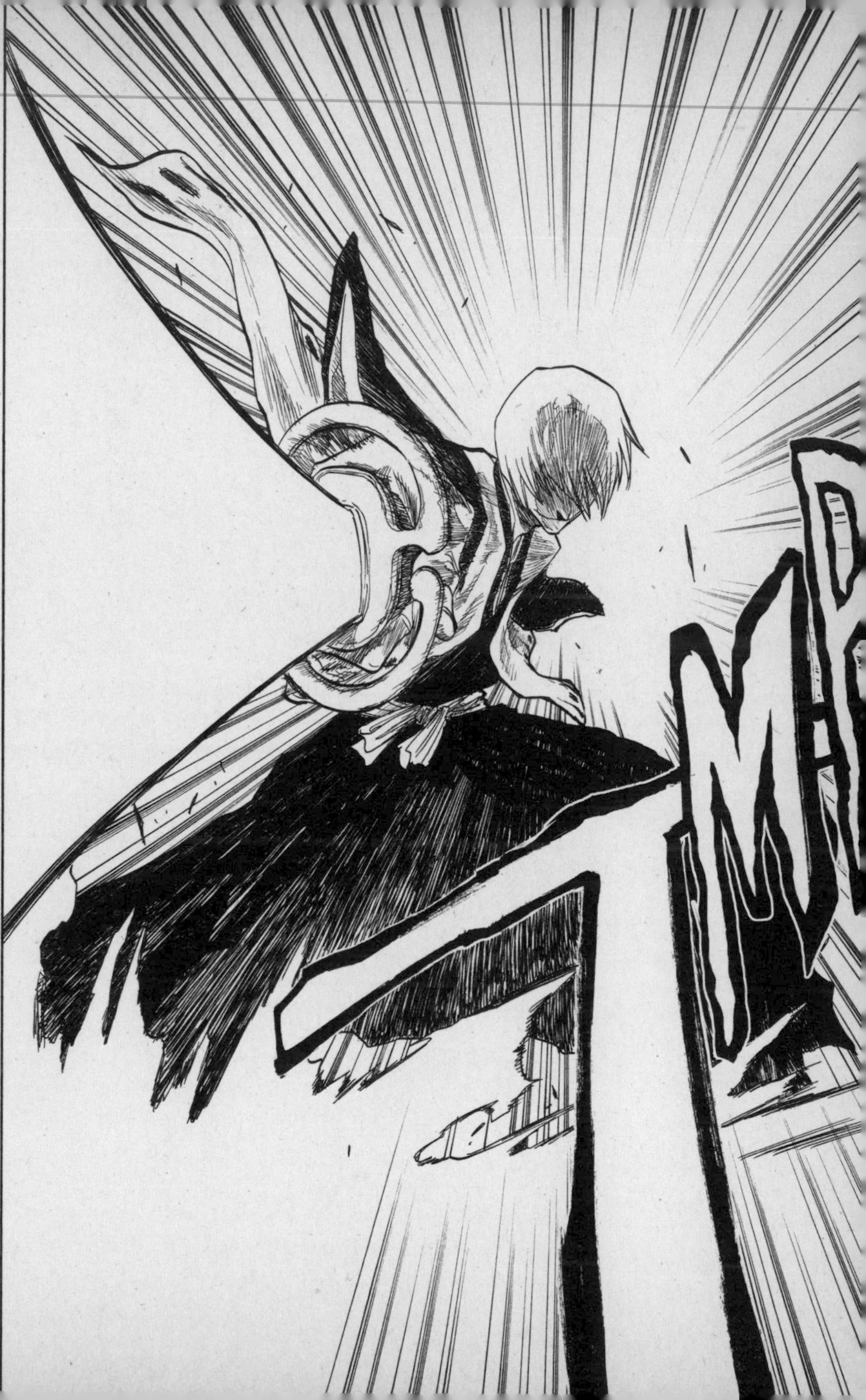

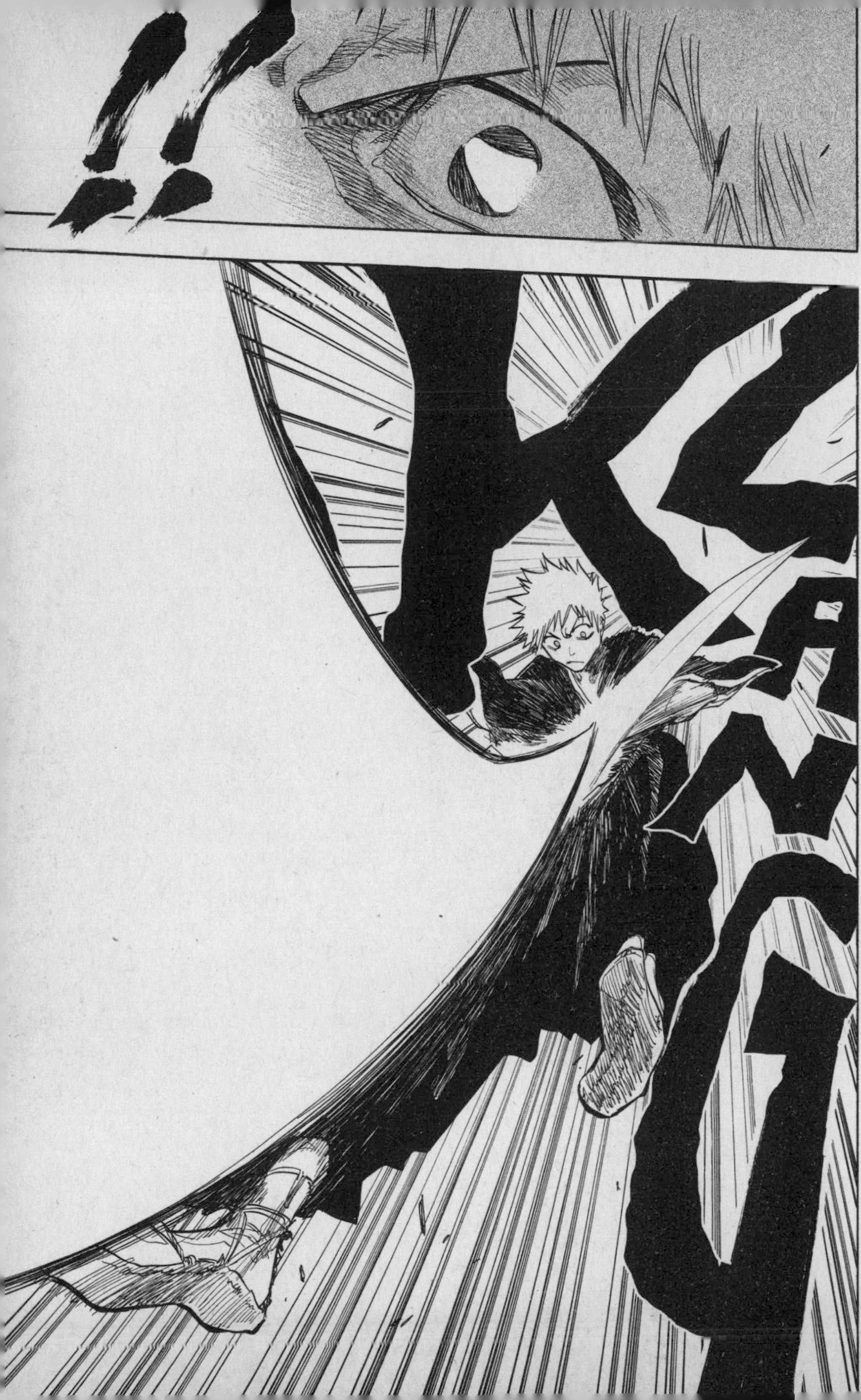
!!

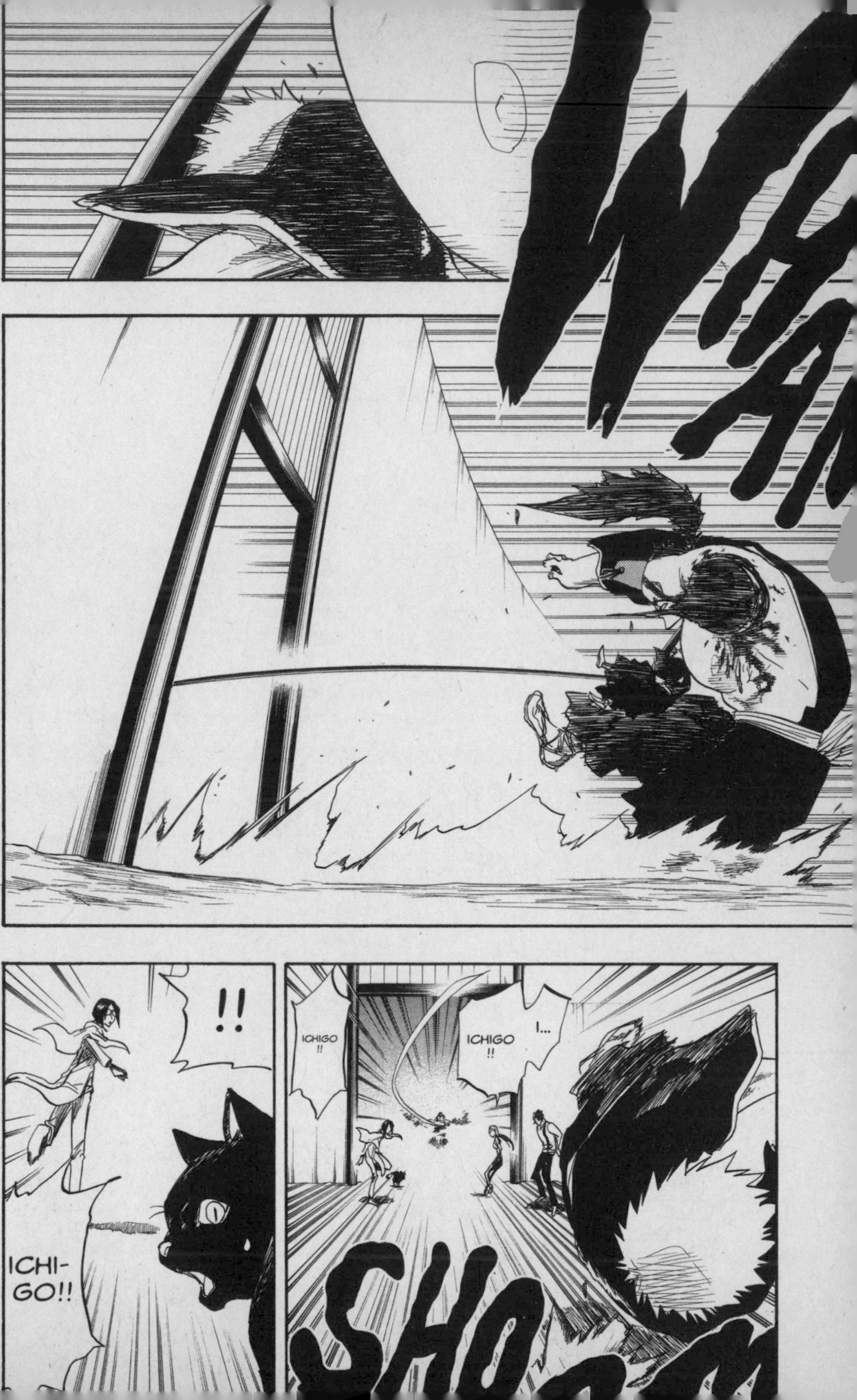
I...
ICHIGO!!
ICHIGO!!
!!
ICHI-GO!!

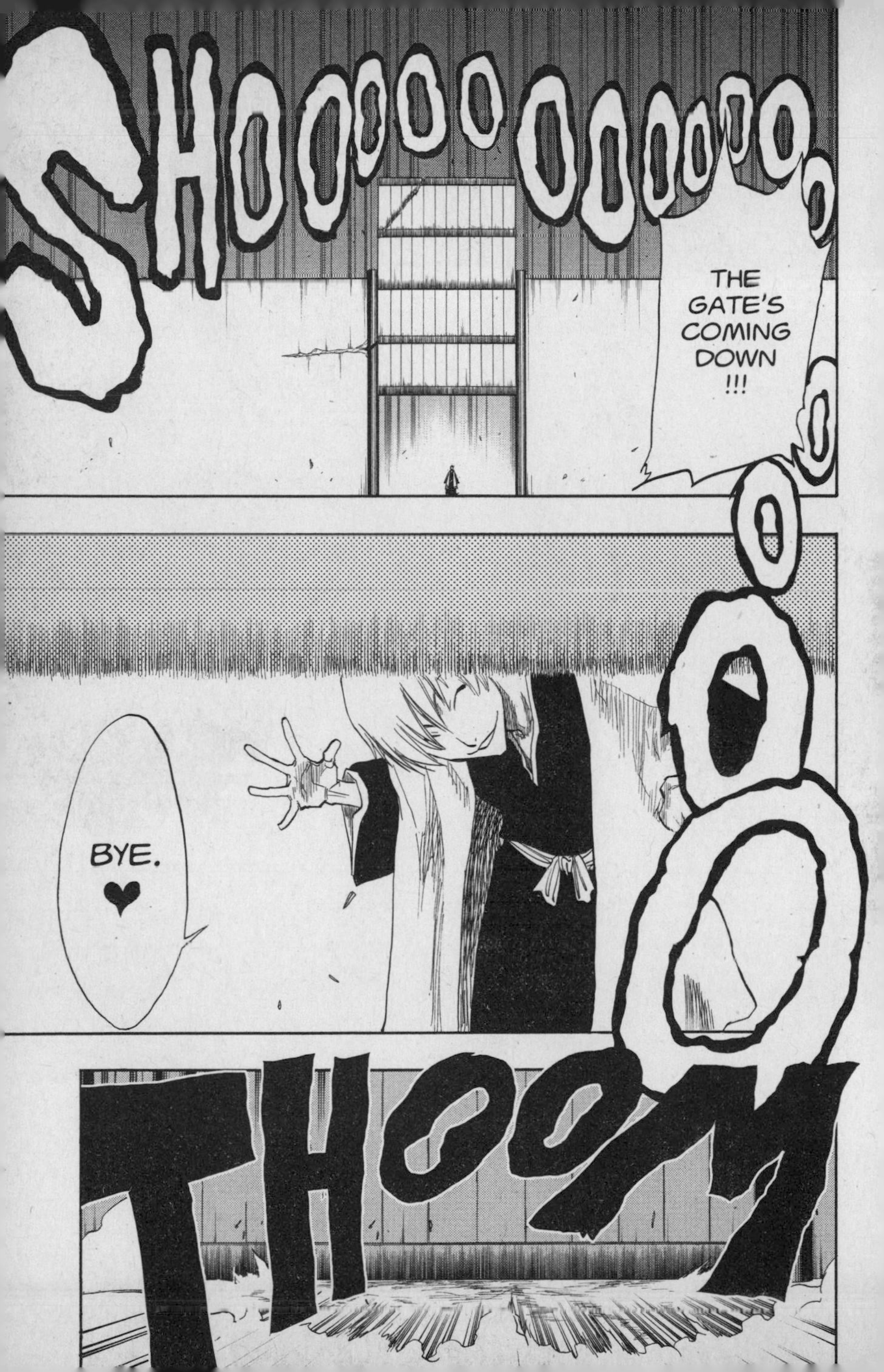
THE GATE'S COMING DOWN!!!
SHOOOOOOOOOOOOO
BYE. ♥
THOOOM

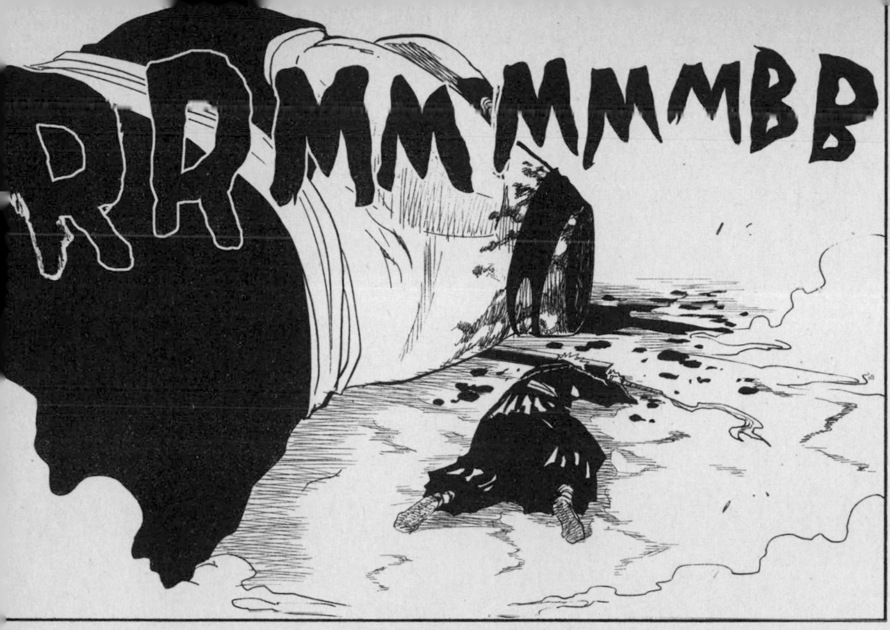
RRMMMMMMBB

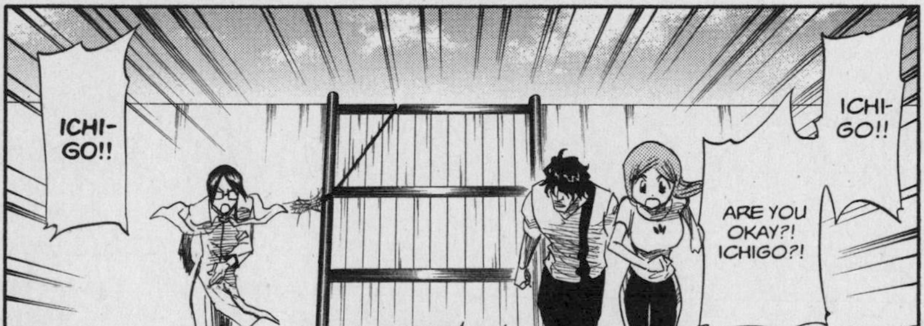
ICHI-GO!!
ARE YOU OKAY?! ICHIGO?!
ICHI-GO!!

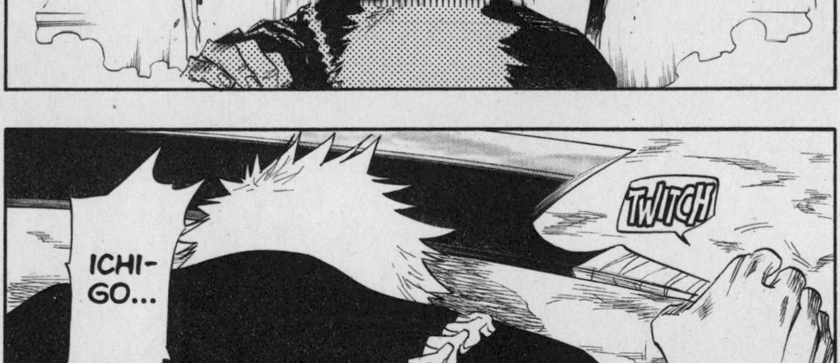
TWITCH
ICHI-GO...

76. Boarrider Comin'

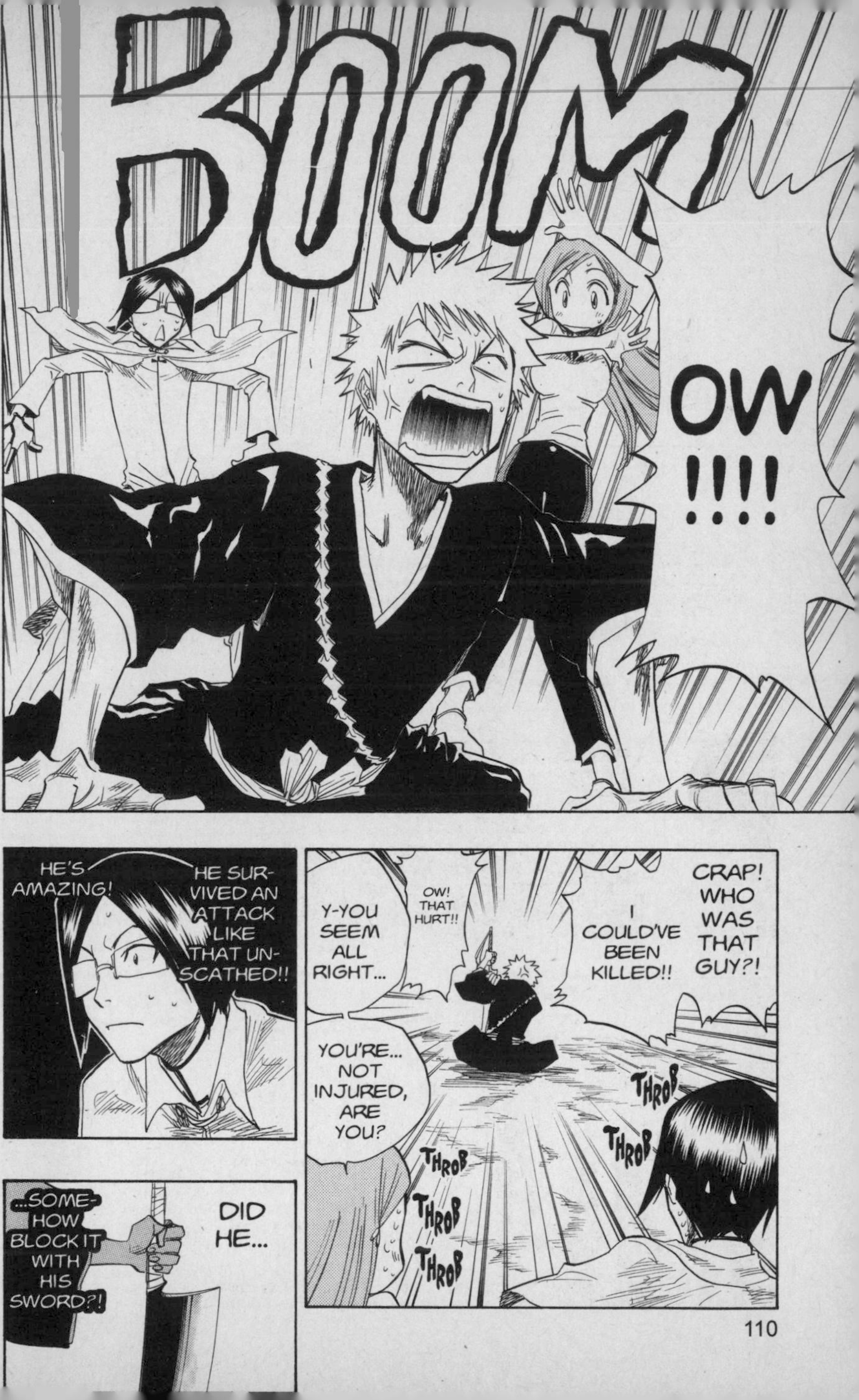
BOOM
OW!!!!
CRAP! WHO WAS THAT GUY?!
I COULD'VE BEEN KILLED!!
OW! THAT HURT!!
Y-YOU SEEM ALL RIGHT...
YOU'RE... NOT INJURED, ARE YOU?
THROB
THROB
THROB
THROB
THROB
HE SUR-VIVED AN ATTACK LIKE THAT UN-SCATHED!!
HE'S AMAZING!
DID HE...
...SOME-HOW BLOCK IT WITH HIS SWORD?!

READ THIS WAY

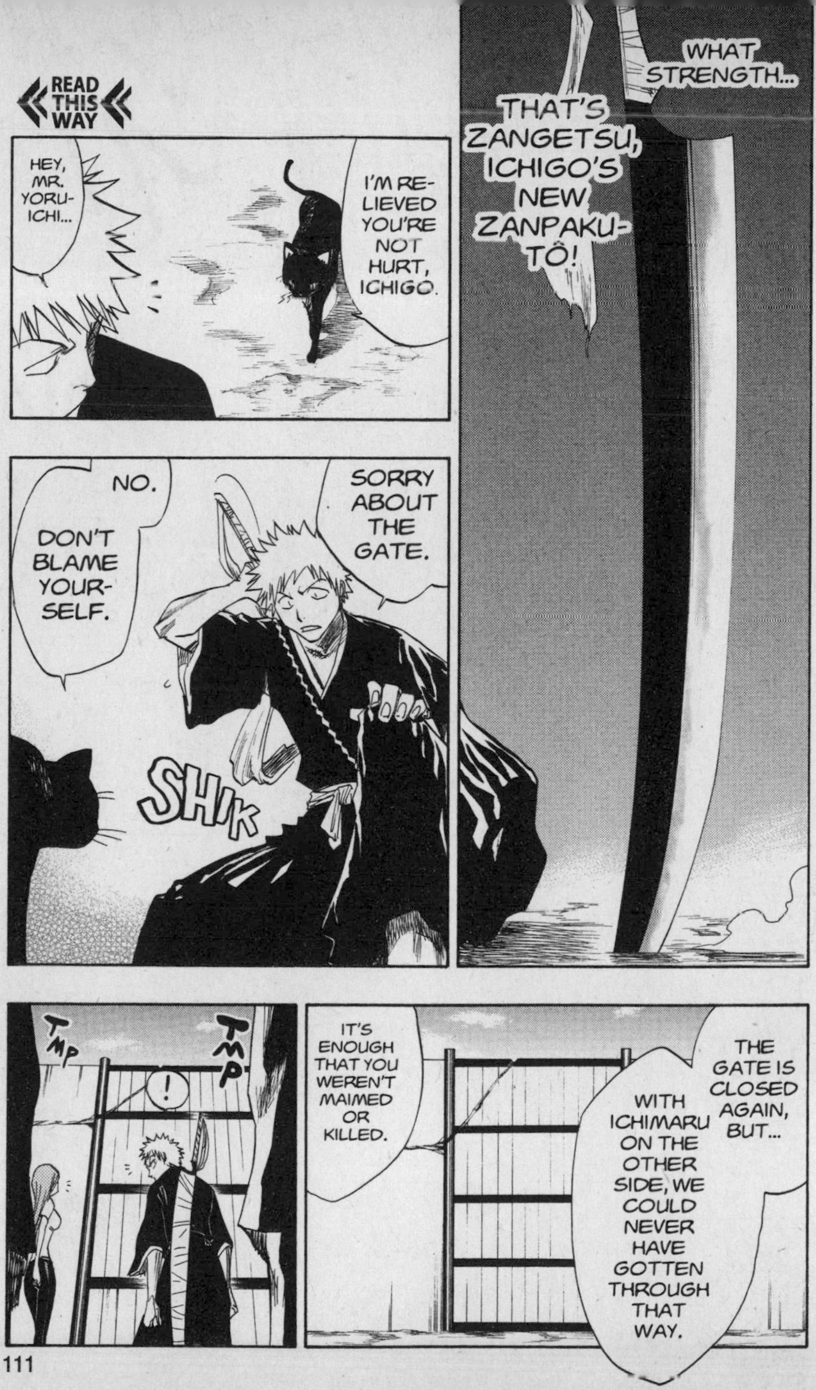
WHAT STRENGTH...
THAT'S ZANGETSU, ICHIGO'S NEW ZANPAKU-TÔ!
I'M RE-LIEVED YOU'RE NOT HURT, ICHIGO.
HEY, MR. YORU-ICHI...
SORRY ABOUT THE GATE.
NO.
DON'T BLAME YOUR-SELF.
SHIK
THE GATE IS CLOSED AGAIN, BUT...
WITH ICHIMARU ON THE OTHER SIDE, WE COULD NEVER HAVE GOTTEN THROUGH THAT WAY.
IT'S ENOUGH THAT YOU WEREN'T MAIMED OR KILLED.
TMP
TMP
!

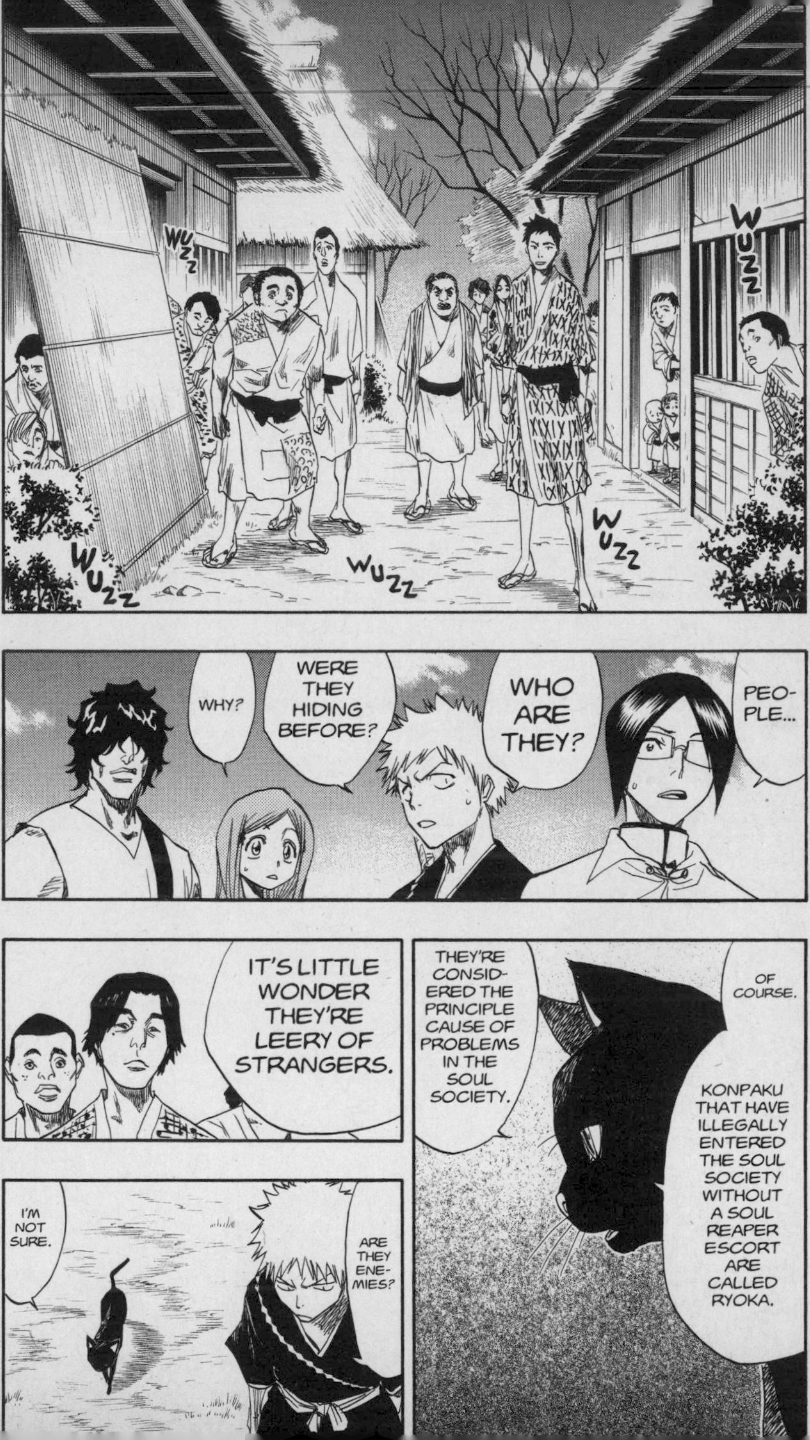
WUZZ
WUZZ
WUZZ
WUZZ
WUZZ
PEO-PLE...
WHO ARE THEY?
WERE THEY HIDING BEFORE?
WHY?
OF COURSE.
KONPAKU THAT HAVE ILLEGALLY ENTERED THE SOUL SOCIETY WITHOUT A SOUL REAPER ESCORT ARE CALLED RYOKA.
THEY'RE CONSIDERED THE PRINCIPLE CAUSE OF PROBLEMS IN THE SOUL SOCIETY.
IT'S LITTLE WONDER THEY'RE LEERY OF STRANGERS.
ARE THEY ENEMIES?
I'M NOT SURE.

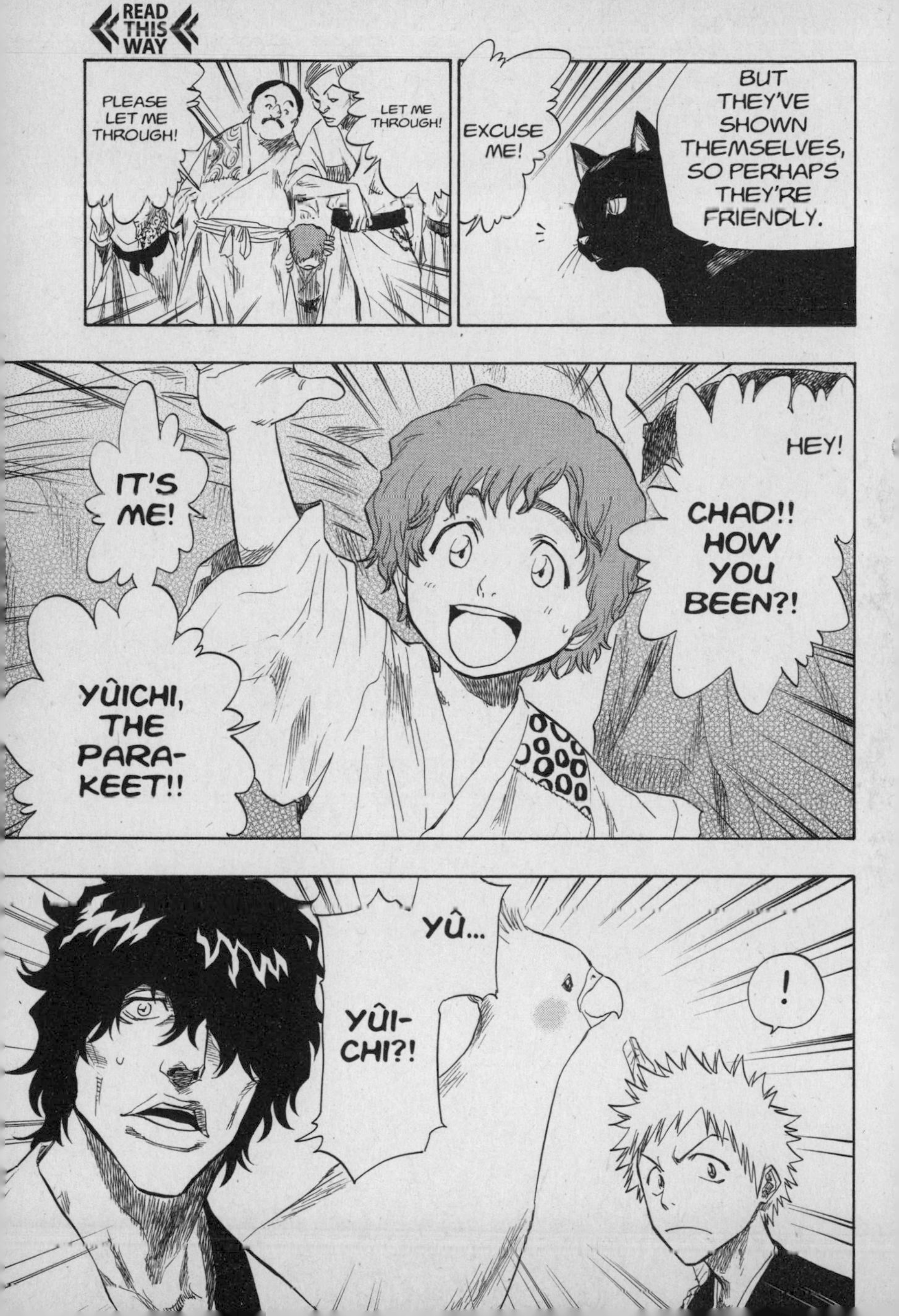
READ THIS WAY
BUT THEY'VE SHOWN THEMSELVES, SO PERHAPS THEY'RE FRIENDLY.
EXCUSE ME!
LET ME THROUGH!
PLEASE LET ME THROUGH!
HEY!
CHAD!! HOW YOU BEEN?!
IT'S ME!
YÛICHI, THE PARA-KEET!!
!
YÛ...
YÛI-CHI?!

76. Boarrider Comin'

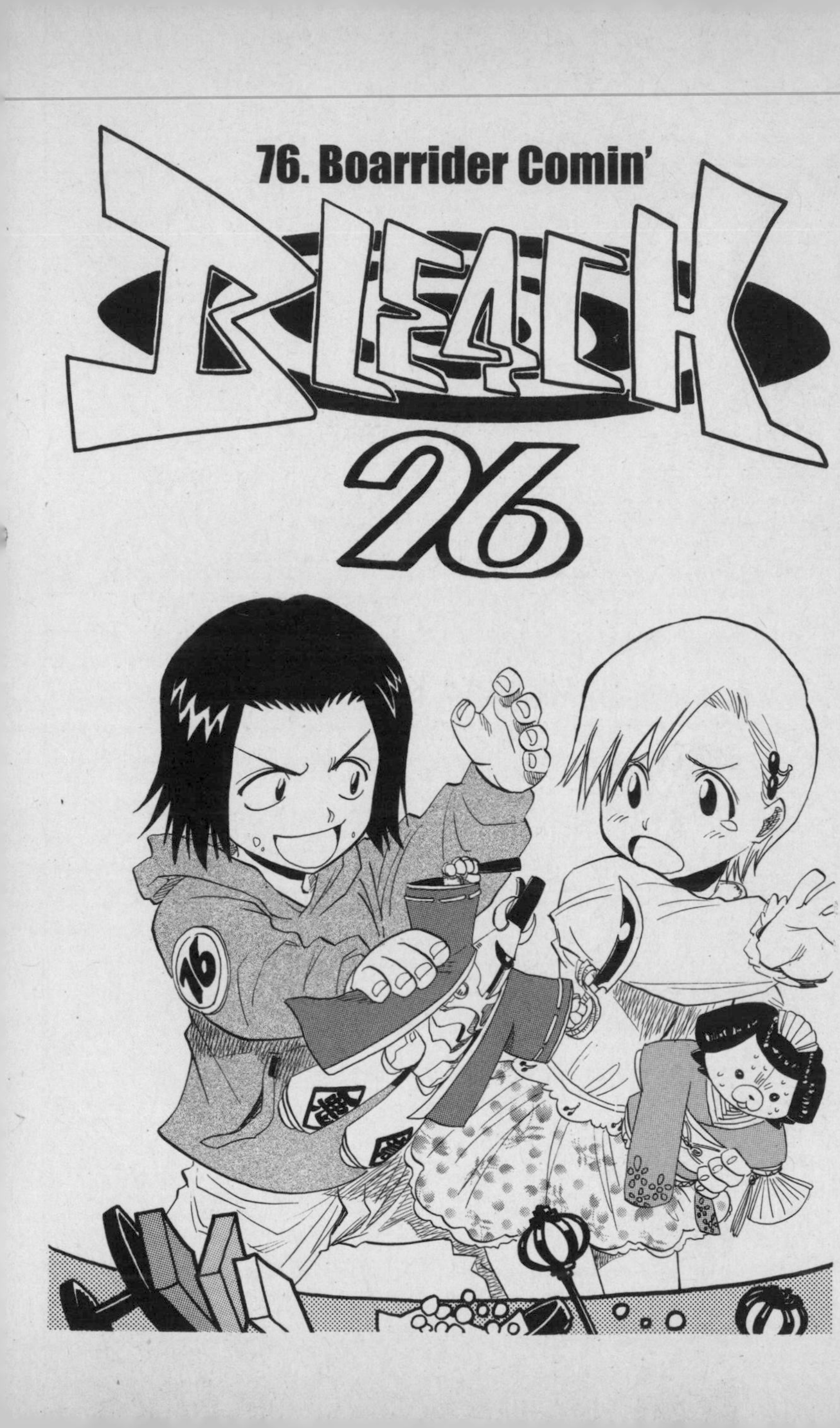

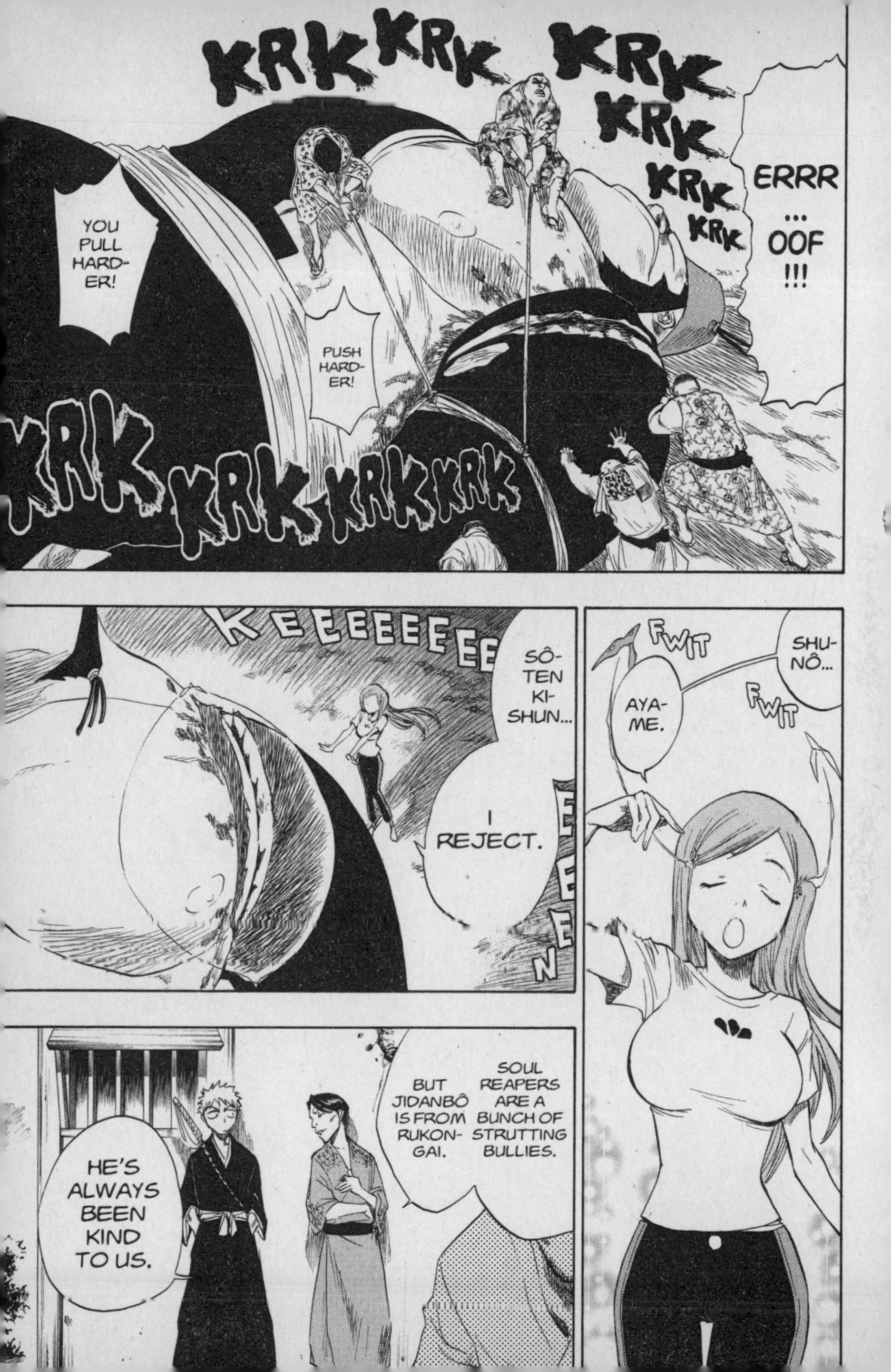
KRKKRK KRK
KRK
KRK
KRK
ERRR ... OOF !!!
YOU PULL HARDER!
PUSH HARDER!
KRK KRK KRKKRK
FWIT
SHUNÔ...
AYAME.
FWIT
KEEEEEEEEEEEEN
SÔTEN KISHUN...
I REJECT.
SOUL REAPERS ARE A BUNCH OF STRUTTING BULLIES.
BUT JIDANBÔ IS FROM RUKONGAI.
HE'S ALWAYS BEEN KIND TO US.

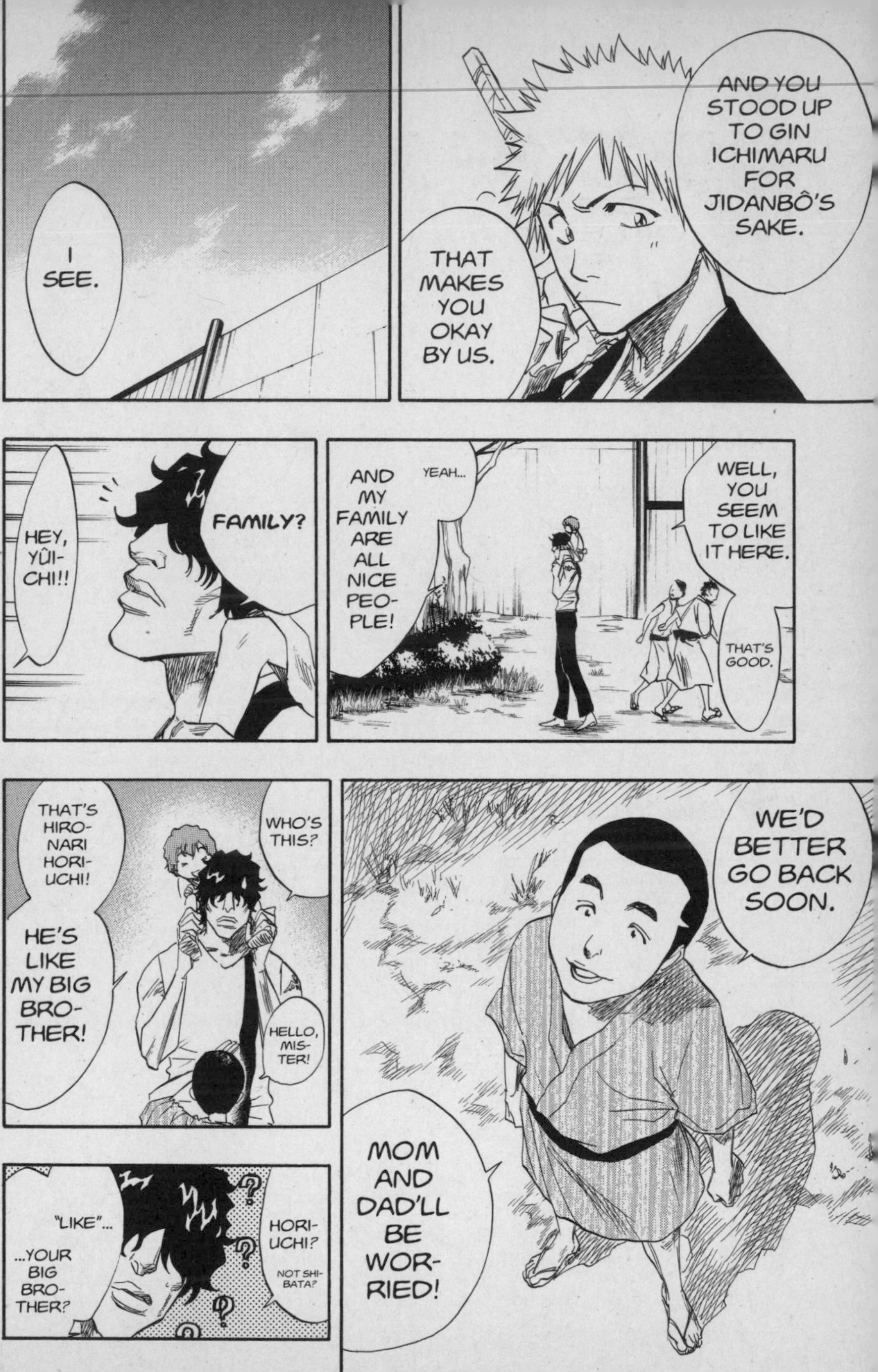
AND YOU STOOD UP TO GIN ICHIMARU FOR JIDANBÔ'S SAKE.
THAT MAKES YOU OKAY BY US.
I SEE.
WELL, YOU SEEM TO LIKE IT HERE.
THAT'S GOOD.
YEAH...
AND MY FAMILY ARE ALL NICE PEOPLE!
FAMILY?
HEY, YÛICHI!!
WE'D BETTER GO BACK SOON.
MOM AND DAD'LL BE WORRIED!
WHO'S THIS?
THAT'S HIRONARI HORIUCHI!
HE'S LIKE MY BIG BROTHER!
HELLO, MISTER!
HORIUCHI?
NOT SHIBATA?
"LIKE"...
...YOUR BIG BROTHER?

READ THIS WAY

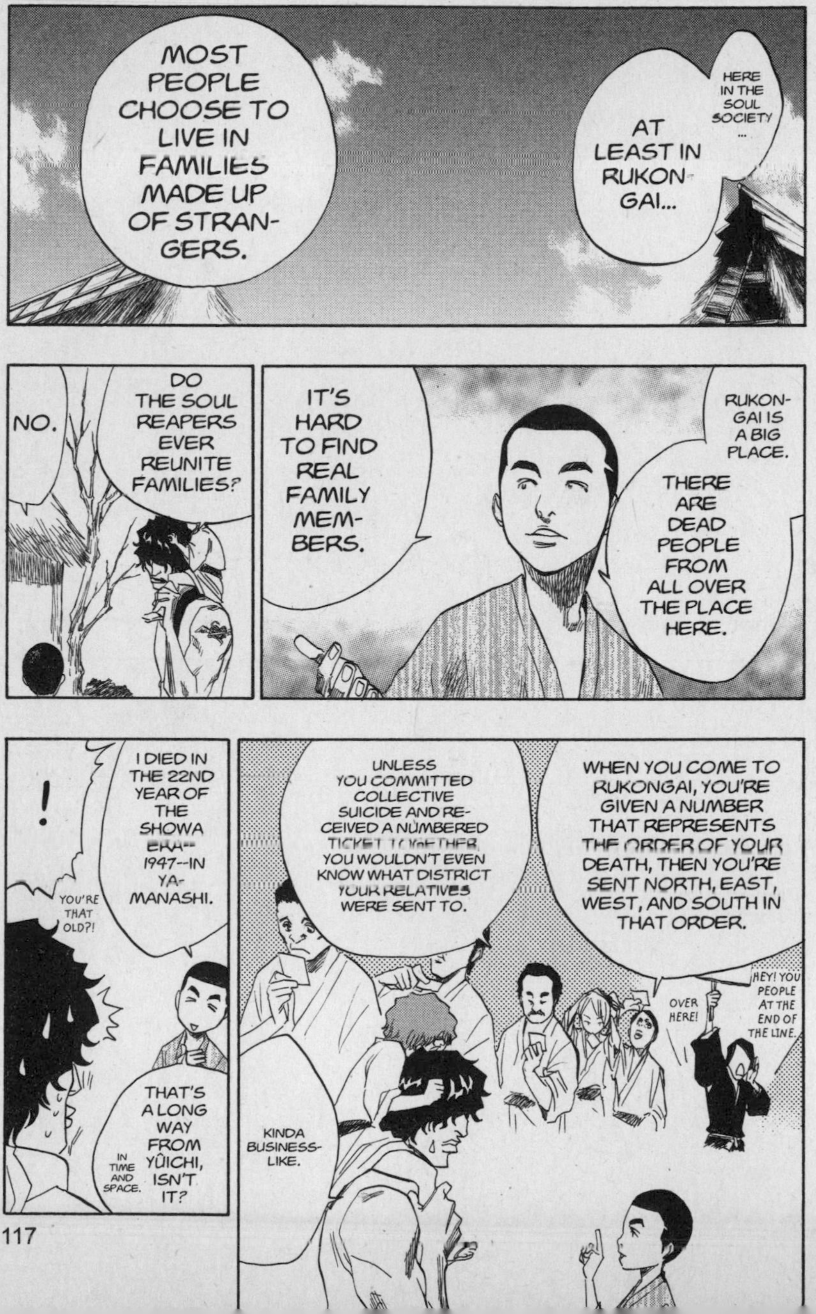
HERE IN THE SOUL SOCIETY...
AT LEAST IN RUKONGAI...
MOST PEOPLE CHOOSE TO LIVE IN FAMILIES MADE UP OF STRANGERS.
RUKONGAI IS A BIG PLACE.
THERE ARE DEAD PEOPLE FROM ALL OVER THE PLACE HERE.
IT'S HARD TO FIND REAL FAMILY MEMBERS.
DO THE SOUL REAPERS EVER REUNITE FAMILIES?
NO.
WHEN YOU COME TO RUKONGAI, YOU'RE GIVEN A NUMBER THAT REPRESENTS THE ORDER OF YOUR DEATH, THEN YOU'RE SENT NORTH, EAST, WEST, AND SOUTH IN THAT ORDER.
UNLESS YOU COMMITTED COLLECTIVE SUICIDE AND RECEIVED A NUMBERED TICKET TOGETHER, YOU WOULDN'T EVEN KNOW WHAT DISTRICT YOUR RELATIVES WERE SENT TO.
HEY! YOU PEOPLE AT THE END OF THE LINE.
OVER HERE!
KINDA BUSINESS-LIKE.
I DIED IN THE 22ND YEAR OF THE SHOWA ERA--1947--IN YAMANASHI.
!
YOU'RE THAT OLD?!
THAT'S A LONG WAY FROM YÛICHI, ISN'T IT?
IN TIME AND SPACE.

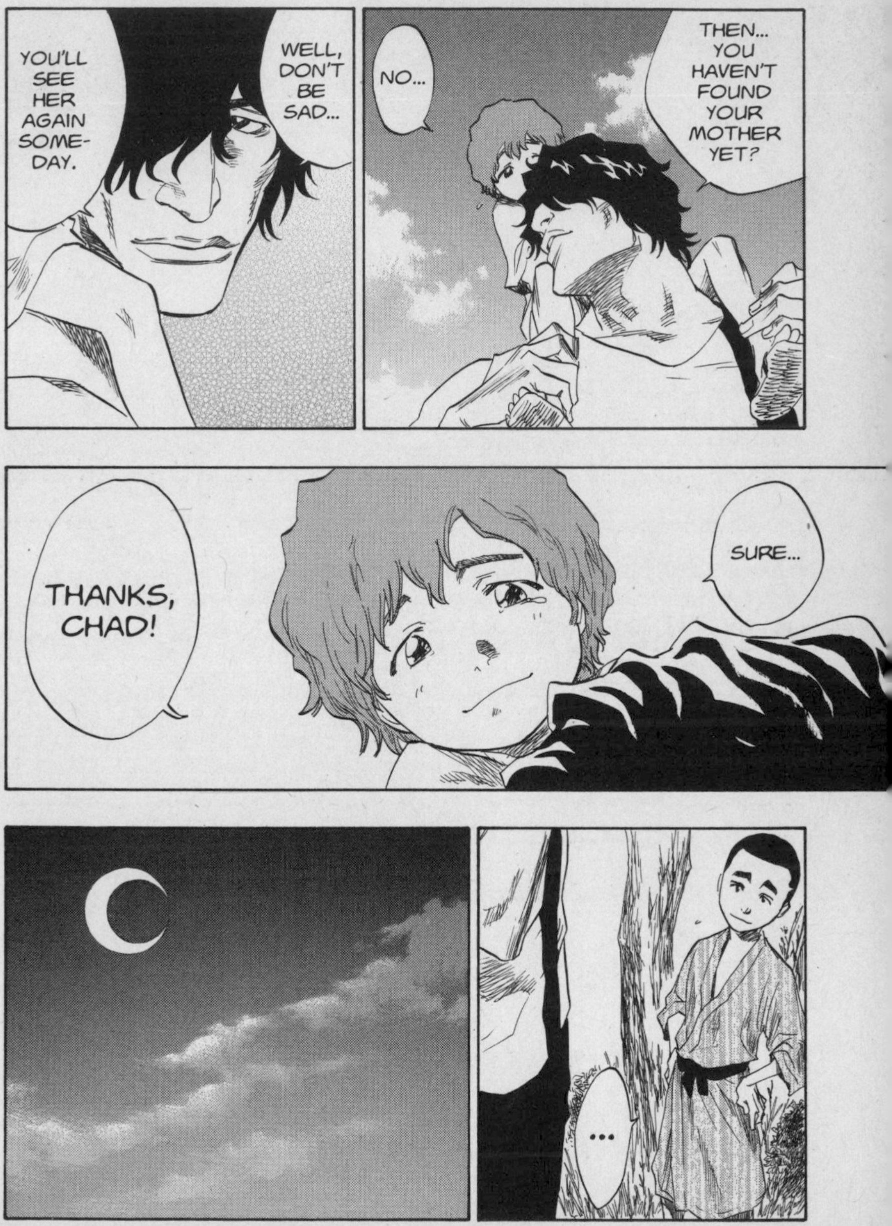
THEN... YOU HAVEN'T FOUND YOUR MOTHER YET?
NO...
WELL, DON'T BE SAD...
YOU'LL SEE HER AGAIN SOME-DAY.
SURE...
THANKS, CHAD!
...

READ THIS WAY

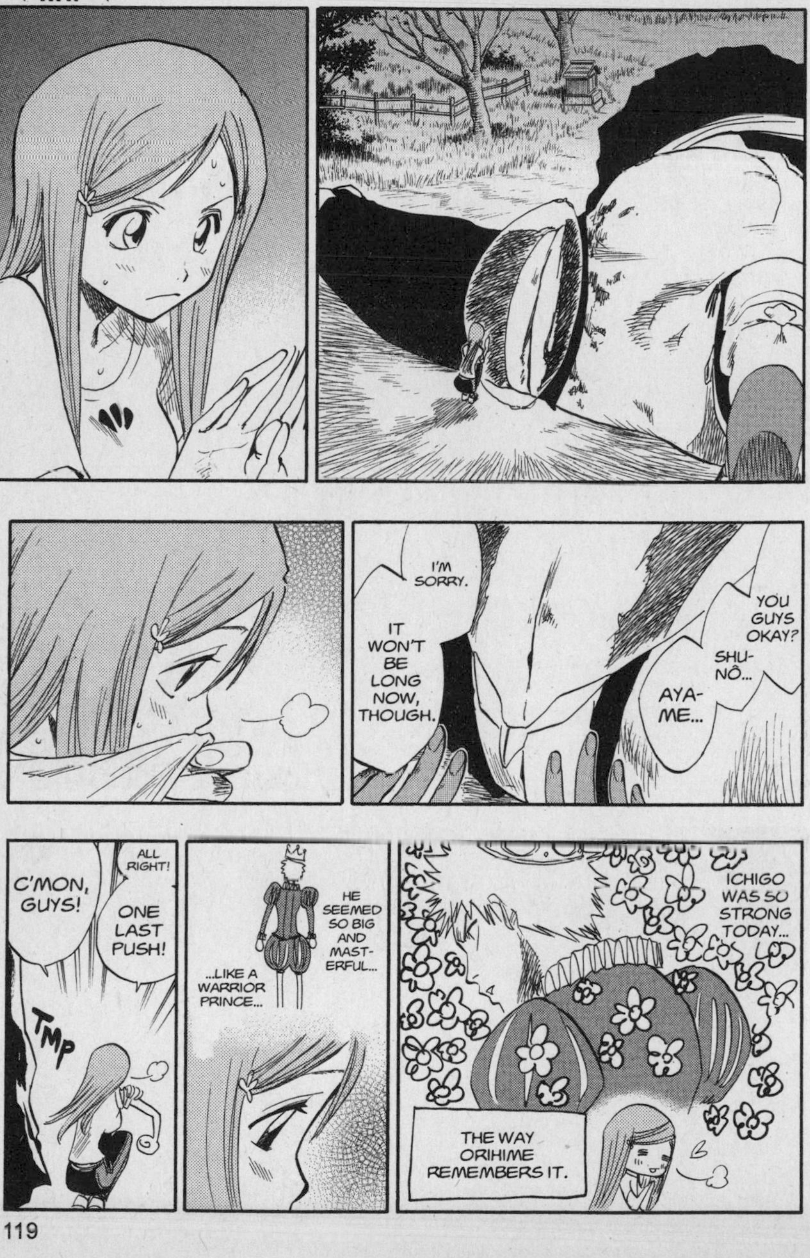
YOU GUYS OKAY?
SHU-NÔ...
AYA-ME...
I'M SORRY.
IT WON'T BE LONG NOW, THOUGH.
ICHIGO WAS SO STRONG TODAY...
THE WAY ORIHIME REMEMBERS IT.
HE SEEMED SO BIG AND MASTERFUL...
...LIKE A WARRIOR PRINCE...
ALL RIGHT!
C'MON, GUYS!
ONE LAST PUSH!
TMP

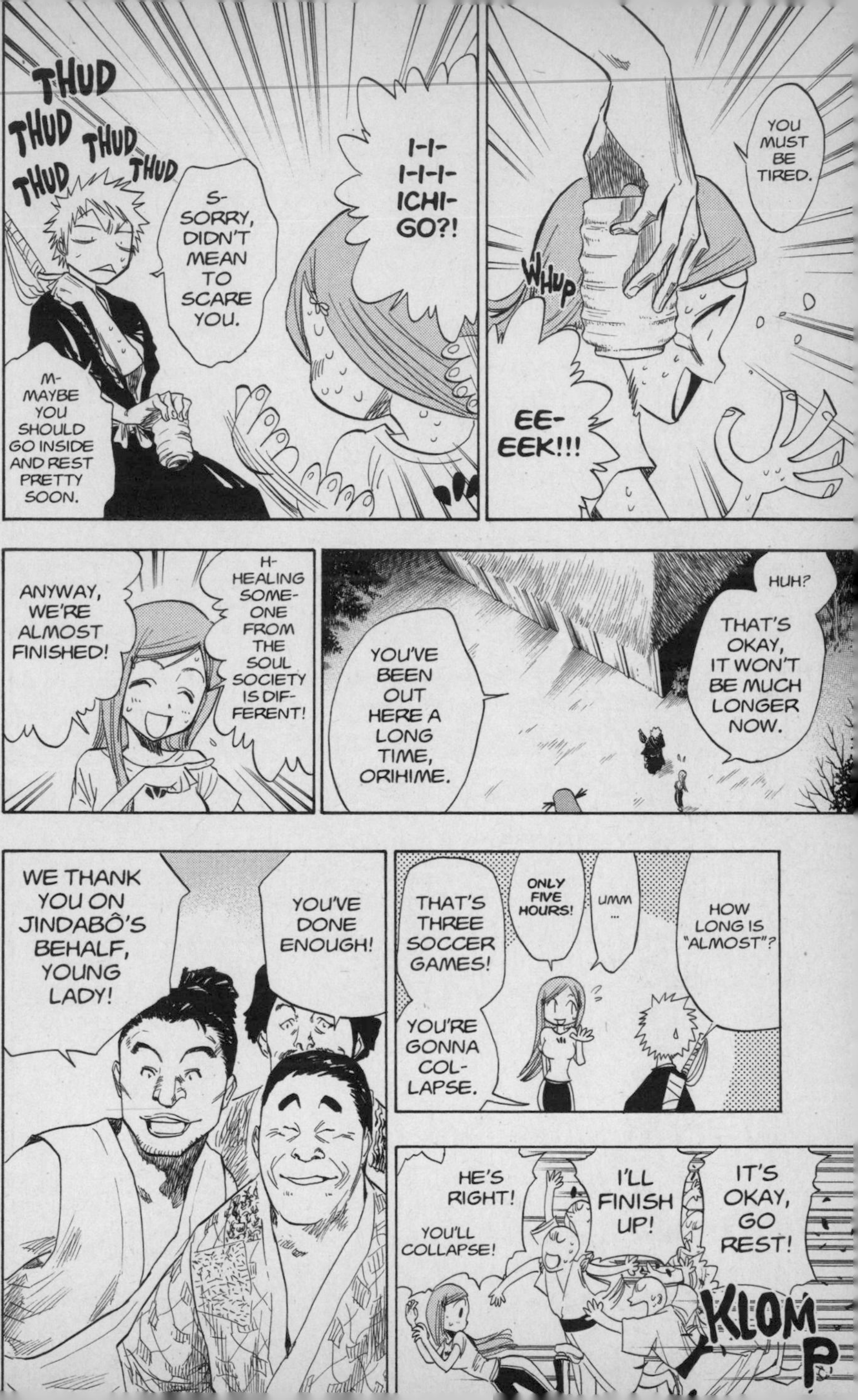
YOU MUST BE TIRED.
WHUP
EE-EEK!!!
I-I-I-I-I-ICHIGO?!
S-SORRY, DIDN'T MEAN TO SCARE YOU.
THUD THUD THUD THUD THUD
M-MAYBE YOU SHOULD GO INSIDE AND REST PRETTY SOON.
HUH?
THAT'S OKAY, IT WON'T BE MUCH LONGER NOW.
YOU'VE BEEN OUT HERE A LONG TIME, ORIHIME.
H-HEALING SOMEONE FROM THE SOUL SOCIETY IS DIFFERENT!
ANYWAY, WE'RE ALMOST FINISHED!
HOW LONG IS "ALMOST"?
UMM...
ONLY FIVE HOURS!
THAT'S THREE SOCCER GAMES!
YOU'RE GONNA COLLAPSE.
IT'S OKAY, GO REST!
I'LL FINISH UP!
HE'S RIGHT!
YOU'LL COLLAPSE!
KLOMP
YOU'VE DONE ENOUGH!
WE THANK YOU ON JINDABÔ'S BEHALF, YOUNG LADY!

READ THIS WAY

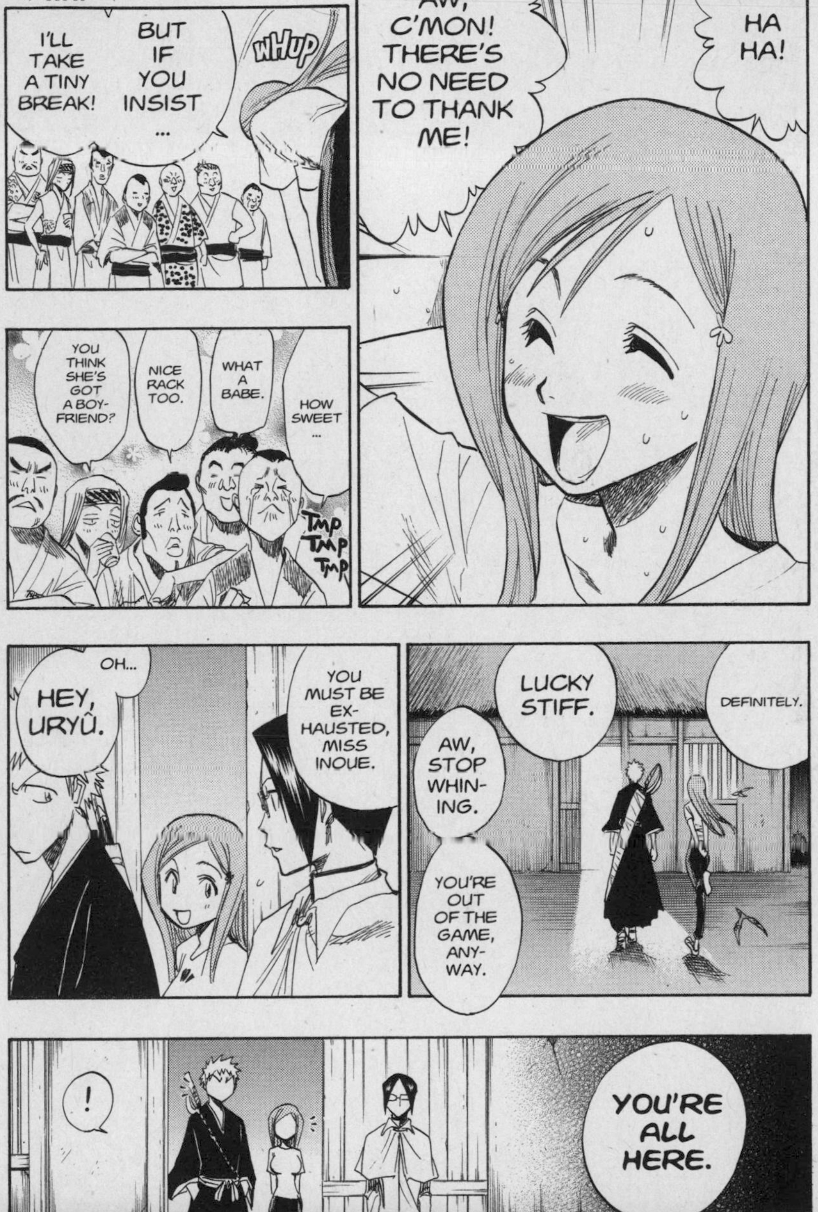
HA HA!
AW, C'MON! THERE'S NO NEED TO THANK ME!
BUT IF YOU INSIST...
I'LL TAKE A TINY BREAK!
WHUP
HOW SWEET...
WHAT A BABE.
NICE RACK TOO.
YOU THINK SHE'S GOT A BOY-FRIEND?
TMP TMP TMP
DEFINITELY.
LUCKY STIFF.
AW, STOP WHIN-ING.
YOU'RE OUT OF THE GAME, ANY-WAY.
YOU MUST BE EX-HAUSTED, MISS INOUE.
OH...
HEY, URYÛ.
YOU'RE ALL HERE.
!

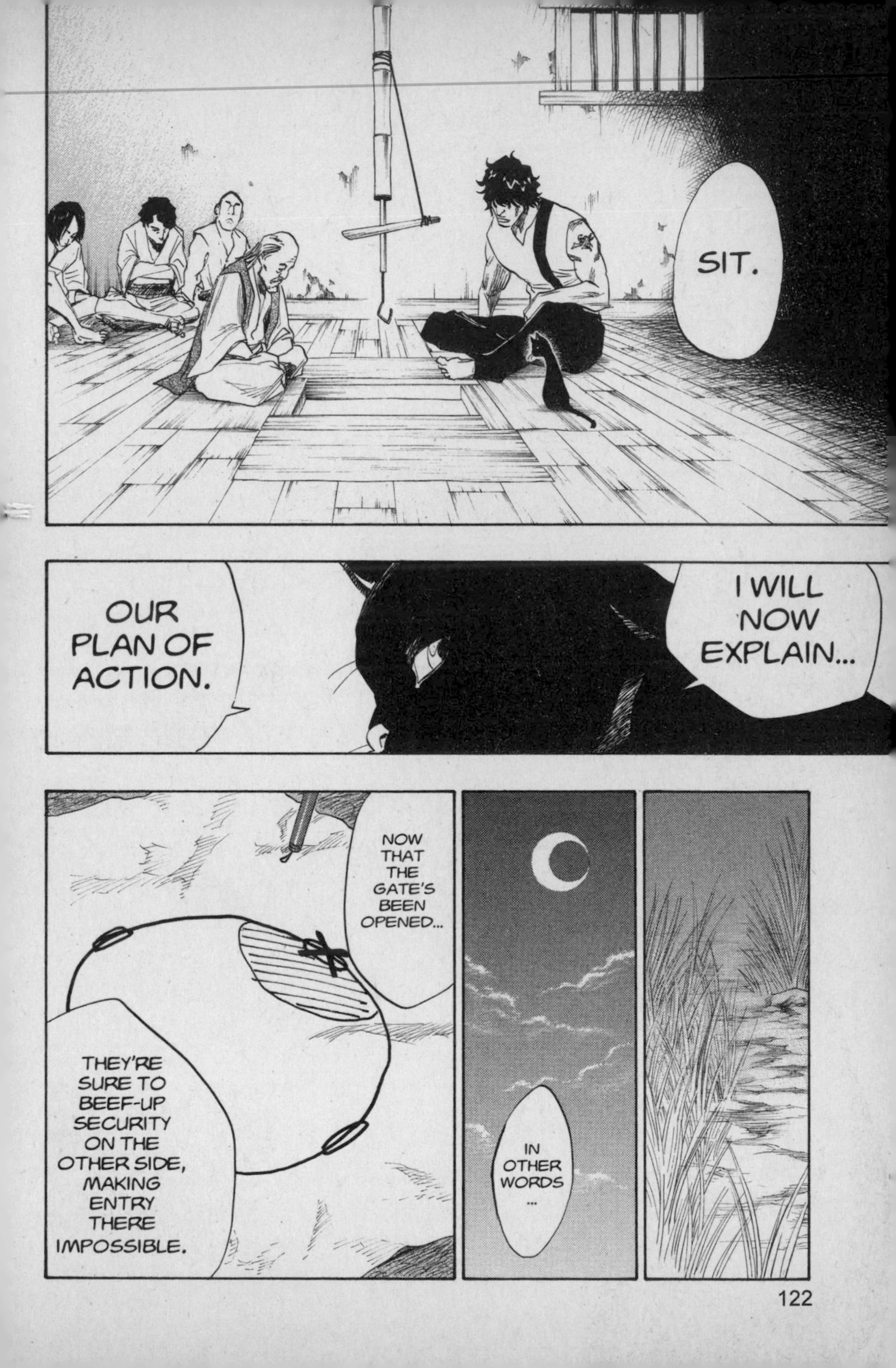
SIT.
I WILL NOW EXPLAIN...
OUR PLAN OF ACTION.
IN OTHER WORDS ...
NOW THAT THE GATE'S BEEN OPENED...
THEY'RE SURE TO BEEF-UP SECURITY ON THE OTHER SIDE, MAKING ENTRY THERE IMPOSSIBLE.

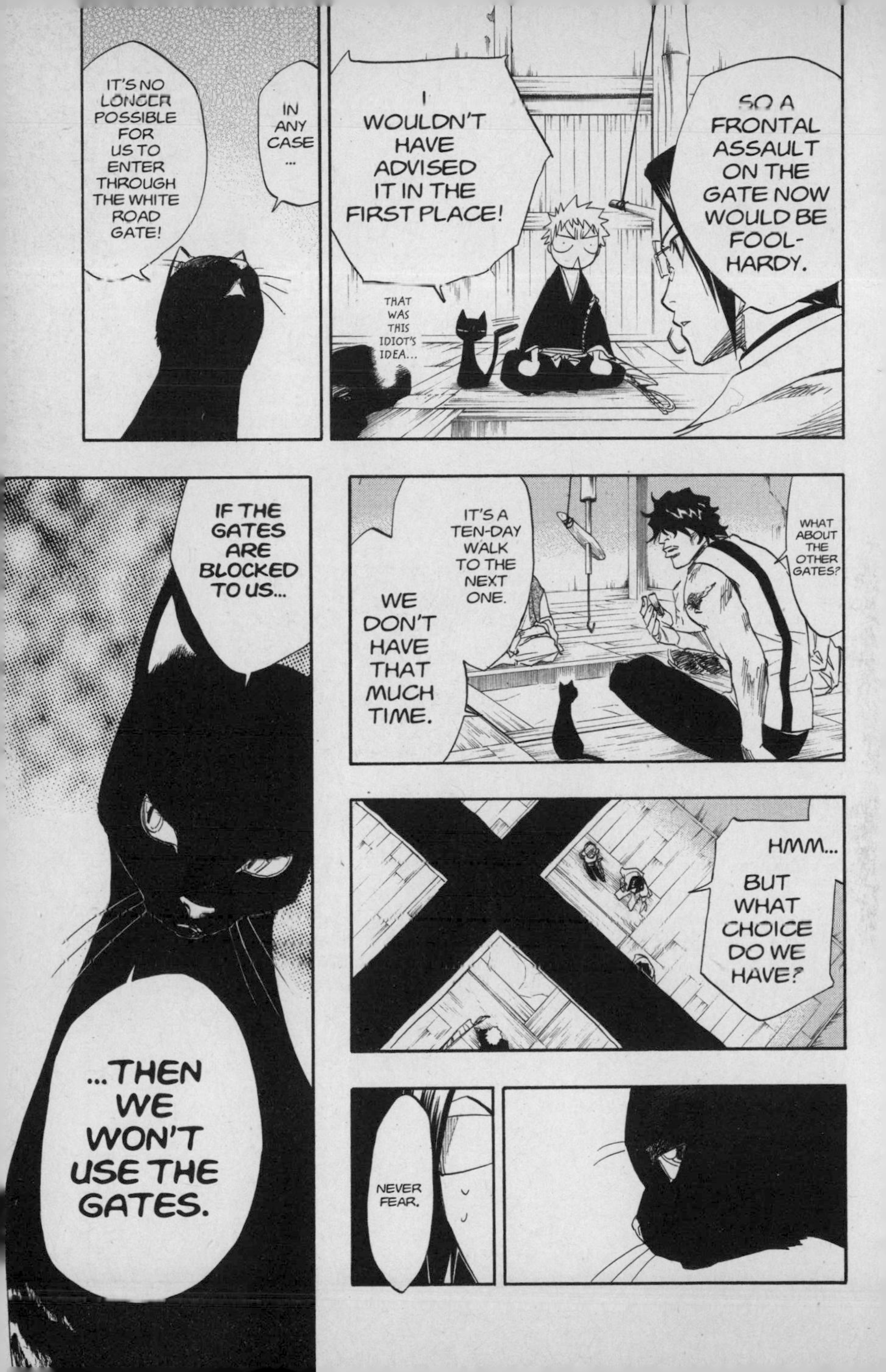
SO A FRONTAL ASSAULT ON THE GATE NOW WOULD BE FOOL-HARDY.
I WOULDN'T HAVE ADVISED IT IN THE FIRST PLACE!
THAT WAS THIS IDIOT'S IDEA...
IN ANY CASE...
IT'S NO LONGER POSSIBLE FOR US TO ENTER THROUGH THE WHITE ROAD GATE!
WHAT ABOUT THE OTHER GATES?
IT'S A TEN-DAY WALK TO THE NEXT ONE.
WE DON'T HAVE THAT MUCH TIME.
HMM...
BUT WHAT CHOICE DO WE HAVE?
NEVER FEAR.
IF THE GATES ARE BLOCKED TO US...
...THEN WE WON'T USE THE GATES.

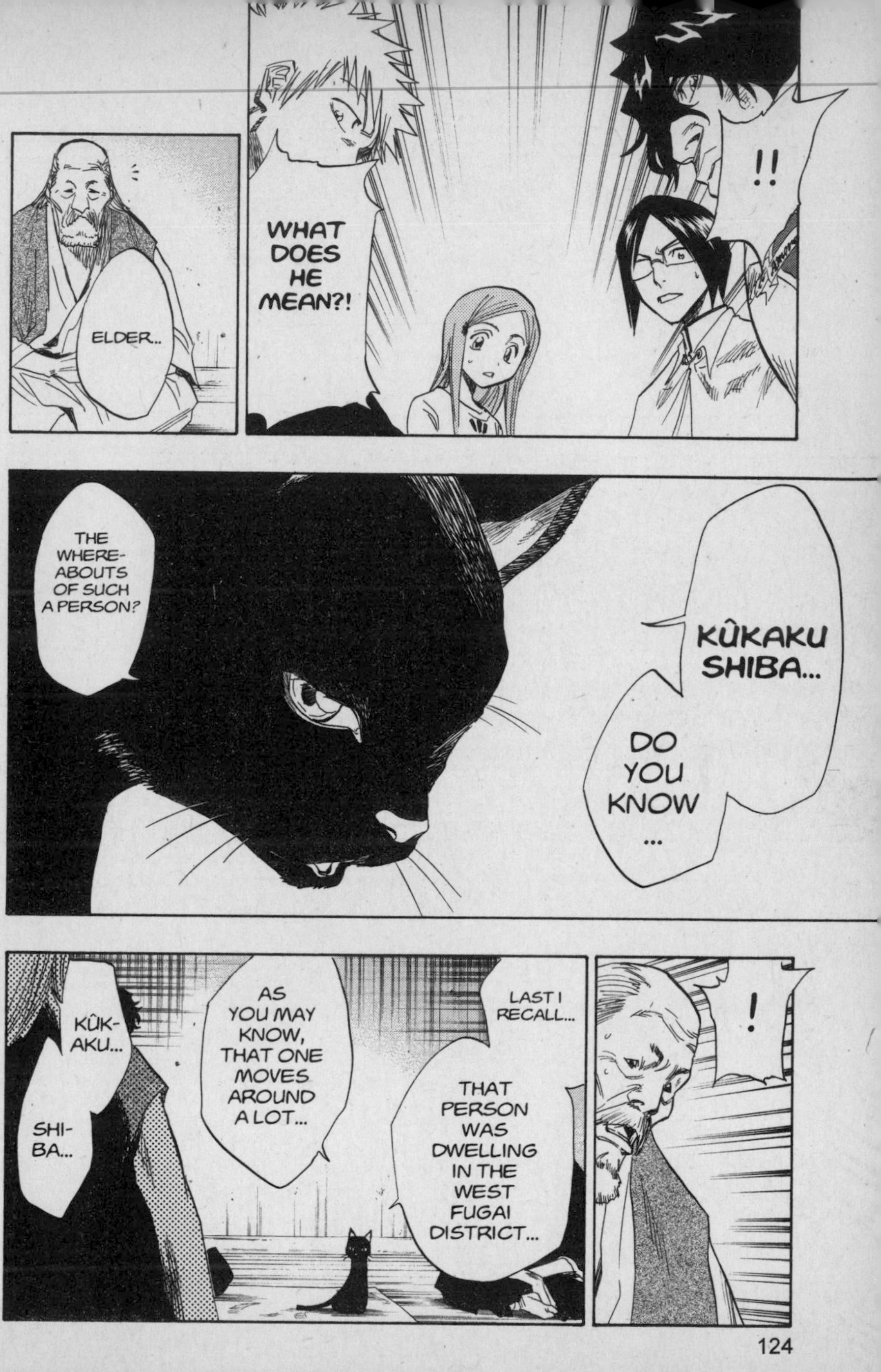
!!
WHAT DOES HE MEAN?!
ELDER..
KÛKAKU SHIBA...
DO YOU KNOW ...
THE WHERE-ABOUTS OF SUCH A PERSON?
!
LAST I RECALL...
AS YOU MAY KNOW, THAT ONE MOVES AROUND A LOT...
THAT PERSON WAS DWELLING IN THE WEST FUGAI DISTRICT...
KÛK-AKU...
SHI-BA...

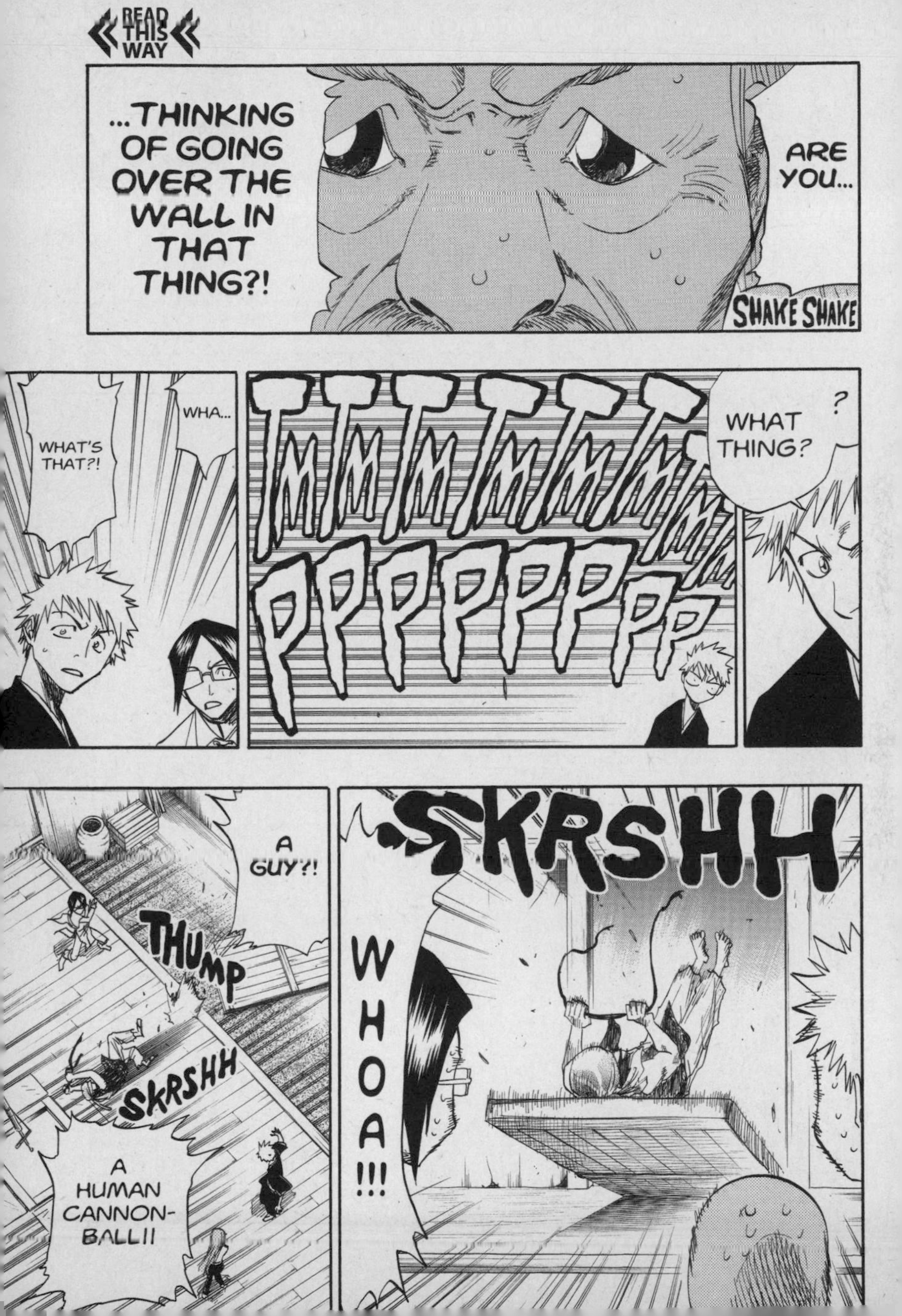
READ THIS WAY
ARE YOU...
...THINKING OF GOING OVER THE WALL IN THAT THING?!
SHAKE SHAKE
?
WHAT THING?
TMMMMMMPPPPPPPP
WHA...
WHAT'S THAT?!
SKRSHH
WHOA!!!
A GUY?!
THUMP
SKRSHH
A HUMAN CANNON-BALL!!

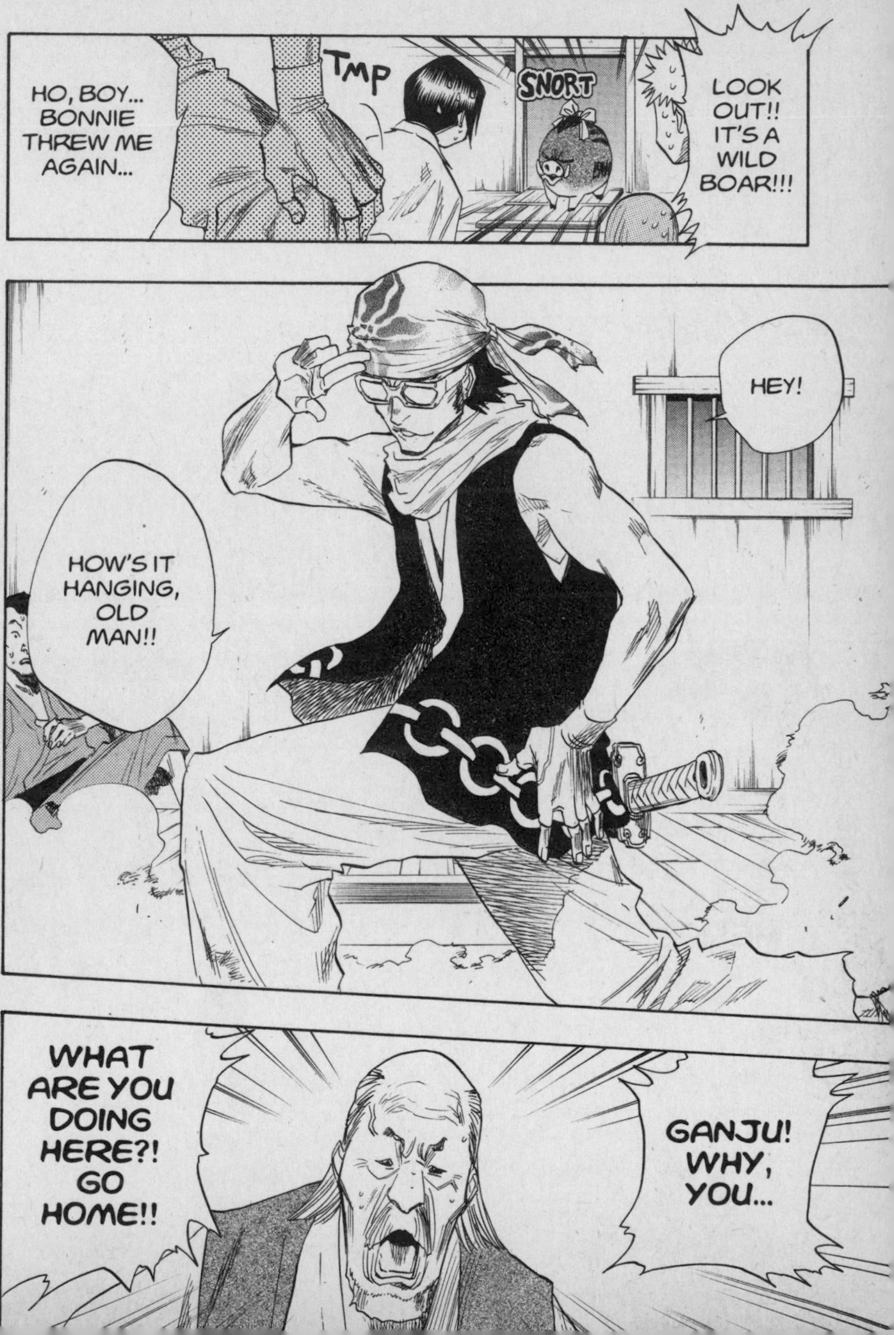
LOOK OUT!! IT'S A WILD BOAR!!!
SNORT
TMP
HO, BOY... BONNIE THREW ME AGAIN...
HEY!
HOW'S IT HANGING, OLD MAN!!
GANJU! WHY, YOU...
WHAT ARE YOU DOING HERE?! GO HOME!!

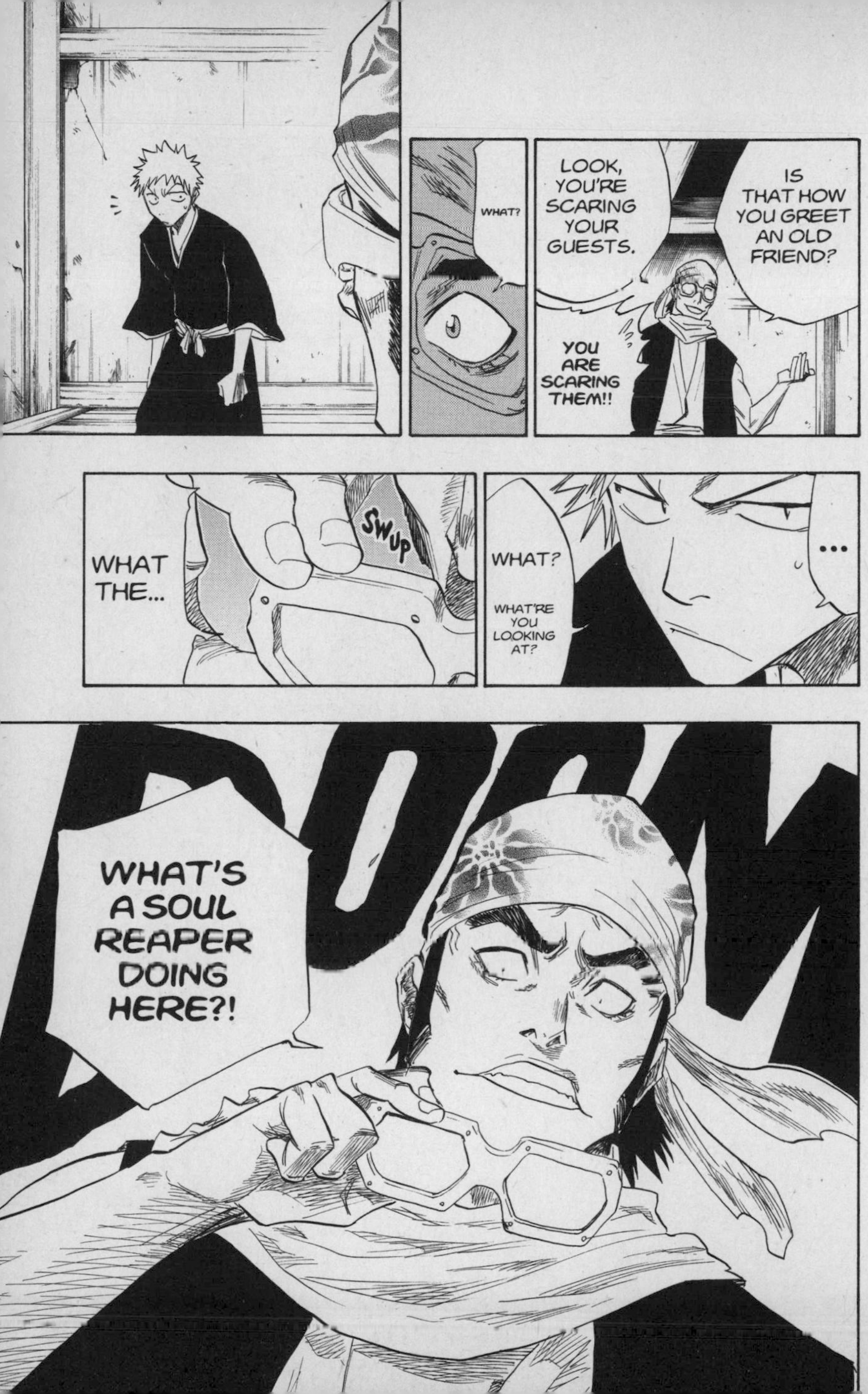
IS THAT HOW YOU GREET AN OLD FRIEND?
LOOK, YOU'RE SCARING YOUR GUESTS.
YOU ARE SCARING THEM!!
WHAT?
...
WHAT?
WHAT'RE YOU LOOKING AT?
SWUP
WHAT THE...
WHAT'S A SOUL REAPER DOING HERE?!

WILL YOU
COME PLAY
WITH ME
AGAIN
SOMEDAY...

CHAD?

77. My Name Is Ganju

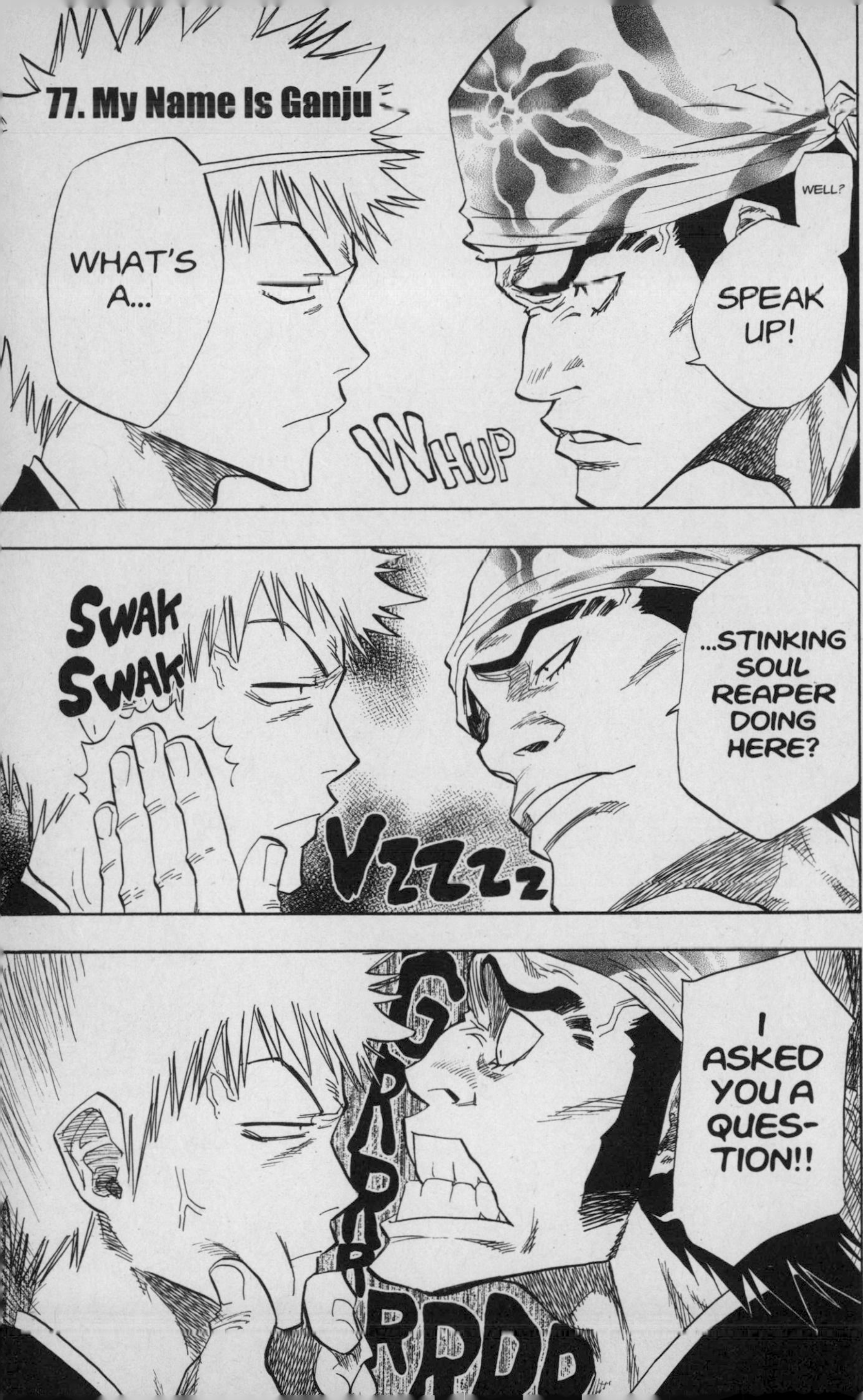
WELL?
SPEAK UP!
WHUP
WHAT'S A...
...STINKING SOUL REAPER DOING HERE?
SWAK SWAK
VZZZz
I ASKED YOU A QUES-TION!!
GRRRRRRPDDD

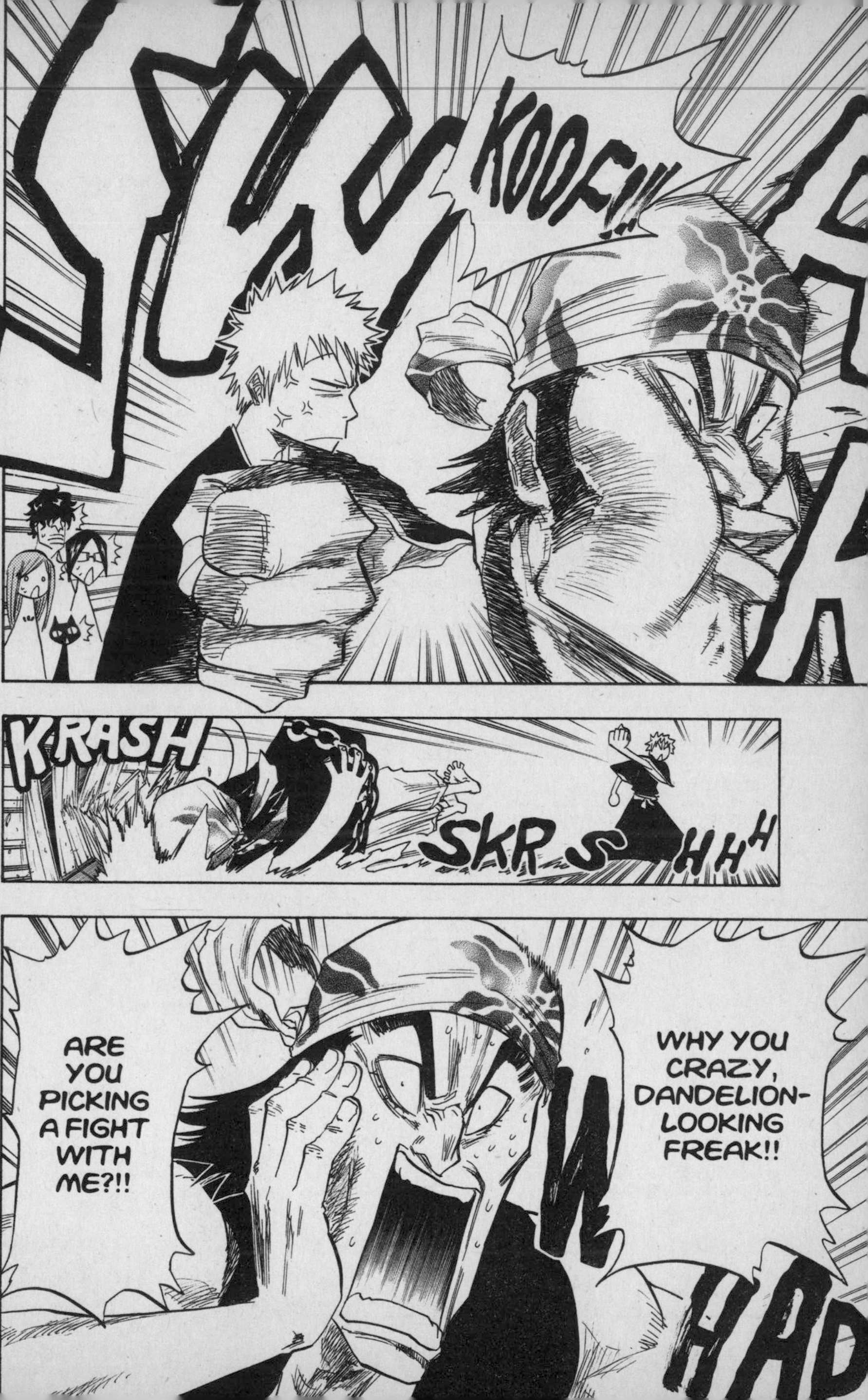
KOOF!!!
KRASH
WHY YOU CRAZY, DANDELION-LOOKING FREAK!!
ARE YOU PICKING A FIGHT WITH ME?!!

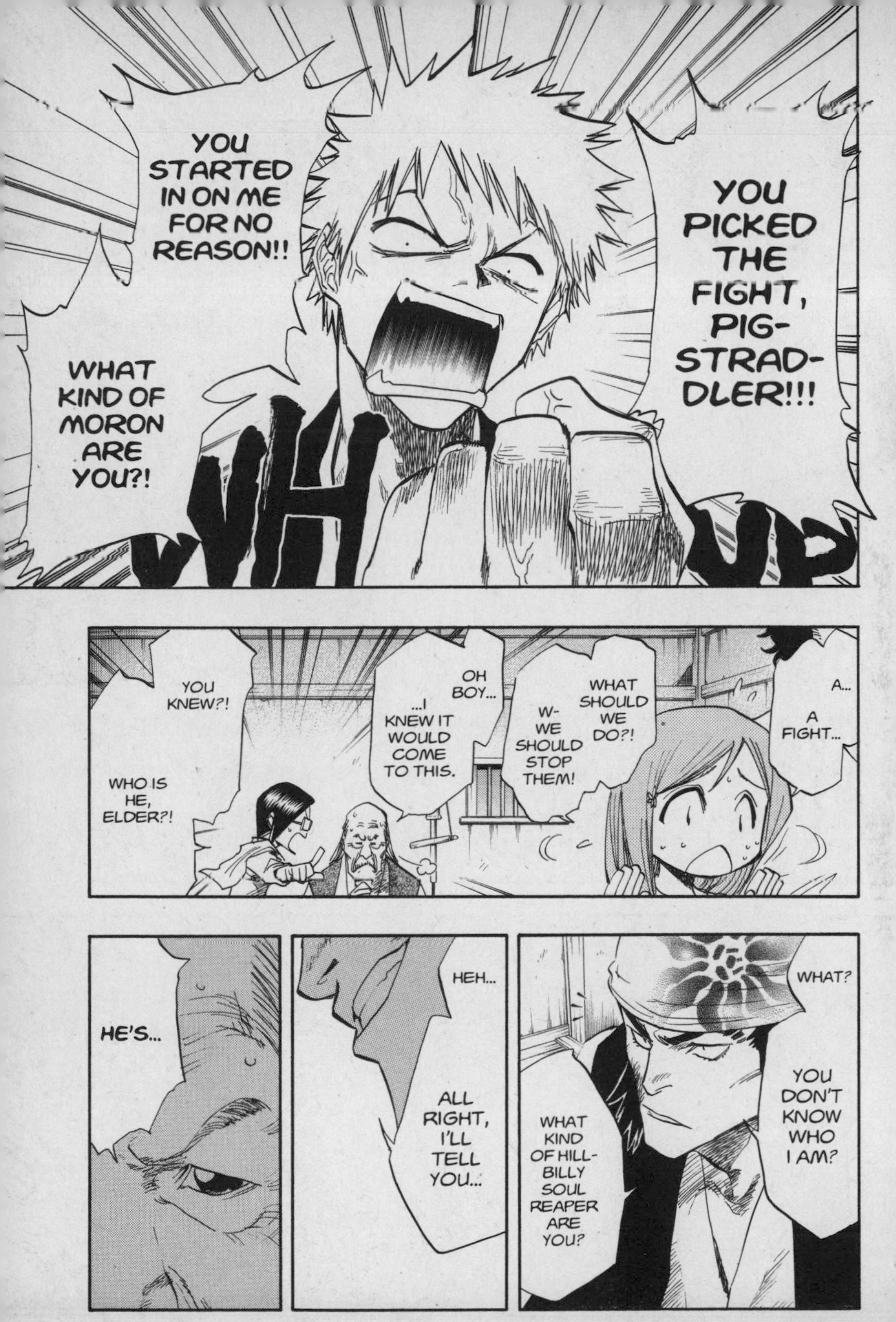
YOU PICKED THE FIGHT, PIG-STRADDLER!!!
YOU STARTED IN ON ME FOR NO REASON!!
WHAT KIND OF MORON ARE YOU?!
A...
A FIGHT...
WHAT SHOULD WE DO?!
W-WE SHOULD STOP THEM!
OH BOY...
...I KNEW IT WOULD COME TO THIS.
YOU KNEW?!
WHO IS HE, ELDER?!
WHAT?
YOU DON'T KNOW WHO I AM?
WHAT KIND OF HILL-BILLY SOUL REAPER ARE YOU?
HEH...
ALL RIGHT, I'LL TELL YOU...
HE'S...

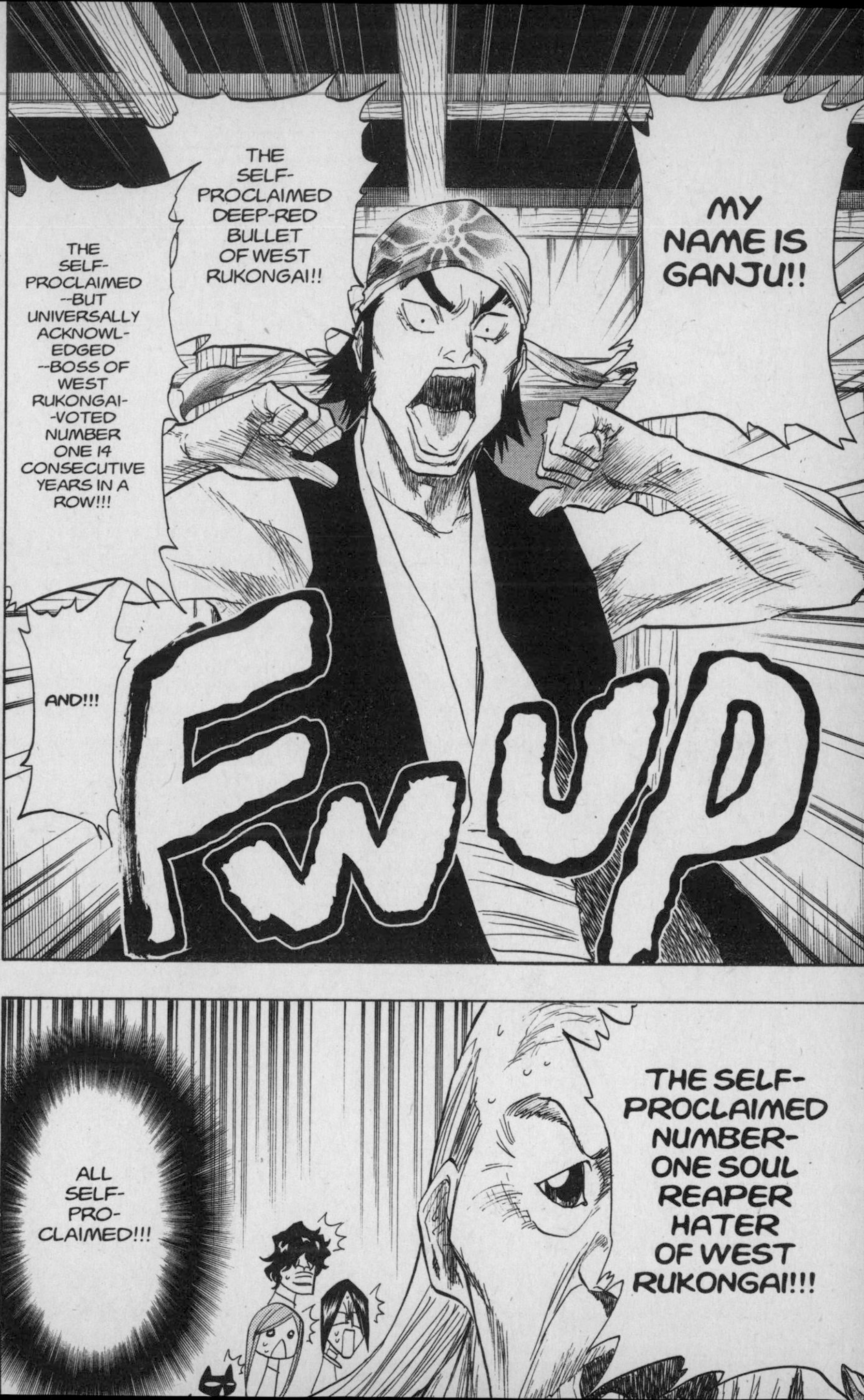
MY NAME IS GANJU!!
THE SELF-PROCLAIMED DEEP-RED BULLET OF WEST RUKONGAI!!
THE SELF-PROCLAIMED--BUT UNIVERSALLY ACKNOWL-EDGED--BOSS OF WEST RUKONGAI--VOTED NUMBER ONE 14 CONSECUTIVE YEARS IN A ROW!!!
AND!!!
FWUP
THE SELF-PROCLAIMED NUMBER-ONE SOUL REAPER HATER OF WEST RUKONGAI!!!
ALL SELF-PRO-CLAIMED!!!

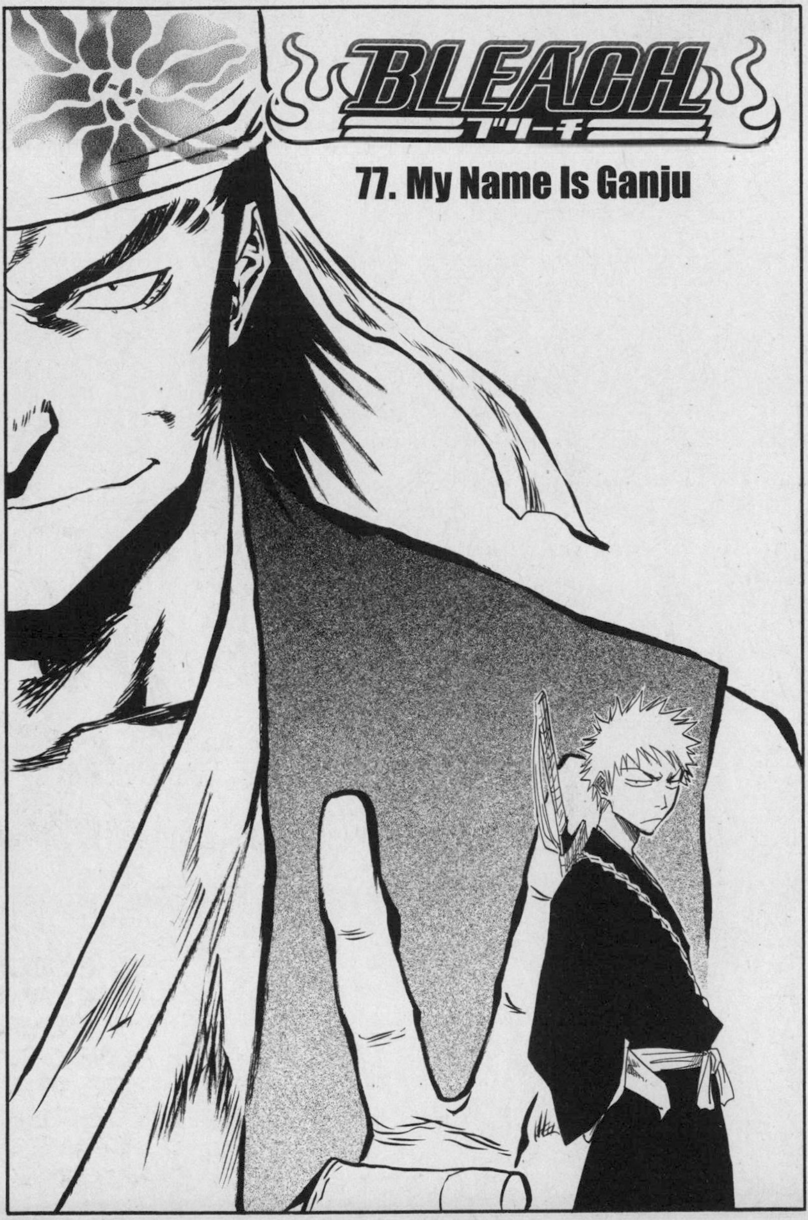
BLEACH
ブリーチ
77. My Name Is Ganju

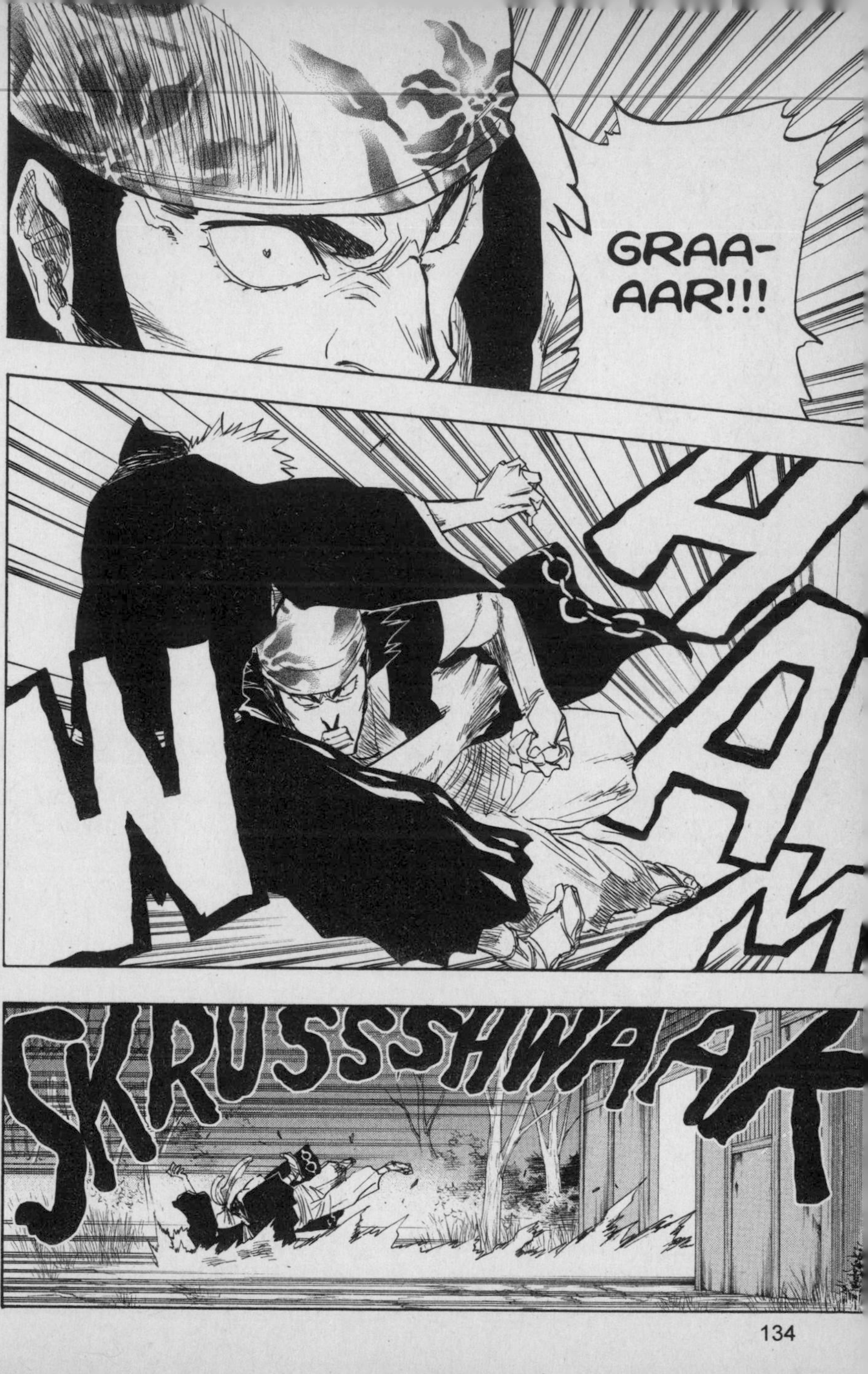
GRAA-
AAR!!!
SKRUSSSHWAAK

READ THIS WAY

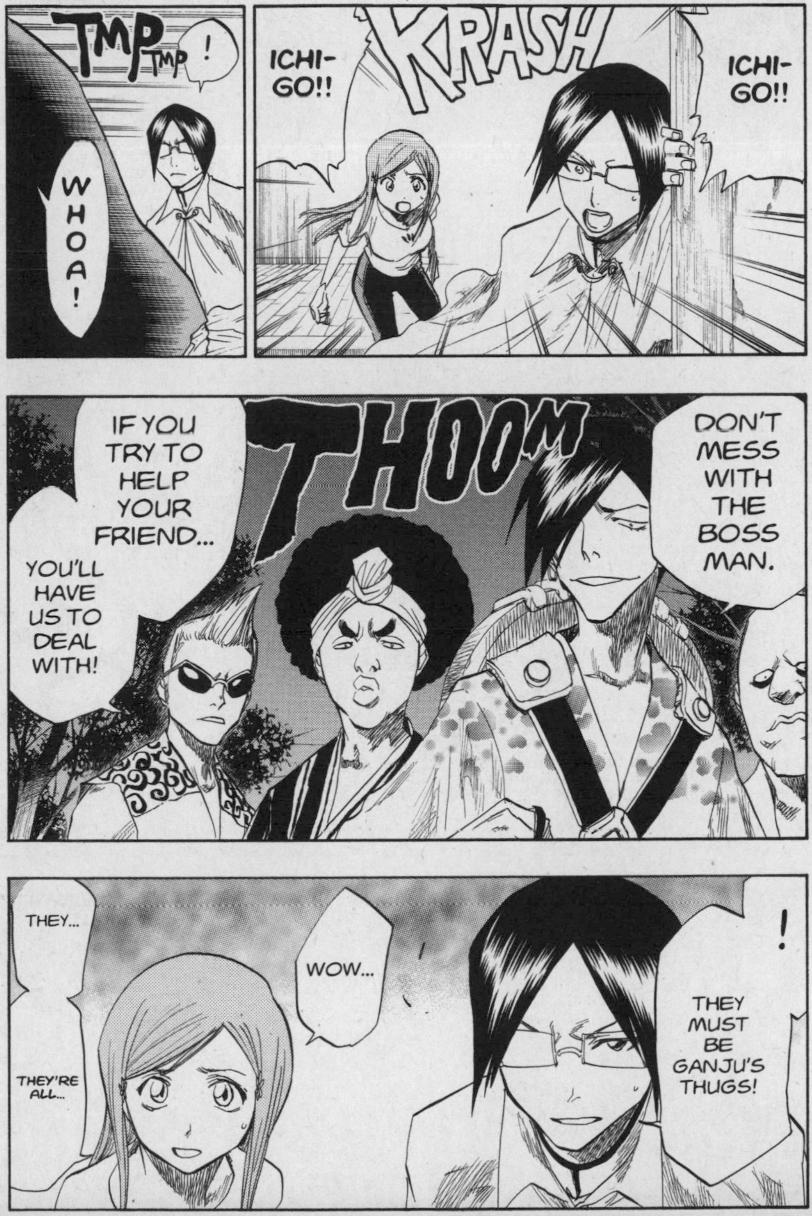

KRASH
ICHI-GO!!
ICHI-GO!!
TMP TMP
!
WHOA!
DON'T MESS WITH THE BOSS MAN.
THOOM
IF YOU TRY TO HELP YOUR FRIEND...
YOU'LL HAVE US TO DEAL WITH!
!
THEY MUST BE GANJU'S THUGS!
WOW...
THEY...
THEY'RE ALL...

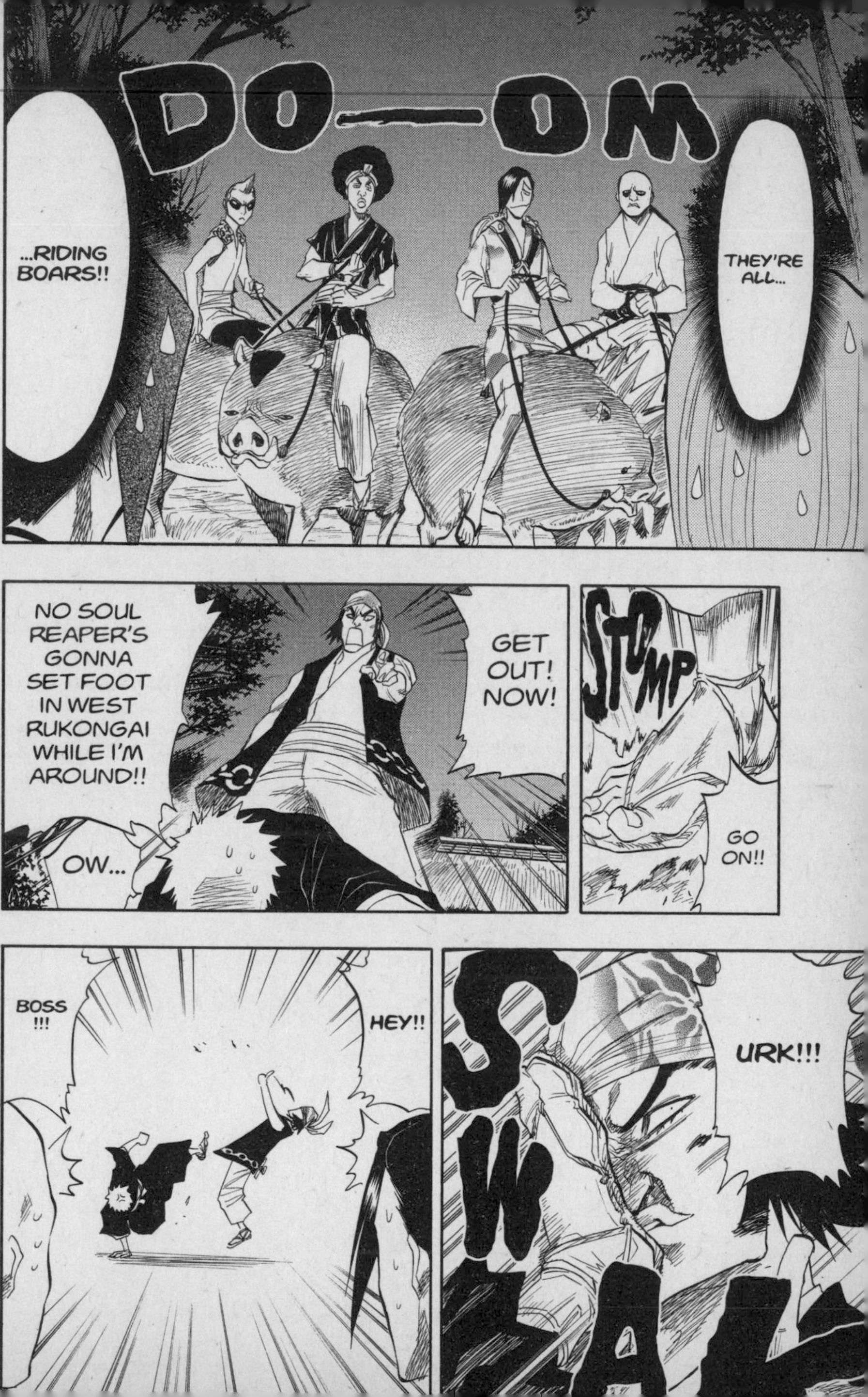
DO—OM
THEY'RE ALL...
...RIDING BOARS!!
STOMP
GO ON!!
GET OUT! NOW!
NO SOUL REAPER'S GONNA SET FOOT IN WEST RUKONGAI WHILE I'M AROUND!!
OW...
URK!!!
HEY!!
BOSS !!!

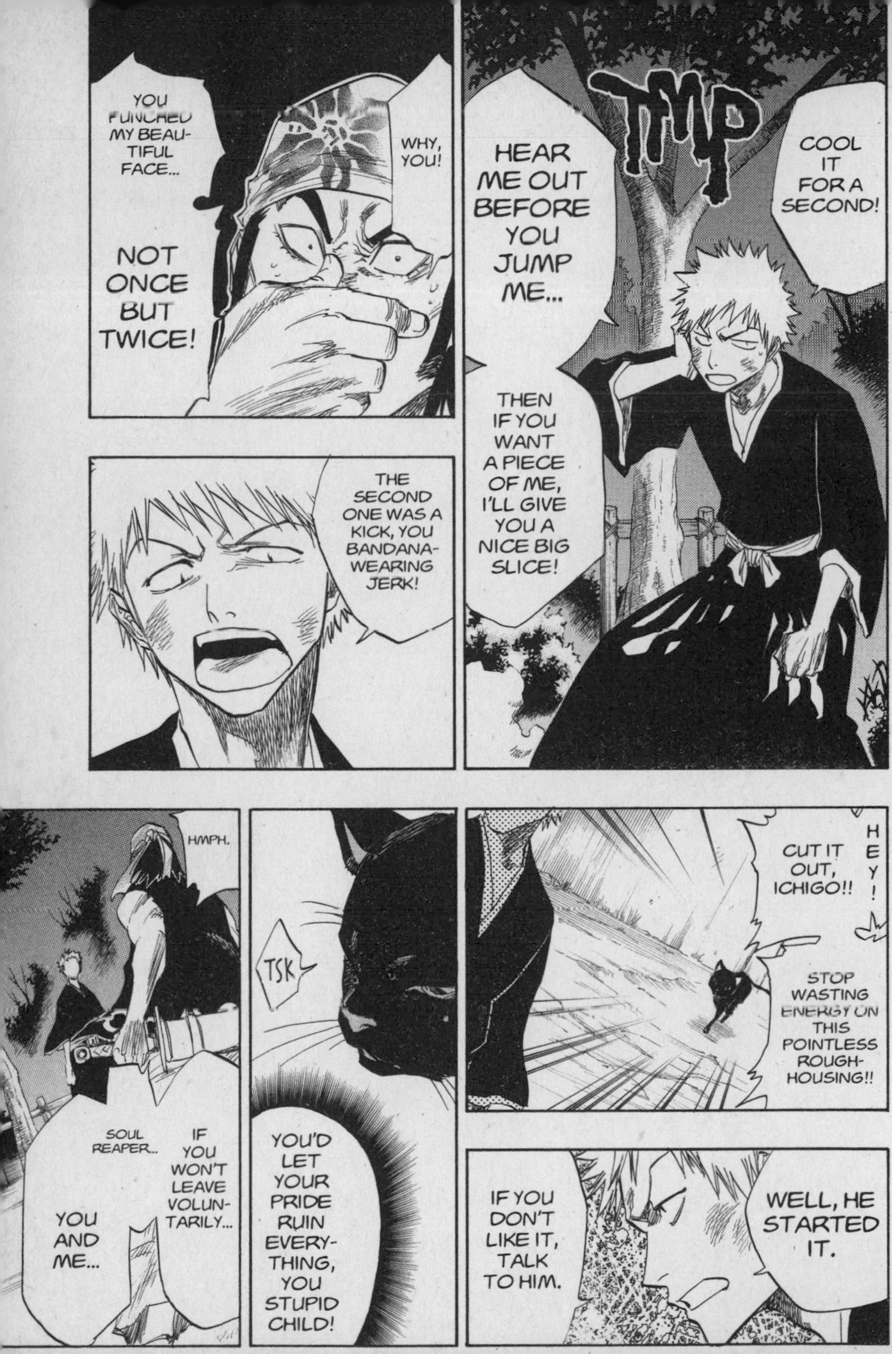
COOL IT FOR A SECOND!
TMP
HEAR ME OUT BEFORE YOU JUMP ME...
THEN IF YOU WANT A PIECE OF ME, I'LL GIVE YOU A NICE BIG SLICE!
WHY, YOU!
YOU PUNCHED MY BEAUTIFUL FACE...
NOT ONCE BUT TWICE!
THE SECOND ONE WAS A KICK, YOU BANDANA-WEARING JERK!
HEY!
CUT IT OUT, ICHIGO!!
STOP WASTING ENERGY ON THIS POINTLESS ROUGHHOUSING!!
WELL, HE STARTED IT.
IF YOU DON'T LIKE IT, TALK TO HIM.
TSK
YOU'D LET YOUR PRIDE RUIN EVERYTHING, YOU STUPID CHILD!
HMPH.
SOUL REAPER...
IF YOU WON'T LEAVE VOLUNTARILY...
YOU AND ME...

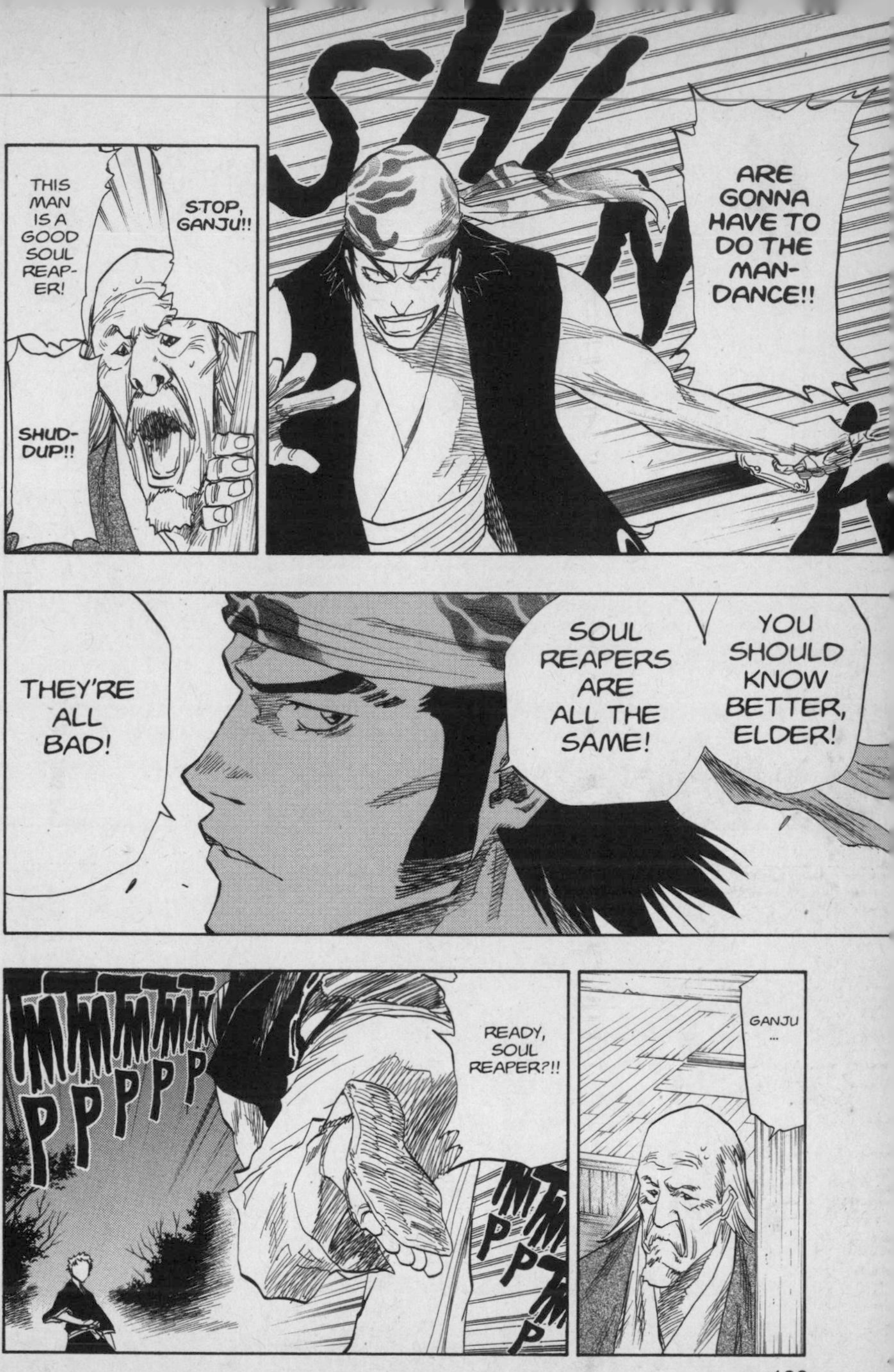
SHI
ARE GONNA HAVE TO DO THE MAN-DANCE!!
STOP, GANJU!!
THIS MAN IS A GOOD SOUL REAPER!
SHUD-DUP!!
YOU SHOULD KNOW BETTER, ELDER!
SOUL REAPERS ARE ALL THE SAME!
THEY'RE ALL BAD!
GANJU ...
READY, SOUL REAPER?!!

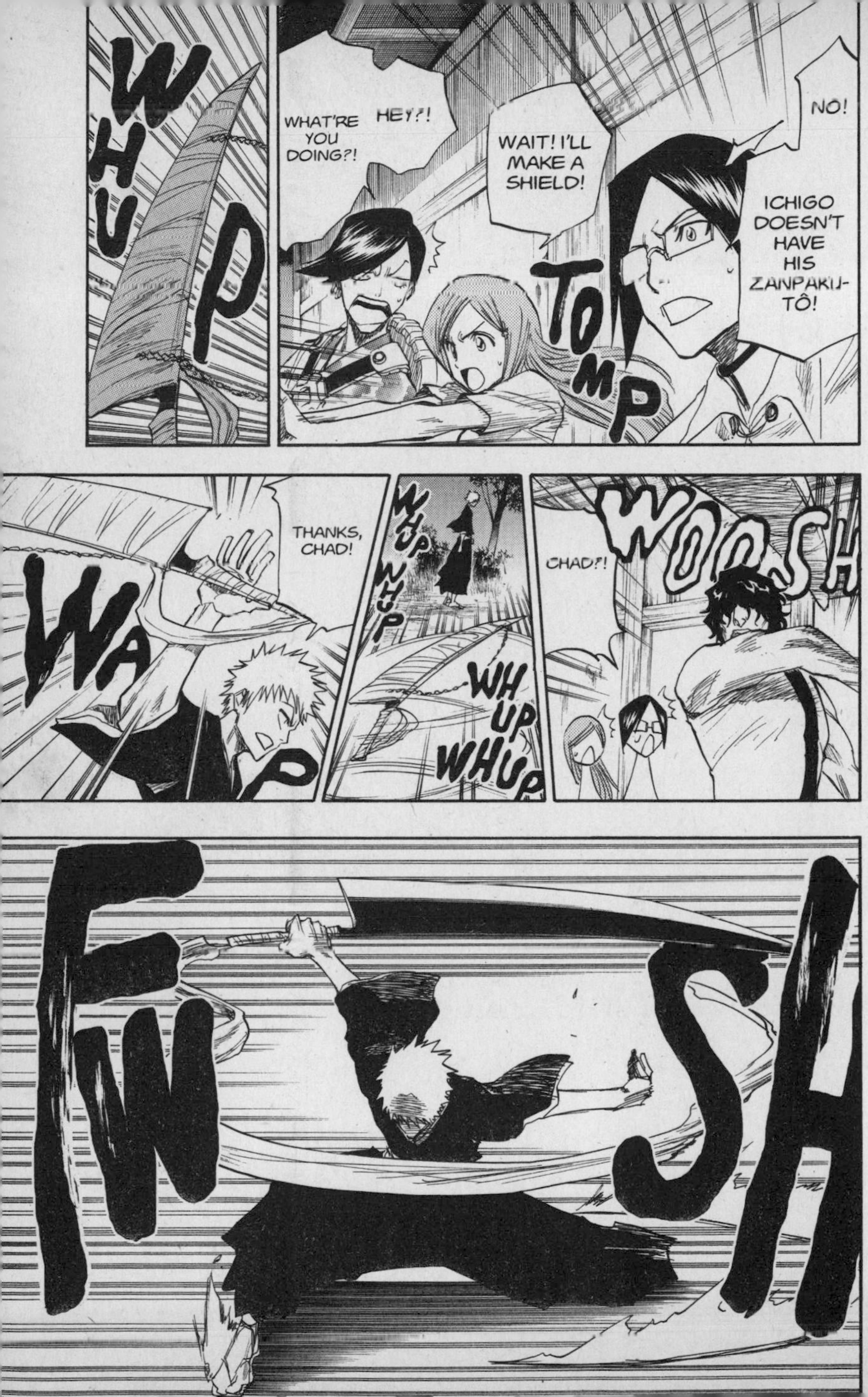
NO!
ICHIGO DOESN'T HAVE HIS ZANPAKU-TÔ!
WAIT! I'LL MAKE A SHIELD!
HEY?!
WHAT'RE YOU DOING?!
TOMP
WHUP
WOOSH
CHAD?!
WHUP WHUP
WHUP WHUP WHUP
THANKS, CHAD!
WAP
FWSH

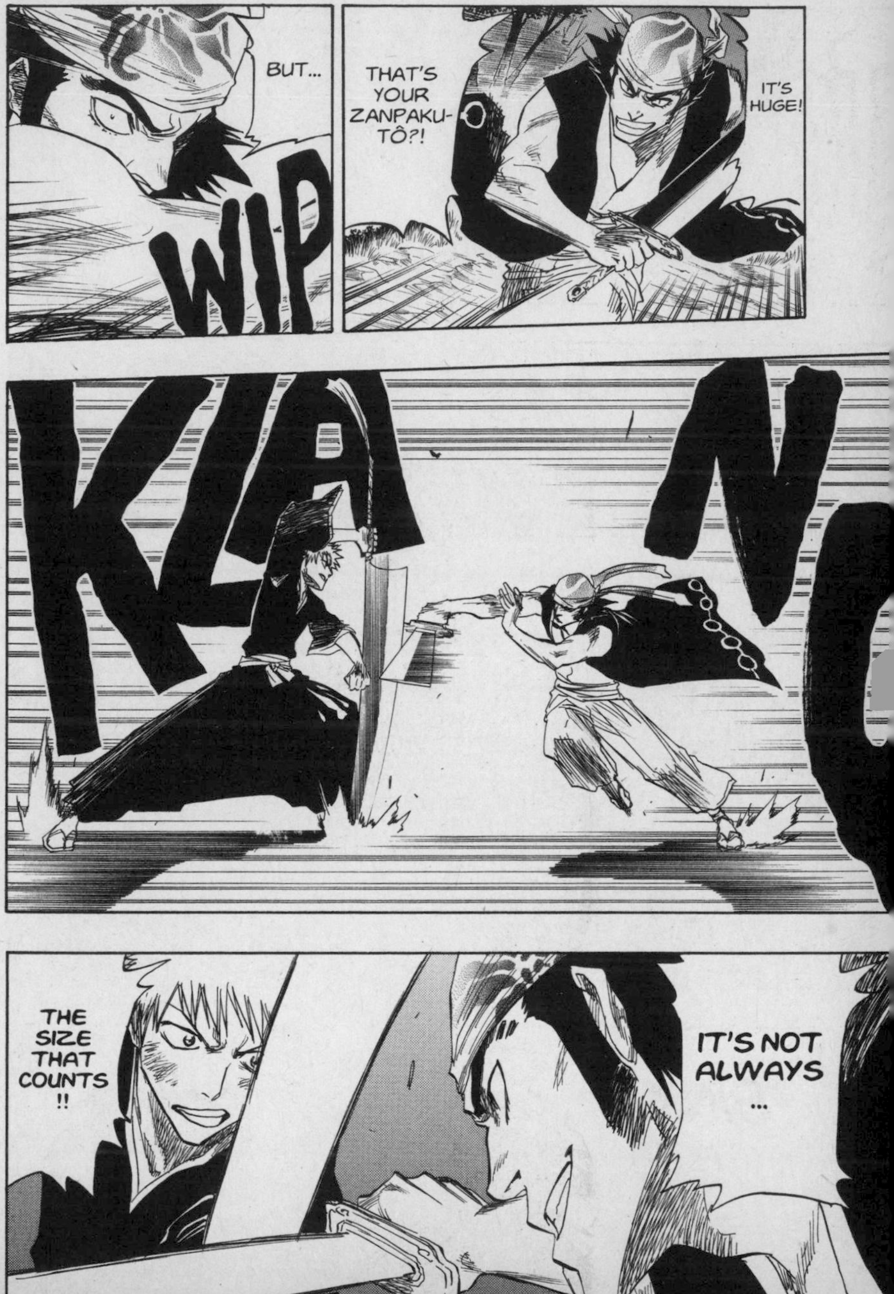
IT'S HUGE!
THAT'S YOUR ZANPAKU-TÔ?!
BUT...
WIP
KLAN
IT'S NOT ALWAYS ...
THE SIZE THAT COUNTS !!

READ THIS WAY

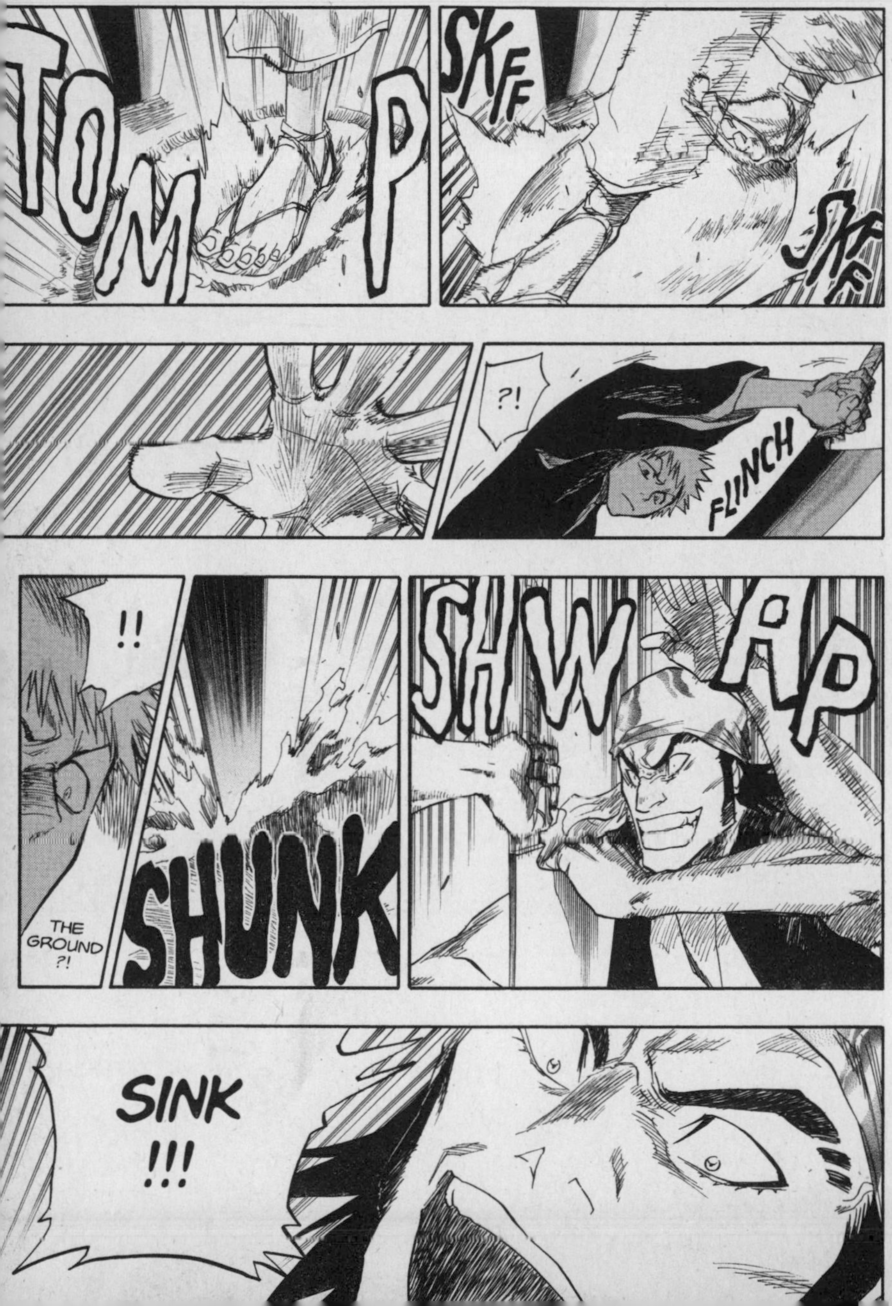
SKFF
SKFF
TOMP
?!
FLINCH
SHWAP
SHUNK
!!
THE GROUND ?!
SINK !!!

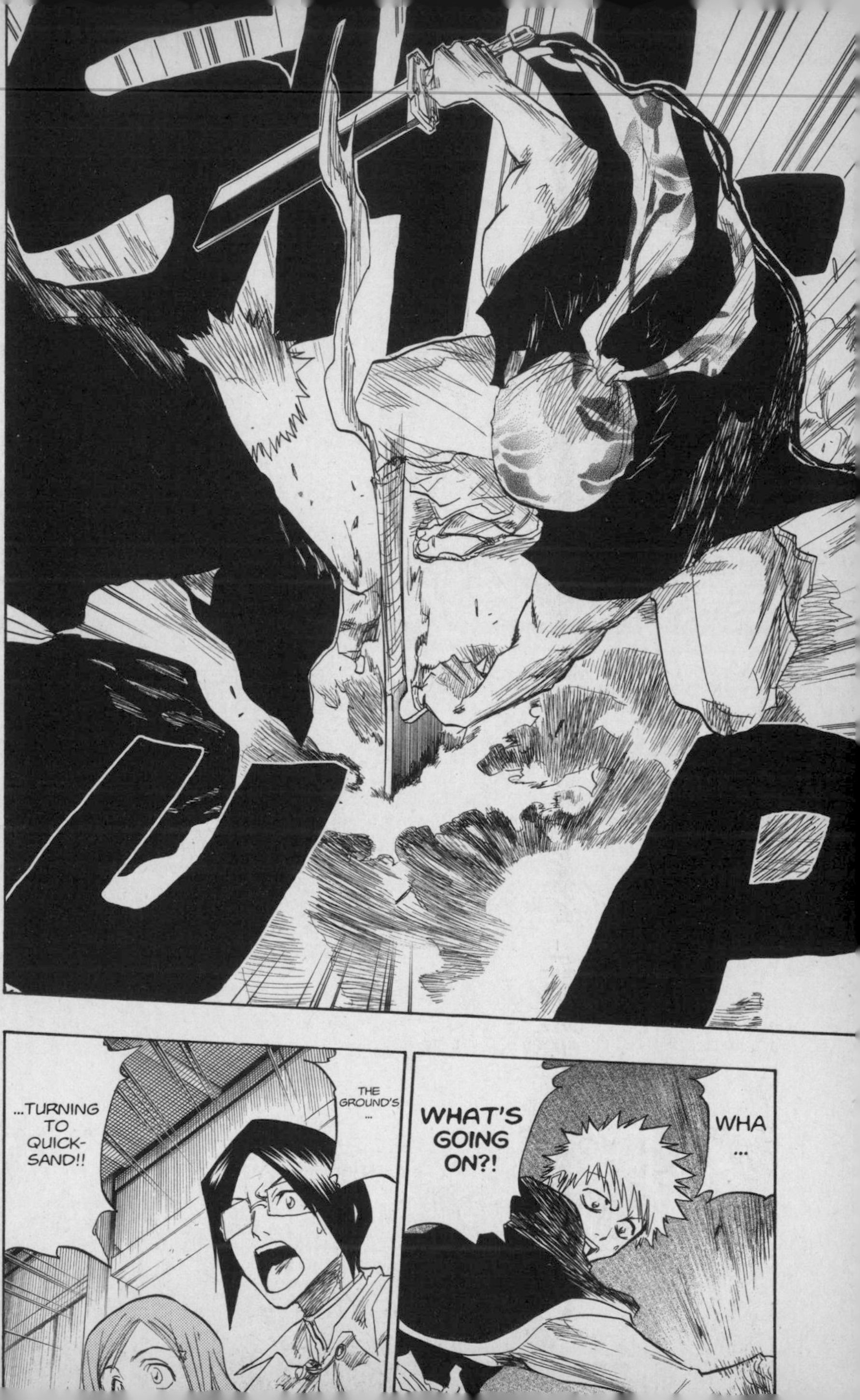
WHA ...
WHAT'S GOING ON?!
THE GROUND'S ...
...TURNING TO QUICK-SAND!!

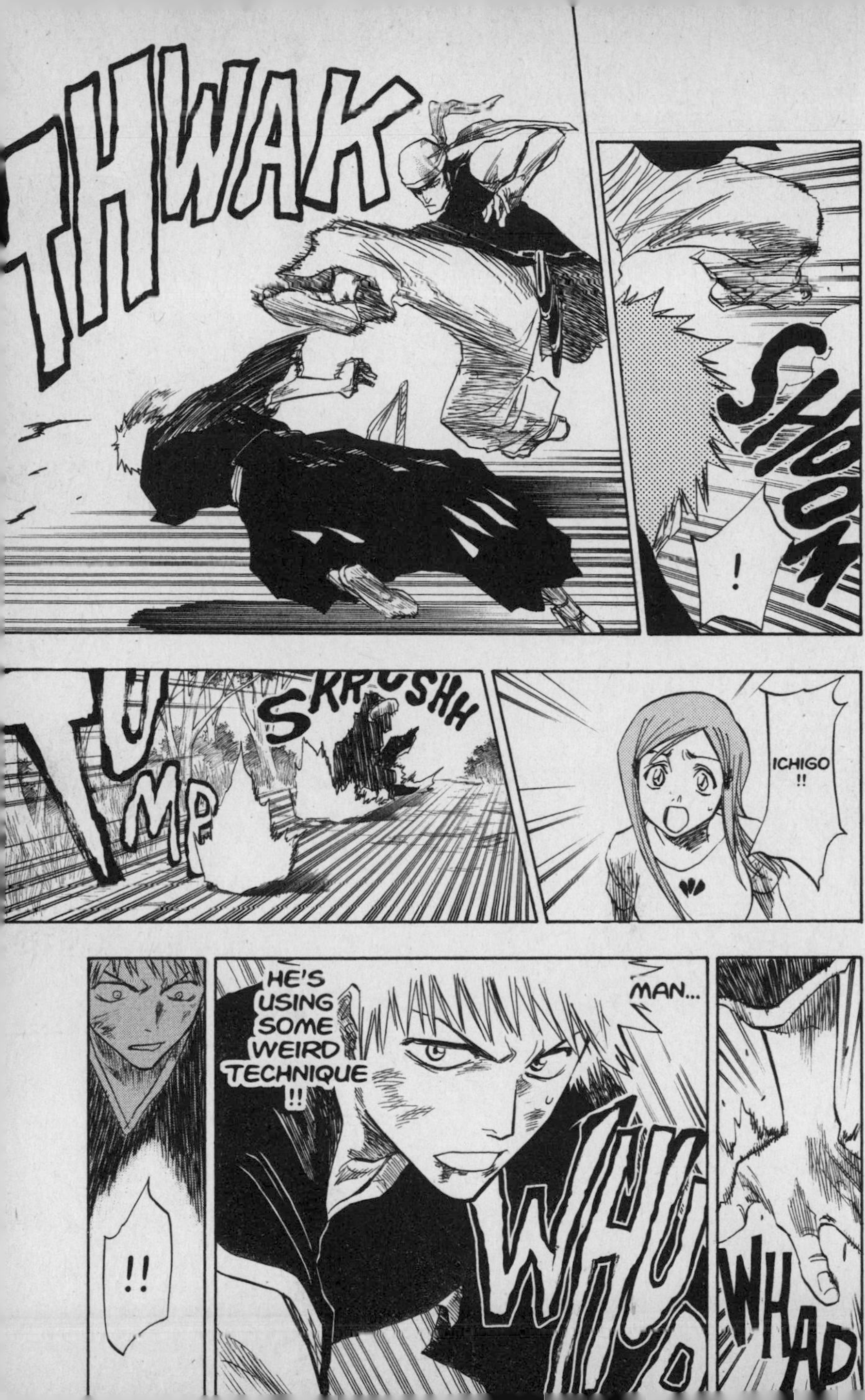
SHOOM
!
THWAK
ICHIGO !!
SKRCSHH
THUMP
WHAD
MAN...
HE'S USING SOME WEIRD TECHNIQUE !!
WHU
!!

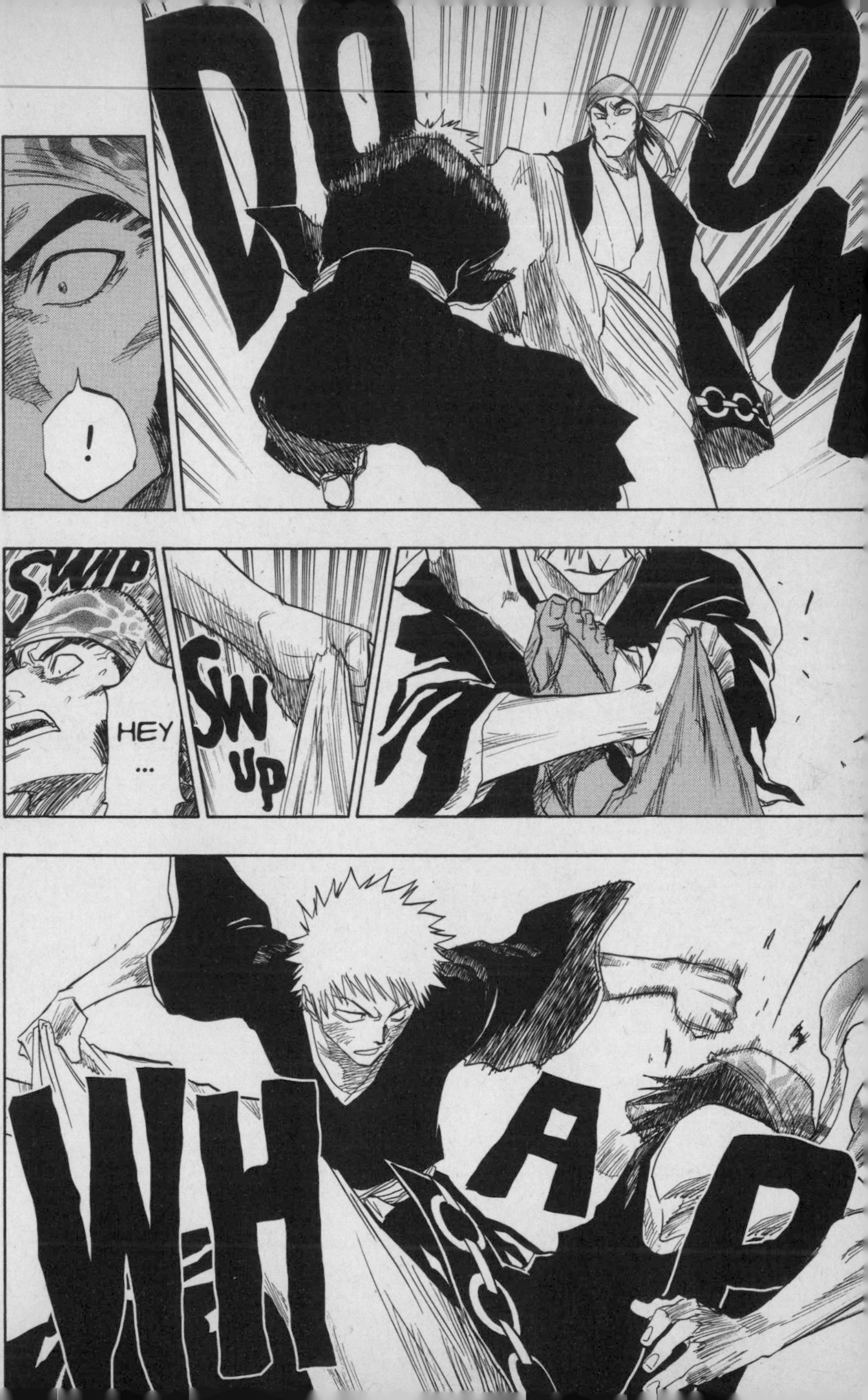

DOOM
!
SWUP
SWIP
HEY ...
WHAP

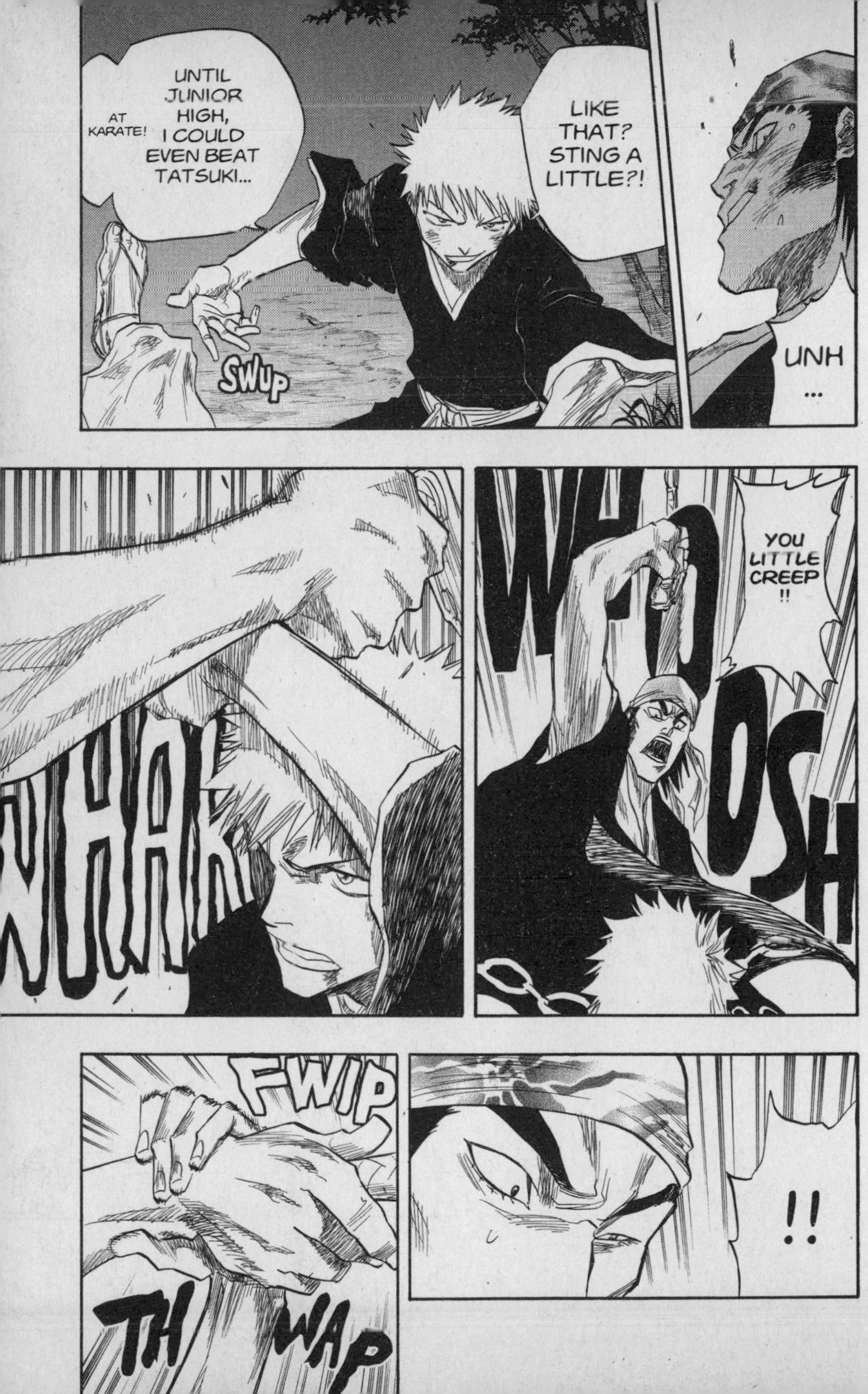
UNH ...
LIKE THAT? STING A LITTLE?!
UNTIL JUNIOR HIGH, I COULD EVEN BEAT TATSUKI...
AT KARATE!
SWUP
YOU LITTLE CREEP !!
!!
F-WIP
THWAP

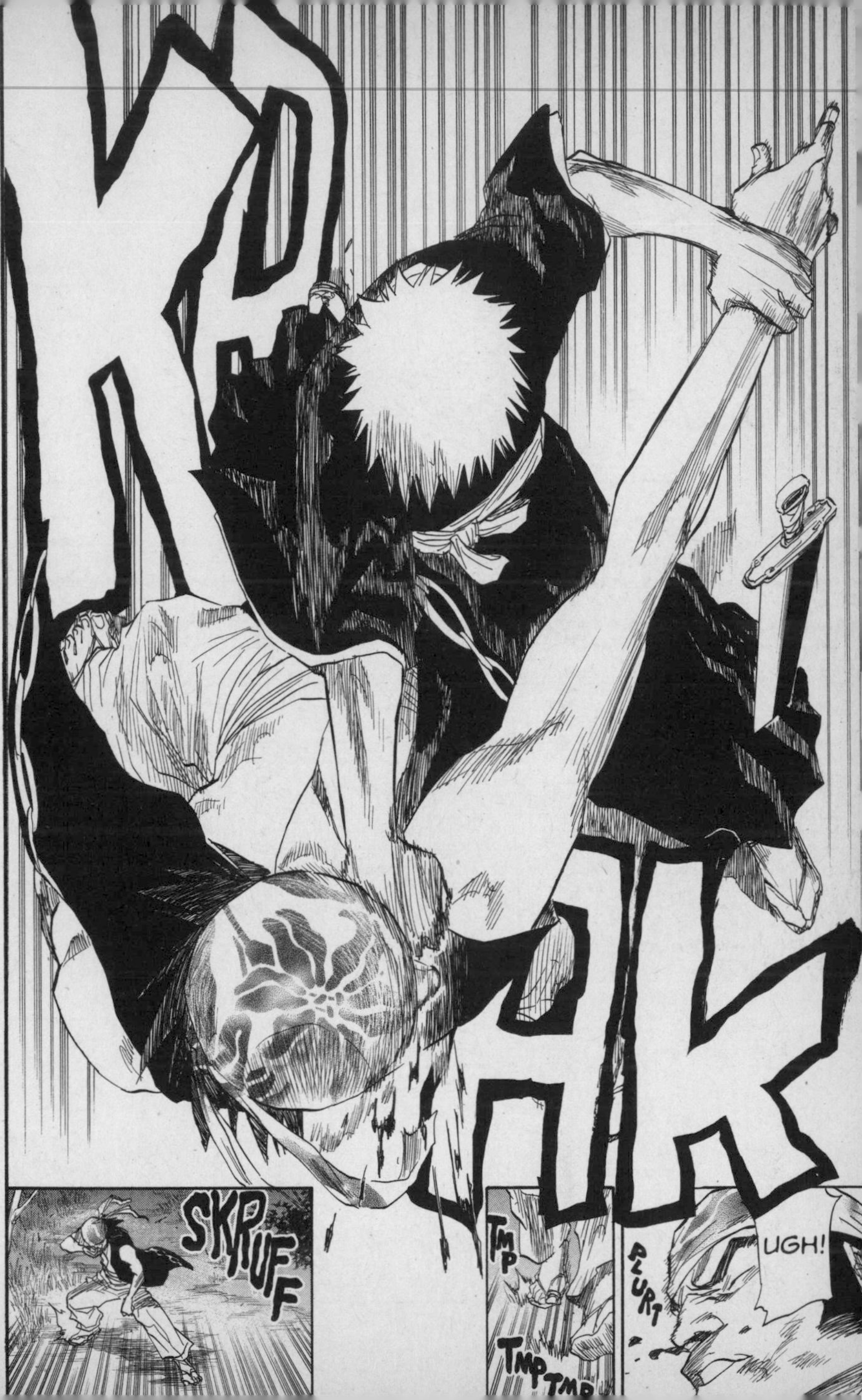
UGH!
PLURT
TMP
TMP TMP
SKRUFF

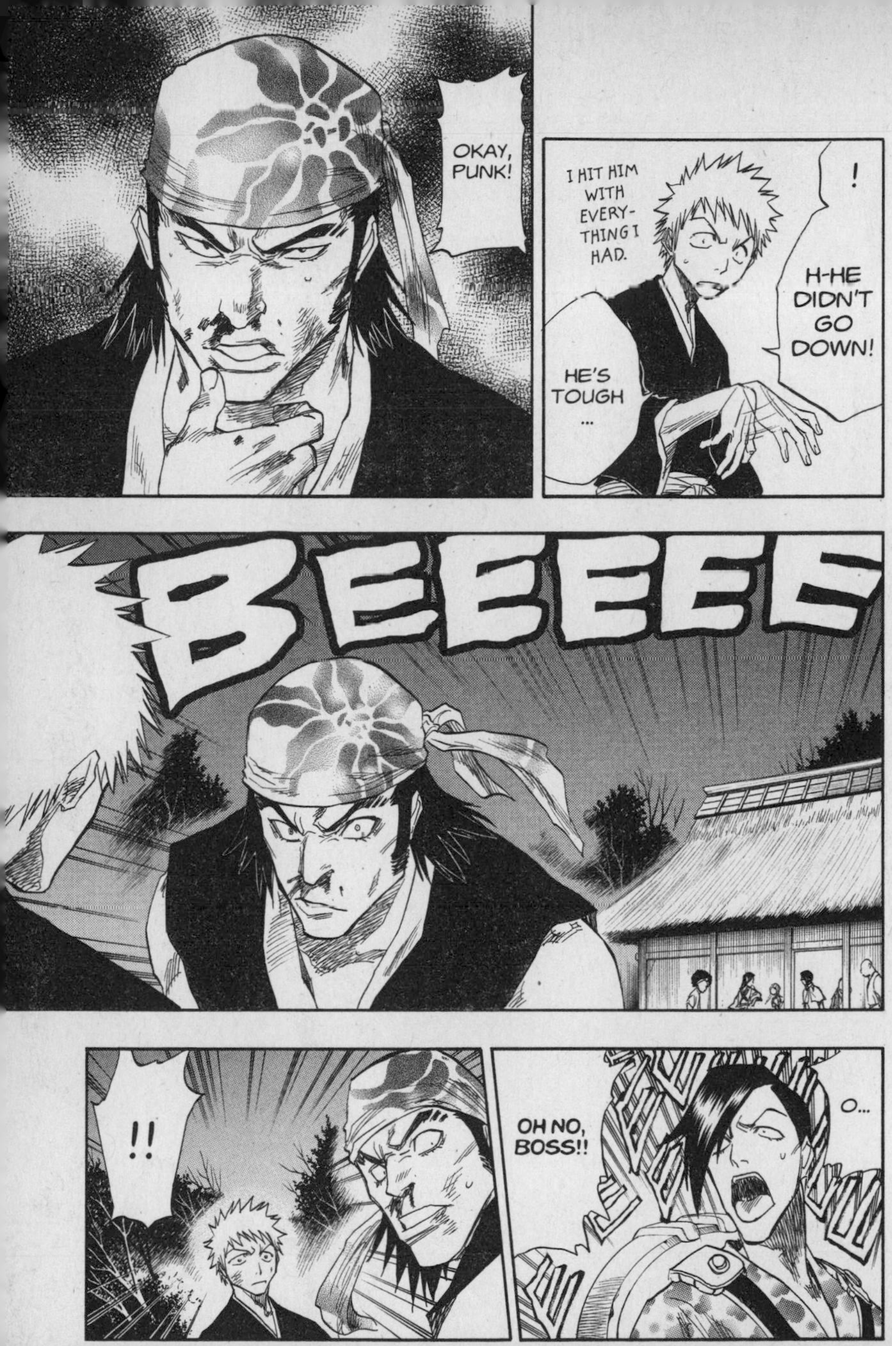
!
H-HE DIDN'T GO DOWN!
I HIT HIM WITH EVERY-THING I HAD.
HE'S TOUGH ...
OKAY, PUNK!
BEEEEE
O...
OH NO, BOSS!!
!!

GANJU'S GANG

TOP
REAL NAME:
KENJI
YAMASHITA
WORST
STREET
FIGHTER.
WORST
ARGUER,
TOO.

FEVER
REAL NAME:
MITSURU
ISHINO
HAS
ABSOLUTELY
NO
RHYTHM.

HAWK
REAL NAME:
TAICHI
MIYAMOTO
HENCHMAN
NUMBER
ONE.
GOOD AT
COOKING.

DUMBBELL
REAL NAME:
SADATOMO
SAIONJI
A GENIUS AT
CARING FOR
ANIMALS.

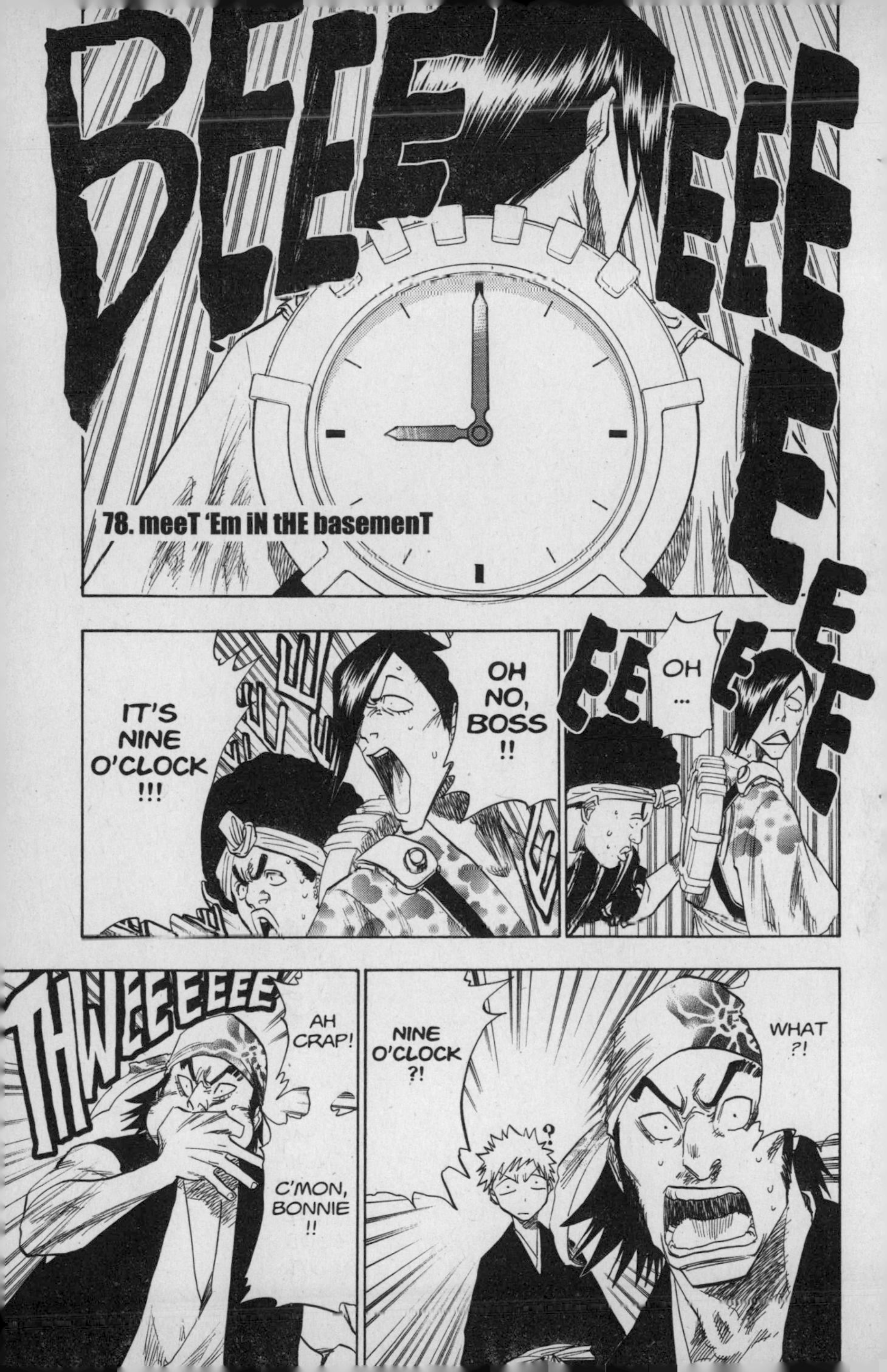
78. meeT 'Em iN tHE basemenT
OH ...
OH NO, BOSS !!
IT'S NINE O'CLOCK !!!
WHAT ?!
NINE O'CLOCK ?!
THWEEEEEEE
AH CRAP!
C'MON, BONNIE !!

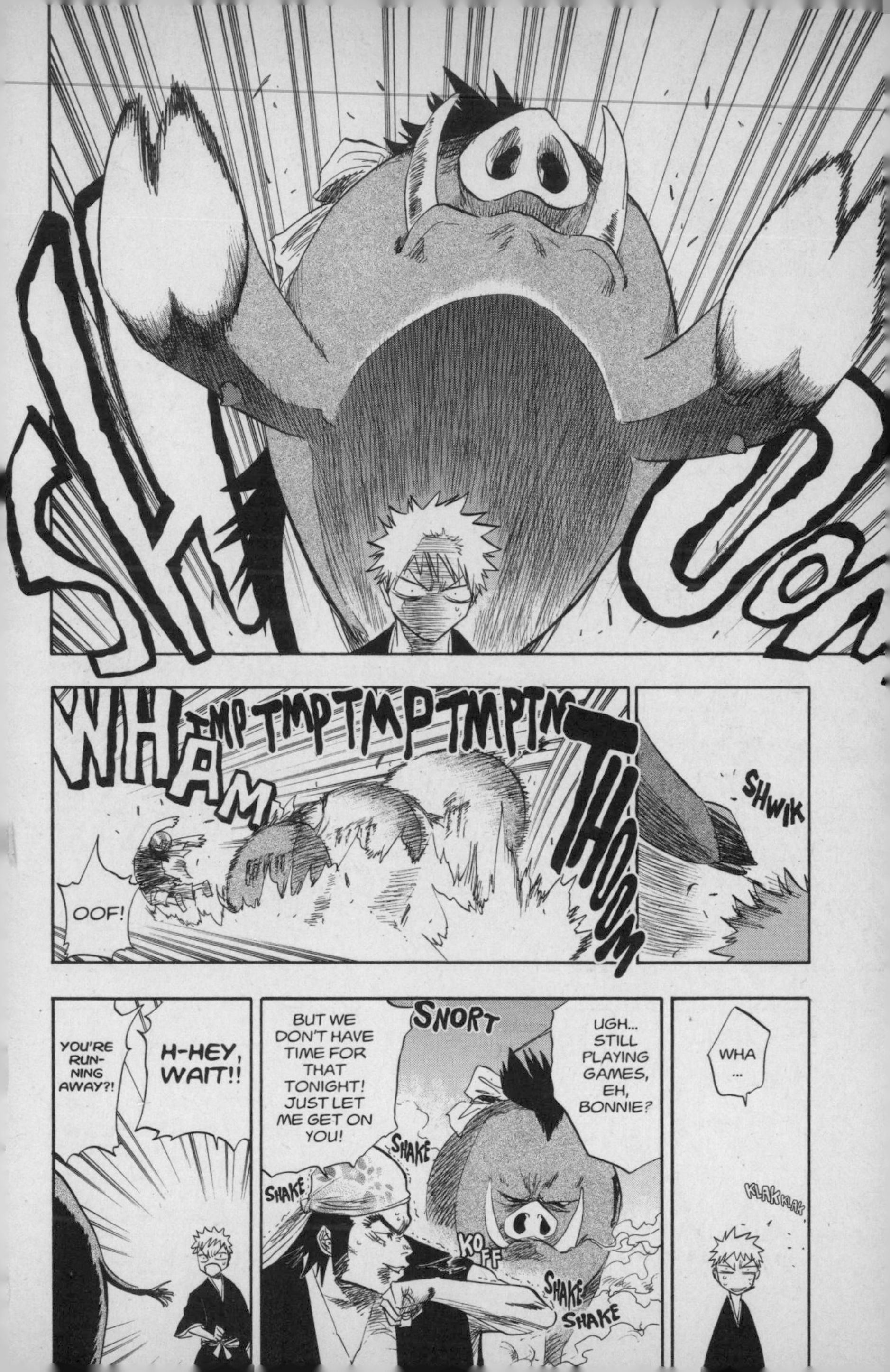
SHWIK
THOOM
TMP TMP TMP TMP TMP
WHAM
OOF!
WHA ...
KLAK KLAK
UGH... STILL PLAYING GAMES, EH, BONNIE?
SNORT
BUT WE DON'T HAVE TIME FOR THAT TONIGHT! JUST LET ME GET ON YOU!
SHAKE
SHAKE
KOFF
SHAKE
SHAKE
H-HEY, WAIT!!
YOU'RE RUN-NING AWAY?!

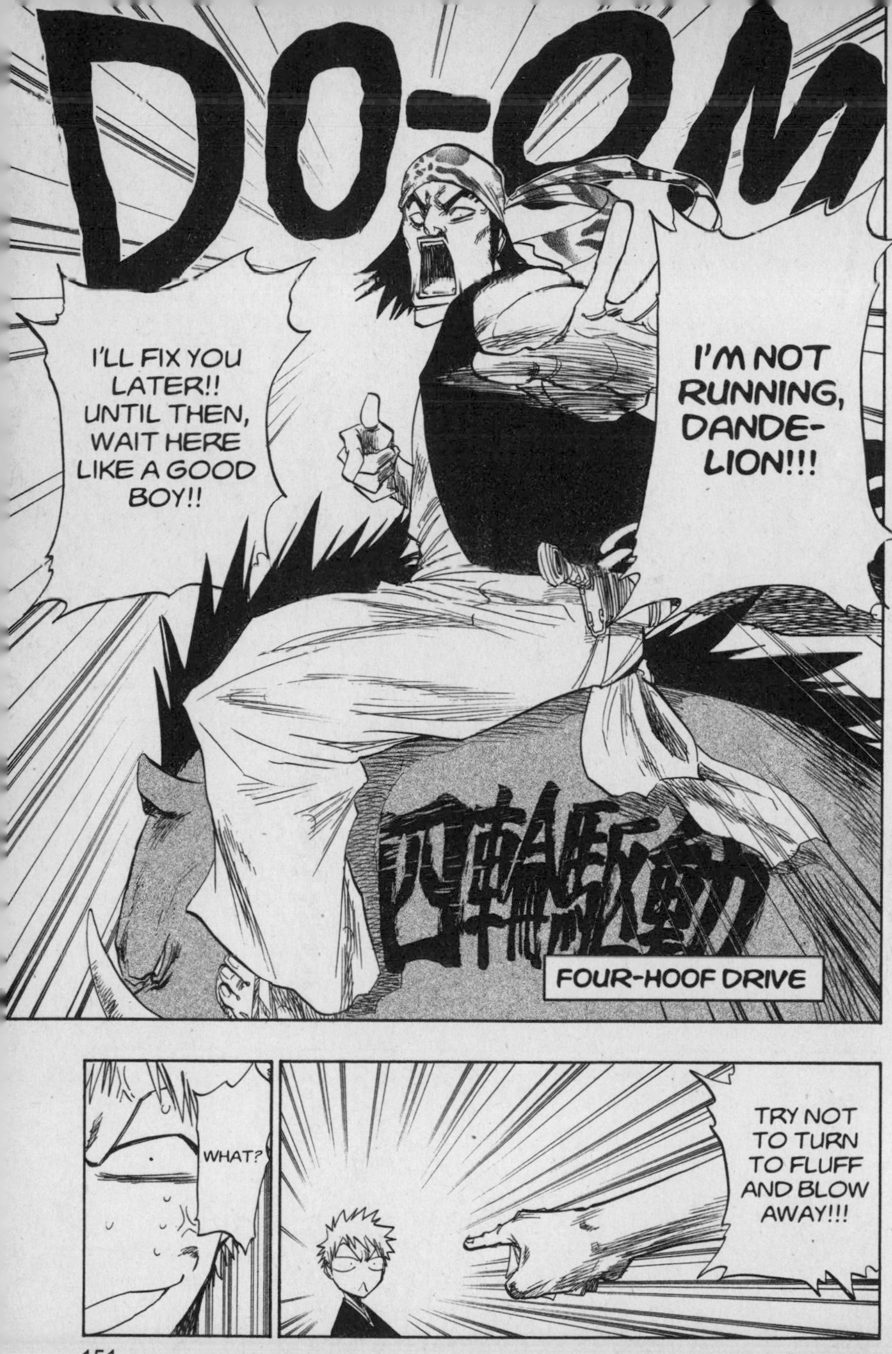
DO-OM
I'M NOT RUNNING, DANDE-LION!!!
I'LL FIX YOU LATER!! UNTIL THEN, WAIT HERE LIKE A GOOD BOY!!
FOUR-HOOF DRIVE
TRY NOT TO TURN TO FLUFF AND BLOW AWAY!!!
WHAT?

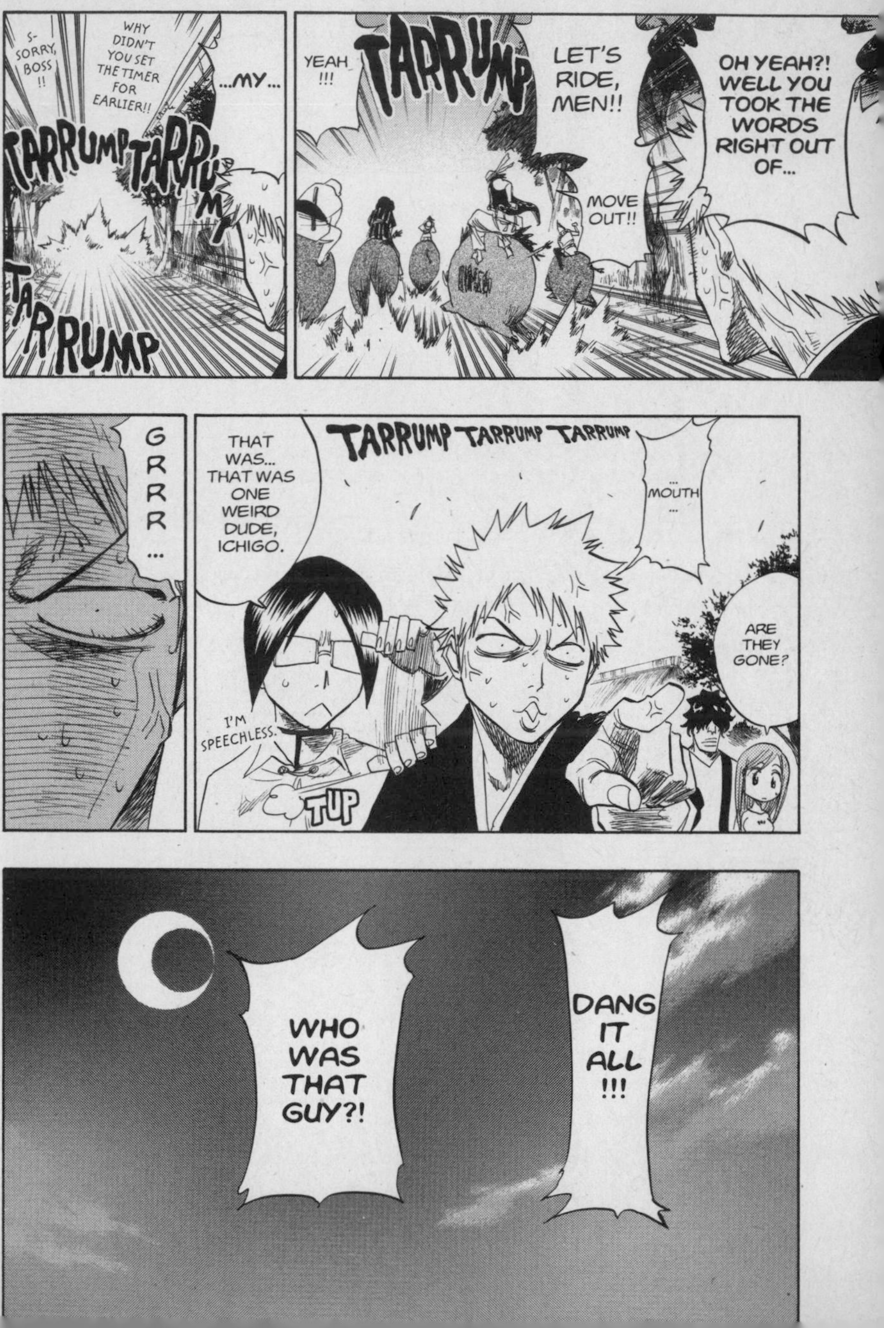
OH YEAH?! WELL YOU TOOK THE WORDS RIGHT OUT OF...
LET'S RIDE, MEN!!
TARRUMP
YEAH!!!
MOVE OUT!!
...MY...
WHY DIDN'T YOU SET THE TIMER FOR EARLIER!!
S-SORRY, BOSS!!
TARRUMP TARRUMP
TARRUMP
...MOUTH...
TARRUMP TARRUMP TARRUMP
ARE THEY GONE?
THAT WAS... THAT WAS ONE WEIRD DUDE, ICHIGO.
I'M SPEECHLESS.
TUP
GRRR...
DANG IT ALL!!!
WHO WAS THAT GUY?!

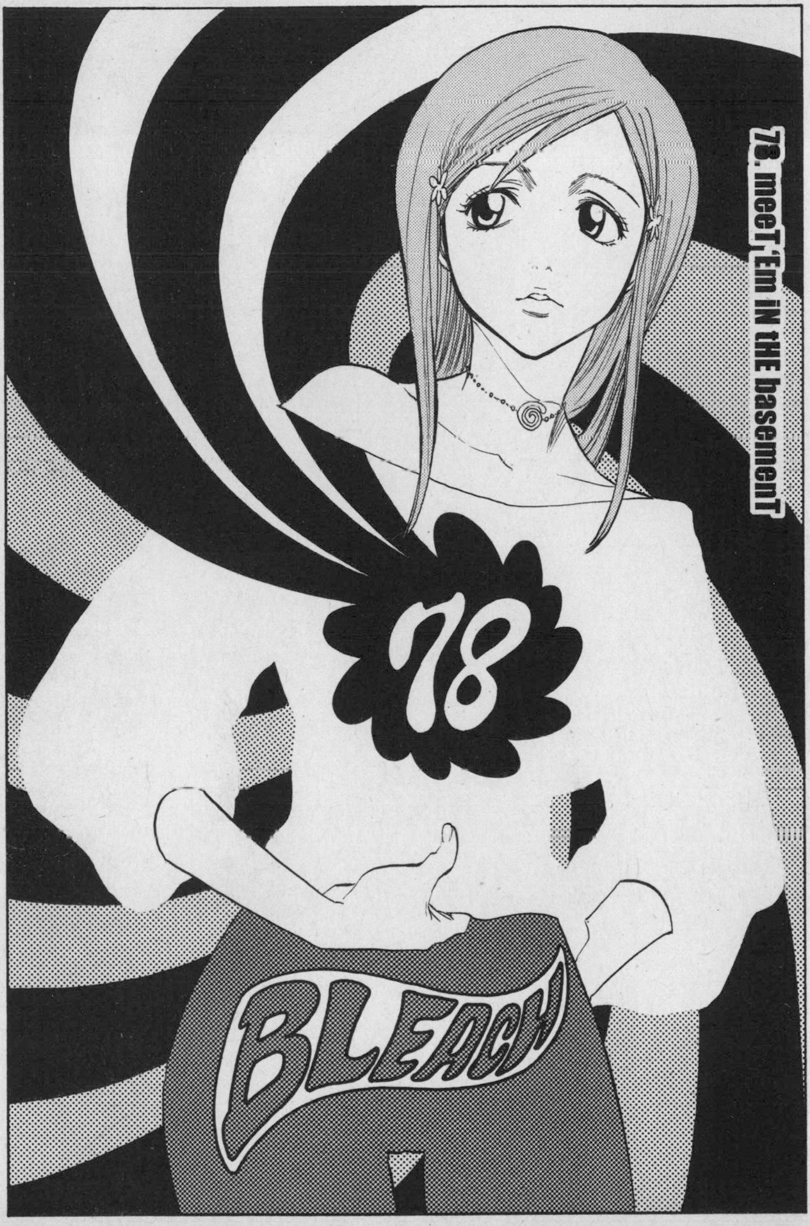
78. meeT 'Em iN tHE basemenT
78
BLEACH

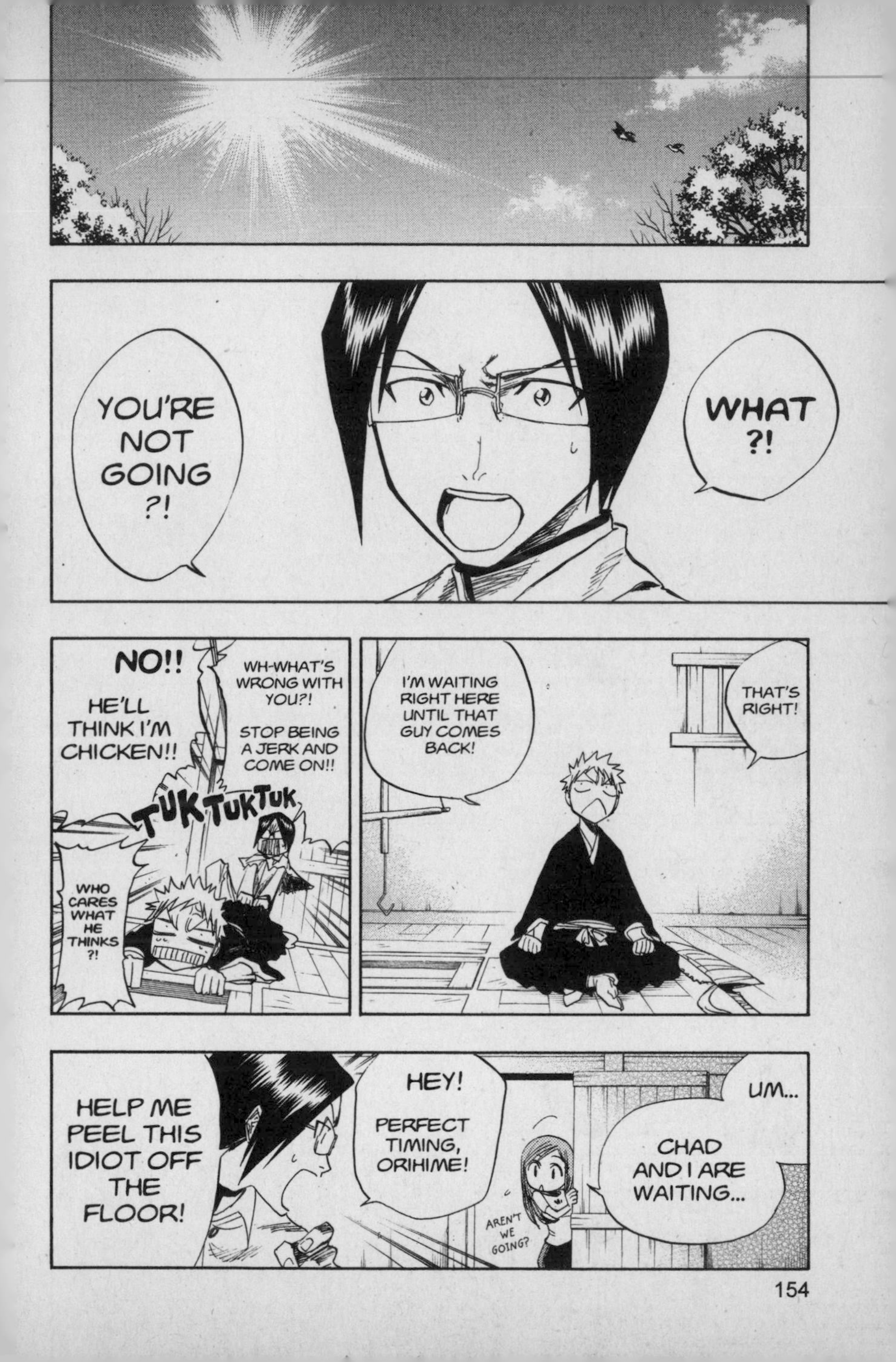
WHAT ?!
YOU'RE NOT GOING ?!
THAT'S RIGHT!
I'M WAITING RIGHT HERE UNTIL THAT GUY COMES BACK!
WH-WHAT'S WRONG WITH YOU?!
STOP BEING A JERK AND COME ON!!
NO!!
HE'LL THINK I'M CHICKEN!!
TUK TUKTUK
WHO CARES WHAT HE THINKS ?!
UM...
CHAD AND I ARE WAITING...
AREN'T WE GOING?
HEY!
PERFECT TIMING, ORIHIME!
HELP ME PEEL THIS IDIOT OFF THE FLOOR!

READ THIS WAY

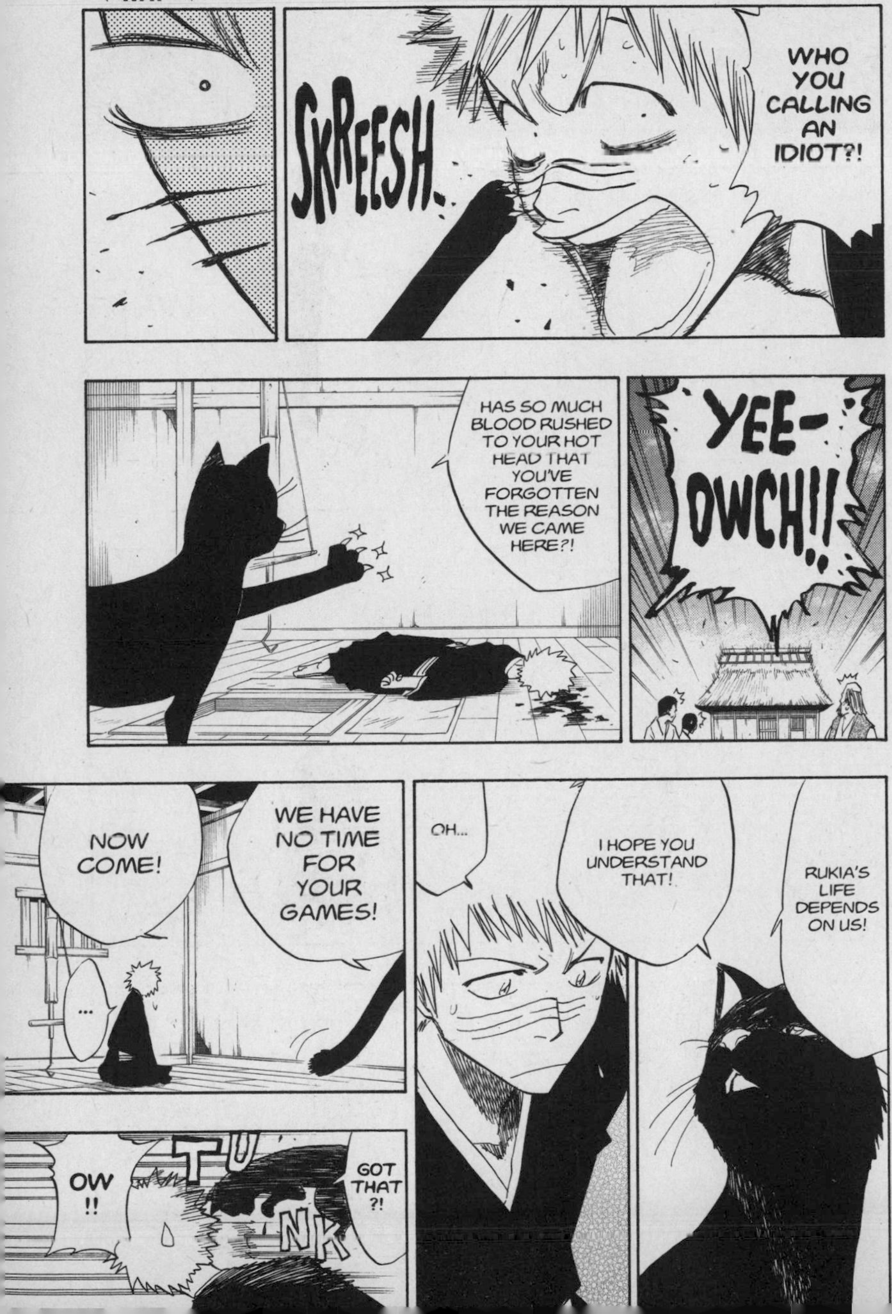

WHO YOU CALLING AN IDIOT?!
SKREESH
YEE-OWCH!!
HAS SO MUCH BLOOD RUSHED TO YOUR HOT HEAD THAT YOU'VE FORGOTTEN THE REASON WE CAME HERE?!
RUKIA'S LIFE DEPENDS ON US!
I HOPE YOU UNDERSTAND THAT!
OH...
WE HAVE NO TIME FOR YOUR GAMES!
NOW COME!
...
GOT THAT?!
TUNK
OW!!

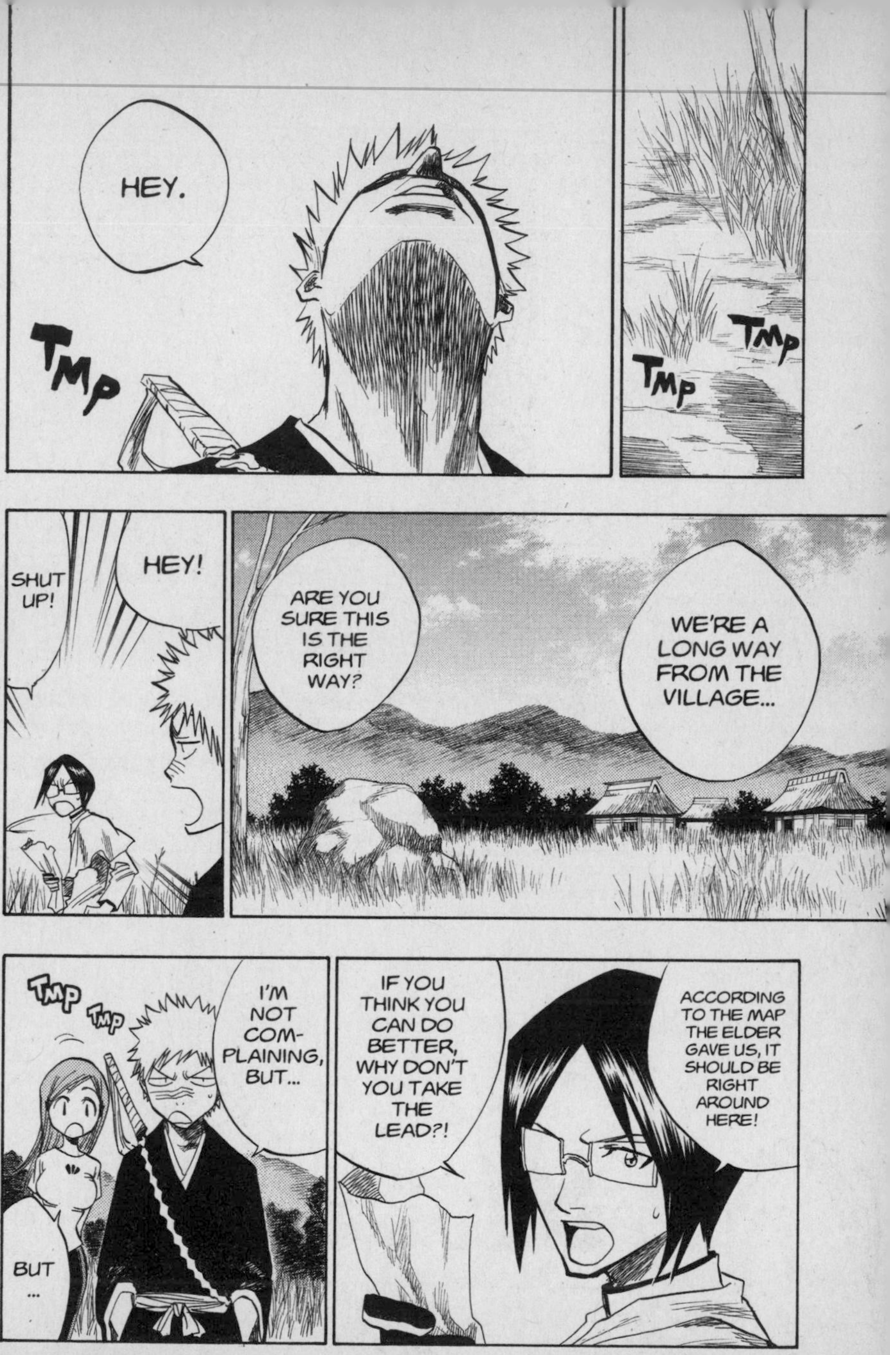
TMP
TMP
HEY.
TMP
WE'RE A LONG WAY FROM THE VILLAGE...
ARE YOU SURE THIS IS THE RIGHT WAY?
HEY!
SHUT UP!
ACCORDING TO THE MAP THE ELDER GAVE US, IT SHOULD BE RIGHT AROUND HERE!
IF YOU THINK YOU CAN DO BETTER, WHY DON'T YOU TAKE THE LEAD?!
I'M NOT COM-PLAINING, BUT...
TMP
TMP
BUT ...

READ THIS WAY

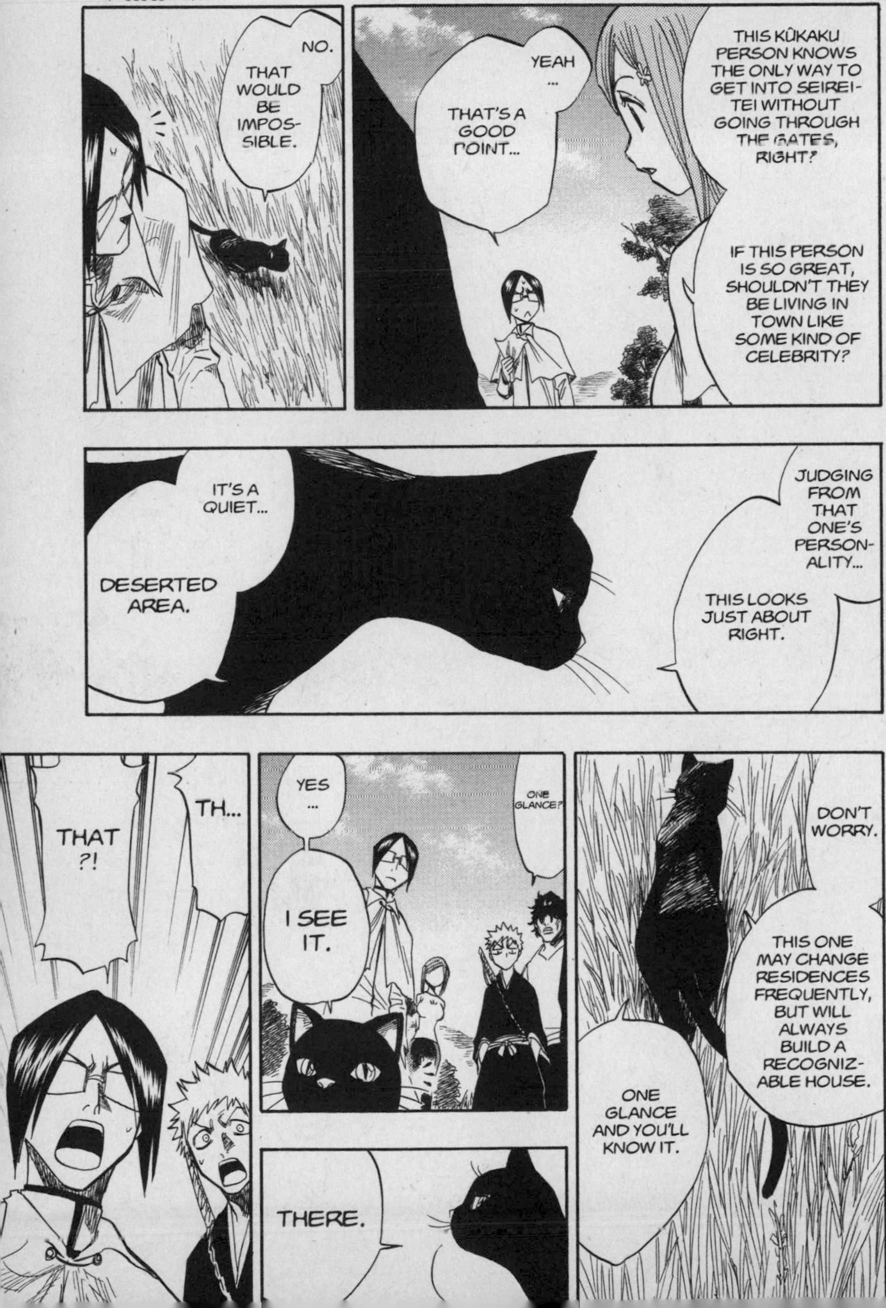

THIS KÛKAKU PERSON KNOWS THE ONLY WAY TO GET INTO SEIREI-TEI WITHOUT GOING THROUGH THE GATES, RIGHT?
IF THIS PERSON IS SO GREAT, SHOULDN'T THEY BE LIVING IN TOWN LIKE SOME KIND OF CELEBRITY?
YEAH ... THAT'S A GOOD POINT...
NO. THAT WOULD BE IMPOS-SIBLE.
JUDGING FROM THAT ONE'S PERSON-ALITY... THIS LOOKS JUST ABOUT RIGHT.
IT'S A QUIET... DESERTED AREA.
DON'T WORRY.
THIS ONE MAY CHANGE RESIDENCES FREQUENTLY, BUT WILL ALWAYS BUILD A RECOGNIZ-ABLE HOUSE.
ONE GLANCE AND YOU'LL KNOW IT.
ONE GLANCE?
YES ... I SEE IT.
THERE.
TH...
THAT ?!

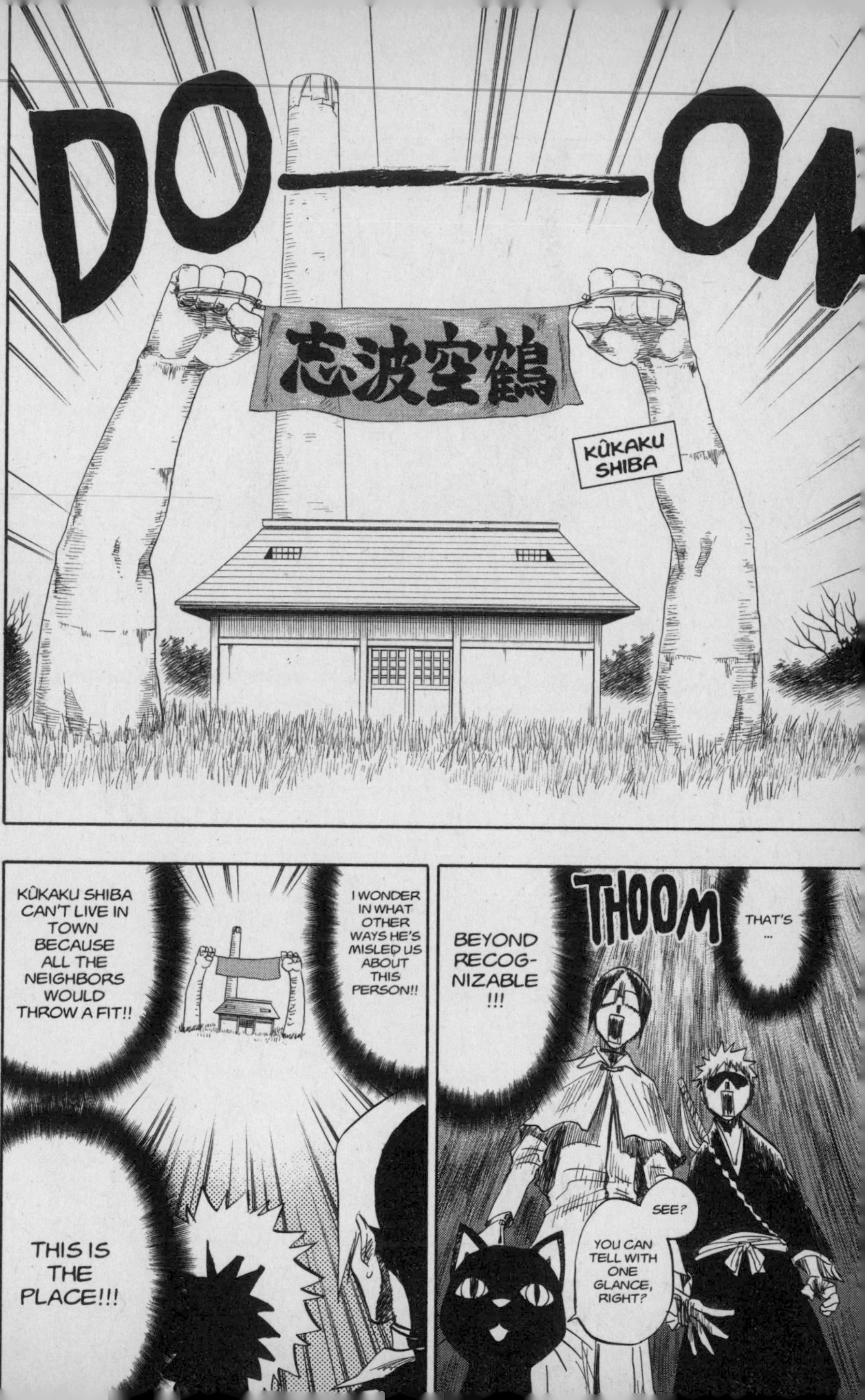
DO—ON
志波空鶴
KÛKAKU SHIBA
THOOM
THAT'S ...
BEYOND RECOG-NIZABLE !!!
SEE?
YOU CAN TELL WITH ONE GLANCE, RIGHT?
I WONDER IN WHAT OTHER WAYS HE'S MISLED US ABOUT THIS PERSON!!
KÛKAKU SHIBA CAN'T LIVE IN TOWN BECAUSE ALL THE NEIGHBORS WOULD THROW A FIT!!
THIS IS THE PLACE!!!

READ THIS WAY

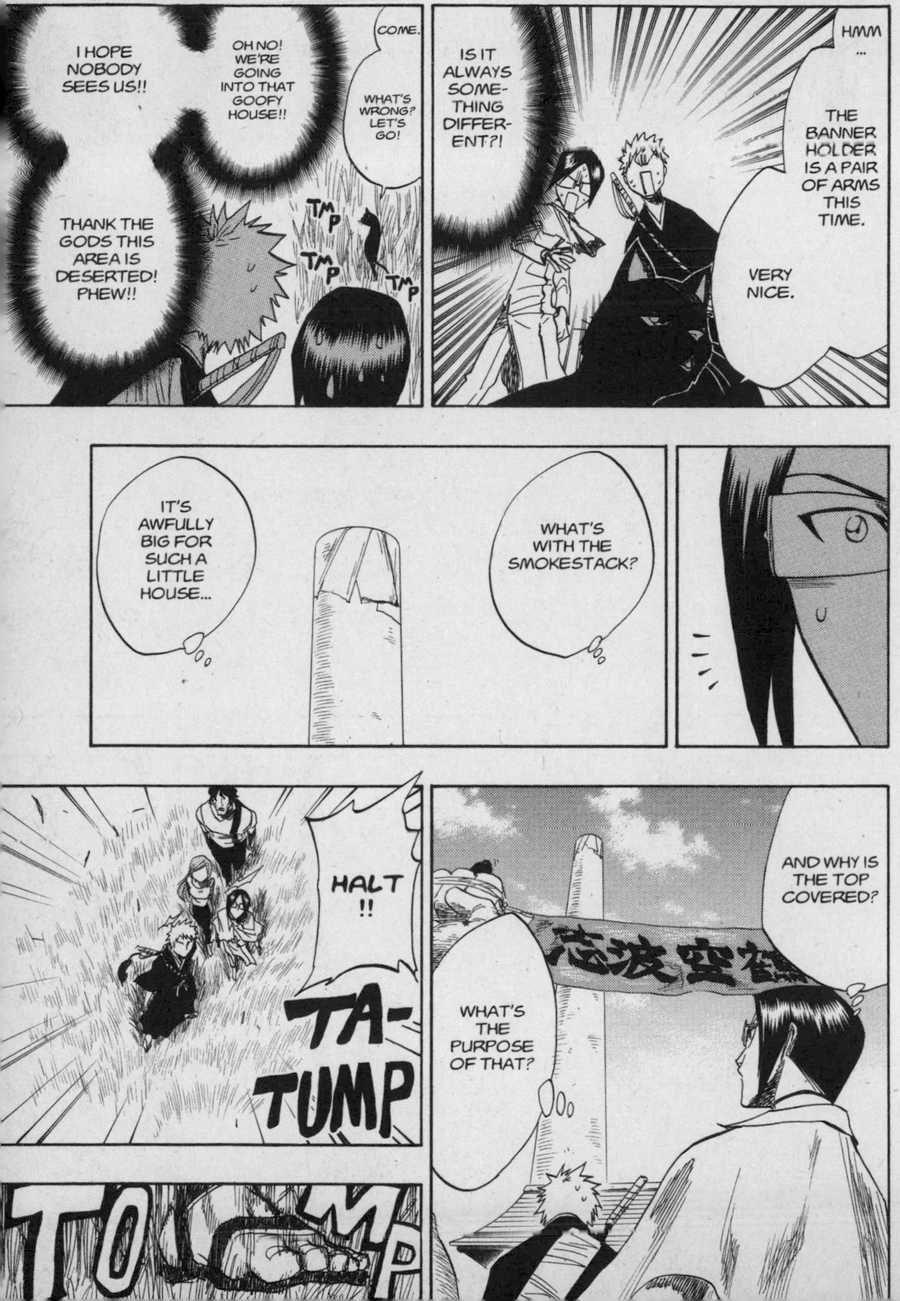
HMM...
THE BANNER HOLDER IS A PAIR OF ARMS THIS TIME.
VERY NICE.
IS IT ALWAYS SOMETHING DIFFERENT?!
COME.
WHAT'S WRONG? LET'S GO!
OH NO! WE'RE GOING INTO THAT GOOFY HOUSE!!
I HOPE NOBODY SEES US!!
TMP TMP TMP
THANK THE GODS THIS AREA IS DESERTED! PHEW!!
WHAT'S WITH THE SMOKESTACK?
IT'S AWFULLY BIG FOR SUCH A LITTLE HOUSE...
AND WHY IS THE TOP COVERED?
志波空鶴
WHAT'S THE PURPOSE OF THAT?
HALT!!
TA-TUMP
TOMP

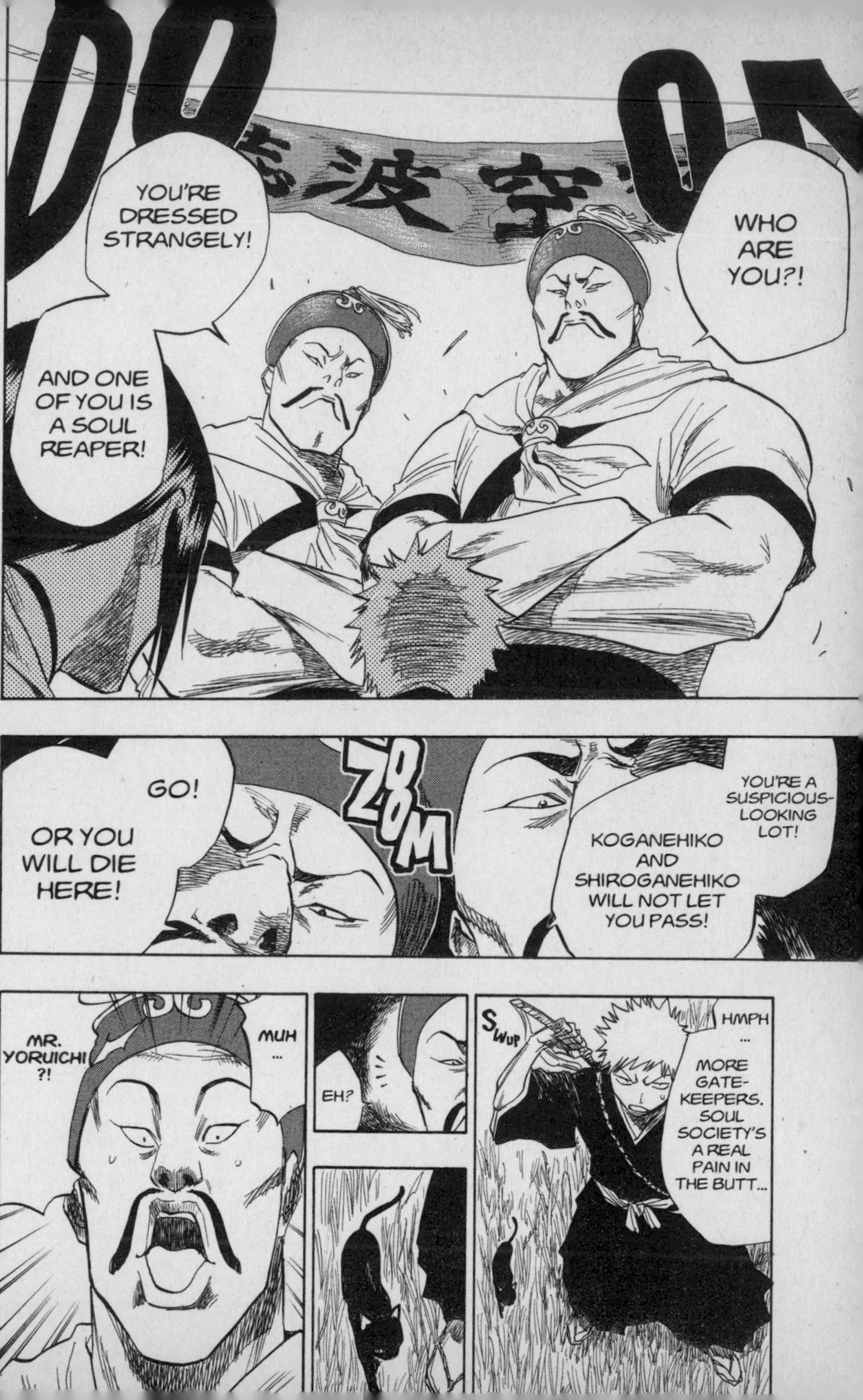
DOON
WHO ARE YOU?!
YOU'RE DRESSED STRANGELY!
AND ONE OF YOU IS A SOUL REAPER!
YOU'RE A SUSPICIOUS-LOOKING LOT!
KOGANEHIKO AND SHIROGANEHIKO WILL NOT LET YOU PASS!
ZOOM
GO!
OR YOU WILL DIE HERE!
SWUP
HMPH ...
MORE GATE-KEEPERS. SOUL SOCIETY'S A REAL PAIN IN THE BUTT...
EH?
MUH ...
MR. YORUICHI ?!

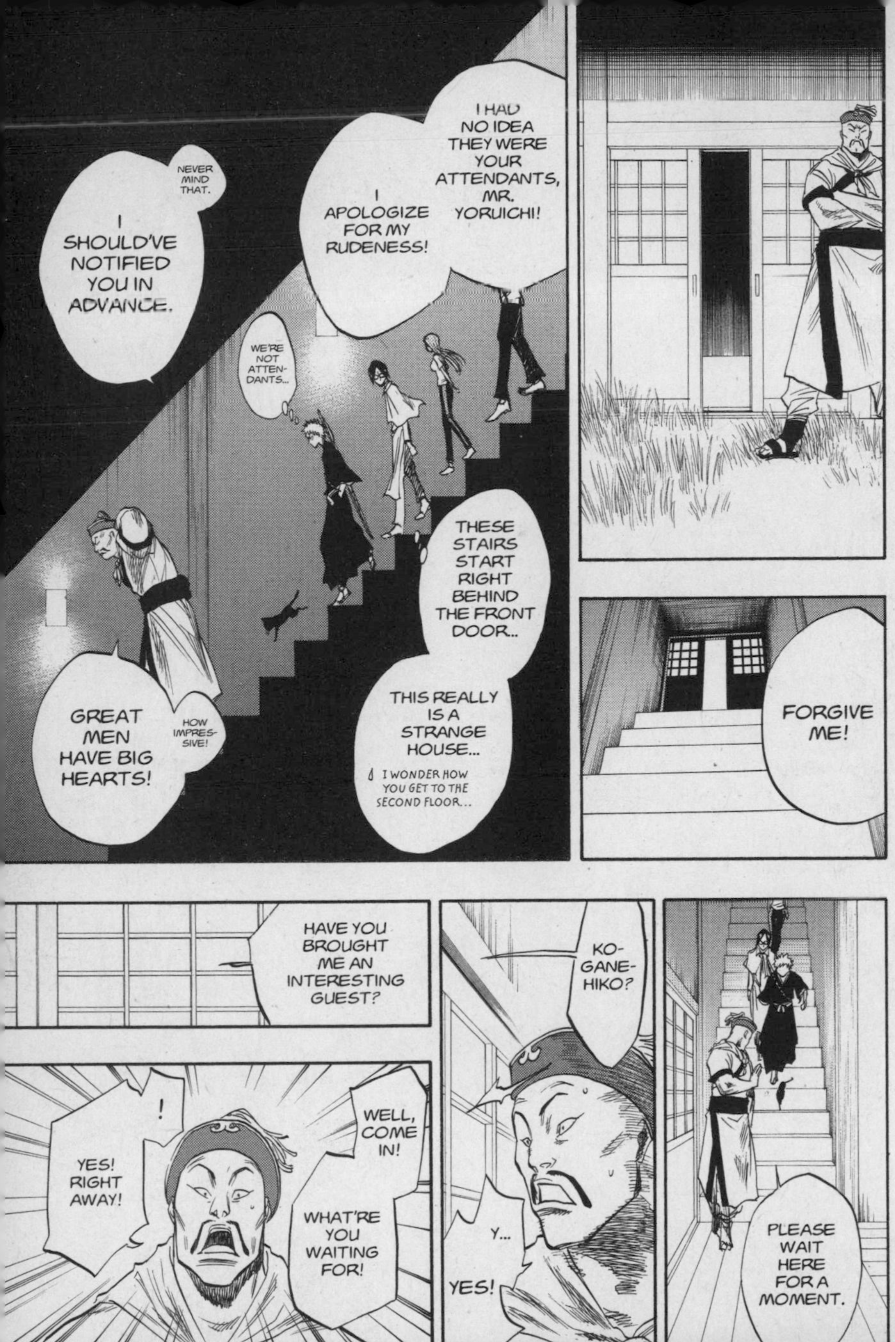
FORGIVE ME!
I HAD NO IDEA THEY WERE YOUR ATTENDANTS, MR. YORUICHI!
I APOLOGIZE FOR MY RUDENESS!
NEVER MIND THAT.
I SHOULD'VE NOTIFIED YOU IN ADVANCE.
WE'RE NOT ATTEN-DANTS...
THESE STAIRS START RIGHT BEHIND THE FRONT DOOR..
THIS REALLY IS A STRANGE HOUSE...
I WONDER HOW YOU GET TO THE SECOND FLOOR...
GREAT MEN HAVE BIG HEARTS!
HOW IMPRES-SIVE!
PLEASE WAIT HERE FOR A MOMENT.
KO-GANE-HIKO?
Y...
YES!
HAVE YOU BROUGHT ME AN INTERESTING GUEST?
WELL, COME IN!
WHAT'RE YOU WAITING FOR!
!
YES! RIGHT AWAY!

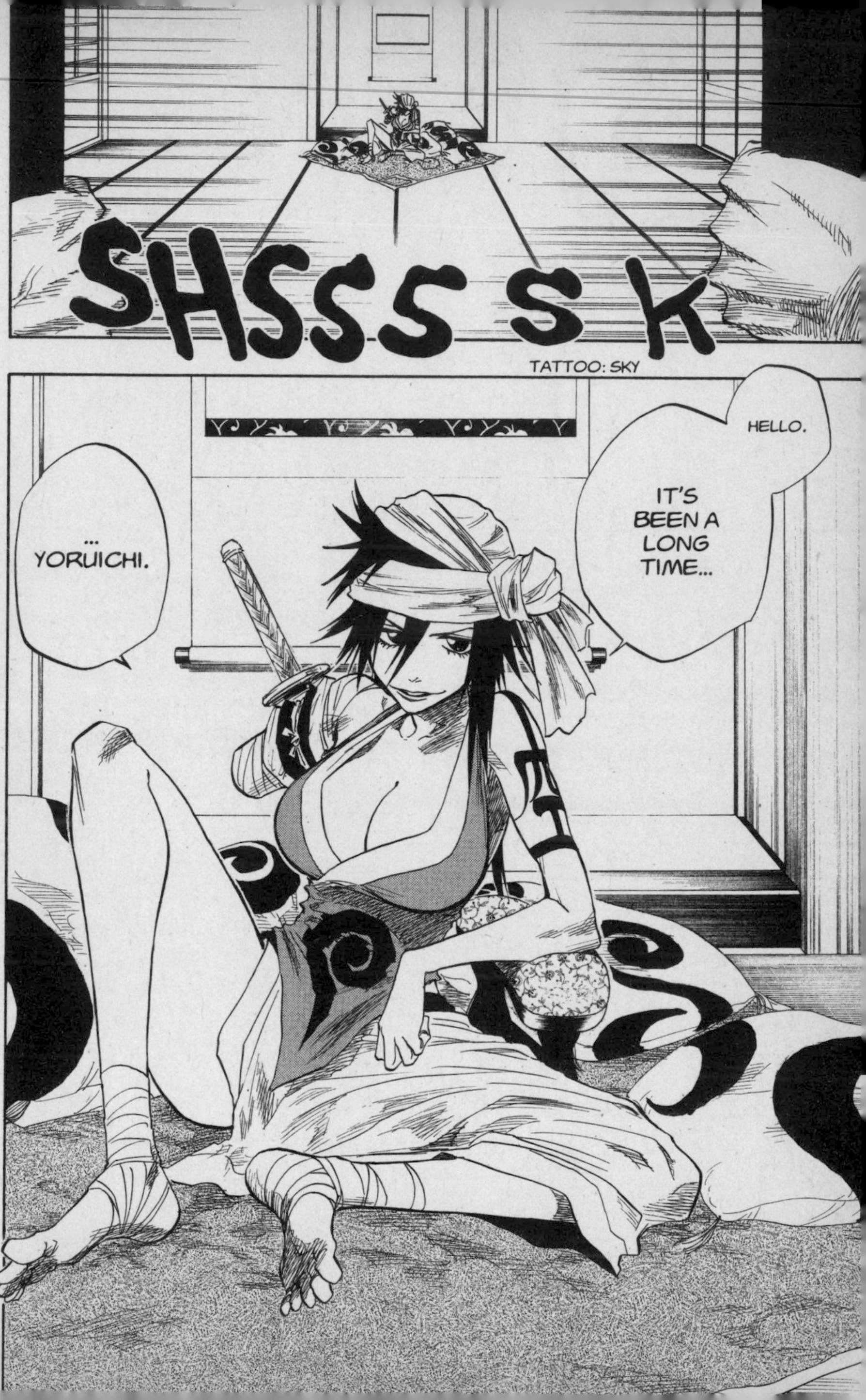
SHSSS S K
TATTOO: SKY
HELLO.
IT'S BEEN A LONG TIME...
... YORUICHI.

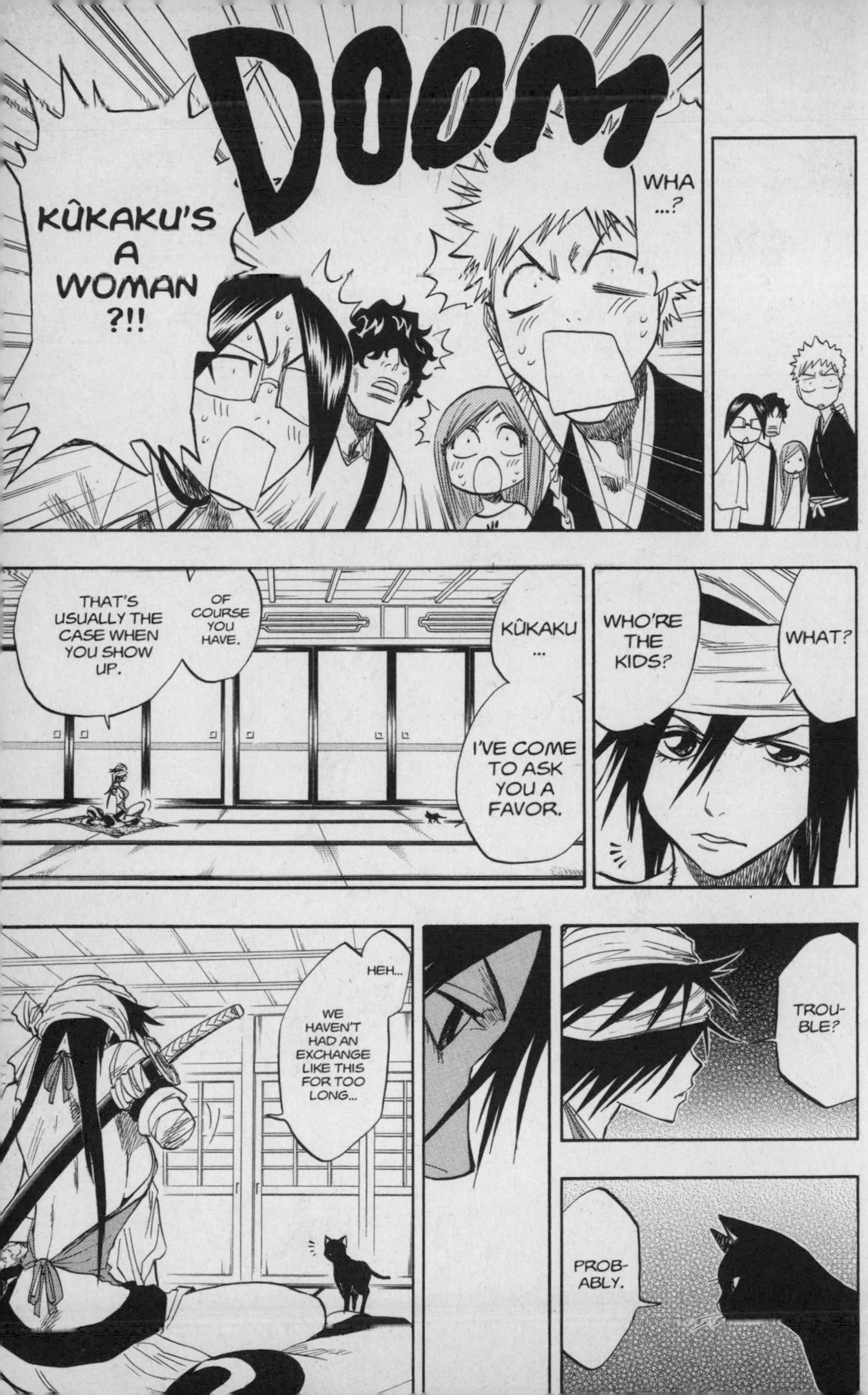
DOOM
WHA ...?
KÛKAKU'S A WOMAN ?!!
WHAT?
WHO'RE THE KIDS?
KÛKAKU ...
I'VE COME TO ASK YOU A FAVOR.
OF COURSE YOU HAVE.
THAT'S USUALLY THE CASE WHEN YOU SHOW UP.
TROU-BLE?
PROB-ABLY.
HEH...
WE HAVEN'T HAD AN EXCHANGE LIKE THIS FOR TOO LONG...

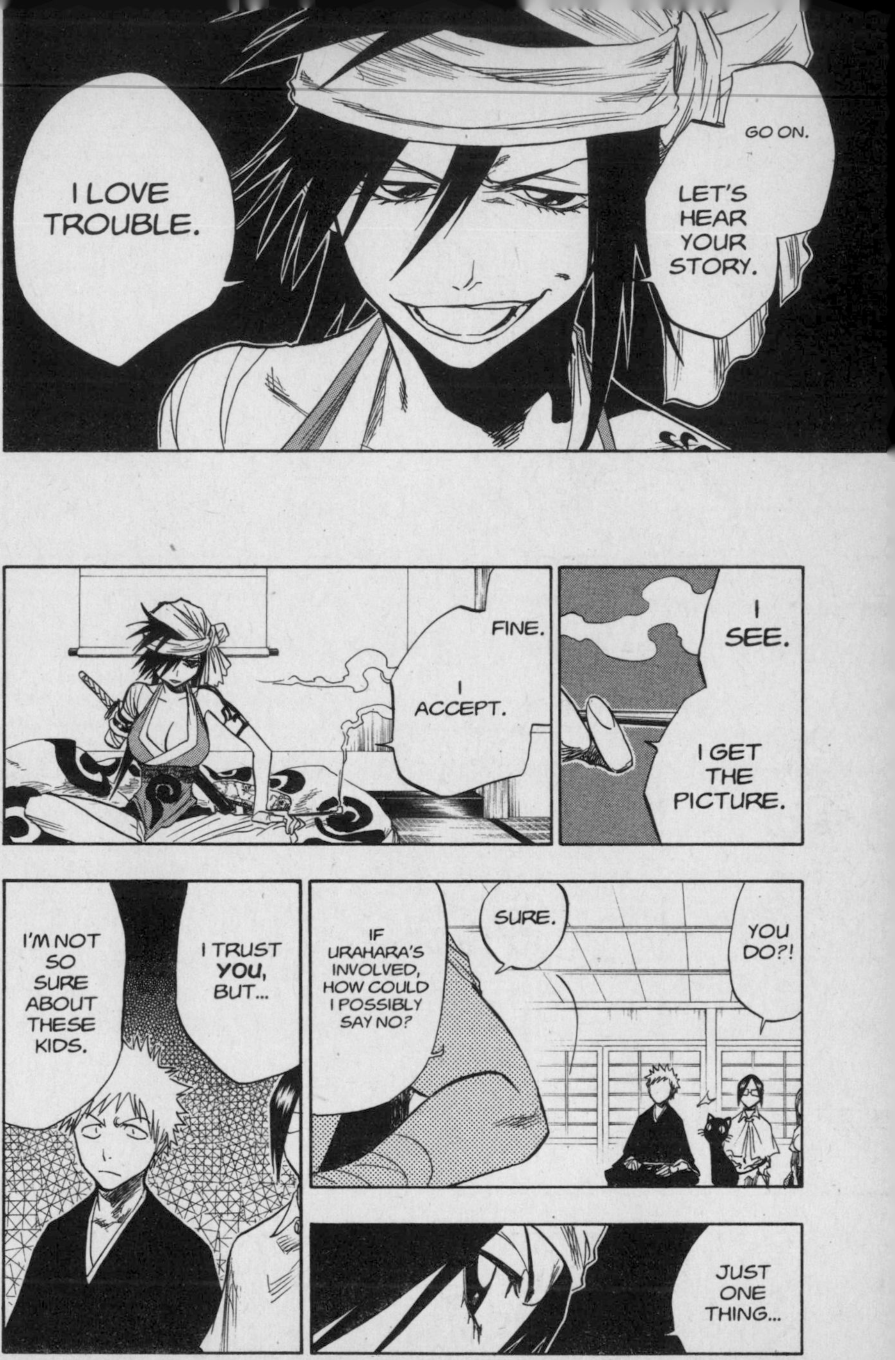

GO ON.
LET'S HEAR YOUR STORY.
I LOVE TROUBLE.
I SEE.
I GET THE PICTURE.
FINE.
I ACCEPT.
YOU DO?!
SURE.
IF URAHARA'S INVOLVED, HOW COULD I POSSIBLY SAY NO?
JUST ONE THING...
I TRUST **YOU**, BUT...
I'M NOT SO SURE ABOUT THESE KIDS.

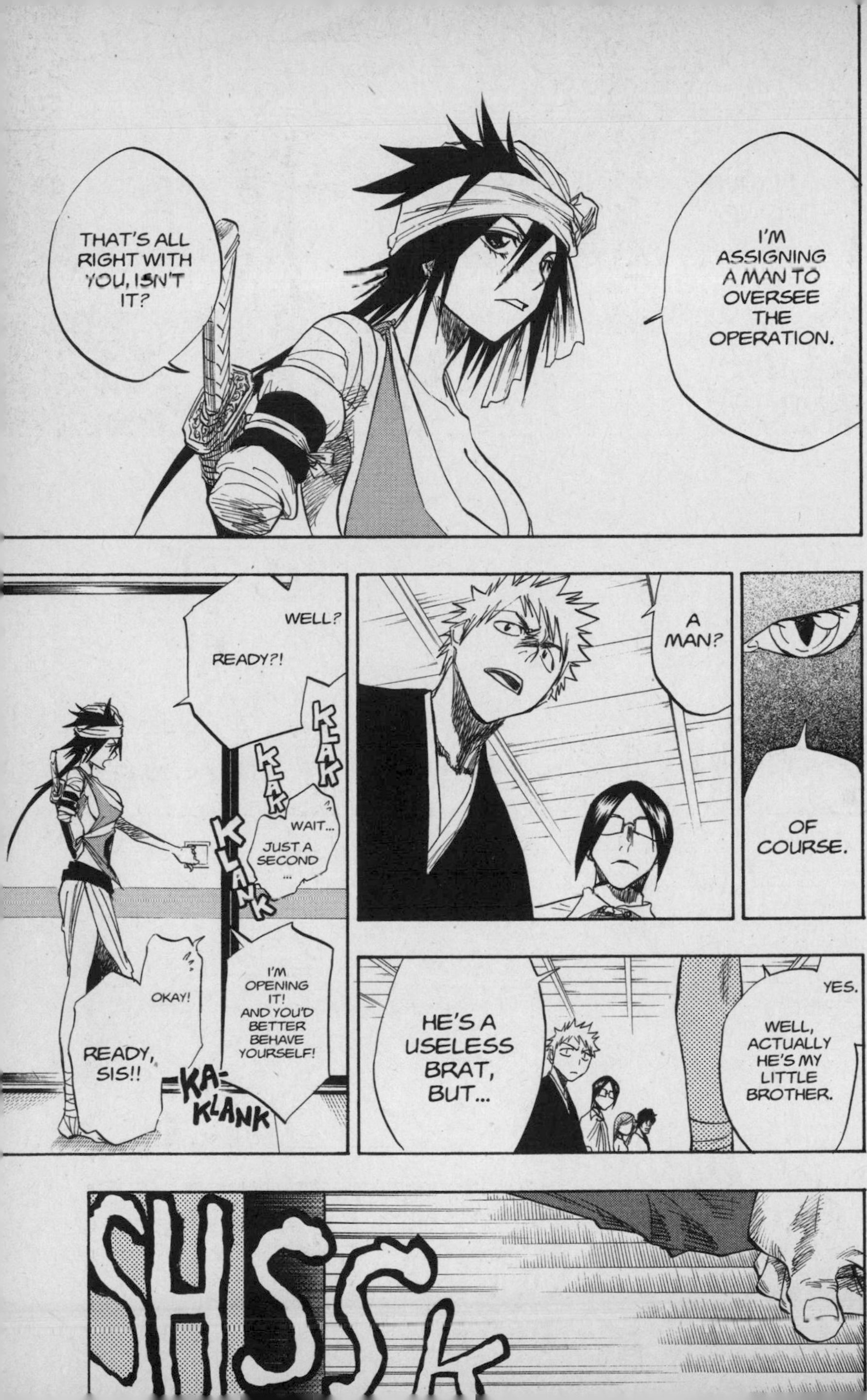
I'M ASSIGNING A MAN TO OVERSEE THE OPERATION.
THAT'S ALL RIGHT WITH YOU, ISN'T IT?
OF COURSE.
A MAN?
YES.
WELL, ACTUALLY HE'S MY LITTLE BROTHER.
HE'S A USELESS BRAT, BUT...
WELL?
READY?!
KLAK
KLAK
WAIT... JUST A SECOND ...
KLANK
I'M OPENING IT! AND YOU'D BETTER BEHAVE YOURSELF!
OKAY!
READY, SIS!!
KA-KLANK
SHSSK

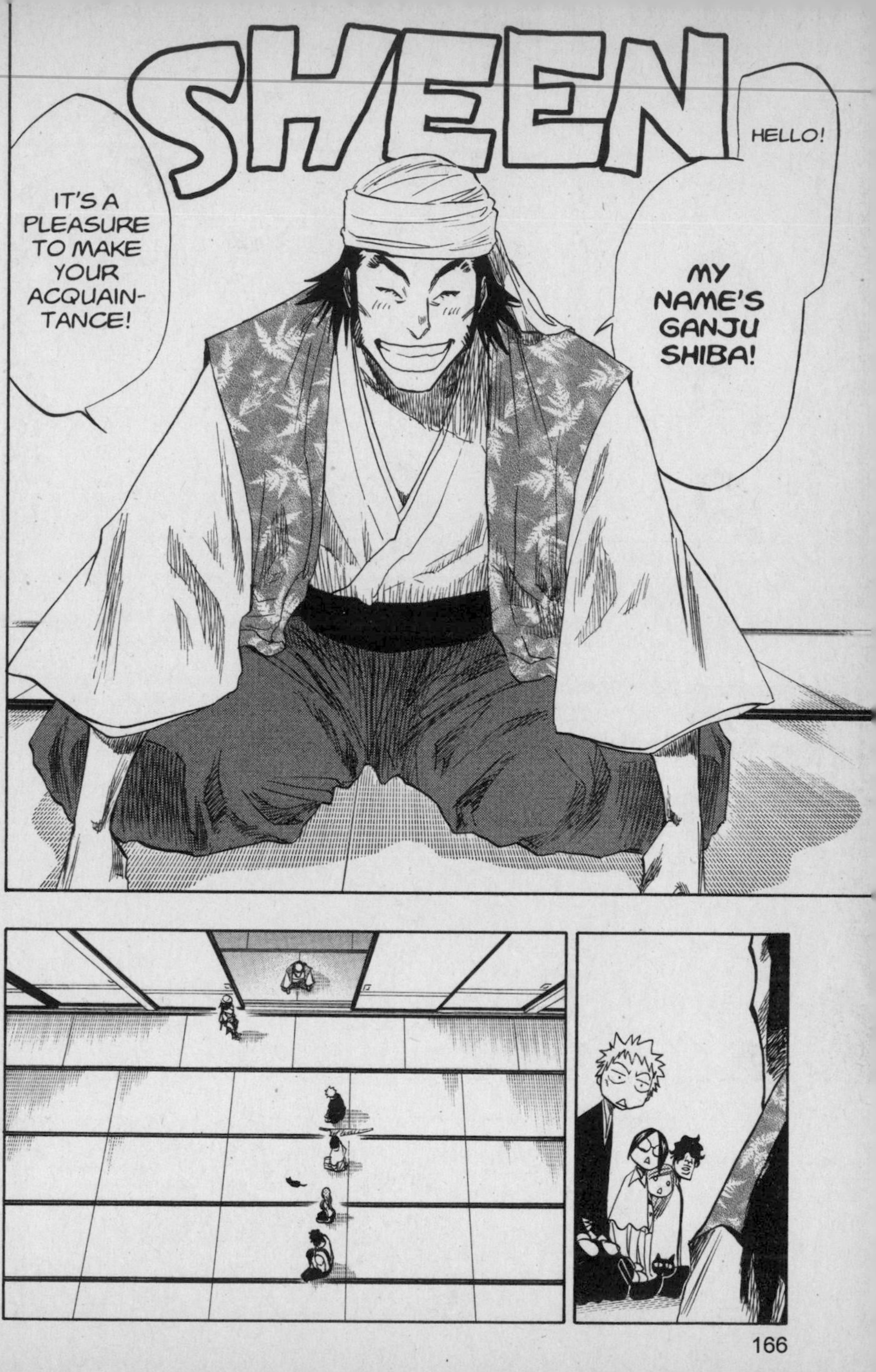
HELLO!
SHEEN
MY NAME'S GANJU SHIBA!
IT'S A PLEASURE TO MAKE YOUR ACQUAIN-TANCE!

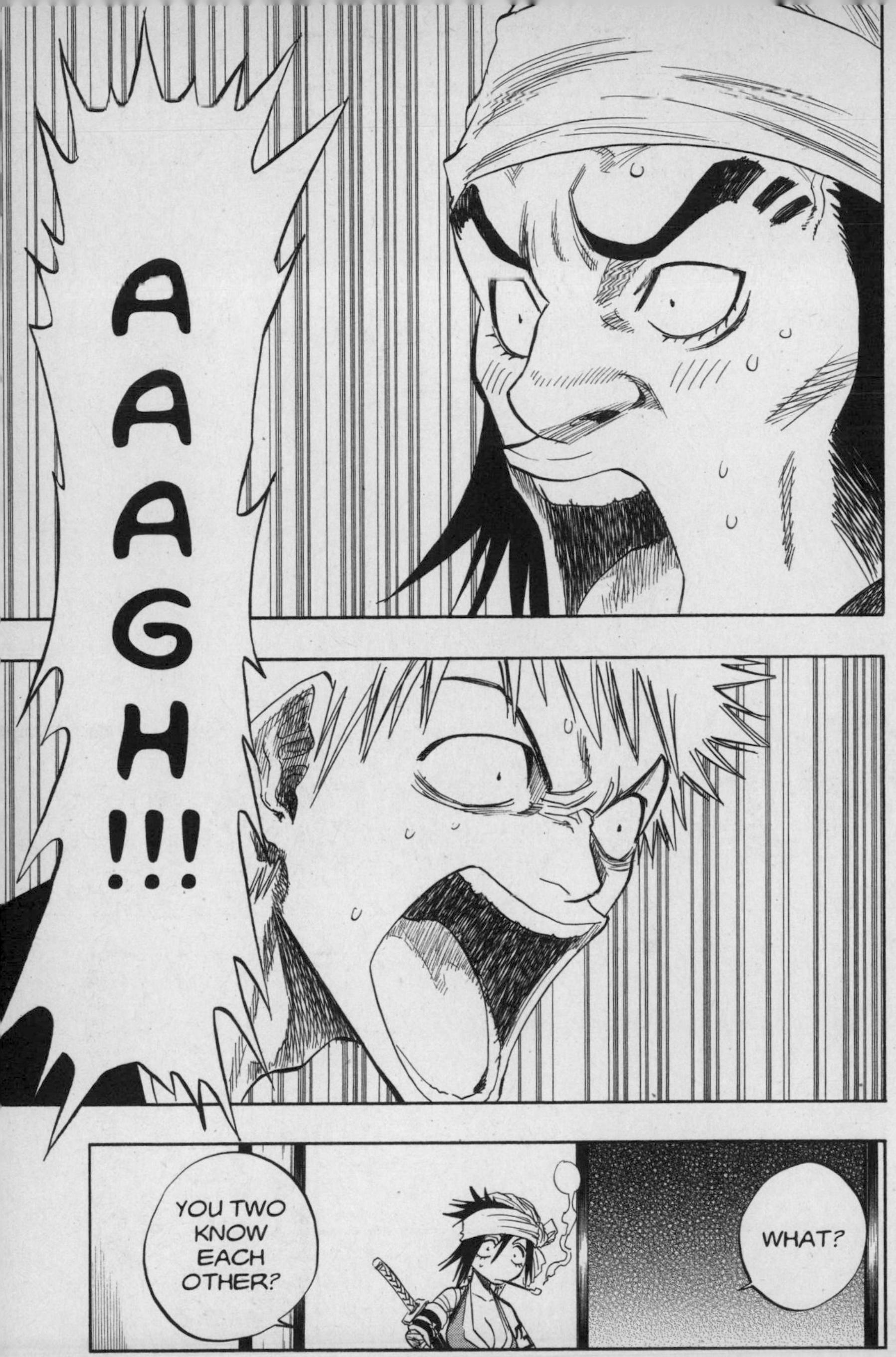
AAAGH!!!
WHAT?
YOU TWO KNOW EACH OTHER?

ICHIGO...

YOU'VE BEEN OVERREACTING TO EVERYTHING SINCE YOU GOT TO THE SOUL SOCIETY.

ARE YOU JUST TIRED OR ARE YOU WORRIED ABOUT US?

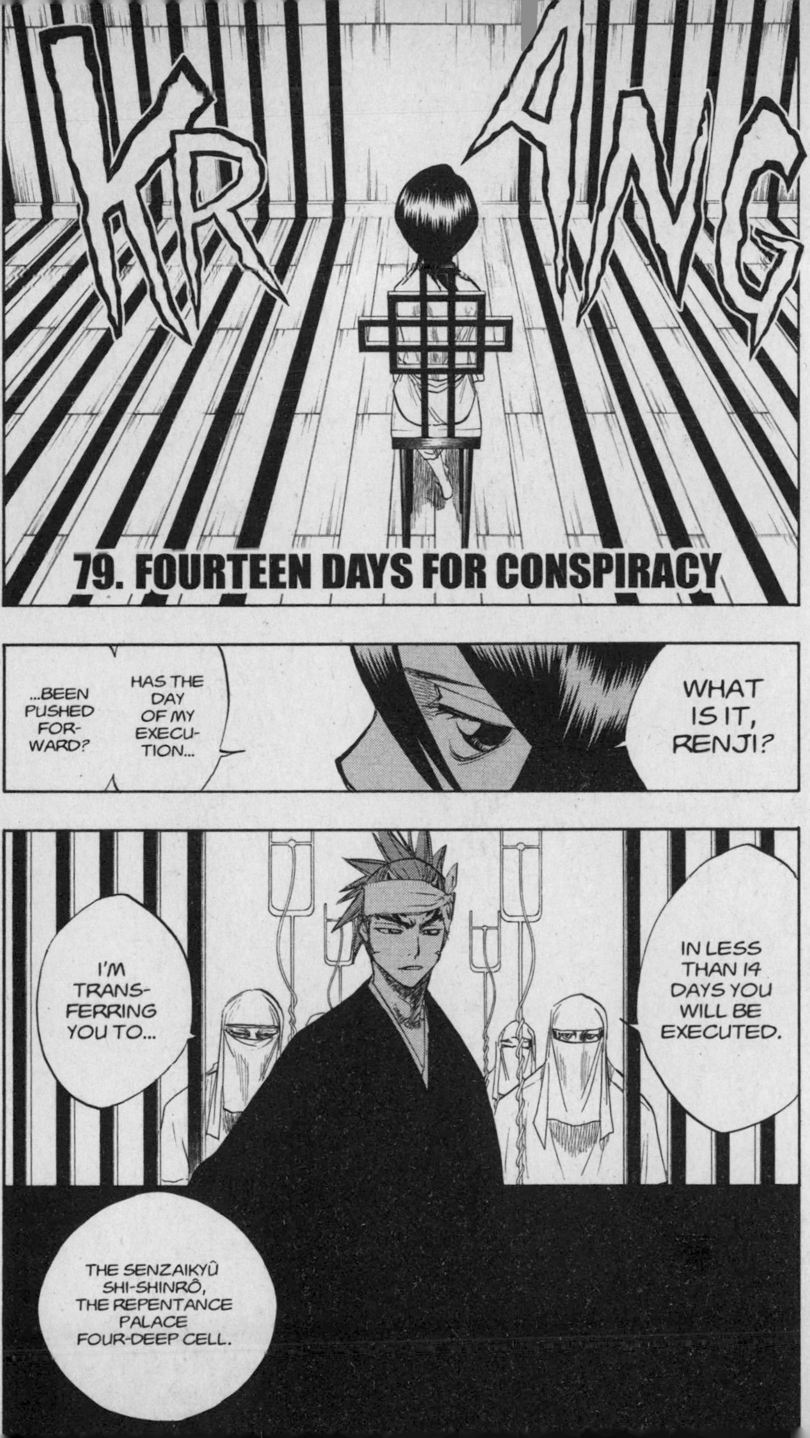
KRAANG
79. FOURTEEN DAYS FOR CONSPIRACY
WHAT IS IT, RENJI?
HAS THE DAY OF MY EXECUTION...
...BEEN PUSHED FORWARD?
IN LESS THAN 14 DAYS YOU WILL BE EXECUTED.
I'M TRANSFERRING YOU TO...
THE SENZAIKYÛ SHI-SHINRÔ, THE REPENTANCE PALACE FOUR-DEEP CELL.

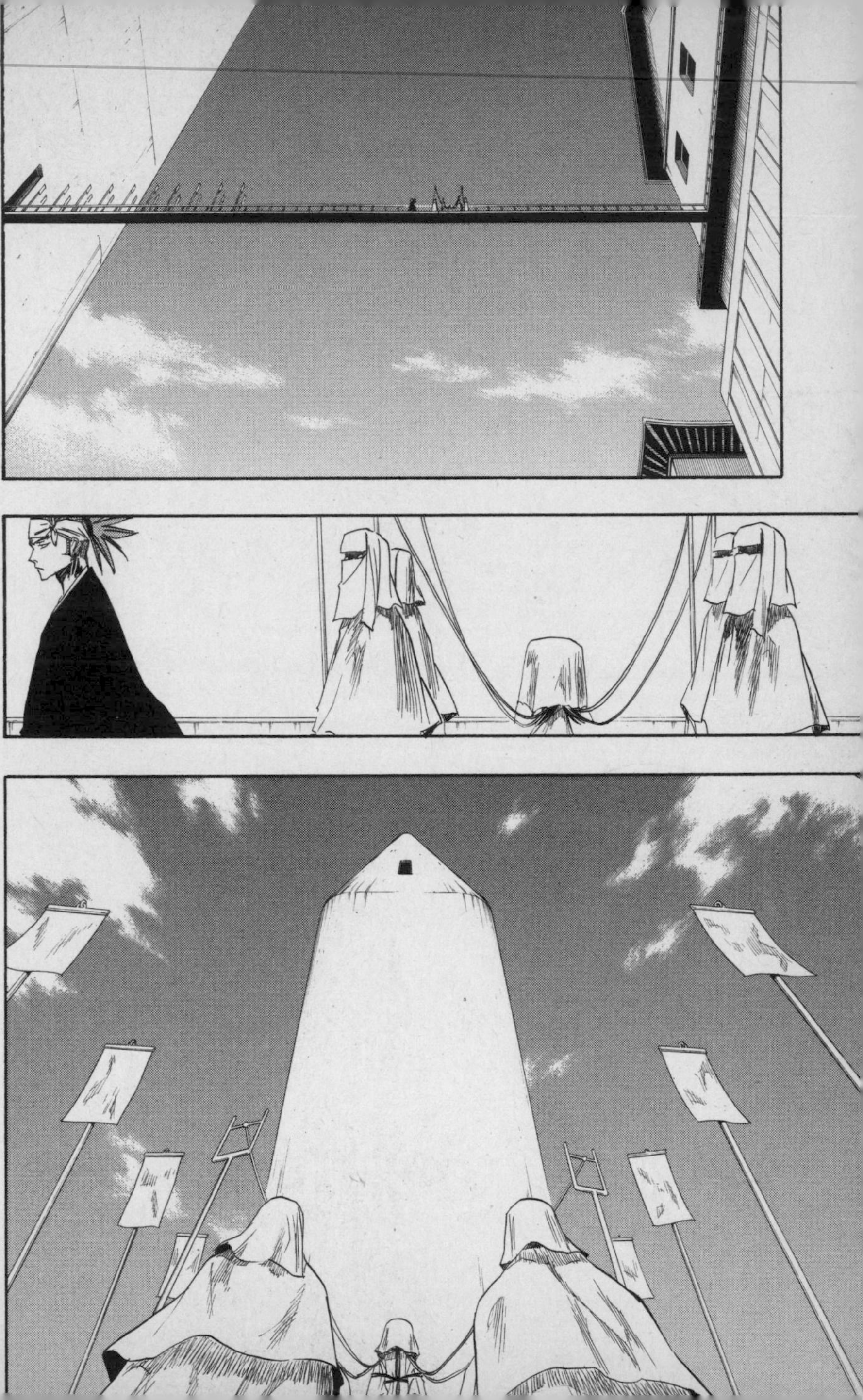

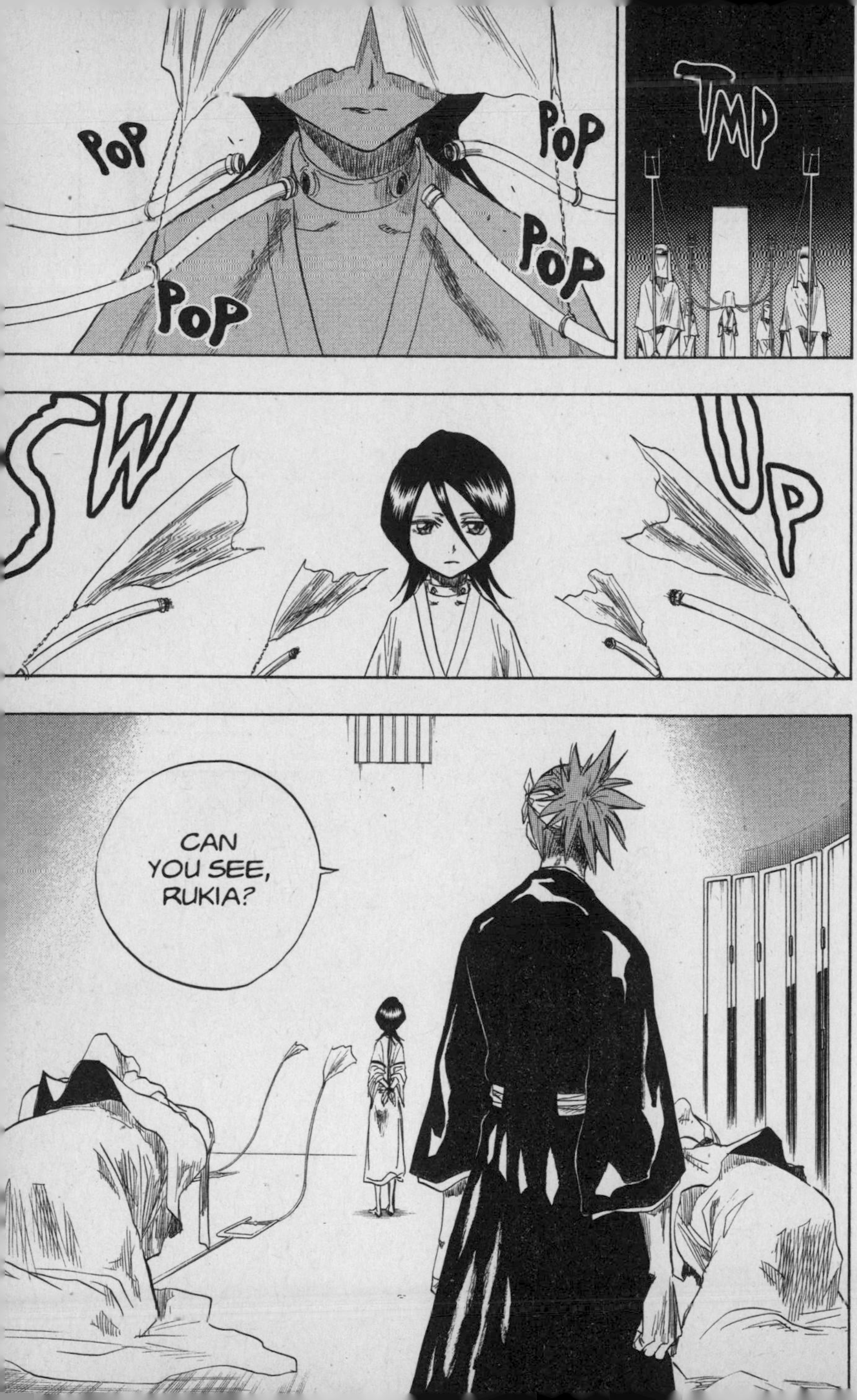
TMP
POP
POP
POP
POP
SWUP
CAN YOU SEE, RUKIA?

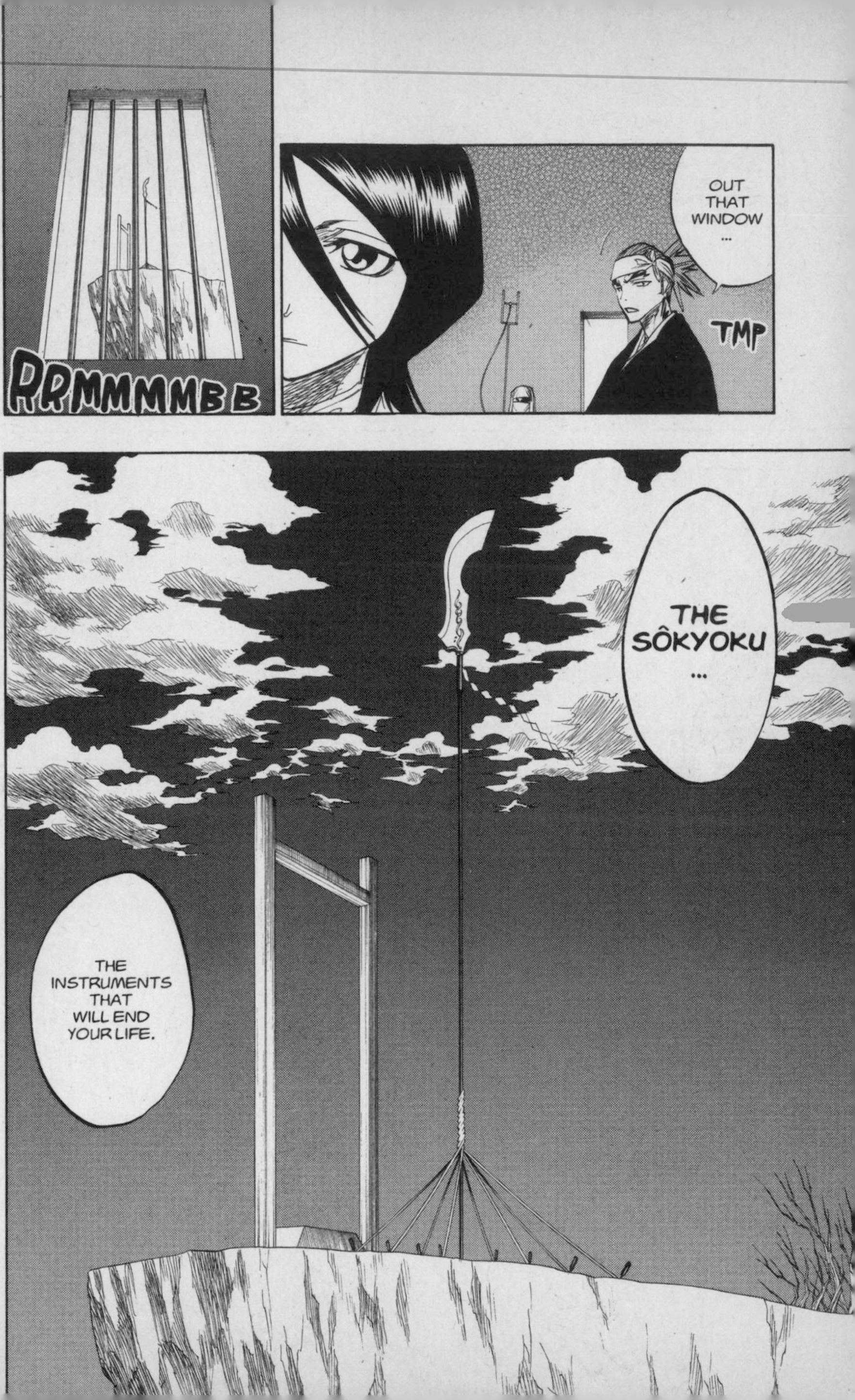
OUT THAT WINDOW ...
TMP
RRMMMMBB
THE SÔKYOKU ...
THE INSTRUMENTS THAT WILL END YOUR LIFE.

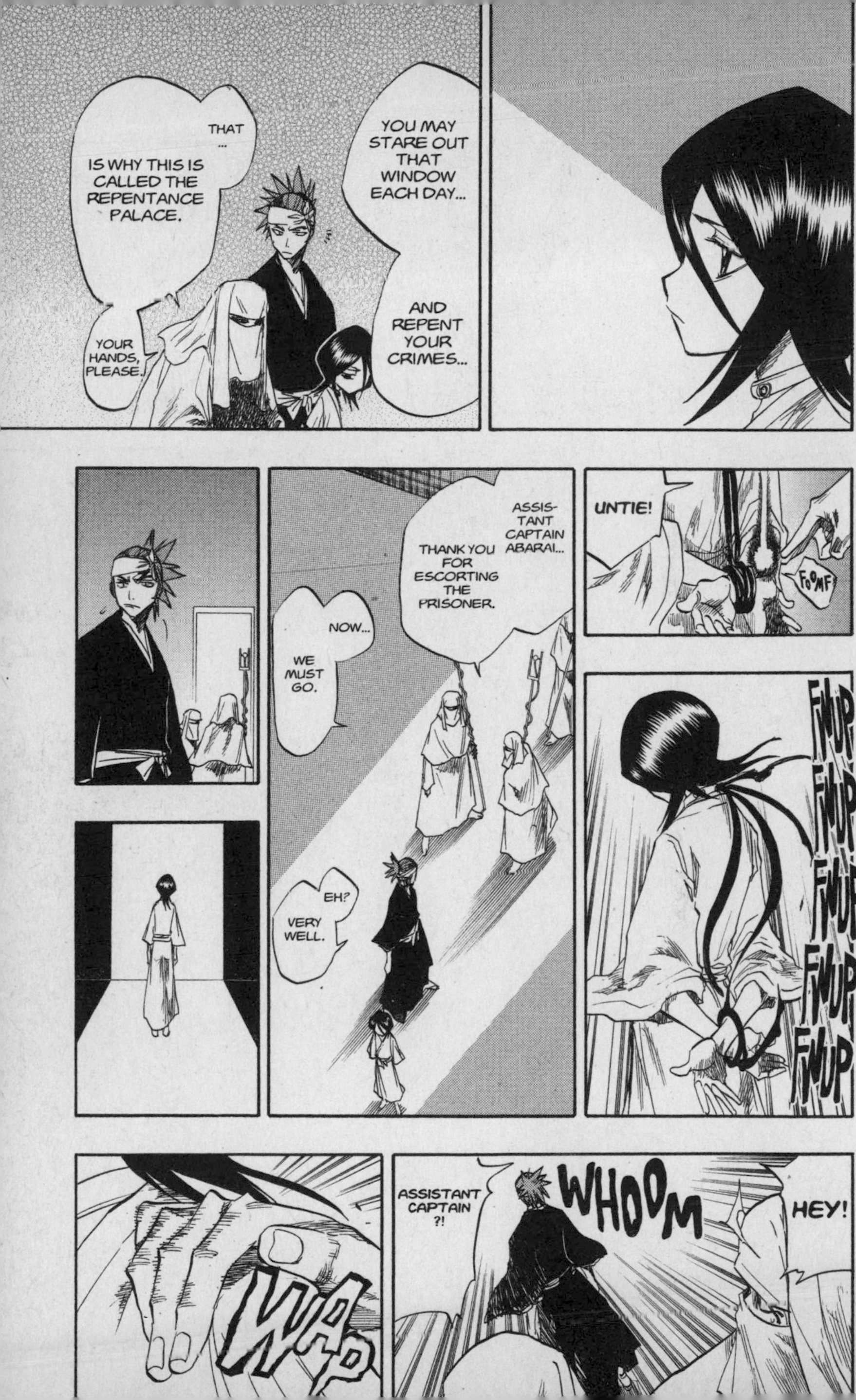
YOU MAY STARE OUT THAT WINDOW EACH DAY...
AND REPENT YOUR CRIMES...
THAT ...
IS WHY THIS IS CALLED THE REPENTANCE PALACE.
YOUR HANDS, PLEASE.
UNTIE!
FOOMF
FWUP FWUP FWUP FWUP FWUP FWUP
ASSIS-TANT CAPTAIN ABARAI...
THANK YOU FOR ESCORTING THE PRISONER.
NOW...
WE MUST GO.
EH?
VERY WELL.
HEY!
WHOOM
ASSISTANT CAPTAIN ?!
WAP

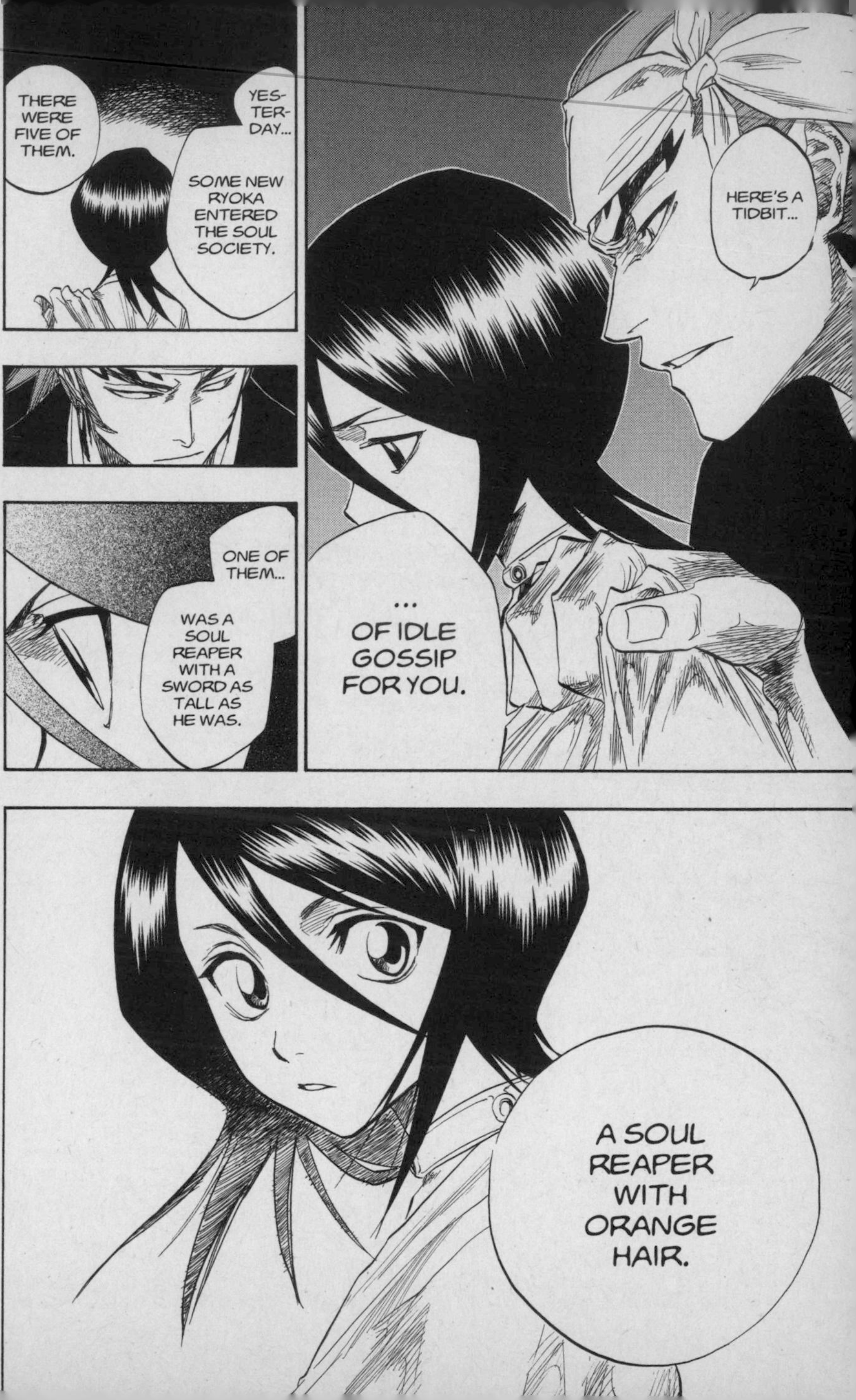
HERE'S A TIDBIT...
...
OF IDLE GOSSIP FOR YOU.
YES-TER-DAY...
SOME NEW RYOKA ENTERED THE SOUL SOCIETY.
THERE WERE FIVE OF THEM.
ONE OF THEM...
WAS A SOUL REAPER WITH A SWORD AS TALL AS HE WAS.
A SOUL REAPER WITH ORANGE HAIR.

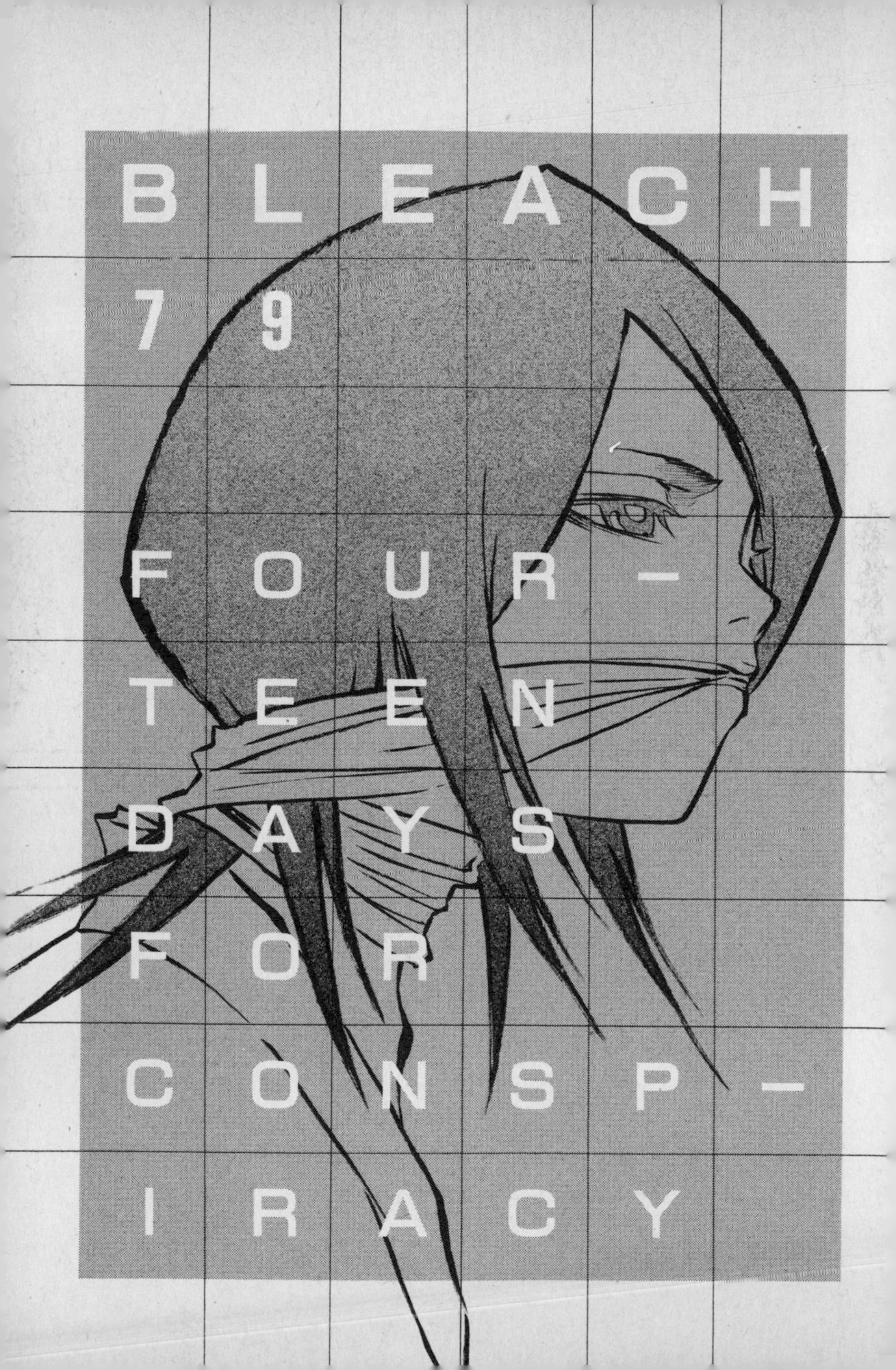
BLEACH
79
FOUR–
TEEN
DAYS
FOR
CONSP–
IRACY

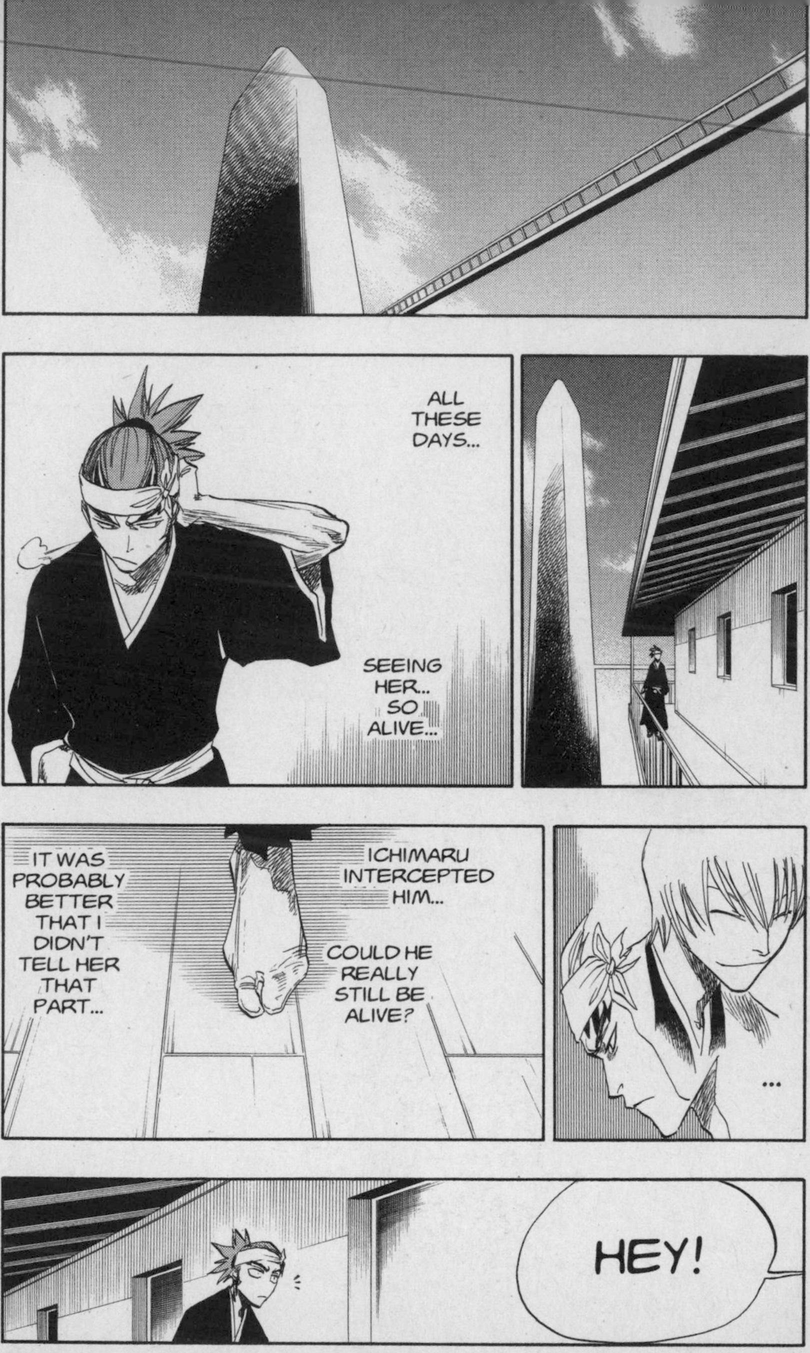
ALL THESE DAYS...
SEEING HER... SO ALIVE...
...
ICHIMARU INTERCEPTED HIM...
COULD HE REALLY STILL BE ALIVE?
IT WAS PROBABLY BETTER THAT I DIDN'T TELL HER THAT PART...
HEY!

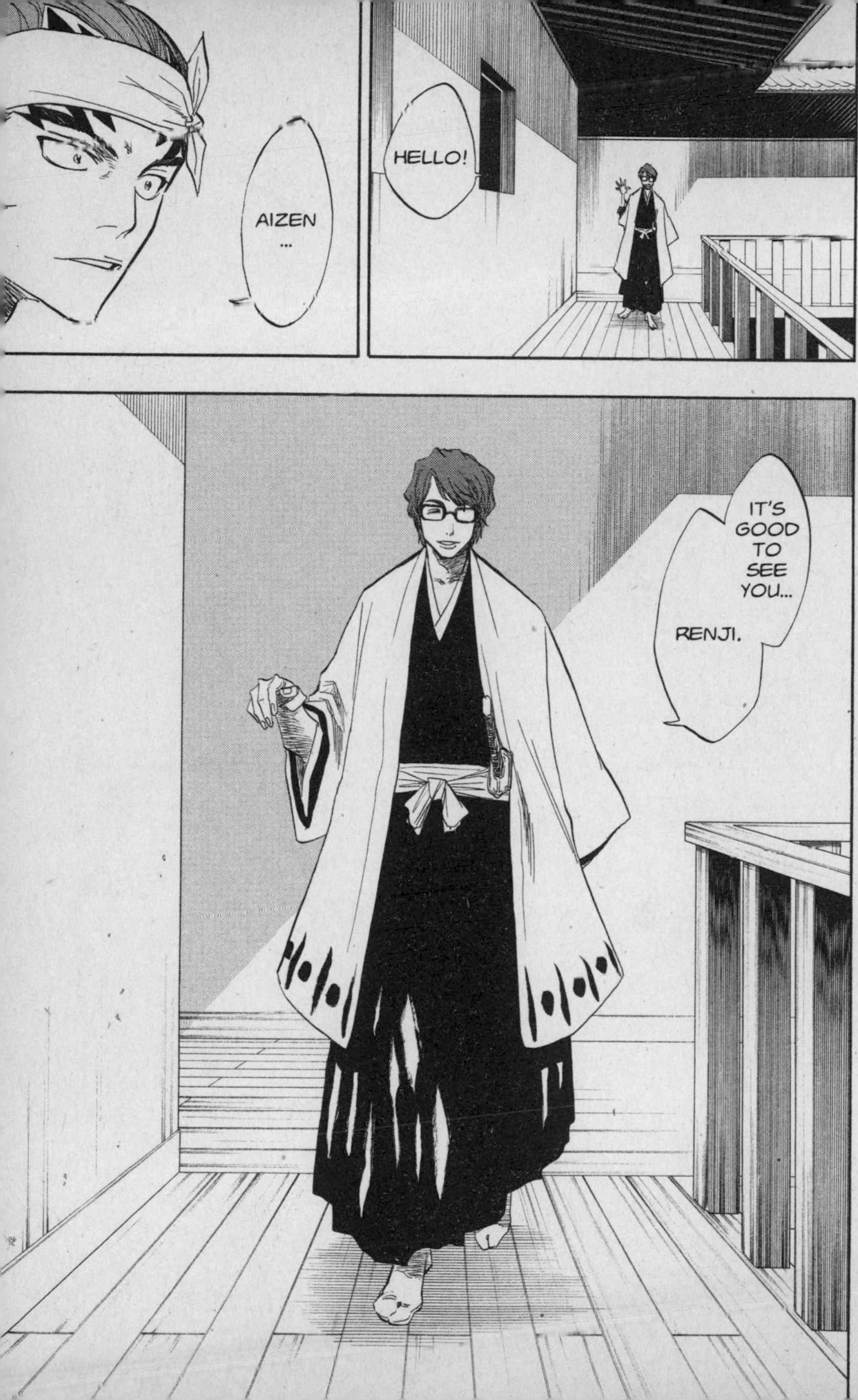
HELLO!
AIZEN ...
IT'S GOOD TO SEE YOU...
RENJI.

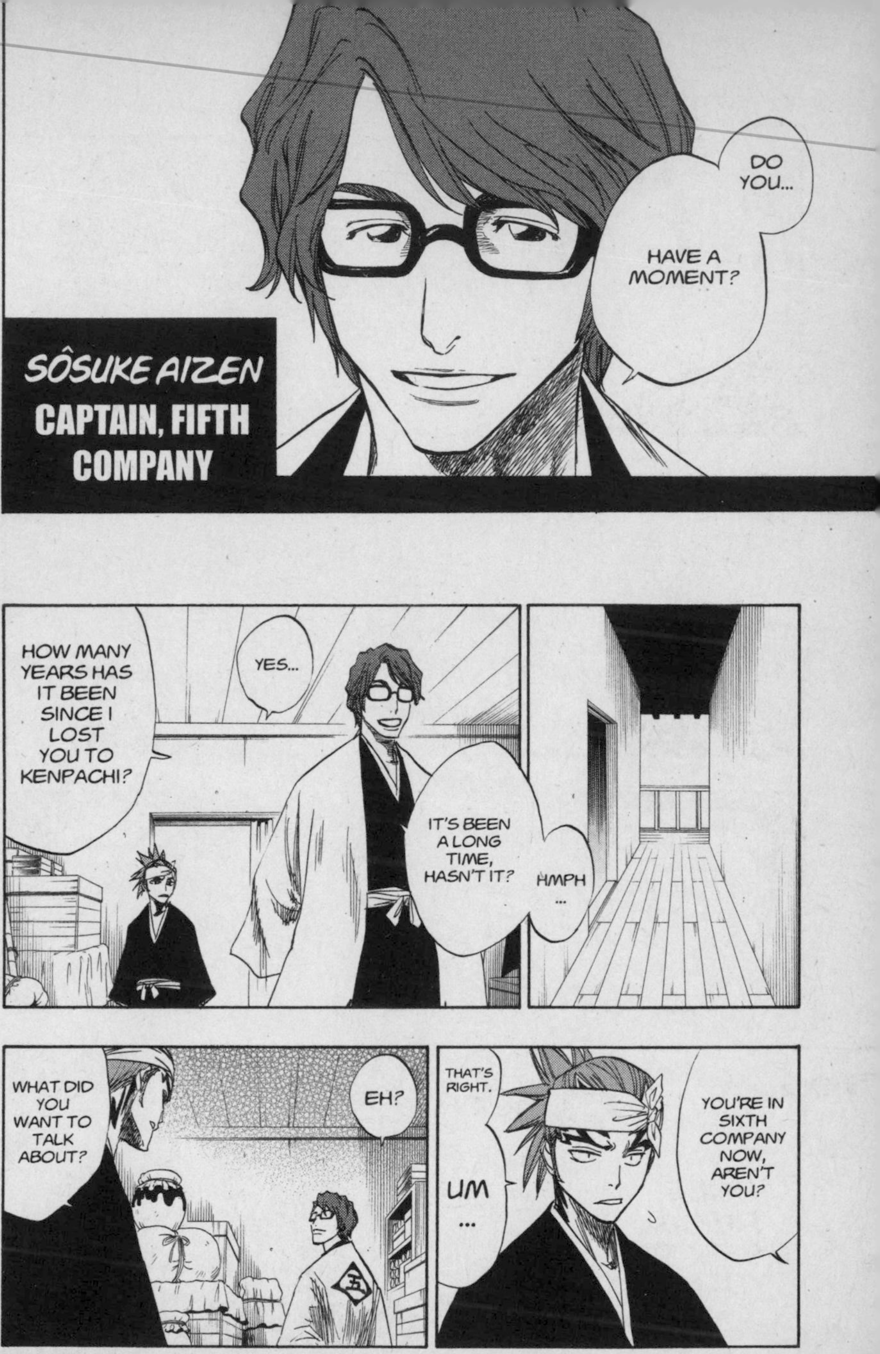
DO YOU...
HAVE A MOMENT?
SÔSUKE AIZEN
CAPTAIN, FIFTH COMPANY
HMPH ...
IT'S BEEN A LONG TIME, HASN'T IT?
YES...
HOW MANY YEARS HAS IT BEEN SINCE I LOST YOU TO KENPACHI?
YOU'RE IN SIXTH COMPANY NOW, AREN'T YOU?
THAT'S RIGHT.
UM ...
EH?
WHAT DID YOU WANT TO TALK ABOUT?

READ THIS WAY

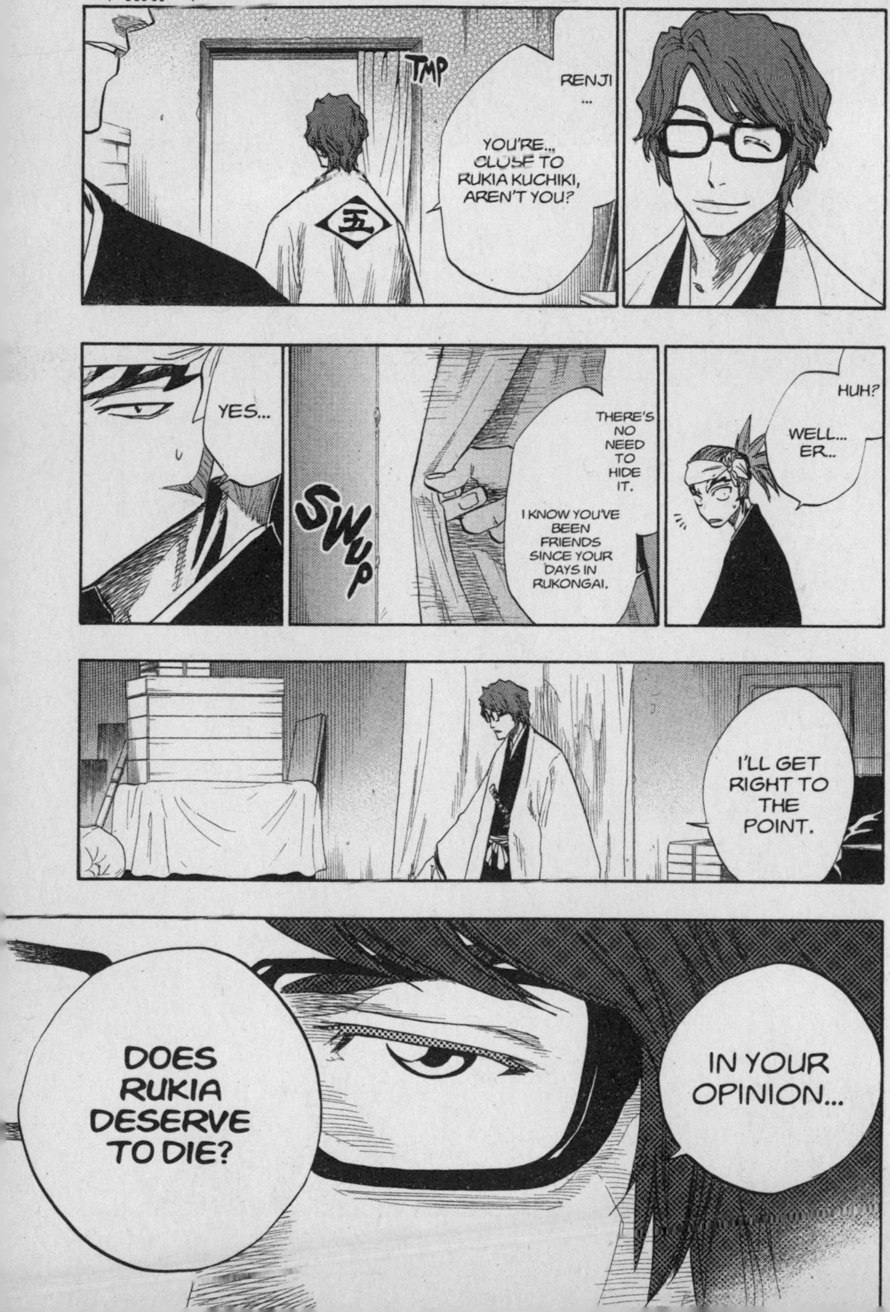
RENJI ...
YOU'RE... CLOSE TO RUKIA KUCHIKI, AREN'T YOU?
TMP
HUH?
WELL... ER...
THERE'S NO NEED TO HIDE IT.
I KNOW YOU'VE BEEN FRIENDS SINCE YOUR DAYS IN RUKONGAI.
SWUP
YES...
I'LL GET RIGHT TO THE POINT.
IN YOUR OPINION...
DOES RUKIA DESERVE TO DIE?

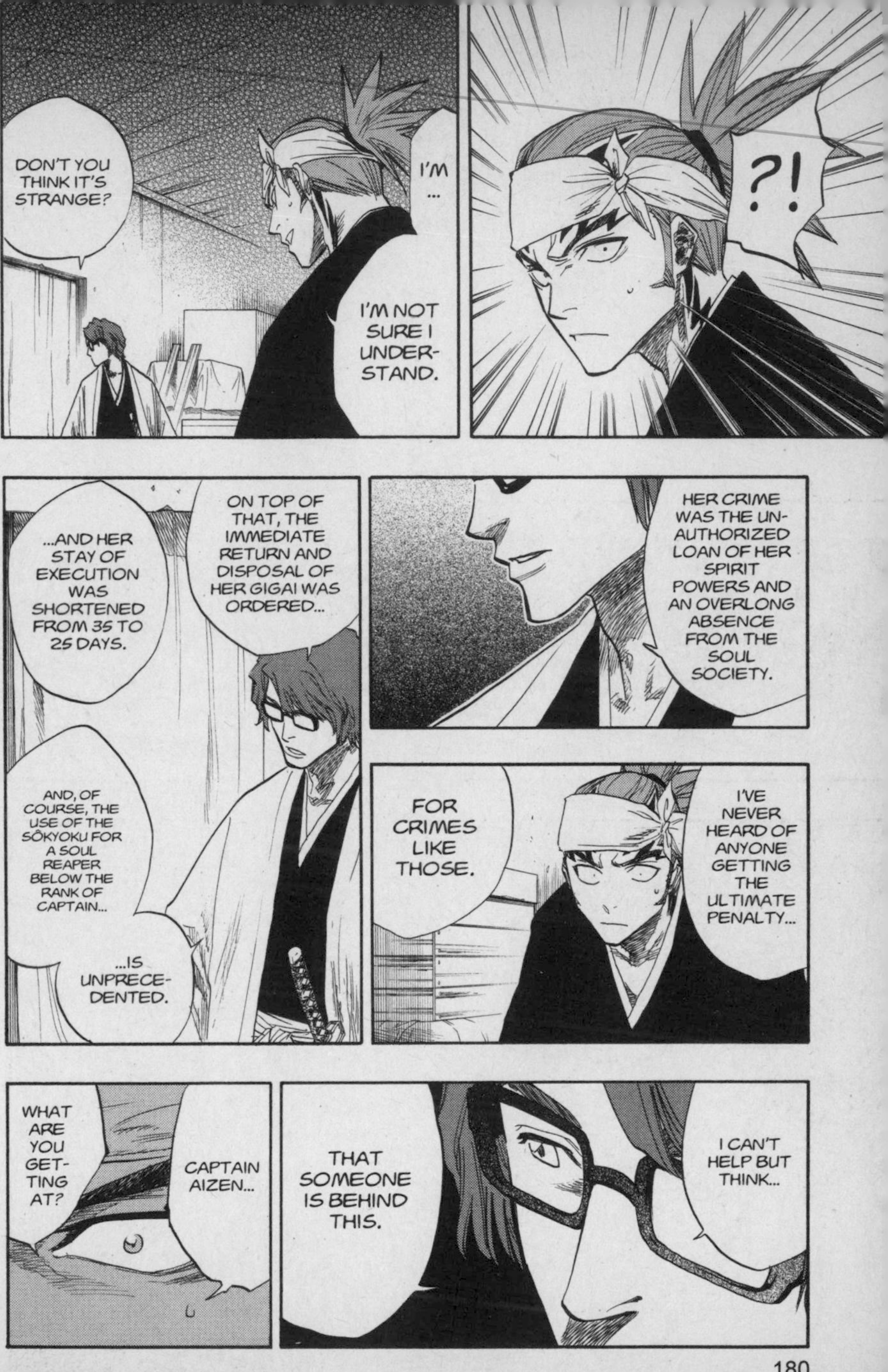
?!
I'M ...
I'M NOT SURE I UNDERSTAND.
DON'T YOU THINK IT'S STRANGE?
HER CRIME WAS THE UNAUTHORIZED LOAN OF HER SPIRIT POWERS AND AN OVERLONG ABSENCE FROM THE SOUL SOCIETY.
I'VE NEVER HEARD OF ANYONE GETTING THE ULTIMATE PENALTY...
FOR CRIMES LIKE THOSE.
ON TOP OF THAT, THE IMMEDIATE RETURN AND DISPOSAL OF HER GIGAI WAS ORDERED...
...AND HER STAY OF EXECUTION WAS SHORTENED FROM 35 TO 25 DAYS.
AND, OF COURSE, THE USE OF THE SÔKYOKU FOR A SOUL REAPER BELOW THE RANK OF CAPTAIN...
...IS UNPRECEDENTED.
I CAN'T HELP BUT THINK...
THAT SOMEONE IS BEHIND THIS.
CAPTAIN AIZEN...
WHAT ARE YOU GETTING AT?

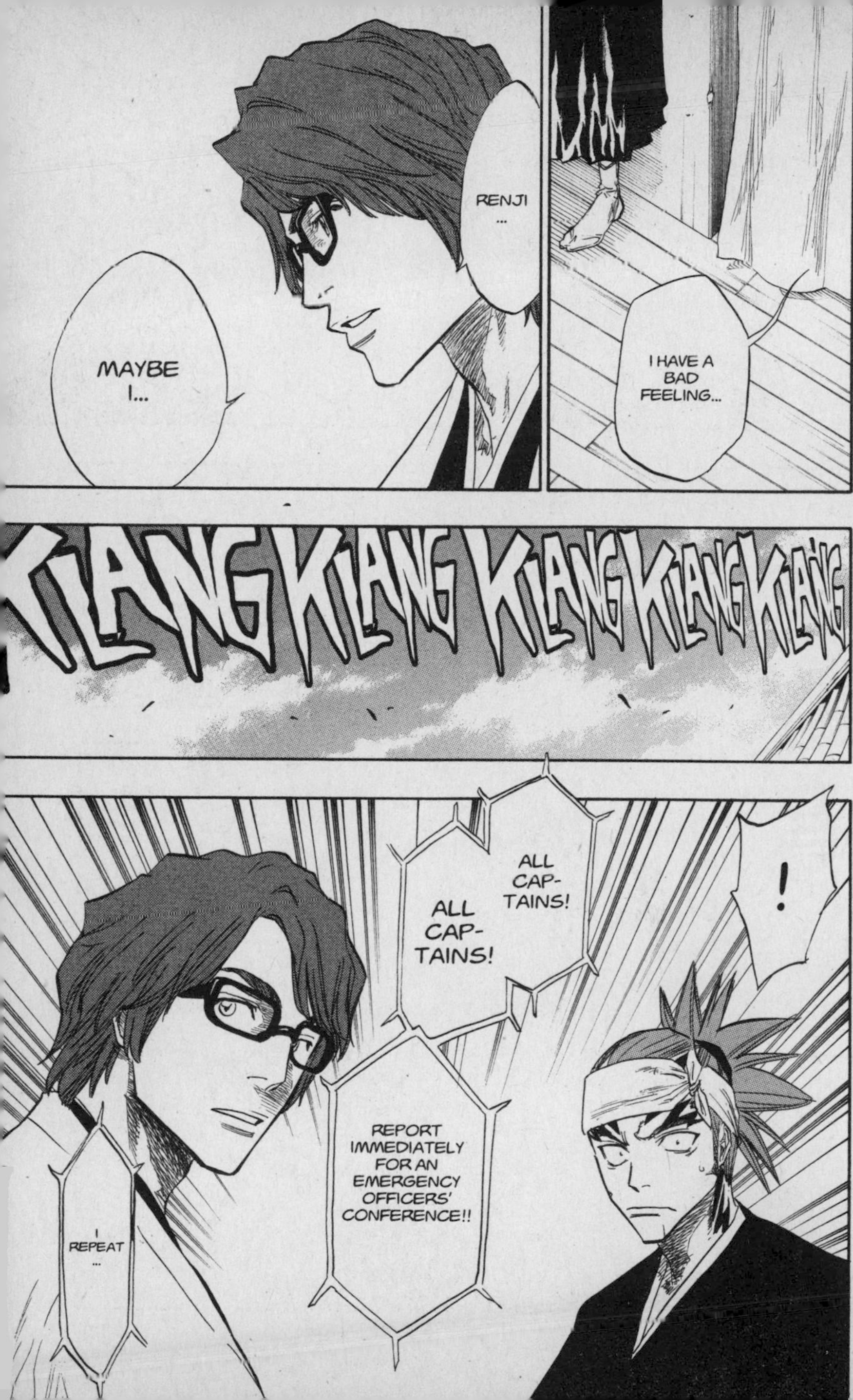
I HAVE A BAD FEELING...
RENJI ...
MAYBE I...
KLANG KLANG KLANG KLANG KLANG
!
ALL CAPTAINS!
ALL CAPTAINS!
REPORT IMMEDIATELY FOR AN EMERGENCY OFFICERS' CONFERENCE!!
I REPEAT ...

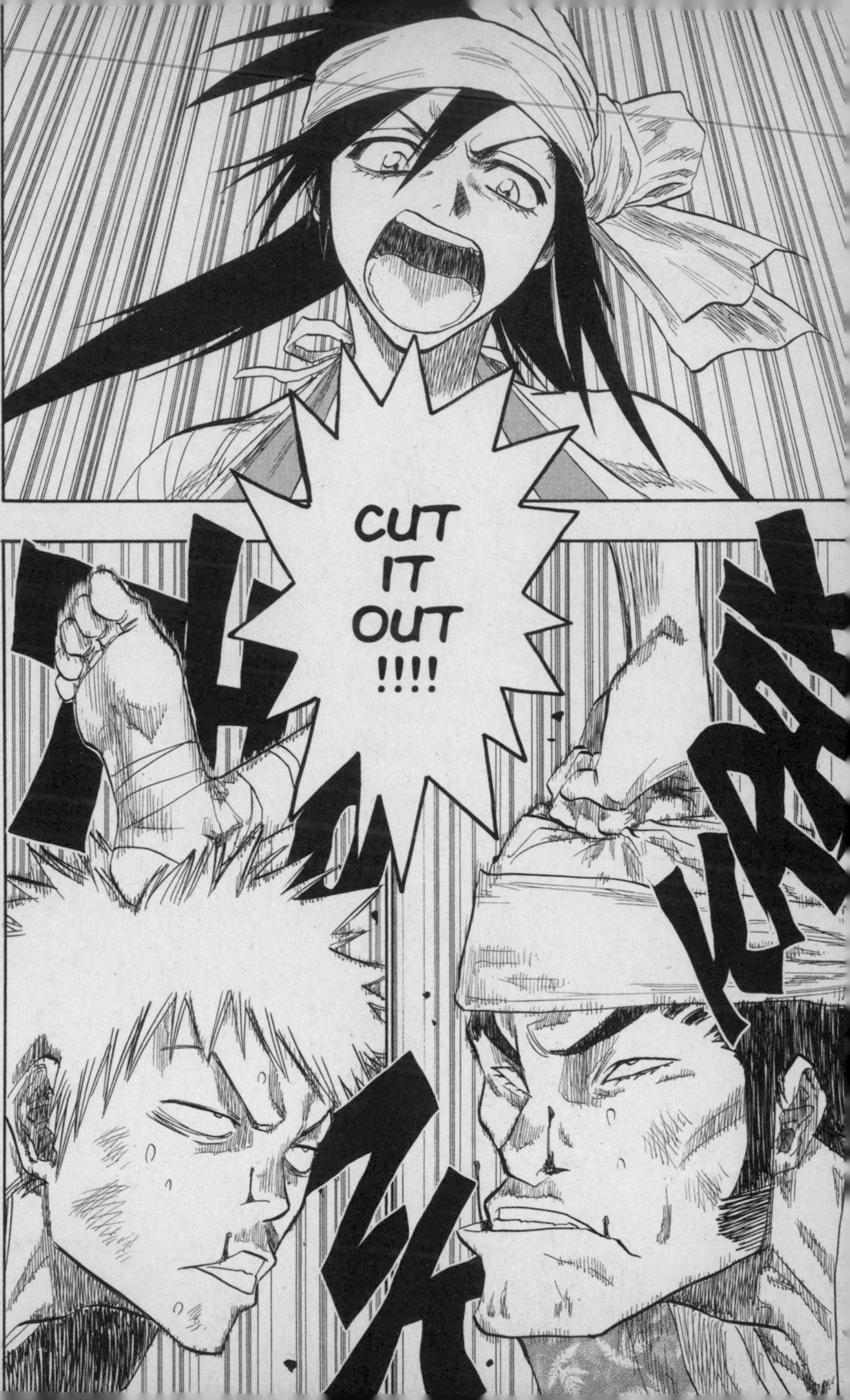
CUT IT OUT!!!!

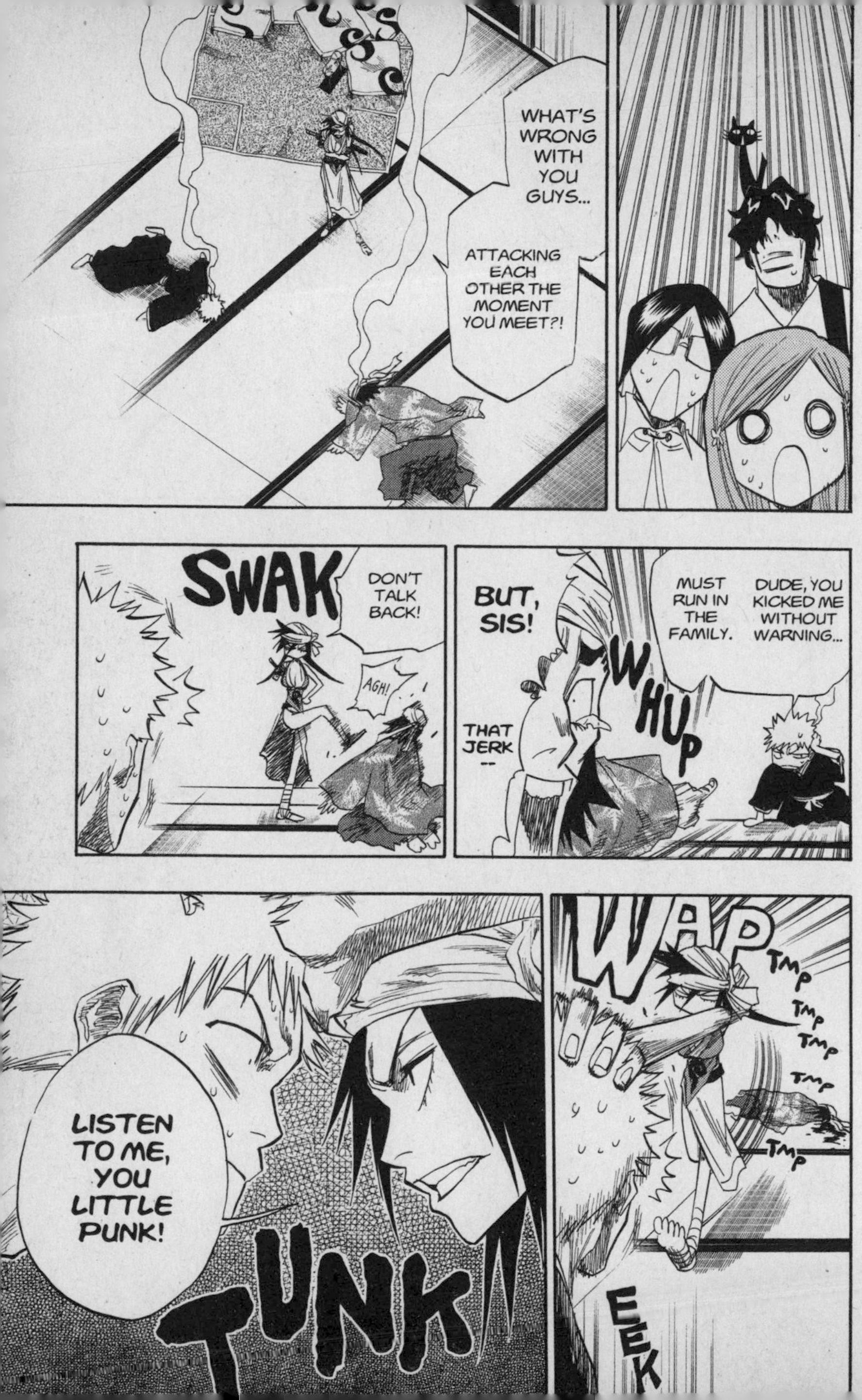
WHAT'S WRONG WITH YOU GUYS...
ATTACKING EACH OTHER THE MOMENT YOU MEET?!
DUDE, YOU KICKED ME WITHOUT WARNING...
MUST RUN IN THE FAMILY.
WHUP
BUT, SIS!
THAT JERK --
DON'T TALK BACK!
SWAK
AGH!
WAP
TMP
TMP
TMP
TMP
TMP
EEK
LISTEN TO ME, YOU LITTLE PUNK!
TUNK

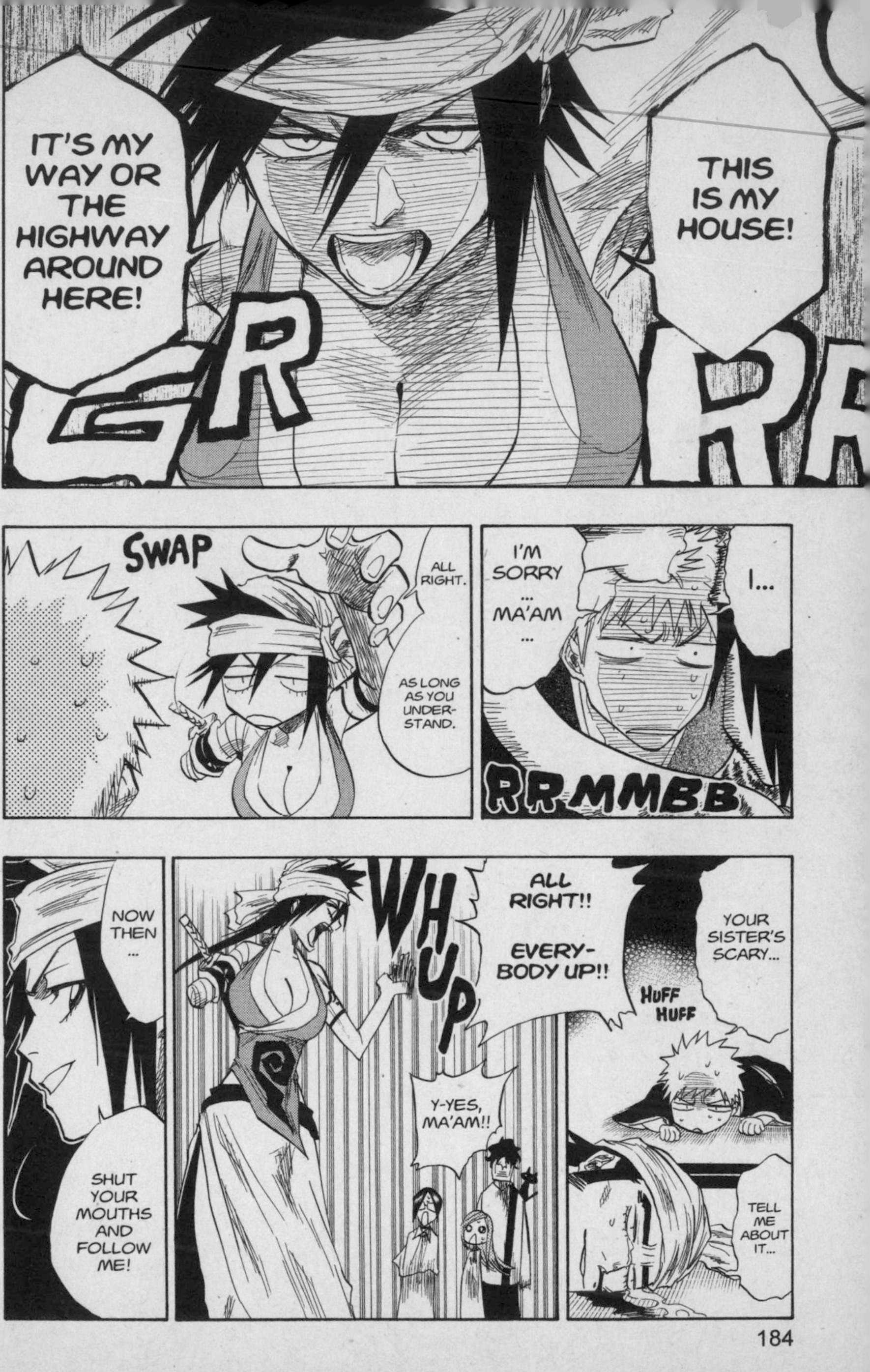
THIS IS MY HOUSE!
IT'S MY WAY OR THE HIGHWAY AROUND HERE!
GRRR
I...
I'M SORRY ... MA'AM ...
RRMMBB
ALL RIGHT.
AS LONG AS YOU UNDER-STAND.
SWAP
YOUR SISTER'S SCARY...
HUFF HUFF
TELL ME ABOUT IT...
ALL RIGHT!!
EVERY-BODY UP!!
WHUP
Y-YES, MA'AM!!
NOW THEN ...
SHUT YOUR MOUTHS AND FOLLOW ME!

READ THIS WAY

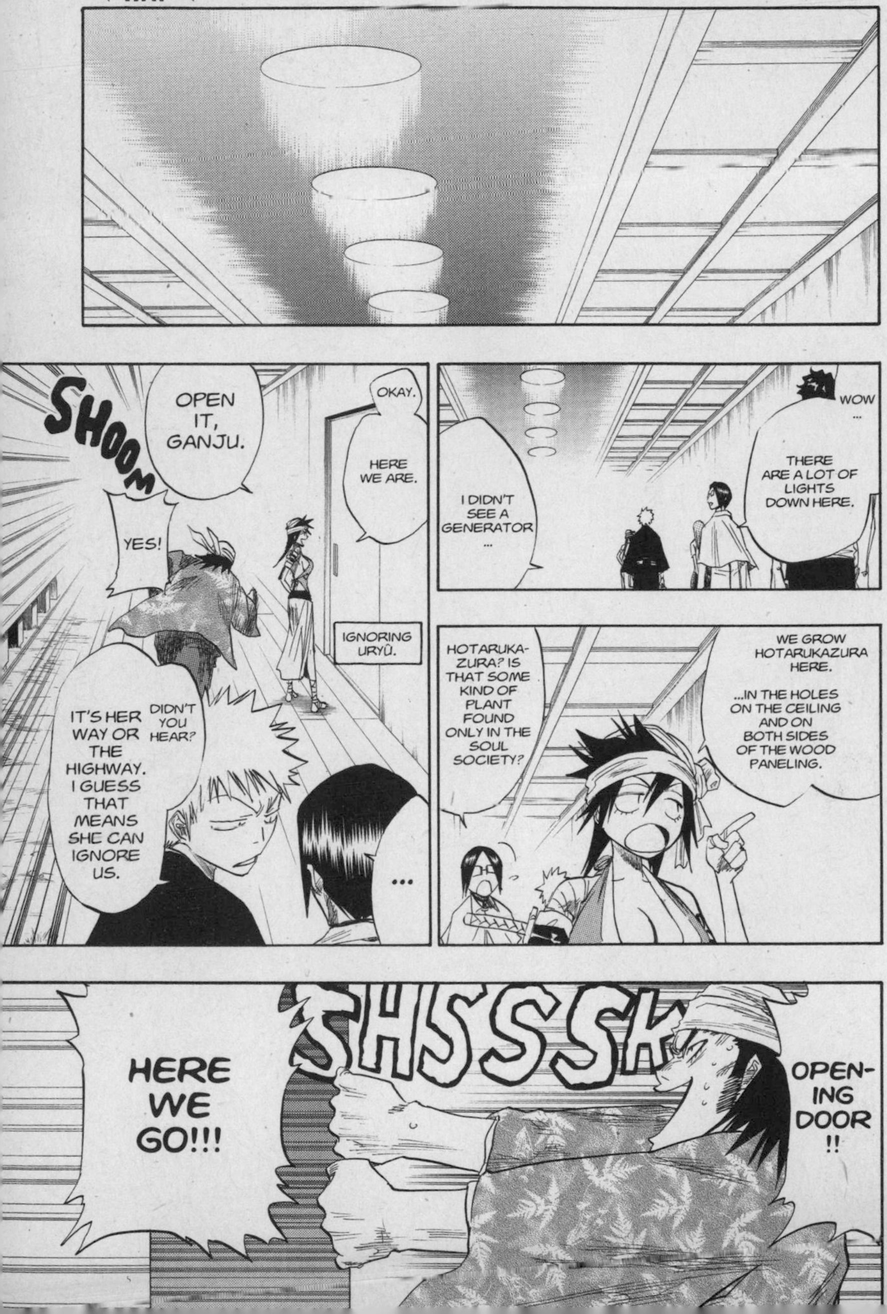
WOW ...
THERE ARE A LOT OF LIGHTS DOWN HERE.
I DIDN'T SEE A GENERATOR ...
WE GROW HOTARUKAZURA HERE.
...IN THE HOLES ON THE CEILING AND ON BOTH SIDES OF THE WOOD PANELING.
HOTARUKAZURA? IS THAT SOME KIND OF PLANT FOUND ONLY IN THE SOUL SOCIETY?
OKAY.
HERE WE ARE.
OPEN IT, GANJU.
SHOOM
YES!
IGNORING URYŪ.
DIDN'T YOU HEAR?
IT'S HER WAY OR THE HIGHWAY. I GUESS THAT MEANS SHE CAN IGNORE US.
...
OPEN- ING DOOR !!
SHSSSK
HERE WE GO!!!

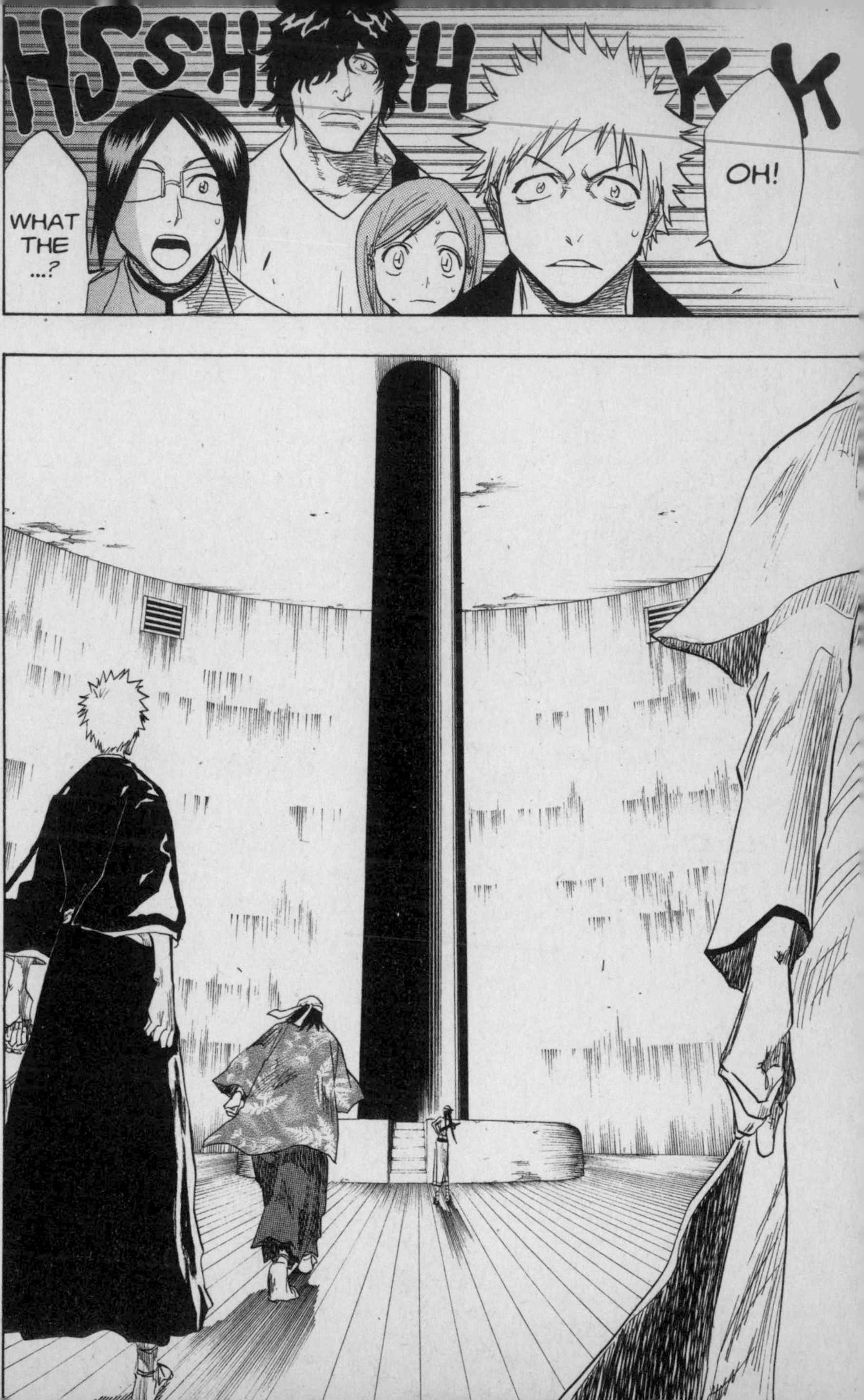
OH!
WHAT THE ...?
HSSHH
KKK

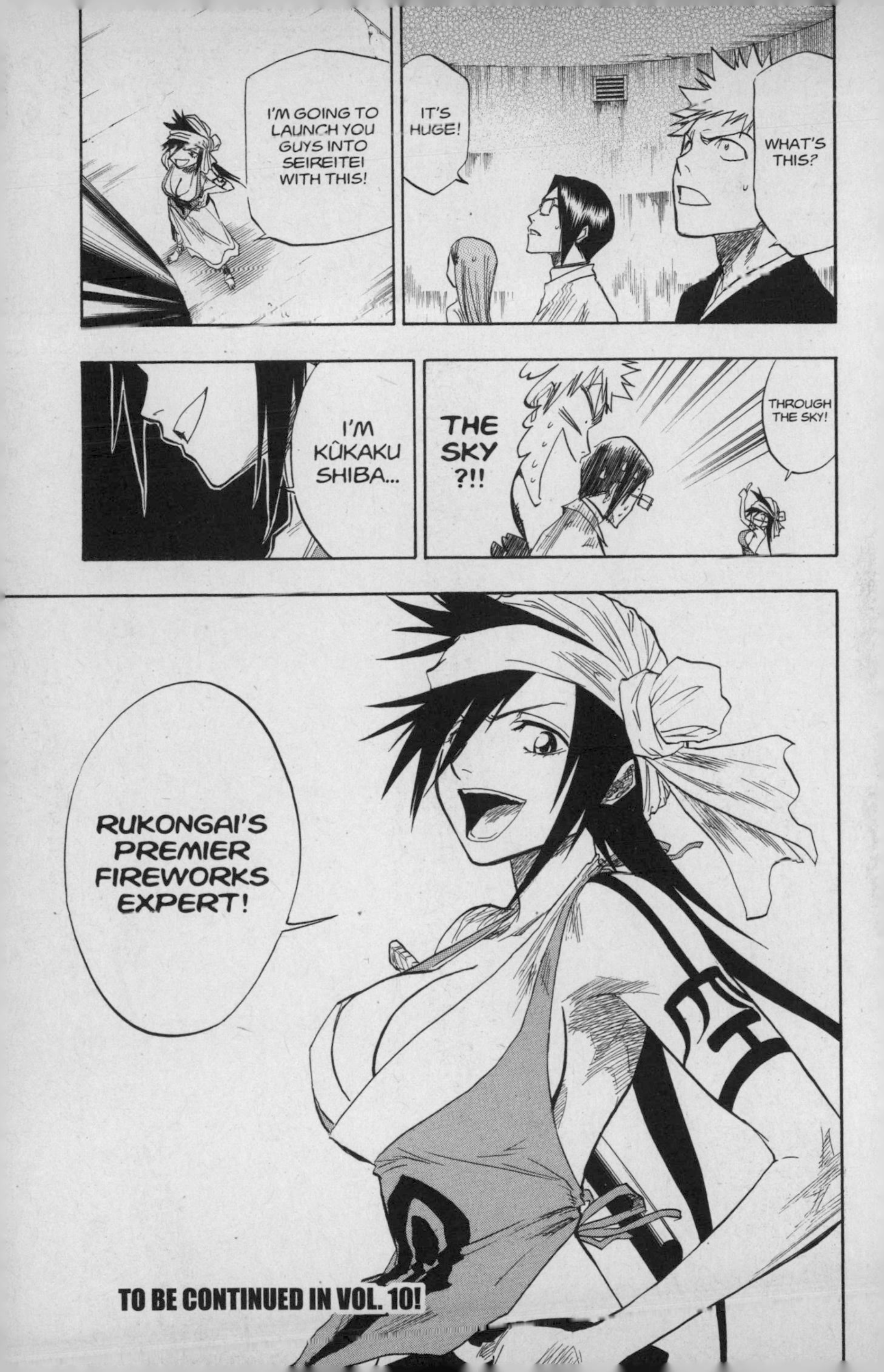
WHAT'S THIS?
IT'S HUGE!
I'M GOING TO LAUNCH YOU GUYS INTO SEIREITEI WITH THIS!
THROUGH THE SKY!
THE SKY ?!!
I'M KÛKAKU SHIBA...
RUKONGAI'S PREMIER FIREWORKS EXPERT!
TO BE CONTINUED IN VOL. 10!

KÛKAKU'S HOUSES--SCULPTURAL ARCHITECTURE (A FEW EXAMPLES)
KÛKAKU SHIBA
TITLE: HANDSTAND
KÛKAKU SHIBA
TITLE: THE CHAMPION
TITLE: FIRST LOVE
KÛKAKU SHIBA
...
THE LATEST VERSION DOESN'T SEEM SO BAD, NOW...

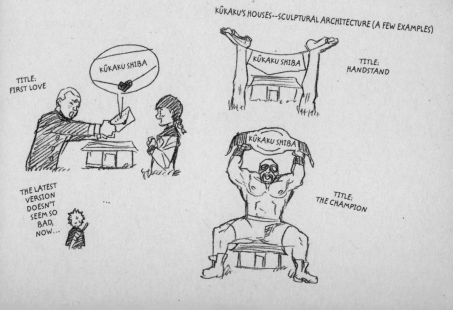

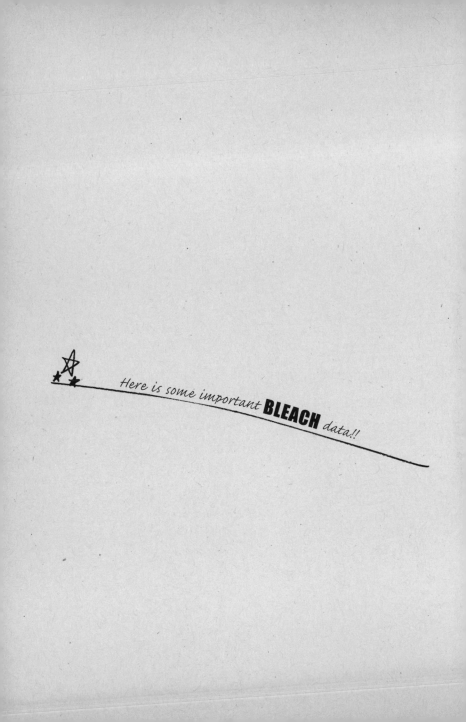

Here is some important **BLEACH** data!!

Thirteen Court Guard Companies	CAPTAIN BYAKUYA KUCHIKI--SIXTH COMPANY	クチキ・ビャクヤ

180 CM

63 KG

D.O.B. JANUARY 31

• 28TH HEAD OF DISTIN-GUISHED ARISTOCRATIC KUCHIKI FAMILY

• WEARS THE KENSEIKAN (PULL STAR SILENCE), AN ORNAMENT ALLOWED ONLY TO NOBLES--A SERIES OF SEMI-TUBES THAT CLAMP TO THE HAIR

• WEARS GINPAKU KAZANO-HANA USUGINU (SILVERY-WHITE WINDFLOWER SILK GAUZE), A SCARF WORN BY GENERATIONAL HEAD OF FAMILY, WOVEN BY A MASTER WEAVER, THE THIRD INHERITOR TO KU-ROEMON TSUJISHIRO. ONE OF THESE COSTS AS MUCH AS TEN HOUSES.

• LIKES BALLOON FLOWERS, MOONLIGHT WALKS, SPICY FOOD

THEME SONG
Giovanni Mirabassi
"Je Chante Pour
Passer Le Temps"
RECORDED IN
"AVANTI!"

Thirteen Court Guard Companies

ASSISTANT CAPTAIN RENJI ABARAI--SIXTH COMPANY

アバライ・レンジ

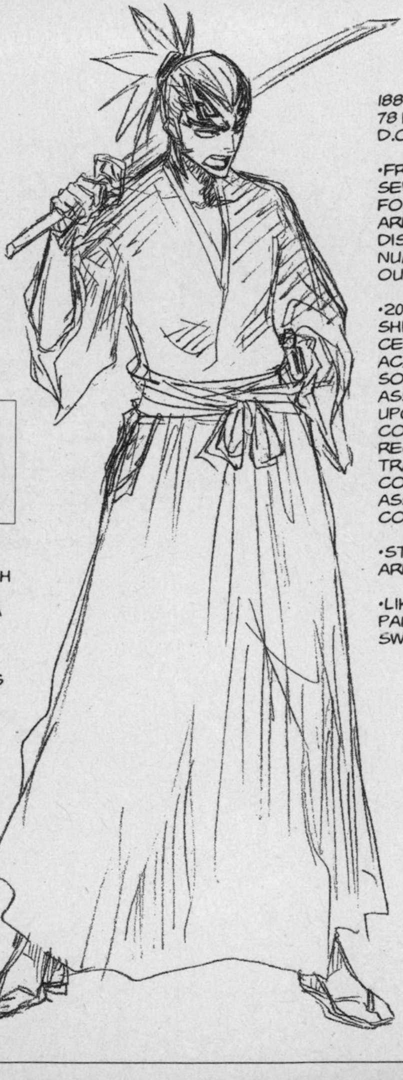

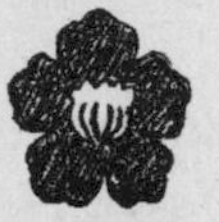

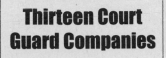

CAPTAIN'S BADGE, SIXTH COMPANY CAMELLIA DESIGN MOTTO: NOBLE REASONING

188 CM
78 KG
D.O.B. AUGUST 31

•FROM INUZURI, RUKONGAI'S SEVENTY-EIGHTH DISTRICT. THE FOUR QUARTERS OF RUKONGAI ARE EACH DIVIDED INTO 80 DISTRICTS. THE HIGHER THE NUMBER, THE MORE DANGER-OUS THE DISTRICT.

•2066TH TERM GRADUATE OF SHINÔ-REIJUTSUIN, THE CENTRAL SPIRITUAL ARTS ACADEMY, ALSO KNOWN AS SOUL REAPER ACADEMY. ASSIGNED TO FIFTH COMPANY UPON GRADUATING, HIS COMBAT ABILITY WAS SOON RECOGNIZED AND HE WAS TRANSFERRED TO ELEVENTH COMPANY. PROMOTED TO ASSISTANT CAPTAIN OF SIXTH COMPANY ONE MONTH AGO.

•STRANGE EYEBROWS ARE TATTOOS

•LIKES TAIYAKI (FISH-SHAPED PANCAKES FILLED WITH SWEAT BEAN JAM)

THEME SONG
HAZU FEATURING
Ill-Bosstino
"NORAINU"
("STRAY DOG")
RECORDED IN
"The NEWBORN"

Next Volume Preview

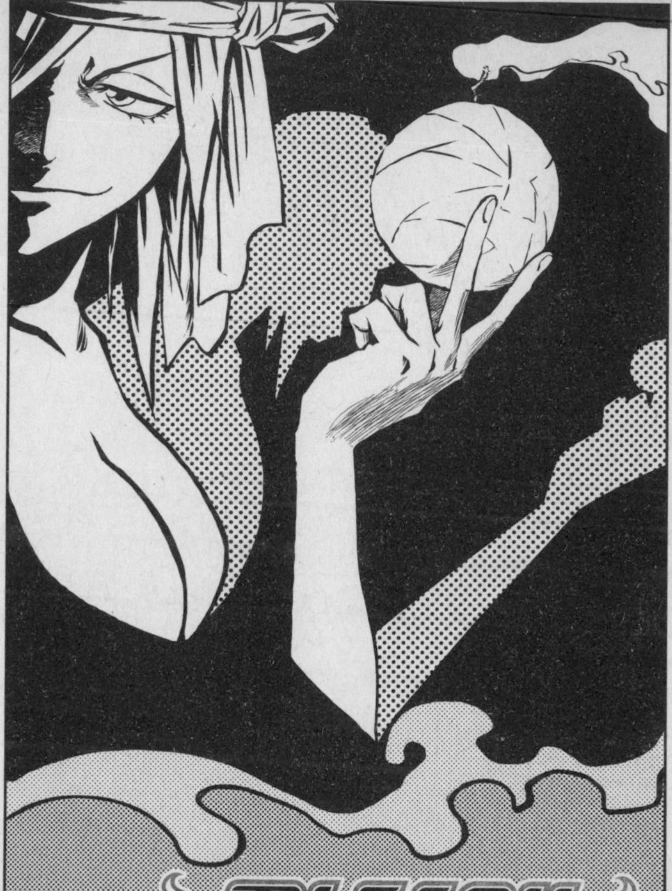
BLEACH
ブリーチ

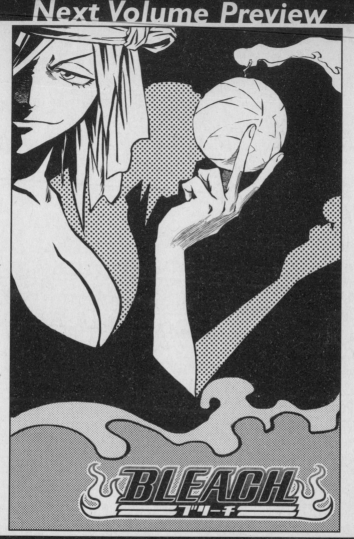

With explosives-expert Kûkaku's assistance, Ichigo's crew is one step closer to finally infiltrating the Soul Society and busting Rukia out of the big house. To successfully break though the Soul Society's powerful barrier, Ichigo will (once again) be forced to control his seemingly endless reservoir of spiritual energy…without blowing everything up. Back at Soul Society HQ, the top captains of the Soul Reapers are assembled so they can figure out how to deal with their unwanted guests.

Available in December 2005

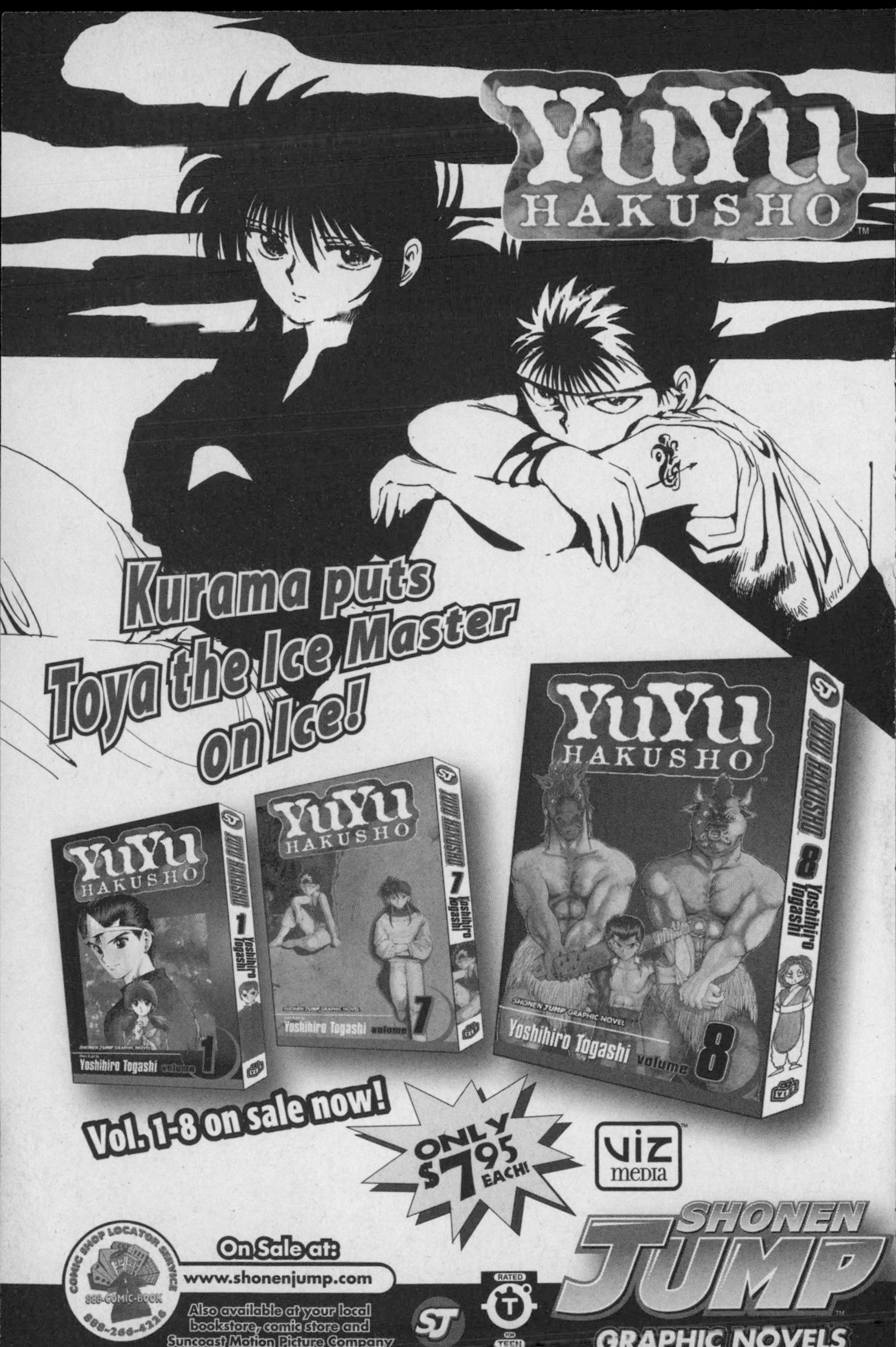
YuYu HAKUSHO
Kurama puts Toya the Ice Master on Ice!
Vol. 1-8 on sale now!
ONLY $7.95 EACH!
viz media
SHONEN JUMP GRAPHIC NOVELS
On Sale at:
www.shonenjump.com
Also available at your local bookstore, comic store and Suncoast Motion Picture Company
COMIC SHOP LOCATOR SERVICE
888-COMIC-BOOK
888-266-4226
RATED T FOR TEEN
YUYU HAKUSHO © 1992 Yoshihiro Togashi

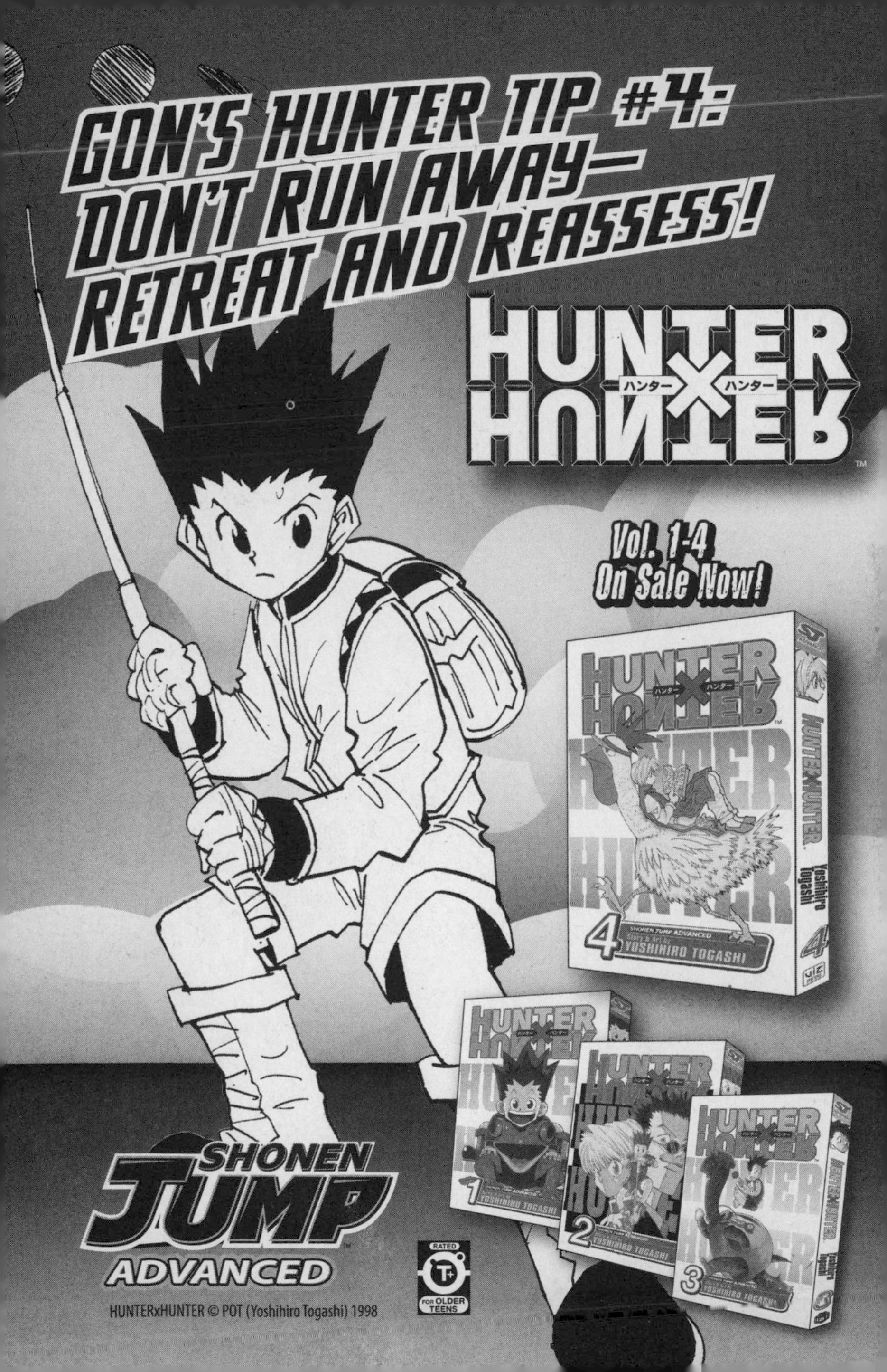
GON'S HUNTER TIP #4:
DON'T RUN AWAY—
RETREAT AND REASSESS!
HUNTER×HUNTER
ハンター ハンター
Vol. 1-4
On Sale Now!
SHONEN JUMP ADVANCED
RATED T+ FOR OLDER TEENS
HUNTERxHUNTER © POT (Yoshihiro Togashi) 1998

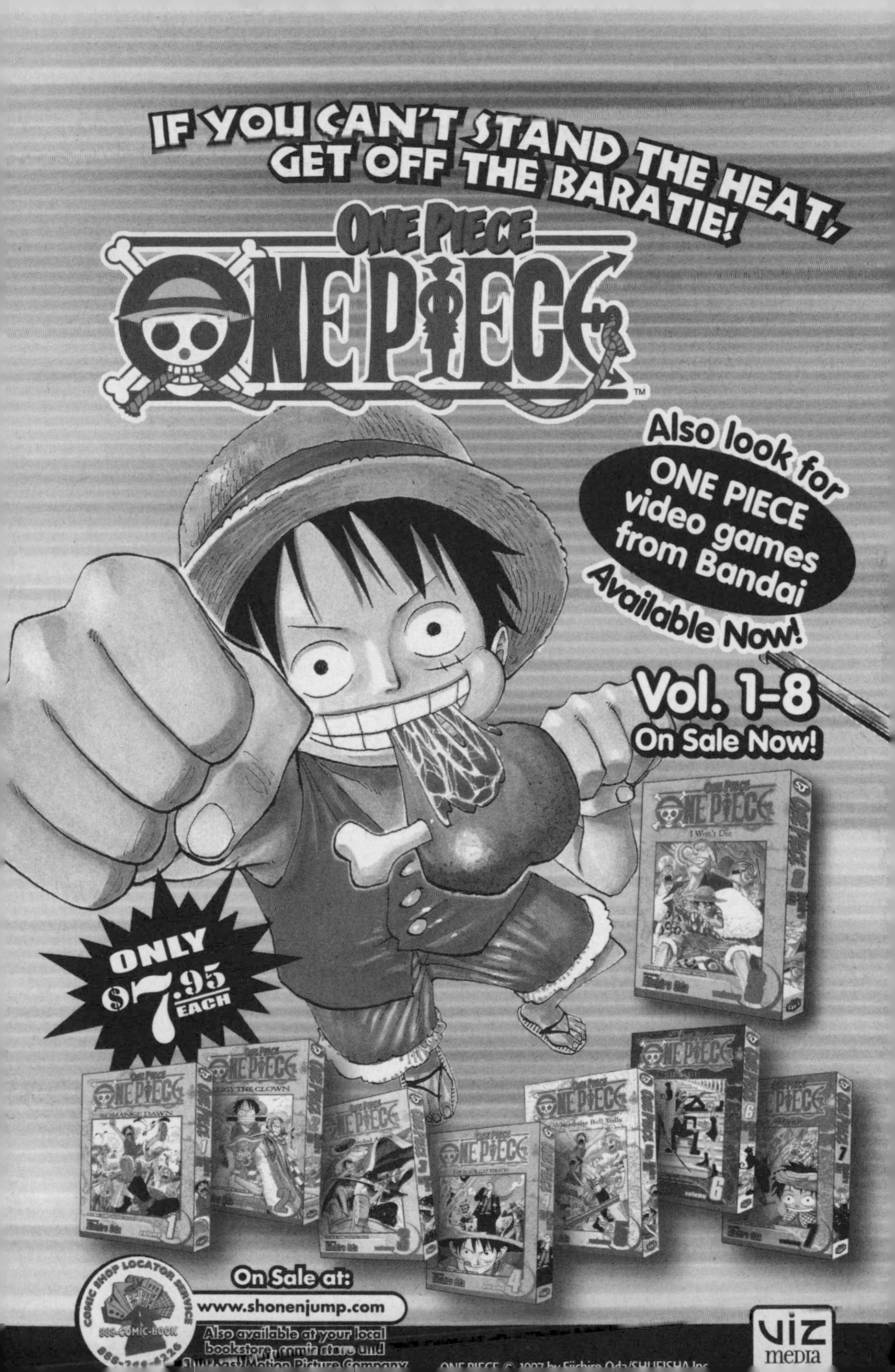

IF YOU CAN'T STAND THE HEAT, GET OFF THE BARATIE!
ONE PIECE
ONE PIECE™
Also look for ONE PIECE video games from Bandai Available Now!
Vol. 1-8
On Sale Now!
ONLY $7.95 EACH
On Sale at:
www.shonenjump.com
Also available at your local bookstore, comic store and
COMIC SHOP LOCATOR SERVICE
888-COMIC-BOOK
VIZ media

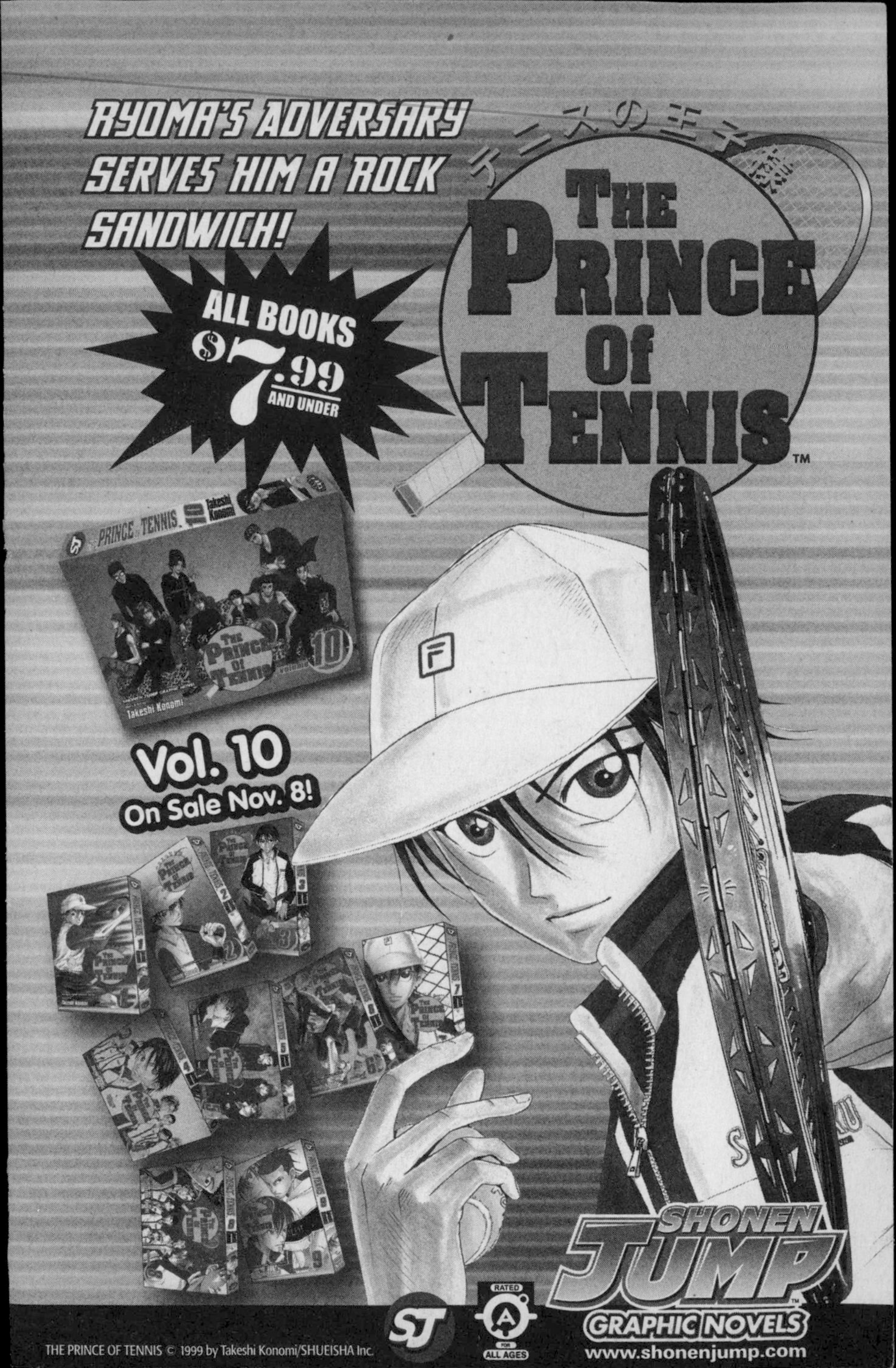

RYOMA'S ADVERSARY SERVES HIM A ROCK SANDWICH!
テニスの王子様
THE PRINCE OF TENNIS™
ALL BOOKS $7.99 AND UNDER
Vol. 10 On Sale Nov. 8!
SHONEN JUMP GRAPHIC NOVELS
RATED A FOR ALL AGES
www.shonenjump.com
THE PRINCE OF TENNIS © 1999 by Takeshi Konomi/SHUEISHA Inc.